VIDEO MEDIA COMPETITION
Regulation, Economics, and Technology

Columbia Studies in Business, Government, and Society
Eli M. Noam, General Editor

VIDEO MEDIA COMPETITION

Regulation, Economics, and Technology

Edited by Eli M. Noam

Columbia University Press
New York   1985

Library of Congress Cataloging in Publication Data
Main entry under title:

Video Media Competition

  (Columbia studies in business, government, and
society)
  Bibliography: p.
  1. Television broadcasting—United States—Addresses,
essays, lectures.   2. Cable television—United States—
Addresses, essays, lectures.   3. Video tape industry—
United States—Addresses, essays, lectures.   I. Noam,
Eli M.   II. Series.
HE8700.8.C6535   1985   384.55′4′0973   85-435
ISBN 0-231-06134-X

Columbia University Press
New York   Guildford, Surrey
Copyright © 1985 Columbia University Press
All rights reserved

Printed in the United States of America

Clothbound editions of Columbia University Press books are
Smyth-sewn and printed on permanent and durable acid-free paper

To my mother and the memory of my father

Contents

Acknowledgments   xi

Introduction   1
   Eli M. Noam

Part One. Empirical Studies of Media Competition

1. The Economics of Pay-TV Media   19
   Jane B. Henry

2. Statistical Evidence of Substitutability Among
Video Delivery Systems   56
   Jonathan D. Levy and Peter K. Pitsch

3. Economies of Scale in Cable Television:
A Multiproduct Analysis   93
   Eli M. Noam

4. The Broadcasters: The Future Role of Local
Stations and the Three Networks   121
   Michael O. Wirth and Harry Bloch

5. The Impact of Competing Technologies on Cable
Television   138
   Kenneth Thorpe

Comment: Empirical Studies of Media Competition   168
   Douglas W. Webbink

Comment: Multichannel Video Competition   174
   Mark S. Nadel

Comment: Analyzing the Critical, Unknown Factor   180
   Stuart N. Brotman

6. Telephone and Cable Companies: Rivals or Partners
in Video Distribution   187
   Walter S. Baer

Comment: Television and Cable Issues   214
   John K. Hopley

7. Prerecorded Home Video and the Distribution of
   Theatrical Feature Films   221
   David Waterman

8. Program Competition, Diversity, and Multichannel
   Bundling in the New Video Industry   244
   Steven S. Wildman and Bruce M. Owen

   Comment: Welfare Analysis and the Video Marketplace   274
   John R. Woodbury

Part Two. The Regulatory Issues in Media Competition

9. The Role of Future Regulation: Licensing, Spectrum
   Allocation, Content, Access, Common Carrier, and Rates 283
   Henry Geller

10. The FCC's Regulation of the New Video Technologies:
    Backing and Filling on the Level Playing Field   311
    Michael Botein

    Comment: The Regulatory Setting   330
    Stephen A. Sharp

    Comment: Competing Technologies and Inconsistent
    Regulation   332
    John D. Abel

11. Antitrust and Video Markets: The Merger of Showtime
    and The Movie Channel as a Case Study   338
    Lawrence J. White

12. Regulation of Broadcast Station Ownership:
    Evidence and Theory   364
    Stanley M. Besen and Leland L. Johnson

    Comment: Antitrust, Concentration, and Competition   390
    Harvey J. Levin

    Comment: Antitrust, Concentration, and Competition   397
    Nolan A. Bowie

Part Three. The International Outlook

13. A European View of Competition and Control in a
    Multimedia Society   405
    Helmet Schäfer

14. New Media in the Third World   416
    Ernest Jouhy

References   441

Contributors   459

Acknowledgments

The discussion of media policy issues is notoriously contentious, given the political, economic, and cultural stakes. In a debate where there is often more heat than light, one of the functions of a university is to generate independent research, and to provide an unbiased forum for its discussion.

To help analyze the emerging new landscape in electronic media, the Research Program in Telecommunications and Information Policy at the Columbia University Graduate School of Business initiated and organized work on the subject, and held a meeting to discuss the findings.

The activities of the Program are supported by a broad spectrum of private organizations and foundations, all of which respect its academic independence.

For this project, we are grateful for the support of the Friedrich Naumann Foundation of Germany. The foundation contributed a welcome and necessary international program component and perspective to the proceedings. We are in particular grateful to its director to the United Nations, Dr. Juergen Wickert. The conference planning was entirely in Columbia's hands, including the selection of the research paper topics, authors, and discussants. For the main studies, authors were chosen from among respected and active researchers of telecommunications regulation, without regard for or, frequently, knowledge of their positions, if any, on the subjects under discussion.

Among the many people who made this book a reality, special credit goes to two people: Roberta Tasley, the executive director of the Program, was the extraordinarily efficient and unflappable administrator of the entire effort. Mark Nadel, an author in his own right of several important studies of mass media regulation, performed various editorial functions; and he was also instrumental in our earlier and wide-ranging search of studies on the economics of mass media, which resulted in nine anthologies based on dozens of mostly obscure materials from filings before the FCC, consultant reports, government studies, and widely scattered academic publications. Many thanks go also to the superb people at the Program, who helped make it happen: John Chapman, Jay Colt, Jonathan Kadis, Claire Kessinger, Florence Ling, Virginia Marion, Timothy Searight, Valere Gagnon, Gina Kovarsky, and Jeffrey Jullich. And special thanks go to my wife, Nadine Strossen, for her supportive and excellent ideas throughout this project.

Introduction

Eli M. Noam

Technological change, entrepreneurial initiative, and regulatory re-orientation, all mutually reinforcing, are transforming the structure of American television. They have increased the number of participants and the means of delivery of video programming, and have put into question the notion of scarcity in broadcasting. It is therefore not surprising that the very concept of regulating the electronic media has been challenged as an affront to the First Amendment. Others, however, argue that the emergence of new technologies is leading to a concentration of power over communications in a handful of major media firms, and that governmental safeguards in the public interest are as important as ever.

This divergence of views has led to spirited debates. One side invokes the alphabet soup of new media—DBS, LPTV, STV, SMATV, VCR, MDS, CATV—while the other waves the banner of public trusteeship. In this exchange, empirical research is usually absent. And when such studies are undertaken or commissioned, the aim is often to provide ammunition, or to supply strategic planners with well-guarded proprietary studies. The purpose of this book is therefore to help generate a body of research work that can illuminate the emerging media landscape, and to make it publicly available.

Although the acronyms of transmission media abound, some of them are not truly "new" media but only extensions of existing ones. One can distinguish between variants of three basic forms of video distribution: over-the-air broadcasting; wire-line transmission; and physical distribution. In earlier and simpler days, "television" consisted of broadcasting on the VHF (very high frequency) band; later the UHF (ultra high frequency) band was added. Several of the new forms of delivery such as MDS (Multipoint Distribution Service) and DBS (direct broadcast satellites) consist merely of broadcasting over frequency bands previously closed to television: in the case of DBS, transmission occurs from the extremely high broadcasting platforms of geostationary satellites rather than earth-bound antennas. LPTV (low power television) and STV (subscription television) are only new uses of existing UHF and VHF broadcasting. On the other hand, most of these newer forms of television (with the partial exception of LPTV) have a very different *economic* foundation from conventional broadcasters, in that they substitute a direct *subscription* relation between viewer and broadcaster, as contrasted with the advertiser-mediated relationship of free television.

Substantially different from broadcasting are recording technologies using videodisk and video cassette recorders (VCRs), and movie theater exhibition, all of which can be subsumed as forms of *physical* (as opposed to electronic) delivery of programming. Also different from-over-the-air broadcasting, though related is the *wireline* transmission of cable television and its companion technology SMATV (Satellite Master Antenna Television, or "private cable"), and—potentially—of distribution over upgraded telephone lines. There also exist hybrid forms of the three basic delivery modes, such as time-delay recordings off-the-air, the cable distribution of various broadcast signals, and the use of telephone lines as an upstream link for broadcasters and cable.

All video distribution media can be viewed as different configurations of national (wholesale) and local (retail) distribution. Given the low marginal cost of distribution relative to the fixed costs of program production, almost all programming is distributed nationwide via satellite, coaxial cable, or by physical means. In local distribution, some "pipelines" are cheap but limited in terms of carrying capacity, while others are expensive but have a wide capacity. Many of the newer media can be differentiated from conventional broadcasting in that they tend to be *multi*channel rather than *single* channel systems of program delivery. This distinction is not technical, but regulatory in nature, i.e., based on ownership rules and spectrum allocation. The distinction between technical and regulatory factors should not be overdrawn; the small spectrum allocation for VHF broadcasting for example is partly based on competing demands from other users of spectrum and its suitability to their technical needs.

It is fundamental that technological ability to use a new form of delivering television images does not assure its economic viability. In retrospect, the year 1983 may have been the high-water mark of expectations that everyone will do well; Cable TV was booming and other

compare this shakeout / ver
w/ possible cable
shakeout

pay-technologies were hopeful of matching that performance. Since then, some shaking out has occurred. STV, which had held its own earlier, began to falter when it began to face cable television head-to-head, thus revealing itself as primarily a transitional method of delivering pay-programming. DBS, which started with more than a dozen hopeful applicants for FCC licenses, has seen a significant attrition in interest, as major firms have at least temporarily dropped out.

Another intricate delivery configuration that disappointed its backers was ABC's now defunct time-delay recording broadcasting *Telefirst* which envisioned pay-programming to be transmitted in the early hours of the morning to subscribers with VCRs preset for recordings. A further fatality along the way were video discs. RCA, which had bet on the disc technology as a major consumer item, discontinued its involvement in light of the overwhelming competition from video cassette (i.e., tape) recorders.

This book is organized in three parts: empirical, regulatory, and international. The first part deals with empirical studies of different aspects of media rivalry.

Since multichannel MDS and high power DBS are in their start-up or planning phases, cost analysis of these pay media is particularly important. Jane Henry's study shows the required investment for DBS to be enormous: a high-powered satellite system carrying 6 to 8 transponders nationwide costs about $500 million (though this can be reduced by a different and more modest deployment of satellites, as the companies have now recognized). Medium-powered satellites are considerably cheaper, and their allocated C-band frequencies are not attenuated by rain as the high-powered Ku-band is. On the other hand, the antenna dish for the high-powered DBS is smaller by 60 to 65 percent. DBS's problems, for Henry, are also its high *marginal* costs per subscriber. While its average costs are comparable to those of cable television, marginal costs are estimated by Henry to be higher. This is due to the need for subscriber dish antenna, amplifiers, descramblers, maintenance, and installation. Monthly DBS subscribers charges are therefore likely to be in the $30–$40 range for five or six channels, as contrasted with $6–$30 for a 36 to 54 channel cable system that may also offer interactive services such as videotex or home banking. This unfavorable comparison is not a death-knell for DBS; in large parts of the country cable is uneconomical due to low population density, and DBS may be an effective transmission vehicle: Henry estimates that DBS will serve 4 million subscribers by 1992, but that is a small fraction of cable's market.

While DBS has received much attention, the more down-to-earth technologies of multichannel MDS and SMATV may prove to be surprisingly resilient. MDS operators may enter and exit cheaply (for less than $1 million) and quickly, and thus can establish themselves early with a 4 to 6 channel system that permits local flexibility. Marginal costs per subscriber are substantially lower than for DBS but higher than for cable. Monthly subscriber charges would therefore be $20–$25, with self-installation possible. These advantages, Henry predicts, are likely to make MDS (also known as MMDS) the strongest overall supplier of pay TV to homes not passed by cable, though not superior to it in direct competition. On the other hand, where population is sparser still, LPTV with a single-channel pay-TV service should not be discounted largely because the cost for a 10-mile radius transmitter is only $8,000–$18,000 and falling. (A studio that could serve several transmitters adds $26,000.) LPTV operating as a pay service would cost $50,000–$70,000 per channel, as compared with MDS's $75,000–$100,000 for a similar transmission radius. Conventional STV, on the other hand, is on its way out. Its break-even point is high, and it is unlikely to be reached or maintained in many places. For Henry, STV's time has come and gone.

While cable television developed spectacularly and in the spotlight of local politics, SMATV—the unfranchised "private cable" of apartment house complexes—grew quietly but steadily to perhaps 600,000 subscribers by mid 1984. This growth and its likely continuation are based on the steady decline in the cost of receiving antennas, which should continue as the new and more powerful satellites and the use of the Ku-band permit smaller earth stations. The capital cost of a typical SMATV system ranges from $30,000 to $40,000 for an addressable system, including installation, and the marginal cost per subscriber is slightly higher than for cable, but lower than for DBS. (However, rewiring and repeaters raises SMATV's marginal cost.) Typical prices for SMATV service are $10–$30 for about a dozen channels, including movie channels, which is somewhat higher than for regular cable with its greater number of channels.

These findings show cable as the most formidable of the pay-TV distributors. The high capital and operating cost of new franchises is pushing cable's cost per subscriber higher, but this is also accompanied by greater channel and service capacity. Its competitors are, nevertheless, likely to find some room in the pay-TV market largely because cable will leave millions of households unpassed. Henry estimates for 1992 a subscriber count for MDS of 8.5 million; for DBS of 4 million; for SMATV of 2.5 million, including DBS and MDS subscribers; and for LPTV, of .75 million.

One of the unexpected developments in the video field was the dramatic increase in the market penetration of video cassette recorders. In 1983, 4.1 million VCRs were sold in the United States. For 1984, this figure was 7.6 million. The explosive growth was anticipated, to some extent, by European sales developments; however, Europeans have usually no viewing alternatives to the limited number of public television channels, and VCRs were seen as fulfilling essentially the role of commercially supplied television programs in the United States. The surge of VCR sales in America now suggests that they are not necessarily a substitute for advertiser supported or pay television. The study by Jonathan Levy and Peter Pitsch is the first empirical investigation of the demand relation among VCRs, broadcast television, and cable. The results lend support to the view that VCRs and broadcast television are *complements,* rather than substitutes, most likely due to VCRs use for time-shifting and librarying. However, the relationship of VCRs and cable is found to be one of *substitutes,* i.e., of rivalry. The authors also find some statistical evidence that pay cable and broadcasting are substituted for each other.

*Inter*media rivalry is not the only form of possible competition. One can also look for *intra*media competition to reduce or eliminate market power. For example, in television broadcasting, an intense rivalry for market share has been prevalent for many years. With the emergence of cable television as an important mass medium, the question arises whether cable, too, will experience internal competition. So far, cable operators compete head-to-head in only a handful of localities. There are a number of institutional constraints to such rivalry, primarily the system of awarding de facto exclusive local franchises. In addition, the primary energies of the industry are focused on the cabling of new areas rather than in invading others' turf and inviting retaliation. With few real-life examples of intracable competitions on record, an empirical analysis must look at the cost and production characteristics of cable television distribution to determine whether cable has economies of scale of such magnitude as to make multifirm production unlikely.

To analyze this question, Eli Noam, the editor of this volume, conducted an empirical investigation based on data for almost 5,000 U.S. cable systems. The statistical results of the model for a multiproduct cost functions shows that the overall economies of scale of cable television operations exhibit a decline of unit cost of about 10 percent per doubling of outputs. These scale economies are moderate in size; they ought to discourage much competitive entry, but they are not likely to prevent it in particularly attractive circumstances; nor would they discourage an invasion across a franchise boundary into new territory. An important observation is that the stand-alone economies of scale of separate product dimensions are smaller than overall economies of scale. This suggests the existence of economies of *scope* of joint operation of transmission and marketing aspects of cable service. Relegating cable to a pure carrier role would therefore tend to make entry easier, but would also increase operating costs. The advantages of integration of transmission and programming to the incumbents are therefore not simply an extension of local distribution power vertically into the programming stage, but also the economies of joint operation.

An important question concerns the effect of new media technologies on conventional broadcasters. The usual expectation has been that these broadcasters will suffer considerably from an erosion of their viewing audience. However, Michael Wirth and Harry Block argue in their study that this process must be analyzed more subtly. On the one hand, the significant demand for programming by new media entrants has raised programming costs for broadcasters, and forced them to spend more on promotion. On the other hand, broadcasters' revenues need not necessarily decline due to the new media. In competing for advertiser dollars, Wirth and Block hypothesize and empirically trace oligopolistic market conditions for nationwide advertising, because many advertisers consider such exposure a "must-buy." Hence lower audience share is not necessarily accompanied by lower advertiser revenues. The authors find the revenue decline only one-fourth to one-ninth as large as previously estimated. Therefore, though broadcasters' profit margins drop, they are still able to earn above normal returns. Of course, if cable becomes

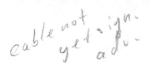

a significant advertising medium, broadcast stations and networks will lose their "must buy" status, as Mark Nadel points out.

In light of the prominent role of cable television, it is an important question to investigate whether the presence of the other pay-media affects cable's profitability. Kenneth Thorpe, in a large-scale empirical study, finds that STV has only a small impact on cable price-cost margins, a result contrasting with earlier findings that regarded STV as a significant competitive factor, at least in the initial phases of cable penetration. Thorpe finds that for every 10 percent in penetration by STV, the price-cost margins of cable operators are reduced by only .05 percent. But he also finds that early STV entry into a media market makes a difference in the short run.

What else affects cable profitability? Interestingly, rate regulation does not, since cable operators can alter the composition of their tiers, particularly after FCC decisions that limit local restrictions on such changes. MSO (multiple system operators) ownership is found to have some impact, suggesting economies of large-scale operation. On the other hand, ownership by MSOs does not affect the number of pay television services, reducing concern that vertically integrated firms would reduce supply to protect their own programming service.

A potentially giant participant in the video transmission is the telephone industry, whose involvement is traced and discussed in Walter Baer's study. Telephone companies, which technologically would seem to be natural providers of cable communications services, are generally restricted from owning a cable system in the area of their telephone operations unless it is leased to an unrelated operator, or located in rural areas. Now that the Bell system has been divested into different components, some of the successor companies are eyeing cable operations and revive in the process the hostility between cable and telephone operators that had centered on pole attachment. Attempts at entry have been made by Wisconsin Telephone, Michigan Bell, Illinois Bell, and Bell of Pennsylvania. In Washington, D.C., the Chesapeake and Potomac telephone company may construct a highly visible cable system. All of these plans, however, are for the ownership of conventional cable systems, entirely separate from the telephone networks—though with possible economies of scope in maintenance and service—and with a tree-and-branch network architecture rather than telephony's switched star-configuration.

But there have also been steps toward integrating narrow-band telephone service with broadband video service in ways more likely to be viable than those of the 3M Company in the 1970s for rural services, a market for which DBS and other broadcasting technologies may prove more economical in any event. The rapid development of fiber optics technology provides a key element of a future broadband digital switched system that could also provide video services. Fiber optical links with a capacity of 1 billion bps have already been tested successfully by Bell Labs. With that technology, eleven standard television channels could be sent over a single fiber strand of a bundle of fibers. At the same time, the network architectures of cable and telephony are moving closer to each other. An example is cable television's "mini-hub" system. In late 1983, Pacific Bell took an important step into more integrated telephone and cable service with its application for the Palo Alto, California, cable franchise. Pacific Bell proposed a partially fiber-optical system, with 80 channels made available to local governments while the company retained control over the remaining capacity for interactive services and for a data network linking Stanford University and other institutions. Key elements of the system would be interconnected with or co-located in the company's general exchange offices.

Cable firms were alarmed at the potential invasion of telcos into their video business; but they have also begun to enter the telco market by providing by-pass capacity for data transmission. This is inevitable. Over time, technological developments and business opportunities will create a competitive overlap. At the same time, there is much room for cooperation, since telephone can provide a cheap and readily available hybrid upstream capability for cable's (and other media's) two-way services.

In addition to over-the-air broadcasting and wire-line transmission, physical distribution of video programming is a basic route of distribution. David Waterman analyzes the economics of such physical distribution and finds that prerecorded video fare can compete successfully as a method of delivery, since it permits distributors a more efficient "unbundled" method of pricing, whereas its competitors must resort to advertiser support or per-channel subscription, at least as long as per-program pay TV is still in its infancy. However, the full potential for prerecorded cassettes cannot be realized today because their suppliers cannot control the subsequent rental pricing of their products because of the First Sale Doctrine of copyright law.

There has been an explosive growth of VCR hardware and software, with a VCR penetration of 13 percent of all households in mid 1984. Video discs, on the other hand, have failed their backers' expectations. The VCR boom is fueled by rapidly dropping unit prices of equipment (to about $300 on the low end). Cassettes sell for about $35–$80, and rent for $1–$5; disks sell for $20–$35. Even at those rental costs, video cassettes would not be price competitive with pay-TV, except that they can appeal to specialized audiences and, more importantly, they provide an effective means to tap the time sensitivity of many viewers for a viewing early in the release cycle. Hence, video recordings affect the time-release patterns of theatrical feature films, which has been the sequence of first and sub-run theaters, pay–TV, television networks, and televisions syndication. If the emerging "home video" now positions itself before or overlapping with pay-TV, it will thus reduce pay-TV's attractiveness to "high-value" consumers. (At the same time, VCRs may also enhance pay-TV for those wishing to create video libraries. The net effect reported by Levy and Pitsch is one of substitution.) Interestingly, theater attendance and revenues in real terms, which had been decimated by early television, has not been affected by the rapid growth of VCRs and pay TV, remaining roughly constant since 1977. At the same time, motion picture production has steadily risen due to greater demand from distribution media.

The last chapter in this section is a theoretical and simulation analysis of the economics of channel bundling. One characteristic of several of the new distribution media is their operation of multiple simultaneous channels. Cable, SMATV, MDS, and DBS can thus provide a portfolio of simultaneous programming, while their single channel rivals can diversify programming only along the dimension of time. In previous years, several economists, including Bruce Owen, had established models of programming choice; Steven Wildman, together with Owen, now extend these models to a multichannel world as well as to situations of mixed pay and advertiser-supporter programming. They argue that the new media have reduced gatekeeper power over access diversity, and that greater content diversity has usually increased consumer welfare, though some viewers may be losers. Owen and Wildman construct models and conduct simulations to show that, under simplifying assumptions, an operator's chosen mix of advertising and pay-TV offerings will be consistent with welfare optimization. When the model is extended to multiple services, it is more difficult to come to generalized findings; but the authors conclude that in a multichannel setting, the number of pay services, relative to advertiser-supported ones, is likely to be larger than the welfare maximizing number, since the consumer benefits of advertiser-supported channels is not taken into account in the cable operator's calculus. Concerning multichannels competition, the authors demonstrate that bundling into tiers can be an affective substituting device for price discrimination, and they analyze different bundling strategies. To the authors, one controversial implication is that as DBS, cable, and MDS achieve significant market penetrations, it may be more efficient to permit local broadcasters to use several broadcast channels in a market rather than the single channel, or to permit a coordination of programming by several broadcasters.

The second part of the book deals with regulatory issues of media diversity. Many developments have occurred in this area, with the Cable Communications Policy Act of 1984 a particular milestone. The first two contributions analyze the "level playing field" in the regulatory treatment of different media. For reasons of historical accident or regulatory lag, unequal rules exist for entry, licensing, content, and public service obligation, among others. For example, the broadcasting group ownership rules limit the number of stations that can be controlled by a single owner, and also restrict them to one channel per local market. Cable operators, on the other hand, can and do own systems at hundreds of locations, and they are usually able to program a good number of channels. On the other hand, cable operators must carry a variety of mandated channels, provide universal service and pay a franchise fee of up to 5 percent of gross revenues.

Three major approaches to regulation of video distribution can be distinguished: first, the print model—with virtually no regulation—which governs video cassette recordings and movie theater distribution; second, the licensing model used in broadcasting and cable television, where a scarce license is awarded in exchange for certain public service obligations or other restrictions; third, the common carrier approach used for MDS, where transmission to program supplier is provided for a set fee, and potentially, for telco distribution. These different types of regulation raise contradictory equity claims. The situation is further complicated by a desire to keep competitors afloat. On the one hand, the equal treatment of all transmission media—a "level playing field"— seems to be an equitable policy; on the other hand, without the "handicapping" of some and preferential treatment of others, several of the media may not be viable—thus denying the public the diversity or other socially desirable goals that they might have offered. In their studies, Henry Geller and Michael Botein trace the tensions between these two conflictive goals; Botein finds the FCC's deregulatory approach full of disparities and inconsistencies, and slow in anticipating interrelations. Because of historic and statutory limitations the FCC cannot insure rapid and equal entry to all media, nor free them from intrusive content regulation. Its "wait-and-see" approach concerning how to classify a technology represents the least harmful strategy. Geller predicts a trend toward deregulation and choice of the regulatory mode by the user, with a tendency toward the print model complemented by some common carrier elements. Cable television, for Geller, has no claim for deregulation as a "video publisher." The licensed "public trustee" concept, on the other hand, has failed in the past, and its aim may be better served by instituting auctions for licenses and spectrum fees, the revenues collected to support social goals. Geller believes that the most practical alternative would be to require a spectrum fee.

When the number of broadcasting outlets was still small, a set of ownership rules had been instituted to reduce the power of any single firm over mass communications nationally, regionally, and locally. Stanley Besen and Leland Johnson examine the empirical and analytical evidence on the effect of these ownership rules. They find that the group ownership rules do not make much difference one way or the other. At least in large markets, the rules have had only a limited effect on anticompetitive behavior—toward program suppliers, advertisers, or competitors—even before considering the effects of new media. Nor do they find that group ownership confers economic efficiencies except perhaps in the production of local news programs. As for the regional concentration rule, they point out that an outright abolition could, in some instances, lead to collusion, but it still might be better to deal with such instances on a case-by-case basis rather than a general rule. There is also only little empirical evidence of the effectiveness of the duopoly and one-to-a-market rules. However, the authors find that the analytic case for these restrictions is stronger, and they favor a case-by-case approach, as they do for cable-broadcast cross-ownership.

Such a case-by-case approach is practiced by the Antitrust Division of the Justice Department, which in recent years has considered a number of cases concerning media industry structure or behavior. Lawrence White describes and analyzes one of these cases involving the merger between two programming services, Showtime and The Movie Channel, respectively the second and third largest pay program suppliers. The merger also joined as owners of the venture three of the six major motion picture distributors: Paramount, Universal, and Warner Brothers, plus Viacom (a major cable firm), Warner Communications, and American Express (co-owners of Warner Amex Cable, another major MSO). Both MSOs also control other cable programming networks.

The proposed merger was evaluated by the Justice Department under the merger guidelines which it had issued in 1982. Analytically, the transaction involved two horizontal mergers in two markets (pay TV services, and studios), as well as a vertical integration issue. As usual, a critical question was how widely to define product markets. Only impressionistic evidence was available, on whose basis markets were defined narrowly as "movie-driven pay services." The Herfindahl-Hirschmann Index of Concentration for movie-driven pay services was very high (above 4,000), and a merger would increase concentration considerably (by more than 400). On the other hand, the Justice Department concluded that entry into the market was relatively easy, and that brand loyalties towards incumbents could be overcome. Thus, the horizontal merger between Showtime-TMC was left unopposed.

On the vertical issue, the Antitrust Division did not find that fears of foreclosure or leverage were justified. But it feared that it might create an ability to raise cost to rivals—a novel theory for the Justice Department—by creating an incentive for a downstream merged firm to seek coordinated behavior among its upstream rivals, in order to raise input prices for its downstream rivals. This led to Justice Department opposition of the vertical aspects of the transaction. Paramount and Universal were then dropped from the ownership, and the merger was approved. Soon thereafter, however, Paramount entered into a five year exclusive distribution agreement with Showtime-TMC.

While the development and penetration of new media has been most rapid in the United States, it would be parochial to neglect developments in other industrialized countries, or the impact of the new technologies on the Third World. The third part of this book introduces some of the many issues involved.

Helmut Schäfer, a participant in the shaping of European media policies, discusses the implications of the remarkable development of VCRs, and of the increased channel capacity of the projected cable and satellite systems. Europeans consider broadcasting a public service rather than a commercial endeavor; the resulting programming traditions of public television, however, are being undermined by the emergence of new media. This has lead to a highly politicized domestic debate on media policies. The emergence of VCRs provides the public with a way to satisfy its program preferences outside the public broadcasting system, and therefore has made part of the political debate moot; it has also put pressure on public broadcasters to satisfy demand for mass entertainment, and thus endangered their ability to provide specialized programs geared to specialized audiences. The introduction of cable is proceeding slowly; recent studies suggest a cable penetration of only 19.5–12 percent by 1992 in Europe, (and much of it of limited channel capacity and more in the nature of master-antenna systems.) DBS, because of its wide coverage, could provide European-wide programming with different language sound tracks, thus taking advantage of economies of scale while furthering the European idea. Governmental telecommunications authorities are likely to have major control over the cable networks, and some public boards are likely to be set up to assure neutrality and balance in private programming. The rapid penetration of VCRs also creates major problems for developing countries. Schäfer sees major challenges for international organizations, and a role for development assistance to reduce the widening gap in broadcasting technology, programming software production, and ease of access.

This theme is considerably expanded upon by Ernest Jouhy, who takes on the task of analyzing the cultural implications of the media developments on less developed societies. The complexity of technology makes it difficult to trace causal relationships, but its general trend has been to increase the cultural and economic dependency of poorer countries, which at the same time also serve as the locations for the production of the equipment that causes such dependency. Programming is much cheaper to import than to produce domestically, and

Western programming, which enhances the image of Western cultural values, is therefore imported, and assumes an important role in fulfilling the need in poor societies for an escapist environment. This creates an escalating trend toward a global and Western culture. Access to video technology becomes an important element in status differentiation, and it puts pressure on those who cannot afford it. To pay for a color TV takes 20 months' wages of an Indonesian peasant, and 10 months' wages of a teacher; and yet the number of TV sets in that country alone rises by 100,000 a year, the combined yearly income of six million peasants. On the other hand, Jouhy forsees the potential for the electronics media and information technology to raise pressures that could lead to a sharing of technology and cultural production between developing and industrialized countries.

What does this all add up to? Still newer forms of delivery, different regulatory policies and technological developments make gazing into the future hazardous. Who would have predicted a few short years ago that the Bell System would be thoroughly dismembered, that VCR penetration would soon approach 20 percent; or that the U.S. Supreme Court, Congress, and the FCC would substantially reduce local and state regulatory powers over cable television? But some conclusions can be drawn. The key video technology of the remainder of this century will be cable television which will become the core of video transmission. Cable's growth has been impressive. Since 1980, the number of cable television subscribers has almost doubled to more than 37 million, there has been a tripling of pay cable households to just under 23 million and a more than fivefold increase in revenue, to nearly $5 billion. Other media are measured, nearly automatically, against cable, as can be seen in the various empirical studies of the authors of this book.

Of the broadcast technologies, STV will not have much of a future, once its transitional role preceding cable has passed, due to its relatively high cost for a single channel. DBS is becoming a substantially weaker mode of distribution than was believed earlier, largely due to the substantial fixed cost in satellites as well as the high marginal cost of subscribers equipment and installation. These necessitate substantially higher subscriber rates for less channels than cable offers; DBS's markets are of two kinds: rural areas unpassed by cable, and urban SMATV and MDS systems which would retail its satellite-beamed programs.

Multichannel MDS may prove to be a surprisingly effective competitor to DBS for uncabled areas, due to its low cost and quick entry potential. In other sparsely populated areas, the lower cost of repeated LPTVs could make it viable for single-channel pay TV. SMATV is also a viable technology; though its existence owes much to regulatory mandates on cable, it can also benefit from a symbiotic relationship with DBS and MDS and from the potential to tailor channel offerings to narrow residential segments. Conventional VHF/UHF broadcasting will stay viable though diminished, since a residual demand for "free" television will remain, and since the present "must carry" rule assures cable distribution. Television's interlinkage by the three national television networks also strengthens it as an advertiser medium.

In physical distribution, prerecorded cassettes are proving to be a powerful and popular way for audiences to achieve control over the content and timing of their viewing. VCRs are part substitute, part complement to cable, and overall a substitute. Theater distribution, by its special social nature, does not seem to be negatively affected by the new pay technologies; it also plays an important role in creating awareness of video products. As to integrated telephone video delivery, the technical potential is there, but it will take substantial maturing of fiber technology, and major investment into the existing telephone networks and switches for this competitor to enter.

Cable's advantages derive from its large and growing channel capacity, its relatively low per-channel cost, and the possibility of linking its video transmission with other communications services. Though it is not inexpensive, it has lower marginal costs per subscriber than many of its competitors. Furthermore, it is already in place in most localities, or about to be so. Hence, its major plant investment is sunk, and in terms of operating cost, cable's economics are favorable for multichannel pay services. Though cable may be dominant in urban and suburban areas, its rivals are operative on the edge of the market, and may be able to enter from their niches of strength such as the rural areas into the cities if, for example pay cable rates are substantially increased. SMATV and MDS, in particular, are multichannel technologies with similar and favorable investment cost per potential subscriber and video channel delivered as cable television. Cable's market power over subscribers may therefore be less than its market share, present or future, would suggest. Nevertheless, investment costs are only part of the barriers to entry. Being as large as it is, the cable industry is surrounded by closely allied program suppliers, and is likely to command the loyalty of many of them against rival delivery systems. Its program offerings may therefore be superior. Thus as cable's high market share in a given locality becomes a reality, and as it begins to operate under the provisions of its new legal regulatory framework, alertness in observation of the effectiveness of competitive constraints is necessary.

PART ONE

Empirical Studies of Media Competition

1

The Economics of
Pay-TV Media

JANE B. HENRY

CONTENTS

  I. Introduction
  II. Cable Television
  III. Satellite Master Antenna Television (SMATV)
    A. Background
    B. SMATV Economics
    C. Pay-TV Economics in Multiunit Dwellings Compared to Single-Family Houses
  IV. Multichannel Microwave Distribution Service (MMDS)
    A. Background
    B. MDS Economics
  V. Direct Broadcast Satellites (DBS)
    A. Background
    B. DBS Economics and Competition
  VI. Subscription Television (STV)
    A. Background
    B. Economics of STV
  VII. Low-Power Television (LPTV)
    A. Background
    B. Prospective Economics of LPTV
  VIII. Conclusion

I. INTRODUCTION

Pay-television programming has grown vigorously in recent years, both in the number of pay-television subscribers and in the quantity of competing subscription services. Over the five years from 1978 to 1983, the number of pay cable subscriptions has increased at an annual rate of roughly 60 percent to over 30 million. In 1983, 29 basic and 10 pay program services were available on cable TV. The number of U.S. homes wired for cable totaled 36,870,000 in 1983, compared to less than half that number—17,135,000 homes—in 1978. Over the five-year period, the number of separate pay cable subscriptions grew at a rate fully four times faster than the increase in basic subscriptions.

While the public's willingness to pay for two- and three-premium channels had not been widely predicted, new suppliers of both programming content and programming distribution have moved quickly to capitalize on the opportunity. A dozen subscription programming services exist today, each trying to duplicate Time Inc.'s highly profitable movie and entertainment network, Home Box Office, which reported 13.7 million subscribers in early 1984.

This paper, will present a competitive cost analysis of cable television and the major noncable pay services: direct broadcast satellite (DBS), multichannel multipoint distribution service (MMDS), satellite master antenna television (SMATV), low-power television (LPTV), and subscription television (STV). Based on an analysis of the economics of each service, I will give an estimate of the cost of each to the consumer, and predict the number of subscribers each will attract by 1992.

II. CABLE TELEVISION

Basic subscription fees and pay tier fees are the major sources of cable revenue. Pay revenues represent about 40 percent of total revenues. The most important factor behind a system's profitability is a high penetration rate, that is, a high ratio of homes that subscribe to homes passed by cable. An average system breaks even when it achieves about a 30 percent penetration, although in some urban systems, breakeven will require a penetration of 45 percent and more to cover the high fixed capital cost.

Because capital costs are so high, ratios of debt to equity range between 1.75 and 3.0. Interest expense has averaged 9.4 percent of sales and will increase. Fixed assets account for 75 percent of the industry's total assets. The average investment per new subscriber runs at about $650 today.

The top ten multiple system operators (MSOs), which serve about three-quarters of all subscribers, invested heavily in the 1979–1983 period to gain market share, backed by well-funded parent companies. The factors that encouraged this surge in construction activity were spectacular growth in cable profits in the late seventies due to a dramatic deceleration of cable construction, the introduction of pay services, and lower interest rates. Today, with cable construction at a high level, the substantial cost of urban construction together with higher interest rates and a more modest view of future revenues from interactive services have caused a retrenchment that is likely to continue. MSOs are also raising rates, and looking for partners who will provide equity relief. Most future growth in cable will occur in urban areas, and roughly 90 percent of new subscribers in the 1980s will be located there. While the *average* cable system cost just over a million dollars in 1981, the average *urban* system requires an estimated $75 to $100 million investment today.

Urban cable systems have the capital characteristics of a modern battleship—a colossal sunk cost—although they also have a higher-than-average potential for return on investment. Thus while the average cable system has less than 5,000 subscribers, profits increase substantially above 10,000 subscribers. Rural systems are generally too small to support enhanced services such as security. The expected higher returns on investment from the large population bases of urban areas, as well as exaggerated hopes for services like videotex, home shopping, and security, created the keen franchising competition of the early 1980s.

Operating expenses increased as a percentage of sales in the 1980s, owing to several factors: costlier franchise negotiations, the increasing share of revenues from pay services (which have a lower profit margin, since cable operators must compensate program suppliers), and the increase in marketing costs. A cable operator passes along about 40 percent of pay subscription fees to the pay service. While substantial discounts exist for the MSO with over 70,000 subscribers, there is no question that basic subscriptions are on the average a more profitable product than are pay subscriptions. Furthermore, in the effort to increase subscriber penetration, and to raise the ratio of pay to basic units, marketing costs rose significantly in the early 1980s.

In the sections that follow, I analyze the economics of competing pay TV delivery services. Several are more expensive than cable—DBS is a good example. Others, like SMATV and in certain areas, multichannel MDS, can skim the cream from a cable system's revenues.

III. SATELLITE MASTER ANTENNA TELEVISION (SMATV)

A. Background

Satellite master antenna television (SMATV) is a simple concept which has become an important and highly profitable business as a result of technological and regulatory trends. In order to bring the wide range of television programming now available by satellite to individual apartments, condominiums, or mobile home units not passed by cable, the SMATV operator installs a television receive-only (TVRO) earth station and connects it by means of suitable wiring to individual television receivers (in effect, a private mini cable system). In early 1984, the National Satellite Cable Association, SMATV's trade organization, estimated total subscribers at 600,000, and SMATV systems at roughly 2,000. As in cable television, a converter may be used to make specific channels on the cable appear at particular locations on the television tuner, and a variety of devices may be used to restrict access to pay television channels to those who have paid for them. SMATV has received increasing attention as major cable MSOs have won franchises in major U.S. cities where a good portion of the choicest apartment units are already served by SMATV.

Most, though by no means all, SMATV systems are installed in apartment buildings. SMATV has been operating for several years in hotels and mobile home parks as well as condominiums, cooperatives, and resort communities. By definition, a localized television distribution system (master antenna television MATV) is a SMATV system if it gets its program feed from one or more satellites and if its distribution cables do not cross a property line. (Once the system crosses a property line, it becomes subject to municipal regulation and may require a franchise—it has turned, from a legal point of view, into a conventional cable television system.) SMATV can serve contiguous apartments, single-family homes, condominiums, or mobile homes which can be reached without crossing a property line. According to a recent FCC ruling, municipalities cannot regulate SMATV (FCC 1983i). If this ruling is upheld, an important advantage of SMATV will be its freedom from potentially burdensome franchise fees (such as the 5 percent fee often charged to cable operators). Still, SMATV operators usually pay between 3 and 10 percent of their revenues to the owner of the multiunit dwelling they serve.

Moreover, the definitions themselves, though useful, are inevitably blurred. Cable Dallas, a major SMATV operator in Dallas, has received a license from the FCC to feed its signals from one location to another by microwave. This means that the SMATV locations supplied in this way do not need to have their own TVRO earth station, so that the cost per location is decreased and smaller groups of housing units—smaller apartment buildings, for example—can be served profitably. SMATV is traditionally seen as a business for small entrepreneurs, but both Warner Amex, and more recently, Cox Cable, have constructed SMATV operations in multiunit dwellings as an interim measure as they are about to wire a city, in an effort to secure their potential subscribers from encroachment by other pay-TV media.

SMATV has been technically possible ever since domestic satellite distribution of signals for cable television began with HBO's first transmissions via RCA's Satcom I satellite in 1975, but it has only become important since 1981. In 1981, there were roughly 150,000 SMATV subscribers in the United States, and by late 1982 the number had exceeded 500,000. The reason for this explosive growth is partly the "discovery" of the SMATV concept by entrepreneurs, but mainly the rapid reduction in the price of TVRO earth stations, reflecting both technical progress and the rapidly accumulated production experience of manufacturers such as California Microwave, M/A-COM, and Scientific-Atlanta.

Two additional forces will promote the continuing growth of SMATV. These are:

1. The launch of new, more powerful U.S. domestic satellite systems, such as Hughes' Galaxy system, allowing smaller and less expensive earth stations to be used by the SMATV operator to provide the same picture quality that larger, more costly earth stations provide today.

2. The availability of advanced satellites operating in the newly exploited Ku-band frequencies, which are more suitable for use with small antennae than the lower-frequency C-band satellites that provide virtually all the television distribution in the United States today. One of the most powerful Canadian Anik C satellites, which operate in the Ku band, is to be tilted so as to provide television distribution service within the United States. Both these developments will accelerate the downward trend in SMATV operators' fixed earth-station costs, thus increasing the profitability of the SMATV business and making it possible to serve smaller groups of households profitably.

At the same time, some obstacles to the development of the SMATV business are also appearing. The most important of these will be the scrambling of pay television channels such as Home Box Office Inc. (HBO), which can presently be received by TVRO earth station owners without charge, though the legal status of such reception is very much in question. In fact, the SMATV industry can be divided into the "legitimate" sector—which receives pay television channels only where the vendor has consented to SMATV relay and receives a percentage of gross tier revenues—and the "pirates." In mid-1982 the former group, organized into the National Satellite Cable Association, counted 250,000 subscribers (and an estimated 325,000 to 350,000 by late 1982), which, compared with an estimated total of 500,000 SMATV subscribers in late 1982, suggests there were perhaps 150,000 "pirate" subscribers at that time.

B. SMATV Economics

1. Trends in SMATV Economics

The SMATV business has very low start-up costs and therefore can generate a quick cash flow for the entrepreneur. Alternatively, the SMATV operator can invest in the longer term by setting up solid customer service and billing operations capable of handling a large subscriber base; investing in addressability for better subscriber control; and investing in new cable wiring within a building, rather than relying on the existing master antenna system wiring. When an SMATV operator makes this level of financial commitment to the pay TV business, his position begins to resemble that of a franchised cable operator. He is investing in the longer term. SMATV is developing in three stages: in the early stage of the business, SMATV was characterized by low capital investment for quick returns, and low percentage-of-revenue compensation paid to landlords. More recently there has been a willingness to invest in sophisticated addressable systems, rewiring, and computerized subscriber management. Landlords now expect a higher percentage of revenue, 7 to 10 percent rather than the 3 to 5 percent fees of early days. In the future multichannel MDS and direct broadcast satellite (DBS) services will allow SMATV operators to receive the signals with only a small investment in capital equipment. For example,

DBS feeds could be set up to provide four to five channels of supplemental programming at a cost of $600 to $800 for the TVRO and related electronics, compared to $20,000 to $25,000 for the same equipment today. It is likely, however, that both DBS and MDS suppliers will give preference to large, well-managed SMATV operators who have invested in sound computerized subscriber management systems.

In the sections that follow, I consider the current economics of SMATV. Although costs and scale vary widely in this industry, I will provide typical values for revenues and costs as supplied by SMATV operators.

2. Capital Costs

a. The Satellite Antenna and Related Electronics. ranges in cost from $6,000 to $35,000, with installation. A 1984 estimate is $17,000 for a four-meter dish aimed at Satcom III-R, the satellite which carries most pay TV programming, and $4,000 for installation.

b. Subscriber Equipment.

i. Nonaddressable. Subscriber equipment costs approximately $80 per subscriber: $50 for a nonaddressable decoder and $30 for installation.

ii. An Addressable System. Table 1.1 supplies estimates for the capital investment in addressable equipment at the head-end office, including microcomputer and software, autodialer and auto-answer equipment, for a total of $14,500. The investment per subscriber for addressable equipment is $143 rather than $80, also detailed in the table.

c. The Wiring from the Earth Station to the Individual Subscriber's Apartment. costs $150 to $200 per unit in a low-rise environment, and $300 to $400 per unit in an urban, high-rise environment. In addition, the SMATV operator may need to invest in repeaters where the building complex is extensive enough to require them. In the calculations that follow, these costs are excluded, since most SMATV operators select buildings that do not require rewiring.

d. Establishment of Administrative Systems, such as customer service operations and billing systems is required for a well-managed

Table 1.1. SMATV Capital Costs: Addressable System with Computerized Subscriber Management, 1983

Investment per subscriber		
Addressable wall unit[a]	$	73
Decoder		25
Installation		45
	$	143

Head-End addressable subscriber management equipment	
Subscriber management software and microcomputer	$10,000
Autodialer	2,000
Data power supply	500
Auto-Answer	2,000
	$14,500

Central programming receive equipment	
Satellite receive antenna and electronics	$17,000
Installation	4,000
	$21,000

[a]For example, Delta Benco Cascade's IT-1-3SM, which allows for three-tier service.

Table 1.2. Comparison of Typical Prices Charged by Three SMATV Operators and a Cable Operator

Cable Operator	SMATV Operator A	SMATV Operator B	SMATV Operator C
Tier 1: $6.00. 38 channels.	Tier 1: $8.95. 9 channels: 5 local channels, CNN, ESPN, Munic. TV.	Tier 1: $8.50. 5 local channels, CNN, ESPN.	Tier 1: $13.50. 12 channels or $7.00 bulk rate.
Tier 2: $16.50. Tier 1 and HBO.	Tier 2: $17.90. Tier 1 and Showtime *or* The Movie Channel.	Tier 2: $18.50. Tier 1, The Movie Channel, and Nickelodeon.	Tier 2: $22.50. Tier 1 and Showtime, $15 bulk rate
Tier 3: $24.50. Tier 1, HBO, and Showtime.	Tier 3: $26.85. Tier 1, The Movie Channel, and Showtime.		Tier 3: None.

SMATV system which operates many buildings in a single urban area. An operator needs 3,500 subscribers to break even, which implies that the SMATV system must pass about 6,000 units. This breakeven estimate assumes that the system is not addressable.

3. Revenues, Operating Costs, and Profitability

SMATV revenues per subscriber are usually slightly higher than the prices charged by cable franchise operators, particularly for basic service. Table 1.2 illustrates the $6 basic price offered by a cable operator for 38 channels compared to the $9 to $13 prices charged by SMATV operators for 12 channels. Prices for a tier adding one subscription movie channel like Showtime or The Movie Channel are slightly higher for SMATV operators: $18 to $22 compared to $16 charged by the cable operator.

SMATV operators achieve a penetration rate of households passed ranging roughly from 40 to 60 percent. A spokesman at a major program supplier to SMATV operators estimates that its affiliates achieve an average penetration of 58 percent.

A pro forma income statement for an SMATV system in a 1,000-unit apartment dwelling is provided in table 1.3. I have assumed that penetration rises from 45 percent in year one to 60 percent in year four, since the demographics of the building in this example favor pay-television penetration. Operating cash flow from this unit reaches $73,000 in the second year and $107,000 in the fourth.

Important cost elements to point out are: fees to program suppliers, the fee to the owner of the building at 7 percent of adjusted revenues per year (gross revenues minus programming fee), and a sales commission of $10 per apartment. Billing, collection, and customer service cost close to $10,000 for management of 500 subscribers in year two.

Investors in SMATV sometimes look for a high level of capital investment to provide a tax shelter through a limited partnership arrangement. This was the case for the building in table 1.3, and the model allows for capital investment in addressability and in an additional earth station to increase the amount of programming available. It does not include rewiring of the apartment building. The higher capital costs are reflected in both depreciation and interest expenses.

Table 1.3. Pro Forma Income Statement for 1,000-Unit SMATV Building

	Year 1	Year 2	Year 3	Year 4
Beginning units	0	450	550	580
Ending units	450	550	580	600
Ending penetration	45%	55%	58%	60%
Average units	360	500	565	590
Average rate, annual	$ 264	$ 290	$ 319	$ 351
Revenue				
Subscriber service revenues	95,040	145,000	180,235	207,090
Installation revenue	9,000	2,000	600	400
Total Revenues	104,040	147,000	180,835	207,490
Expenses				
Programming fee	29,664	45,320	56,333	64,708
Owner's fee	5,206	7,118	8,715	10,247
Sales commission	4,500	1,000	300	200
Guide	1,512	2,100	2,373	2,478
Billing and collection	3,240	4,500	5,085	5,310
Customer service	3,780	5,250	5,933	6,195
Maintenance	4,320	6,000	6,780	7,080
Bad debt	1,901	2,900	3,605	4,142
Total Expenses	54,123	74,188	89,124	100,360
Operating cash flow	49,917	72,812	91,711	107,130
Depreciation expense	16,983	19,443	20,585	21,024
Income before interest, fees/and taxes	32,934	53,369	71,126	86,106
Interest expense	13,694	16,004	17,184	17,758
Management fees[a]	14,904	15,700	18,384	20,949
Net income before taxes	4,336	21,665	35,558	47,399
Income taxes	2,168	10,833	17,779	23,700
Net profit	2,168	10,832	17,779	23,699

[a]Administrative fee: 10% gross revenues; construction management fee: $10 per unit installed.

C. Pay-TV Economics in Multiunit Dwellings Compared to Single-Family Houses

Cable operators in many cities have created an opportunity for SMATV by being slow to wire apartment buildings. Their reluctance to wire apartments and other multiunit dwellings and to concentrate on construction that passes single-family houses is due to several factors. Apartment buildings have higher churn (turnover) rates than single-family houses, since the apartment population is more mobile; there are higher incidences of decoder boxes being stolen, and more incidents of bad debt and bounced checks with apartment residents. These and other variables are compared in table 1.4, which is based on a 1982 survey of pay-TV operators serving both apartments and single-family houses. Decoder boxes were stolen nearly twice as often by apartment dwellers, and disconnects for a variety of reasons were higher in a multiunit environment. On the basis of these observations, table 1.5 calculates the additional expense incurred by an operator serving 100 apartment-dwelling subscribers rather than 100 single-family houses.

The highest costs are $140 extra to serve 100 apartment dwellers for disconnecting subscribers who do not pay their bills, and $89 for disconnecting subscribers who voluntarily discontinue service. The fig-

Table 1.4 Pay-TV Economic Characteristics of Households
Multiunit Dwellings vs. Single-Family Households

	Single-Family Houses (Cable TV's natural market)	*Multiunit Dwellings (SMATV's natural market)*
Stolen box	100 Index	183
Bad debt loss	100	166
Bounced check	100	160
Nonpay disconnects ("hard discos")	100	119
Sales orders cancelled before installation ("erosion")	100	126
Service call required	100	119
Voluntary disconnects	100	112

SOURCES: CableVision; Communications Studies and Planning International.

ures are based on two elements: the cost of each item and the average frequency with which it occurs in each environment. Therefore, while disconnects are only 12 to 19 percent higher in an apartment setting, their frequent occurence in any pay-TV system generates the highest marginal cost.

It is important to note that addressability allows the SMATV to significantly reduce many of the costs shown in table 1.5. A large component of any disconnect is the cost of sending a service technician to the dwelling to pick up the decoder box and adjust the wiring. With addressability, the disconnect can be accomplished in 8 to 10 seconds by a central computer, which may even be located in a distant city. Subscribers who are late with payments can also be controlled closely by temporarily switching off their service.

Finally, the addressable system illustrated in table 1.1 allows the operator to put a low-priced decoder box (cost $25) in the subscriber's apartment and to control tier levels with a "wall tap," placed permanently in the wall of the apartment unit and having the dimensions of an electrical outlet. In a nonaddressable SMATV system, decoder boxes cost $50 to $75. Stolen boxes are, therefore, clearly less of a problem in

Table 1.5. Higher Cost of Pay-Television Business in Multiunit Dwelling Setting (not an addressable environment)

	Marginal Cost for 100 Multiunit Households vs. 100 Single-Family Houses per Year	Higher Incidence Multiunit Household vs. Single-Family House
Nonpay disconnect	$140	19%
Voluntary disconnects	89	12
Service call required	36	19
Sales orders cancelled	33	26
Bad debt loss	26	66
Bounced check	21	60
Stolen box	4	83

SOURCE: Dallas-based cable operations in single-family households compared to Dallas-based multiunit pay TV operation.

NOTE: Average frequency for multiunit dwellings (SMATV) compared to average frequency for single-family households, times cost per incident per year, times 100 households.

an addressable system using wall taps. Service calls can also be reduced
if the operator uses the $25 boxes, since these can be inventoried with
the apartment manager for quick replacements. This often makes it
unnecessary to send a service technician to the apartment.

IV. MULTICHANNEL MICROWAVE DISTRIBUTION SERVICE (MMDS)

A. Background

With several major 12- to 20-channel multichannel microwave distribution services (MMDS) in the start-up stage, MMDS is likely to become
the most profitable of the "cable substitutes," and also the largest in
terms of the number of subscribers. MMDS is likely to attract over 8
million subscribers by 1992, compared to only 5 to 6 million subscribers for the next largest of the new pay TV media, DBS. In urban areas
where cable construction promises to be very expensive, MMDS could
move in early and establish a consumer penetration which the cable
system, launched later and priced higher, would not be able to challenge
very easily.

MMDS has several important economic advantages: the headend capital investment to launch an MMDS system is under one million dollars,
and its operating costs are lower than those of DBS. Subscriber equipment costs about $150 to $175, compared to an estimated $380 to $480
for DBS subscriber equipment and installation. As a result, MMDS can
underprice its competitors in cable and DBS, while offering more channels than DBS.

In theory, a total of 29 channels are available for MMDS entertainment services, a significant increase over the *two channels* which the
FCC authorized for multipoint microwave distribution service (MDS) in
1962. Microband, owned by Tymshare, operates MDS pay-TV systems
in 75 cities, transmitting Home Box Office, for example, as a single-
channel service to roughly 60,000 subscribers in the New York area.
Another eight channels are awarded by the FCC through a lottery. The
FCC awards two four-channel grants per market (*four channels* to one
operator). Applicants include all three networks, large group broadcasters, cable MSOs, newspapers, SMATV operators, and existing MDS
operators like Microband. An additional *three channels* become avail-

able in mid-1985 on Operational Fixed Service (OFS) channels. Finally, and most importantly, an additional twenty channels are available on the Instructional Television Fixed Service portion of the spectrum (ITFS channels). A major MMDS activity is therefore to sign deals with universities and other nonprofit institutions likely to have ITFS licenses. Instructional channels were poorly utilized. For example, only 5 percent were in use in 1980. All major MMDS applicants are seeking to negotiate deals with educational institutions, who are allowed (as of April 1984) to sell the bulk of time on their channel or channels to an entertainment service like an MMDS operator.

Like subscription television, MMDS broadcasts a scrambled signal to a special antenna and decoder at a private home or multiunit dwelling. MMDS, however, has much lower capital and operating costs than STV. The signal range of MMDS is about 25 to 30 miles; an important limitation of MMDS is that it requires line-of-sight transmission.

Multipoint distribution service (MDS) is a microwave-fed communications service used primarily for the distribution of pay television as well as business and government data in metropolitan areas. It was created in 1962 when the Federal Communications Commission set aside a high-frequency portion of the electromagnetic spectrum, 2.15 to 2.16 GHz, for the distribution of local communications services to the public. Regulated as a common carrier service by the FCC, an MDS operator (also known as the MDS licensee) constructs a low-power transmitting facility, generally with a reach of 15 to 30 miles, and leases time to outside parties for communication services of their selection. The MDS signal is picked up by a microwave receiving dish on an apartment roof or subscriber home. For multiunit subscribers, coaxial cable distributes the MDS signal from the dish to the building units. A down-converter changes the microwave signal into the frequency of a conventional television channel.

When MDS was created, it was expected that private business and Instructional Television Fixed Service (ITFS) communications would be its primary use. No one envisioned that it would take more than ten years for commercial MDS services to develop, and that afterwards MDS would become one of the major methods of delivering pay television in urban areas. CableVision estimates that in 1983/84 MDS systems in the United States broadcast single-channel pay television programming to 600,000 subscribers in apartments, hotels, motels, and single-family homes.The local nature of the MDS signal can be turned into a programming advantage. Unlike DBS, which transmits a single program format to the entire country, MDS has considerable flexibility in the selection of local programming and in the ways that programming can be delivered to the station transmitter.

While these advantages cannot materially challenge the superior value delivered by cable television, they do make multichannel MDS the strongest overall competitor for pay TV services to homes not passed by cable.

Originally conceived as a means of transmitting business data, MDS has attracted pay-TV entrepreneurs because technology advances have dropped the price of an MDS antenna to $100 to $150. Prior to this change in subscriber economics, the natural market for MDS was limited to reception clusters like apartments and hotels, where the cost of the receiving equipment could be spread over many subscribers.

B. MDS Economics

According to industry sources, single-channel MDS services for subscriber entertainment cost an average of $16 in 1982. This monthly price compares favorably with the average monthly fee for cable and for subscription television, which averaged about $21 per month in 1982. However, the monthly service charges are likely to increase for multichannel MDS. The discussion of MDS economics that follows focuses on the economics of multichannel MDS service.

1. Headend and Subscriber Equipment Costs

The costs of an MDS system are subject to several variables: the physical configuration of the market served; whether a 10-watt or a 100-watt transmitter is used; whether or not a satellite receiving dish is installed; whether down-converters and antennas are bought separately or as combination units; whether the signal is scrambled; and whether the system is addressable or not.

Headend costs for multichannel MDS stations range from $700,000 to $900,000. A system equipped for satellite signal reception could cost an additional $100,000 to $120,000. Both a CCC/CBS multichannel MDS proposal and a Microband multichannel MDS proposal target station capital costs at well under $1 million, and include the cost of satellite-fed programming.

Subscriber equipment costs, in 1984, were between $150 and $200; if the MDS system is addressable, 1984 costs per subscriber are estimated as $220 to $300. Addressability adds a revenue stream from pay-per-view events, allows closer control of subscribers who pay late, and reduces service calls.

2. Subscriber Pricing

The low equipment costs for multichannel MDS, both at the station transmitter site and for the SMATV operator or the individual sub-scriber home, make multichannel MDS one of the strongest noncable pay-TV competitors in markets where topography favors MDS trans-mission.

According to estimates based on the FCC filings of CCC/CBS and Microband, an installation fee of $50 and a monthly fee of $20 to $23 for a five- to six-channel MDS service will provide a good income return to MDS suppliers as well as a healthy subscriber growth. This assumes that the MDS supplier is willing to amortize the cost of MDS subscriber equipment and installation over a 24-month period in order to gain faster market penetration. Accordingly, $5 a month is budgeted to amortize the subscriber equipment, and $15 to $18 a month is allo-cated for profit, programming, customer service, and billing. Alter-natively, the MDS supplier could charge the subscriber the full price of subscriber equipment and installation, $150 to $200, and reduce the monthly fee to $15 to $18.

3. Breakeven and Market Size

Cash flow breakeven in a typical MDS city is only 4,000 to 5,000 subscribers, compared to 45,000 to 50,000 subscribers for subscription television (STV). This lower breakeven will allow MDS to serve many markets that STV cannot enter. I expect MDS stations to bring multi-channel pay TV programming to uncabled parts of large urban areas by establishing more than one MDS transmitter in a city. Los Angeles would be a good example.

Very small population centers, on the other hand, will often be served better by low-power television (LPTV). Although LPTV offers only one channel, its start-up cost (well under $50,000 for the headend) allows LPTV to reach small population clusters that would not be economical for MDS.

V. DIRECT BROADCAST SATELLITE (DBS)

A. Background

On June 23, 1982, the FCC cleared the way for direct-to-home transmission of premium entertainment services via very high-powered satellites. When this kind of service is available, satellite receiver dishes placed on top of a home or apartment building will be able to pick up five or six full television channels for home viewing. At least three of these channels will be delivered without advertising. The DBS concept essentially streamlines the delivery of pay television programming. High-powered satellites in a fixed position 22,300 miles above the earth transmit programming (beamed from a program supplier) directly to subscribers' homes equipped with dish-shaped receiving antennas two to two-and-a-half feet in diameter.

While DBS will not be a major competitor for cable, it does have a market in areas which cannot be served profitably by cable, and to SMATV operators both inside and outside cable franchise areas. The point/multipoint distribution architecture of DBS gives it advantages in serving sparsely populated areas and in delivering pay-per-view more economically than cable. Despite these advantages, it is doubtful that the DBS market will be able to support more than two fully integrated competitors, since it is likely to have only five to six million subscribers by 1990 (a 15 to 20 percent share of U.S. households not passed by cable). The high capital requirements of DBS have already narrowed the field.

The technological concept that makes direct-to-home satellite broadcasting possible is the use of high-powered satellite signals which can be received by small TVRO (television receive-only) antennas, affordable to a mass consumer market. Business planning for DBS services has assumed considerable pricing flexibility, based on the assumption that DBS will serve areas without competition from cable TV. Early prices are $30 to $40 for five channels of programming, and a $300 to $400 installation charge. Competitors will differentiate themselves on price; Comsat has signaled its intention to do so.

The basic concept of "interim DBS" is the use of medium-powered satellites, which are available at a lower cost than the high-powered satellites necessary for "true DBS" but require larger and more expensive subscriber dish antenna and electronics to receive and amplify the weaker signal.

The success of interim DBS services depends on the resolution of two key questions: (1) *How expensive* the subscriber equipment will be; 1985 forecasts range from $550 to $750, depending on the DBS company consulted. (2) *How effective* the entire system (particularly the subscriber receiving antenna and electronics) will be in creating a high-quality picture.

The key issue behind an economic assessment of DBS is the advantage of high-powered DBS relative to medium-powered DBS. Stated differently, at what price does the far higher cost of high-powered satellite transmission justify the reduced cost of the dish antenna to the consumer? The market price for a medium-powered transponder, for example, was about $10.5 million. Each pay-TV channel requires one transponder, and most services back up their transponders with a standby. A high-powered transponder costs an estimated $14.5 to $15 million. Comsat's Satellite Business Systems (SBS) asked $17 million but found no buyers.

Advances in the technology of consumer dishes and backup electronics, especially low noise amplifiers, have dramatically altered the outlook for DBS by making it possible to capture signals from medium-powered satellites on small dishes. In the trade-off between investment in the sky and investment on the ground, Comsat/STC chose to invest in the sky, and will transmit a very high-powered Ku-band signal capable of being picked up by a two-foot dish (three in some areas). United Satellite's strategy, on the other hand, is to broadcast on a medium-powered C-band satellite, requiring three- to four-foot dishes at a reported cost of $650 to $750 including installation.

It is important to note that dish technology has improved so rapidly that today, a one-meter dish is sufficient to pick up the HBO signal from Galaxy, which is a stronger-than-average medium-powered (C-band) satellite. Galaxy's effective radiated power (EIRP) is 39, compared to about 30 for conventional C-band satellites. For comparison, the EIRP of the high-powered SBS transponders offered at $17 million is 48.

The C-band, medium-powered DBS service has two important advantages:

1. Price

High-powered transponders are at least five times as expensive as medium-powered transponders. To illustrate, a high-powered satellite carrying six to eight transponders costs about $500 million. Assuming eight transponders, the cost of each was about $60 million, compared to a market price of $10.5 million for a medium-powered transponder. C-band transponder prices reflected a glut, and have continued to soften in 1984, as almost as many transponders are scheduled to be launched as are already in orbit.

2. Performance

High-powered satellites transmit a signal that can be received by a dish 50 to 65 percent of the diameter of a medium-powered satellite. However, rain attentuates the Ku-band signal, but does not attenuate the C-band signal.

B. DBS Economics and Competition

DBS's pricing flexibility will be a key factor in its successful market penetration. In this section I will first compare DBS to cable on the basis of its marginal capital cost and provide an estimate of fixed construction costs for DBS. Second, I compare DBS to multichannel MDS, emphasizing subscriber equipment costs. Third, I compare DBS to low-power television services.

It is increasingly clear that DBS will have to price at a relatively high level to cover fixed costs and return a profit. It is also likely that DBS will encounter significant price competition in parts of both rural and urban markets from LPTV and multichannel MDS. In urban areas, multichannel MDS will offer significant price competition to DBS and provide the same product. DBS should do better in those urban areas that have many apartments and condominiums—these offer DBS a natural partner in the SMATV operators who wire multiunit dwellings, and they will also be the areas that cable operators wire last (see the above section on SMATV economics.) In rural areas, DBS will meet competition from low-power television services.

1. Competition with Cable

Given spectrum allocations, cable can offer more channels than DBS. While a Browne Bortz study (1981) established that pay-television subscribers tend to concentrate their viewing on four or five channels, it is also clear that when offered identical prices, consumers will favor the choice of 36 or 54 channels rather than 5 or 6. DBS can deliver up to half a dozen entertainment channels, as well as many one-way text channels. DBS will not, however, offer two-way text and information channels for such services as home shopping and home banking. The capability for interactive services on DBS is technologically possible but prohibitively expensive. Cable clearly dominates in its ability to offer a broad range of entertainment and information services.

Second, comparing the two services on price, it is less well known that DBS is at a price disadvantage relative to cable. The average installed capital cost per subscriber is roughly the same for cable and DBS, but the *marginal* capital cost, that is, the equipment investment for one more subscriber added to an existing system, clearly favors cable. This is owing to appreciably lower cable converter costs compared to DBS home receiver costs, as shown in table 1.6.

Table 1.6. Cable and DBS Capital Investment Per Subscriber

	Average Cost	*Marginal Cost*
Cable	$500–$600	$120–$160
DBS	$500–$650	$230–$240

Source: CSP International.

Note: Assumption: Pay TV services delivered to individual homes, not units of multiunit dwellings.

Table 1.7 Estimated Cost of System Construction,
Comsat ($ million)

Construction/Preoperational Costs	First Year
Satellite development and launch	$252.0
Ground System	13.0
Capital investment in rented indoor electronics and outdoor microwave units	31.8
Program production equipment	3.5
Administrative/start-up costs and working capital	93.0
Subtotal	$393.3

Source: Satellite Television Corporation FCC Application.

a. Capital Costs. Comsat's Satellite Television Corporation filed its view of the capital investment necessary to launch DBS (table 1.7). The development and launch of Comsat's satellites were estimated at $252 million. Industry observers believe this cost, which accounts for 64 percent of early capital investment, will be considerably higher. STC has announced, in addition, a $25 million marketing budget to launch DBS. More important, Comsat has been criticized for taking a system-design approach that dramatically increased the cost "in the sky"—the $252 million figure—to achieve a small reduction in the diameter of the dish on the subscriber's roof.

b. Subscriber Equipment Costs. The cost of a receiver dish, low noise amplifier (LNA), decoder, and installation for DBS could very well be the key to its success or failure. There is a large area of uncertainty surrounding these costs in 1986 and 1987, but one can make some useful observations. In late 1984, the subscriber equipment needed for DBS could be bought for about $600. In the two years that follow, Comsat expects subscriber equipment to drop to $350 to $400. Oak Industries, which decided not to pursue its initial interest in DBS, projects substantially higher figures. The unknown variables here are how fast suppliers will move down the cost curve of accumulated production experience. The problem is that the experience curve for DBS equipment is going to be fragmented among several suppliers. Economies of scale will also reduce costs, but again, they will be distributed over competing equipment suppliers. These factors make it difficult for suppliers to agree on the probable cost of subscriber equipment in 1986 and 1987.

Oak projects subscriber equipment prices at least 15 to 20 percent higher than Comsat's $300 to $400 estimate. The company is essentially skeptical about the ability of advances in chip technology to drive down the price of the LNA while maintaining its efficiency. Oak's stategic moves are undoubtedly due in part to its judgement that subscriber equipment costs will be higher than originally expected. Thus it withdrew from its "interim DBS" business, which was to have been launched in 1983, and decided to make SMATV operators an integral part of its business planning for DBS in 1986.

2. Competition with Multichannel MDS

Several factors could make multichannel MDS a formidable competitor to DBS for households not passed by cable.

a. Quicker Entry. Multichannel MDS can be launched at a capital cost of under $1 million per station, according to CBS and Microband, and CBS estimates that stations can be built in only six months. Multichannel MDS should have a good one- to two-year lead on DBS and enjoy the favored position of an entrenched pay-TV supplier. While both services will offer roughly the same four- to six-channel capacity in their early stages, MDS can capitalize on its programming flexibility.

b. Greater Programming Diversity and Flexibility. DBS must send national, homogeneous programming across the entire continent. MDS, on the other hand, tailors programming to appeal to the audience in its 20 to 25 mile range. It can offer local sports or movies selected for a regional appeal, and has many ways to get the programming to the MDS transmitter, such as satellite feeds or physical distribution of video tapes or films.

c. Lower Subscriber Equipment Costs. Table 1.8 compares subscriber equipment costs for DBS and MDS services, accepting Comsat's low ($300–$400) estimate. Comparative equipment costs for multichannel MDS are roughly only $175 to $250. Given these equipment costs,

Table 1.8. Multichannel MDS Subscriber Equipment Costs Compared to DBS

	Multichannel MDS[a]	*True DBS*
Total subscriber equipment costs[a]	$175–$250	$300–$400
Hypothetical subscriber pricing		
Installation fee	$50	$100
Total monthly fee	$20–$23	$30–$33
Amortization of equipment	$5	$15
Programming, billing, etc.	$15–$18	$15–$18
Total	$20–$23	$30–$33

SOURCES: Comsat, Microband, CSP International.
[a]Includes receive antenna, LNA, decoder, and installation.

multichannel MDS can price lower than DBS. As shown in the table, MDS could charge $50 for installation and $20 to $23 a month. Furthermore, MDS could offer self-installation of equipment purchased at a retail store, while for DBS, a trained installer must spend roughly four hours.

3. DBS Competition with Low-Power Television (LPTV)

DBS stands a good chance of competing in low-density rural markets, where the number of homes per square mile is too low to attract an MDS operator. These rural markets, however, will also be attractive to low-power television (LPTV) operators. Total transmitter and studio costs of a normal ten-mile-range LPTV station are only about $40,000, with transmitter cost at about $8,000 to $10,000 and falling, in real terms, at about 5 percent per year.

4. DBS Feeds to SMATV Operators

Because they can deliver DBS service to many apartments via the apartment MATV system, SMATV operators are a good initial market for DBS. The DBS receiving equipment and programming package will allow SMATV operators to make a profit serving far smaller multiunit dwelling complexes than they can now. Today, SMATV needs a complex of over 500 units to be profitable. Since an SMATV system needs roughly 3,500 subscribers in a city to reach breakeven, the ability to increase penetration of smaller buildings with a DBS partnership, improves the outlook dramatically for SMATV.

VI. SUBSCRIPTION TELEVISION (STV)

A. Background

Subscription television (STV) is a single-channel pay-TV service which is broadcast in scrambled form for part or all of a day over conventional UHF and VHF television channels. Scrambling is meant to insure that only those television sets equipped with a decoder box can receive the movies and sports programming. STV transmits a standard broadcast signal via a UHF channel to a subscriber's special antenna, decoder, and standard television receiver. STV headends, located in or near major cities at a VHF station, receive programming both by physical distribution (i.e., reels of movies are flown to the STV station) and by satellite (e.g., a live pay-per-view boxing match). The signal is scrambled at the local transmitter site and unscrambled by a decoder attached to the subscriber's television receiver. The decoder costs about $120 to $150. In 1984, *CableFile '84* reported a total of 1,324,000 STV basic subscribers, using mid-1983 counts, compared to 1,349,150 counted by CableVision in 1982. While STV apparently managed to maintain its nationwide level of subscribers, the number of systems dropped from 29 in 1982 to 25 in 1983. More important, where cable and SMATV are actively being developed, STV subscriber counts drop quickly—for example, in early 1982 Dallas had over 100,000 STV subscribers, and by mid-1983, only 54,000.

STV operators typically enter the business by purchasing UHF channels or, if cross-ownership regulations prohibit that approach, by leasing channels during either evening or weekend hours or on a 24-hour basis from a UHF station owner. An easing of FCC rules has made entry into the STV market simpler.

STV operators purchase their films and sports rights directly from producers, or buy the programming packages of other STV operators. Their main program offerings include 40 to 45 movies per month, sports, occasional pay-per-view events, and an adult tier of late night programming.

The fact that subscription television (STV) has attracted so much attention as a challenger to cable television's dominance has little to do with the underlying business strength of STV. With its single-channel programming, unenhanced broadcast signal, and relatively high price, STV is not a real competitor to cable, and has trouble attracting and retaining subscribers even in areas which are not passed by cable.

Industry observers have given STV services consideration because they have a large subscriber base and because they provide clear competition to cable television in Los Angeles. In 1983, with just over 1.3 million subscribers, STV had more than twice as many customers as the second most popular noncable pay-TV service, MDS. STV began in 1976 and experienced fast growth because its large, well-funded entrants saw it as a short-lived opportunity to make money on pay television before cable arrived in the major cities; it was expected to mature very rapidly. Subscriber bases were built up fast through heavy mass media advertising, particularly television ads. Since the STV signal could be instantly broadcast to all homes within the UHF signal range from the first day of operation, subscribers could easily get service after the quick installation of a roof antenna and receipt of a decoder box to unscramble the movie and sports programming. The early demise of STV has been postponed as the politics of cable franchising has lengthened the pre-cable period.

Nevertheless, the 1.3 million subscriber base of STV severely tested the abilities of system operators to manage the installation and the back paperwork in the peak years of 1980 and 1981. Most operators alienated subscribers during this period, as they could not handle their unexpected growth and still provide good customer service.

An influential study of cable and its competitors published in 1982 by Browne, Bortz, and Coddington (Pottle and Bortz 1982) showed STV as a substantial competitor to cable. The study was commissioned by the National Cable Television Association (NCTA) to impress on Washington that cable faced substantial competition from other media. In its effort to avoid regulation, the cable industry argued that it did not have a "monopoly" position in franchised areas—the view held by some legislators and FCC staff in Washington—because there was competition from other pay-TV services. Using subscriber data gathered in Los Angeles (the most favored of STV markets for several unusual reasons), the Bortz study clearly implied that STV could hold its own against cable competition. In fact, Los Angeles STV subscribers declined from over 500,000 in 1982 to 271,000 in June 1983.

In commissioning the Bortz study and directing its slant, the NCTA did not imagine the news would reach beyond Washington to Wall Street. Yet ironically, the net result of cable's desire to appear part of a healthy competitive battle in Washington was to damage its ability to raise capital on Wall Street, as well as some short-lived attention to STV as a serious long-term business.

In fact, STV has fundamental problems as a business. Before STV, pay-television executives marveled at the astounding appetite of the American people for pay-TV services. STV definitely tests the limits of that appetite. With one channel of indifferent signal quality priced at approximately $21 a month, STV operators have attempted to establish a business at the outer frontier of what people will pay for uninterrupted movie programming. Systems which are striving to reach breakeven find it difficult to attract new subscribers, even with free installation offers.

Even though subscribers for adult-only programs seem to be on the rise, STV churn rates (i.e., the percentage of all subscribers who disconnect in any month) are running at 5 to 6 percent per month, as compared to between 3 and 4 percent per month for pay cable. Churn is costly for a business where a serviceman must visit a subscriber's house to install equipment and again to pick up the expensive decoder box whenever a subscriber disconnects. An STV subscriber must maintain a subscription for about 18 to 22 months for an operator to break even. Today, many STV subscribers drop service well before 18 months.

B. Economics of STV

STV systems with less than 40,000 subscribers are suffering substantial cash losses. The causes of their disappointing performances are:

(a) Subscriber disconnection (churn) is much higher than expected, running at 5 to 6 percent per month rather than the 2 to 3 percent projected.

(b) Piracy of the STV signal has deprived operators of significant revenues.

(c) The $20 to $22 monthly subscription price has caused bad debts to rise.

(d) Difficulties have arisen with STV technology. In particular, the decoder boxes placed in subscriber homes to unscramble programming have not proven as reliable as expected.

1. The Basics

Revenues and expenses per subscriber are provided in table 1.9. Revenue projections are based on a price of $21 per month for standard service, and the assumption that 40 percent of the subscriber base also takes a $5 adult tier.

General operating and administrative expenses, totaling about $33 per subscriber per year, include: customer service telephone inquiries, billing, and service technician visits to fix subscriber equipment—e.g., to change defective decoder boxes or to reorient antenna.

Origination expenses are a fixed cost that can be roughly allocated to subscribers. For a system with 50,000 subscribers, the cost of leasing time from the UHF station and operating the STV studio runs at about $5 per year per subscriber.

Marketing to established subscribers involves actions aimed at preventing voluntary subscriber disconnect. Programs to discourage churn

Table 1.9. Summary of STV Economics, Revenues, and Expenses per Subscriber, 1982 Estimates

Annual revenue per average subscriber for programming service[a]		$265
Annual continuing expenses per average subscriber		
Programming	$75	
Semivariable general and administrative	18	
Operating	15	
Origination	5	
Remarketing	4	
		$117
Cost of acquiring one new STV subscriber		$180
Cost of one subscriber disconnect		$ 40

SOURCE: Communications Studies and Planning International.

[a]Less bad debt and late pay allocation. Assumes basic service price is $21 per month, 40% of subscriber base take adult tier at $5 per month. Also assumes an average STV system of 50,000 subscribers.

have recently been given more attention, and usually range from $2 to $10 per subscriber per year; for purposes of the calculation, $4 is assumed.

2. Breakeven Calculations

In the early days of STV, operators planned to reach breakeven at 20,000 to 25,000 subscribers. As marketing costs skyrocketed in the effort to acquire subscribers as quickly as possible, hefty advertising budgets and sales costs made breakeven an elusive goal for nearly all STV systems. Breakeven in 1980–1982 was often at over 100,000 subscribers per station.

Recently, STV systems have shifted their focus to cost-cutting rather than spending to acquire that new subscriber. The breakeven calculation shown in table 1.10 illustrates an STV station which has reduced expenses to achieve breakeven. Annual fixed costs are roughly $5.2 million a year. The annual gross margin is calculated at $147 a year. Therefore, the station's breakeven is 35,000 subscribers. For STV stations which have not reduced costs, breakeven ranges from 60,000 to 80,000 subscribers.

3. Implications for the Future Development of STV

This overview of STV economics raises two important concerns about the business. First is the high cost of churn. The cost of replacing subscribers who disconnect is roughly $160 to $180 and the cost of the disconnect is about $40, including office paperwork as well as the service technician visit. As the competing pay TV services, such as multichannel MDS and DBS, enter STV's urban markets, STV systems

Table 1.10. STV Operating Breakeven

Fixed Costs	$5.2 million	
Monthly revenue per subscriber		$ 22.00
Variable costs per subscriber		9.75
	Monthly gross margin	$ 12.25
	Annual gross margin	$147.00

Source: Communications Studies and Planning International.
Note: Breakeven equals $5.2 million ÷ $147 = 35,000 subscribers.

will find their churn rates rising, and the cost of acquiring new subscribers even higher.

Second, since STV systems have high breakeven subscriber levels, there will be a point when many STV systems, faced with competition from four- and five-channel systems as well as the growth of cable television, realize that they cannot hope to reach breakeven. In the mid-1980s, many STV stations will, in all likelihood, sell their subscribers to competing pay-TV stations at prices ranging from $135 to $175 per subscriber (1983 dollars). In some cities, multichannel MDS operators may offer to acquire the office operations of STV stations— customer service, billing, those service technicians directly employed by STV, and general management. The STV "window" has existed largely because cable franchising battles and the slow machinery of urban politics have decelerated cable penetration of important urban areas.

VII. LOW-POWER TELEVISION (LPTV)

A. Background

Low-power television is the first new conventional TV service to be approved by the FCC in over twenty years. The possibility of owning a relatively low-cost broadcast station with a broadcast radius of up to 40 miles has created great excitement from a wide range of entrepreneurs, including newspaper publishers, nonprofit organizations, minority businesses, and well-known national corporations. The licensing of these new stations, according to the FCC, will promote more diversity in media ownership, since start-up costs of less than $50,000 should not prohibit any organization or business from embarking upon this kind of television venture.

The first low-power TV stations came about when some television translator operators succeeded in obtaining FCC waivers of rules to broadcast locally made programming and to record and reschedule playback of programs being received from high-power broadcast stations whose signals were being boosted. In 1983, the FCC approved the service as a broadcast service in its own right. Although it is limited to substantially less power than full power UHF and VHF broadcasters, as

Table 1.11. Comparison of Effective Radiated Power of Low-Power Television and Full-Service Broadcast Television

	UHF	*VHF*
LPTV stations	2,500–20,000 watts	100 watts
Full-power broadcast stations		
Channels 2–6		100,000 watts
Channels 7–13		316,000 watts
Channels 14–69	5,000,000 watts	

SOURCE: FCC Broadcast Bureau.

illustrated in table 1.11, its stations can still cover a radius of 5 to 40 miles, depending on topography and climate.

LPTV is currently defined by the FCC as a "secondary service," which in practical terms means that low-power stations may receive signal interference from but not cause signal interference to such "full service" licensed communications facilities as full-power broadcast stations. Though this "secondary" status is likely to have little technical impact on LPTV stations in rural and semirural areas, avoiding interference with other broadcasters may become a problem for LPTV operators in the urban TV markets.

Because the maximum transmission power of LPTV stations is low, LPTV transmission sites must be in or quite close to the target broadcast area. The choice of UHF or VHF signals for a specific LPTV station varies, depending upon the kind of obstruction or interference the signal may encounter. For instance, choosing a low-band VHF signal is preferable if homes in the target broadcast area are surrounded by hills, buildings, or trees. However, if the signal encounters man-made interference, a UHF channel is a superior choice. UHF is therefore usually better for a station which attempts to reach homes in urban areas.

A survey of ideas for LPTV which have appeared in several FCC applications gives a further view of how companies and individuals are thinking about the proposed service. An early application was submitted, for instance, by the Community TV Network (CTN), a group of black attorneys who formerly worked for the FCC. They proposed to broadcast satellite-delivered programming geared for black audiences during the day and to carry subscription TV service from Wometco during prime-time hours. Programming would be carried in a number of cities, including Denver, Indianapolis, Louisville, Tampa, Houston, New Orleans, Memphis, Kansis City, Missouri, St. Louis, and Dallas. CTN estimated that its program facilities, transmission equipment, and satellite equipment would cost approximately $130,000.

It is important to note that, contrary to its image, LPTV is not simply a broadcasting service for rural audiences, since it also has a significant potential to reach major-market audiences. In rural markets, LPTV could function as a pay service to individual subscribers, but in major markets LPTV revenues are much more likely to come from advertising. While the focus of this article is the new pay media, it is worth understanding advertising-supported LPTV.

An LPTV operator could acquire LPTV stations in major markets, each one with a signal radius of 7 miles, for example, and cover a good portion of an ADI. A boosted signal, provided it is noninterfering, can boost LPTV output further. In nearly all major markets, LPTV and translator applications have been filed, and awards will be made in the LPTV in late 1985 and 1986. The lottery has begun with applications from the most rural taken first. There are noninterfering frequencies still available in nearly every major market. Recently, however, the FCC made it more difficult for LPTV to find noninterfering frequencies in major cities, because it ruled that it would not consider an LPTV application that was *potentially* interfering, that is, one that conflicted with a full-power TV station that was only at the application stage. Sears' Allstate Venture Capital, for example, has funded Neighborhood TV, a new venture located in Phoenix, Arizona, which has translator applications in virtually every major market. Neighborhood TV has filed a translator application in Boston for channel 61. Recently, a full-power UHF application for channel 62 has been filed, so the Sears-backed application will be declined.

B. Economics of LPTV

With all the discussion of low-power television's extremely low cost, some observers are worried that many applicants have not correctly appraised the true investment that may be required. Though considerably less expensive then full-power transmission facilities, a 1,000-watt transmitter for a 20 to 30 mile broadcast radius may cost between $60,000 and $100,000. The cost of originating programming and/or purchasing programming for the station will boost costs higher by about one half.

Even these figures, however, are low compared to the investment that the Bemidji, Minnesota, LPTV station has made. Though many LPTV observers may feel that high investment will be uncharacteristic of future low-power operations, it is useful to examine the Bemidji station to see how choices about quality of service and the size and topography of the service area may affect an entrepreneur's decisions about justifiable costs. Bemidji's channel 26 is the only commercial station serving a town of 11,500 people. The 1,000-watt transmitter for the station was erected on a 457-foot tower at a site seven miles north of town. Under normal circumstances, a low-power signal such as this might have a radius of approximately 20 miles, but because of the relatively flat terrain, the reach of the station is boosted to a 50-mile radius. The result is that channel 26 reaches a service area containing approximately 40,000 people who are not reached by more than one full-power TV station or by a cable service.

Channel 26 is run as a commercial station supplemented by STV, and its owner, who has built five full-power broadcast stations in his career, decided that an investment of approximately $800,000 was warranted. The company has spent $463,000 for construction and $600,000 per year for its total operation. About $100,000 has been spent on a mobile production unit and $102,000 for a building. Programming begins at 8:00 A.M. with syndicated shows from a satellite, an hour of local news, a local TV magazine program on local people and events, and satellite-delivered weather forecasting.

Channel 26 contracted with SelecTV in Los Angeles to provide subscription programming via satellite from 7:00 P.M. until sign-off to supplement revenues from local advertising. The STV service was initially offered for $18.50 a month, and the goal of the station was to sign on 1,500 subscribers in the first year.

In the pay-TV market, economic forecasts show that LPTV delivery may be competitive with MDS. In fact, LPTV is projected to have lower direct and retransmission costs than the other two pay-TV delivery systems. Table 1.12 offers some comparison.

Although small entrepreneurs might be inclined to approach venture capital firms for LPTV financing, many financial experts would be hesitant to advise this approach. Because such firms take between 40

Table 1.12. Comparison of Projected Costs of LPTV and MDS

	LPTV	*MDS*
Cost per channel	$50–$70,000	$75–$100,000
Operations and mainte- nance per channel	$6,000/year	$9,000/year
Subscriber equipment, 1984/85	$150 decoder	$200

and 80 percent of the company, many feel that the small businessman could do better by soliciting commitments from groups of local investors or from a single wealthy member of the community. While venture capital firms are accustomed to financing enterprises with more national and regional visibility, local investors would be more likely to appreciate the services that an LPTV operation will bring to the community that they know.

VIII. CONCLUSION

Today, noncable pay-TV services have attracted a total of roughly 2.75 million subscribers. In 1992, they are likely to account for about 14 million subscribers, a cumulative increase of over 500 percent. The probable distribution of these subscribers among the noncable pay-TV services is given in table 1.14.

By 1990 pay-cable penetration of households passed by cable will be about 60 percent. This figure is based on the assumption that the market for noncable services lies outside the areas passed by cable—cable dominates wherever it is provided. Given this 60 percent penetration rate, by 1992 there will be an estimated 32 million U.S. households not passed by cable. Of these, 40 to 45 percent are likely to subscribe to one or more of the pay-TV services in table 1.13, for a total of about 14 million subscribers. The current penetration of existing noncable services into households not passed by cable is only 8 percent.

Multichannel MDS, DBS, and SMATV will dominate this growth of new pay-TV services.

Based on an analysis of the economics of the new pay-TV media, as well as an understanding of the marketing advantages each service possesses, the outlook for each service in the early 1990s can be estimated. Assessing the attractiveness of each of these "cable substitutes" as a business opportunity raises three key questions:

— Which of the cable substitutes is likely to attract the most subscribers in 1992?
— What level of investment does it take to secure a competitive position in one of the new pay-TV media today?
— Which services are likely to be the most profitable ones in the 1990s?

Among the new pay-TV media, multichannel MDS is likely to attract the greatest number of subscribers in the early 1990s (see table 1.13). Of a total of 14 million subscribers to noncable pay TV services, I estimate that MMDS will attract roughly 8.5 million, compared to the 4.0 million that DBS is likely to attract, and the 2.5 million subscribers SMATV could serve in the early 1990s.

Multichannel MDS could successfully challenge cable in urban areas that are expensive to wire, since major 12- to 20-channel MMDS systems could price the monthly subscription at $20 to $25 and offer two to three premium service channels in the package. MMDS has greater pricing flexibility than DBS, its major competitor along with cable, because the cost to build a transmission station for MMDS with a signal range of 25 to 30 miles is under $1 million. DBS capital costs range from $70 to $500 million, and it should be noted that the competitor who tried to launch a medium-powered DBS service at an estimated $70 million in capital costs, United Satellite, failed in 1984 and was absorbed by STC.

Table 1.13. Projected Subscriber Counts for Several Noncable Pay-TV Services in 1992 (United States only)[a]

	Millions
Multichannel MDS	8.5
Direct broadcast satellite	4.0
Satellite master antenna television	2.5
Low-power television	0.75
Subscription television	0.0

[a]The estimated number of subscribers in 1992 for each pay service was derived by weighing many factors, together with the competitive cost analysis which is the subject of this essay. Taken into account, for example, were signal strength, channel capacity, the projected distribution of households among multiunit dwellings (by size of the MDU), households in rural areas not served by cable, households in areas with a housing density attractive to MMDS, and the households in urban areas that may not receive cable by 1992.

[b]I assume that the majority of SMATV subscribers receive either MMDS or DBS feeds, or both; thus SMATV subscribers may be counted twice or even three times, causing an apparent total of 15.75 million subscribers when the total should be only 14 million.

Furthermore, MMDS subscriber installation fees could be priced much lower than DBS installation fees. The cost of subscriber installation and equipment for DBS is estimated at $380 to $480, compared to about $150 to $175 for MMDS. The practical result of MMDS's lower headend and subscriber equipment costs is that MMDS will be able to price subscriber installation fees at promotional levels (amortizing some of the equipment cost over monthly fees), while DBS subscriber installation fees are likely to remain above $300. For cost comparisons, see table 1.14.

With the availability of Instructional Television Fixed Service (ITFS) channels to MMDS entertainment services, the total number of channels theoretically available to an MMDS operator is 29. In practice, most MMDS systems will probably offer 12 to 20 channels. Most of these systems will be launched very soon, since MMDS does not require a long lead time, and since MMDS is eager to establish consumer franchises in markets that will be served in the future by cable or by DBS. In addition to the 6 to 7 million subscribers MMDS is likely to serve in single-family dwellings in 1992, it should also serve between 1 and 2 million subscribers through SMATV operators, where MMDS becomes a low-cost program feed to SMATV.

Direct Broadcast Satellite (DBS) cannot compete head to head with multichannel MDS in markets where the MMDS signal is a good one. It offers fewer channels at a higher price: 4 to 5 channels for a $300 installation fee and a monthly fee in the $30 range, compared to MMDS's 12 to 20 channels priced at about $25 a month with a $100 to $180 installation fee. Driven to very rural markets by MMDS, DBS is unlikely to attract more than 4 million subscribers by 1992, enough to support only two competitors at most.

While DBS has the clear advantage of serving virtually any household within the continental United States, its high cost puts it at a disadvantage to multichannel MDS. More important, the cost to the subscriber for multichannel MDS receiver equipment could easily be priced under $100, while the DBS subscriber equipment will cost $200 to $300. A key assumption is that MMDS operators subsidize part of the subscriber equipment cost, just as DBS does now. As shown in table 1.14, DBS's capital costs are of a completely different order of magnitude.

Table 1.14. Comparison of Pay-TV Services

	Transmission Capital Investment	Cost of Equipment and Installation per subscriber	Likely Number of Channels Offered	Estimated Reach of Potential Subscriber Households	Average Transmission Investment per Potential Subscriber Reached	Average Transmission and Subscriber Investment per Potential Subscriber	Average Capital Investment per Potential Subscriber and Video Channel Offered
DBS (high power)	$400 million[a]	$380–480	5–7	50 million[d]	$8	$440	$75
Cable Television (700,000 city)	$75–100 million	$150–175	35–54	150,000	$600	$765	$17.20
STV[b]	$1–2 million	$175–250	1	120,000[b]	$12.50	$200	$200
MDS[b]	$1 million	$175–250	10–20	100,000[b,d]	$10.00	$220	$14.60
SMATV[c]	$30–40 thousand	$150–170	10–30	500[c]	$70	$230	$11.50
LPTV[b] (pay)	$200 thousand	$175–200	1	60,000[b]	$3.50	$190	$190

NOTE: This table was compiled and estimated by Eli Noam from various economic and technical information in Jane Henry's paper, in order to compare the order of magnitudes in question.

[a] $400 million assumes building a high-powered system.
[b] Assumes broadcasting in a 700,000 metropolitan area.
[c] Assumes 500-unit building, addressable system, direct satellite feed. Building not rewired.
[d] Not including feed to SMATV systems.

Satellite Master Antenna Television (SMATV) should attract between 2 and 3 million subscribers by 1992. Since it is essentially a small cable system within the confines of a privately owned multiunit dwelling, and protected by a contract between the owner of the property and the SMATV system, SMATV has sound business characteristics. Due to its low barriers to entry and high cash returns on investment, however, SMATV has attracted many small competitors who are poorly financed. The crowded field will undergo consolidation, and by the early 1990s addressable SMATV systems will serve apartments and condominiums with as few as 25 units each, using cheap MMDS and DBS feeds. As the table readily demonstrates, the lowest subscriber equipment costs are held by cable, STV, and SMATV. STV can be ruled out as a competitor, since it offers only one channel. SMATV's investment per subscriber, even assuming an addressable SMATV system, is a low $150 to $170. This fact, together with the barrier to entry posed by SMATV whenever an SMATV operator signs an exclusive contract with a building owner, makes it a powerful competitor against any pay-TV service. By 1990, the majority of SMATV systems will be served by low-cost DBS and MMDS feeds, expanding their channel capacity beyond the offering of current programming received from SatCom III-R.

Low Power Television (LPTV), with a signal range of only 6 to 10 miles, faces difficulties in selling and creating advertising because of its small scale. LPTV will largely be an advertising-supported service, with LPTV stations linked in networks to sell advertising more efficiently. Pay-television subscribers to LPTV could reach between 500,000 and 750,000 by 1992. Pay LPTV will compete with DBS, MMDS, and VCRs. The initial capital cost to build an LPTV headend is about $200,000.

2

Statistical Evidence of Substitutability Among Video Delivery Systems

JONATHAN D. LEVY and
PETER K. PITSCH

CONTENTS

  I. Introduction
 II. The Model
    A. Introduction
    B. The Dependent Variables in the VCR Equations
    C. The Independent Variables in the VCR and Cable Equations
    D. Dependent Variables in the Cable Equations
    E. Hypothesized Signs
    F. Geographic Coverage
 III. Problems of Methodology
    A. The Partial Equilibrium Assumption
    B. The VCR May Be Both Substitute and Complement
    C. Joint Estimation
    D. The Opportunity Cost of Time
 IV. The Results
    A. Simple Correlation Coefficients
    B. The VCR Results
    C. The Cable Results
  V. Conclusions
Appendix

I. INTRODUCTION

The sharp increase in the number of television broadcast stations in the last two decades, combined with the development of various new home video delivery systems, has brought the existing broadcast regulatory structure into question. If consumers can turn to close substitutes, the imposition of ownership and program content restrictions on full-power television stations may be superfluous or even counterproductive. For example, in 1982 an estimated 80 percent of television households were receiving five or more signals (Levy and Setzer 1982:81). While the rapid growth of traditional broadcasting services in their local markets in itself may justify elimination of ownership and content regulation, the arrival of new services can reinforce this conclusion. If the relevant product market for broadcast stations, according to standard antitrust analysis, includes all other means for distributing video programming—cable television, satellite master antenna television (SMATV), low-power television, direct broadcast satellites (DBS), multichannel MDS, and home videocassette recorders (VCRs), it is highly unlikely that broadcasters have significant market power in these local markets.

Market power refers to the ability of a firm or group of firms to profit by raising the price of a product or service above its cost. Two extensions of the concept are needed in order to apply it to video markets. First, quality must be considered. A reduction in the quality of a service (e.g., video programming) at constant price may be an exercise of market power. Second, advertising supports television broadcasting. There is no "price" paid by viewers for programming; advertisers pay broadcasters for exposures to viewers. Because VCRs and cable are currently both pay media, their impact on television advertising markets is slight. Radio and print provide the major substitutes for television advertising. This article will not address itself to that topic.[1]

The primary issue, then, is diversity and quality of programming. The presence of rival delivery systems is likely to improve the quality of broadcast programming. Movies, both theatrical and "made for TV," are staples of broadcast programming. The availability of inexpensive rental cassettes provides viewers with an alternative, one that broadcasters are likely to find increasingly important to consider as VCRs spread. The possibilities of substitution are present even for less similar programming. The advertiser-supported nature of television dictates that it appeal to the mass market. Pay media can appeal to more specialized interests. The possibility that viewers may shift from (mediocre) general-interest programming to specialized programming is likely to stimulate improvements in the quality of programs with mass appeal.

Substitution possibilities extend beyond entertainment programming. Information can also be presented via VCRs, and it is possible that video equivalents of magazines may develop. Even political messages may be distributed by VCR. (This method was used by Ayatollah Khomeini while in exile, for under the Shah, his access to the media was restricted. The fact that it is currently hard to imagine this technique being used in the United States is due perhaps to the wide diversity of readily available viewpoints here.)

If, then, the menu of alternatives available to viewers (and, indeed, speakers) is so wide, regulation of broadcast programming content or commercial messages will not improve consumers' lot. The same analysis supports the FCC policy of not regulating pay-television rates (and preempting state regulation). Indeed, it might support the case against regulation of basic cable rates.

One purpose of this study is to estimate the demand for VCRs and cable in order to obtain some statistical evidence on the substitution of these sources of programming for traditional broadcast service. Previous staff reports of the FCC's office of Plans and Policy have suggested that such substitutability may exist in the case of cable and VCRs (Levy and Setzer, 1982; Gordon, Levy, and Preece 1981; Setzer, Franca, and Cornell 1979). This paper will also attempt to obtain quantitative evidence on substitutability between cable and VCRs.

The next section develops a supply-and-demand model for VCRs and cable service, and describes the data set used to estimate it. The third section discusses the methodological problems arising out of using a state by state model as well as other features of the model. The fourth section describes the results of the data analysis. The final section summarizes our findings and presents suggestions for future research.

II. THE MODEL

A. Introduction

This section develops the empirical models for estimating VCR and cable demand. The basic exposition is presented in some detail for the VCR model, then more briefly for the cable model. Following the expositions is an examination of some methodological difficulties with the underlying model.

The models are simple partial equilibrium ones in which it is assumed that the quantity demanded (of VCR or cable services) is determined by income, population, tastes, own prices, and the prices of substitute and complement goods. The supply is assumed to be perfectly elastic in the relevant range. This assumption appears reasonable in light of the fact that the model is estimated on cross-sectional data.[2] The model can thus be written as:

(1) $Q_{VCR}^d = Q_{VCR}^d [P_{VCR}, P_{cable}, P_{TV}, P_{movies}, P_{cassettes}, Y, N, T]$
(2) $P_{VCR} = K$
(3) $Q_{VCR}^s = Q_{VCR}^d$

where the following definitions obtain:

Q_{VCR}^d = quantity demanded of VCR services
P_{VCR} = price of VCRs
P_{cable} = price of cable service (see subsection B.3.b.)
P_{TV} = "price" of television services (see subsection B.3.c.)
P_{movies} = price of movies
$P_{cassettes}$ = price of cassettes (see below)
Y = income
N = population
T = tastes
Q_{VCR}^s = quantity supplied of VCR services
K = the constant price of VCRs

Equation (2) reflects the perfect elasticity of supply assumption. Substituting (2) into (1) and (1) into the equilibrium condition (3) yields the following reduced-form equation (dropping superscripts):

(4) $Q_{VCR} = Q_{VCR} [K, P_{cable}, P_{TV}, P_{movies}, P_{cassettes}, Y, N, T]$.

As noted above, the model is estimated on cross-sectional data. Data availability and certain conceptual constraints dictate the modeling strategy. The consumer has several video distribution channels from which to choose, some of which are available on a local basis only (e.g., cable, broadcast television, and movies). For VCR services the market may be broader, since the availability of rental cassettes probably is similar across the country. While the local selection may be narrower outside the big population centers, differences are unlikely to be great. Furthermore, cassettes are available for rental on a mail-order basis as well. In any event, market-specific data are needed to examine interactions among the various products. Unfortunately, the least aggregated data available for VCRs are on a state-by-state basis. Data on movies are available for only a limited number of metropolitan areas, and therefore are not included. Although figures are compiled by state every five years, the most recent data are too old.[3]

Even though cable and broadcast markets are local in nature, the VCR data availability dictates using state figures for cable and broadcast television as well. The variables are constructed in such a way as to reflect actual market conditions as closely as possible.

The estimation of equation (4) using state data means that two independent variables drop out of the equation. It seems reasonable to assume $P_{cassettes}$ is constant across states.[4] It is also assumed that each state's population has the same distribution of tastes. This would clearly not be the case if people chose their state of residence on the basis of television availability. Nor would it be true if states varied by age of population or size of household. It is assumed that such variations are insignificant (but see note 9). Hence tastes also drop out of the equation. This leaves the following basic estimating equation:

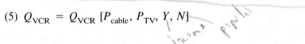

$$(5) \quad Q_{VCR} = Q_{VCR} [P_{cable}, P_{TV}, Y, N]$$

B. The Dependent Variables in the VCR Equations

Data are available on VCR sales to dealers for 1979–1982, on a state-by-state basis. The latest data available on the other relevant variables are also for 1982. Thus, 1982 is the year for which the statistical analysis is made. The ideal VCR variable would consist of the flow of VCR services provided during 1982 by the VCRs in consumer hands then. Such a variable could be constructed by determining the stock of VCRs available and applying a pure rental rate to it. Although the home VCR was introduced to the public in 1975, sales records are only available beginning in 1978 (Electronic Industries Association 1983).[5] Table 2.1 shows the 1978–1982 sales to dealers. The sum of 1979–1982 sales to dealers is 4.7 million, while an estimated 4.5 million were in use at the beginning of 1983. (Electronic Industries Association 1983:16–18). Thus, sales to dealers and final sales are in rough correspondence, even taking into account the 400,000 VCRs sold in 1978. While the VCR is a durable product, some VCRs probably had been scrapped by 1982, and it is likely that most of those scrapped were older models. Thus it is reasonable to take 1979–1982 sales to dealers as an estimate of VCRs in consumers' hands.[6]

Table 2.1. VCR Sales to Dealers

Year	Sales to Dealers
1978	401,930
1979	475,396
1980	804,663
1981	1,360,988
1982	2,034,797

SOURCE: Electronic Industries Association (1983:18).

To convert this stock to a flow of services requires a pure rental rate. At least two issues arise in choosing such a rate. First, there have been significant improvements in the quality of VCRs over time. Thus the value of the services provided by a 1979 VCR is probably lower than that of a 1982 model. Second, the market rates for VCR rentals are probably overestimates. VCRs are usually rented for short periods of time—either periods of peak demand or perhaps for gathering information before a purchase. Also, the normal VCR rental includes some sort of maintenance provisions.

In the absence of a better way to deal with these problems, the initial form of the dependent variable will be simply the total number of VCRs in use. Had there been no problem with quality change, the transformation of the stock to a flow would have been accomplished by simply applying a fixed rental rate to the stock of VCRs. In that event, using the total stock as the dependent variable would not affect the statistical significance of the relevant coefficients, although their magnitude would be affected. Even with the quality differences, as long as there are no important differences in the quality mix across states, the significance of the results will be unaffected. Table 2.3 shows that the sales by state in each year are highly correlated with one another. Finally, table 2.1 indicates that 73 percent of the VCRs in use are 1981 or 1982 models, which suggests that the problem of quality change may not be that important.

An alternative form of the dependent variable is VCR penetration— the fraction of television households that own a VCR.[7] As the results reported below suggest, the total VCR variable seems to be more a reflection of the size of a state (in population and total income) than of anything else. The VCR penetration variable in effect holds state size constant and allows a more detailed analysis of other explanatory variables. The results in section IV and in the appendix include both of these dependent variables, along with a few transformations of them.

C. The Independent Variables in the VCR and Cable Equations

This subsection describes the independent variables used in the analysis and indicates the sources of the data. The independent variables include income, population, and broadcast and cable TV prices.

1. Income

The basic income data come from U.S. Department of Commerce (1983c). Total and per capita disposable personal income (i.e., after taxes) are available. Because choices such as VCR purchase and cable subscription are made on a household basis and because of the use of data on television households (see subsection 2 of this section), it is desirable to have a household income variable. Household income data are not available for 1982, and a series was therefore constructed on the assumption that the average household has three members. As long as there are no systematic differences in household size across states, the statistical significance of the results is unaffected (although the magnitude of the coefficient would be wrong if the average number of people per household were different).[8] However, there may be more retired-person households in Florida, there may be larger families in the South or West, and there may be variations in household size associated with income. It is assumed that these differences are not important.[9]

2. Population

Since a television receiver is required to make use of VCRs, cable television, and broadcast television, it is appropriate to limit attention to those who own receivers. The decision to make use of these video delivery systems is generally made on a household basis; so data on television households per state are employed. The data are collected by Arbitron and reported by Television Digest, Inc. (1983:20–36). Nationwide, 98 percent of households have television. The lowest penetration is 96 percent, achieved in one state. Most states have 98 or 99 percent penetration. It should be noted that the income data are for the entire population, not just for television households. If it is true that households without television receivers are of relatively low income, then the income data used slightly underestimate the income of television households.

3. Other Prices

a. General Considerations. The price of cable or broadcast television services has several components. The first is the out-of-pocket price. For basic cable or pay cable service, this is the monthly rate paid. For advertiser-supported broadcast television service, this price is zero, although the price of the television receiver is relevant. A second component of the "price" of service is availability. For example, the price of cable service to a home not passed by cable is infinite. The third component is the quality of the service. For example, the quality of broadcast television service is related to the number of channels available (the same is true for cable). Some of the prices mentioned have the character of "access charges." The price of basic cable service buys the subscriber not only basic service but access to pay service. The price of a television receiver buys "access" to broadcast television. These principles are applied in the discussions of the specific price variables.

b. Cable Prices. Paul Kagan Associates (1983b) provides state data on the number of homes passed by cable systems and on the average monthly basic and pay (per channel) rates in each state.[10] Two measures of the availability of cable service are used. The first is simply the number of homes passed by cable. The second is the fraction of television households in the state passed by cable. For homes not passed by cable, the price of cable service is, for all practical purposes, infinite. There are limited exceptions, which are ignored in this study. SMATV provides service akin to basic and pay cable, but its penetration was negligible, with an estimated 100,000 subscribers nationwide at the end of 1982 (Paul Kagan Associates 1983d:1). One-channel pay service is also available via multipoint distribution service (MDS) and subscription television (STV). However, by the end of 1982 these accounted for only 2.4 and 7.9 percent of pay subscriptions, respectively (Paul Kagan Associates 1983d).[11]

Homes passed by cable face out-of-pocket prices for basic and pay services.[12] As Dunmore and Bykowsky (1982:3–12) have shown, the prices relevant for basic cable demand are the basic rate and the composite (basic plus pay) rate. A viewer will subscribe to basic cable if he values it above the basic rate, *or* if he values it below the basic rate but his valuation of pay cable is sufficiently greater than the pay cable rate that the value of basic plus pay service is greater than the composite rate. In this event, he will find a basic subscription worthwhile just to gain access to pay cable.

Similar reasoning within the Dunmore-Bykowsky framework suggests that the relevant prices for pay service are the pay rate and composite rate. In order to choose pay service, it is necessary for the value placed on basic plus pay service to be greater than the composite rate. However, this is not sufficient. The value placed on pay service alone must also be above the pay rate. If the first condition were true because basic service was very highly valued but pay service was not, then only basic service would be purchased.

This reasoning has clear implications for the appropriate form of the cable demand equations. In each case the analysis takes into account the interplay of pay and basic services. However, for the VCR equation the implications are less clear. Both pay and basic cable may be substitutes or complements with respect to VCRs. Because the composite rate is the sum of the basic and pay rates, all three cannot appear in the same equation. Hence various combinations of cable price variables will be tried.

There are also quality differences across cable systems. The number and composition of channels in basic service differs from system to system, as does the availability of pay services. The movie channels may be of differing qualities, though there is no a priori way to assess the differences. This problem will be unimportant if the average quality does not differ across states. One possible proxy for different quality levels is the subscriber-weighted average number of channels available per state, but the data to calculate this measure were not available.

c. Television "Prices." As noted above, viewers pay no direct price for television programming. While it is necessary to pay an "access charge" by purchasing a television receiver, this study includes only television households. Also, receiver prices are unlikely to vary significantly across states. In order to derive a "price" proxy for broadcast television, quality considerations must be introduced.

When product prices are compared, it is necessary to specify the quality as well as the quantity of product available at a given price. For example, if two television receivers each cost $400, and were identical except for the fact that one of them had remote control and the other did not, it would not make economic sense to say that their prices were the same. By analogy, the quality-adjusted price of broadcast television service becomes lower as the number of stations available increases.

These considerations suggest using the average number of television broadcast stations available per household as a proxy for the "quality-adjusted price" of television service. As the number of stations available goes up, the "quality-adjusted price" goes down. The data collected come from Arbitron Television (1983). It is assumed that television households can receive every station in their ADI market. While this procedure is open to some criticism, particularly if conclusions about specific markets are attempted, it is likely to be fairly accurate for aggregate station availability estimates. For a brief discussion of the pros and cons of using ADI markets for station coverage, see Levy and Setzer (1982). For a pointed critique of the ADI procedure, see FCC, Network Inquiry Special Staff (1980:105–12). In addition to average total stations available per state the average numbers of VHF and UHF stations available are also compiled separately.

D. Dependent Variables in the Cable Equations

The Kagan Census provides data on basic cable subscribers and pay cable subscriptions by state. (Some homes subscribe to more than one pay cable service.) The cable equations were run after the VCR ones, and with the benefit of that experience it became clear that the dependent variables worked better on a "per television household" basis rather than on a "total" basis. Hence the dependent variables in the cable equations are "per television household" and transformations thereof. The basic estimating equation is:

(6) $Q_{cable} = Q_{cable} [P_{cable}, P_{TV}, Y/N]$

As in the VCR case, it is assumed that the supply of cable service is perfectly elastic to homes passed. Hence P_{cable} includes the share of homes passed by cable as well as the subscriber fees. As noted above, two subscriber fees are relevant for basic cable demand and two for pay cable demand. The equations are specified accordingly.

The cable quantities are basic subscribers and pay *subscriptions* from Paul Kagan Associates (1983b). In the pay case, households subscribing to more than one pay service are counted more than once. Hence in

principle the pay household share could be above one. Data on unduplicated households are not available by state.

E. Hypothesized Signs

This subsection specifies the hypothesized signs of the independent
variables. The income and population variables are hypothesized to
have positive signs. The signs of the cable and television broadcast
variables indicate whether these services are substitutes or complements with respect to the dependent variable.

A positive sign on the variable for the average number of television
stations available indicates complementarity. That is, a larger number of
stations available, which corresponds to a lower "price" of television
service, is associated with higher consumption of the dependent variable. A negative sign would indicate substitution. Thus, if VCRs are
used primarily for "time-shifting" or "librarying" of broadcast television programming (see section III.B. below), the sign would be positive
in the VCR equation. If broadcast and cable television are substitutes,
the sign would be negative in the cable equations.

The cable price variables represent prices of alternative products in
the VCR equation and own prices in the cable equations. In the former
case, a positive sign on the homes-passed variable indicates complementarity and a negative sign substitution. Thus, as the share of homes
passed by cable rises, the "price" of cable falls; if this price decline is
associated with a decrease in VCR use (i.e., a negative coefficient) then
a substitution relationship is indicated.

The pay, basic, and composite cable subscription rates are standard
prices. In the VCR equations, positive coefficients imply substitution
and negative ones complementarity. In the cable equations, it is hypothesized that the cable price variables are negatively associated with cable
quantities. Hence the hypothesized signs are negative for the subscrip-
tion-rate variables and positive for the homes-passed variable.

F. Geographic Coverage

As noted above, the data are by state. Data availability limitations
dictate that the sample consist of the 48 contiguous states.

III. PROBLEMS OF METHODOLOGY

This section considers four additional methodological problems with the model. First to be considered is the lack of equilibrium in the VCR market; second, the fact that a VCR can serve as both a substitute and a complement to broadcast and cable television. This is followed by brief discussions of the implications of not estimating VCR and cable equations jointly, and of differences among households in the opportunity cost of time.

A. The Partial Equilibrium Assumption

The VCR is a relatively new product. Nationwide penetration in 1982 was only 10 percent of households, but it is growing rapidly (*Videoweek,* January 2, 1984, p. 5). Clearly, the assumption made in the preceding section that the VCR market is in equilibrium, is not valid. Yet this problem cannot be alleviated in a purely cross-sectional analysis. In a time series study of the demand for computers, Chow (1967) grappled with the problem of estimating demand in a growing market. He combined a "natural growth" model based on the Gompertz curve (similar to the logistic) with a comparative statics model in which computer demand is a function of price and total output of those sectors using computers as an input. The result was an equation including the comparative statics parameters and the lagged stock of computers. The Batelle model of VCR demand, also a time series study, utilized another standard technique—a stock adjustment model. This model, which explicitly assumes that the market is not in equilibrium, also yields an equation which includes a lagged value of the dependent variable (Cronin et al. 1983:32–34). Both of these techniques require estimation on time series data, which data are not available here.

The effect of not accounting for the lack of equilibrium is unclear. If every state were at the same point on the growth curve (Gompertz or logistic), then the basic results would not be affected, although the magnitude of the coefficients would be. Moreover, the estimated coefficients are not presented as tools for predicting future VCR (or cable) penetration: so miscalculation of the *size* of the coefficients would not affect the conclusions of the analysis regarding relationships among the various video products. On the other hand, it is not obvious that every state is at the same point on the growth curve. VCRs were not introduced simultaneously in every state (major cities got them first). While it is unlikely that the lag in availability was significant and thus it is reasonable to assume that each state started at roughly the same point, it is possible that the parameters of the growth curve differ systematically across states. Furthermore, the differences in the diffusion rate may well be functions of some of the independent variables in the present model. Thus if, for example, VCRs and cable are substitutes, states with low cable penetration may have faster diffusion rates. The phenomenon would bias coefficients away from zero.

B. The VCR May Be Both Substitute and Complement

As the debate over the application of copyright laws to home taping reveals, there is more than one possible use for a VCR (*Sony v. Universal Studios,* 1984). In particular, VCRs may be used to record broadcast (or cable) programming for viewing at a different time. This activity encompasses "time-shifting" and "librarying." The former refers to recording a program that one is unable to view when it is broadcast and viewing it at a more convenient time. The latter entails recording a program for repeated later viewing, a program that one may actually watch while recording. In both cases, the VCR functions as a complement to television; that is, as use of the VCR increases, so does use of television.

To understand the phenomenon properly requires a careful definition of the term "use." Normally, there is a direct relationship between the quantity consumed of products that are complements. Here, however, it is possible that the VCR use is complementary to television use and yet television use in terms of hours viewed does not increase. For example, one may have watched ten hours per week of television before acquiring a VCR. Afterward, one may still watch ten hours per week but a totally different ten hours. It is possible that one's preferred programming is broadcast at times when one cannot watch it. Hence, VCR use may increase the *utility* of television even without increasing viewing time (unless one counts the time spent recording programs with no one watching). Indeed, it is possible that VCR use may increase the utility of television while reducing viewing time. At the other extreme, all viewing of VCR-recorded programming could represent a net increase in viewing. Of course, intermediate situations are possible too.

This complementary use of VCRs has implications for programming diversity. The VCR, while not increasing the diversity available in the marketplace, does allow the viewers to provide themselves with the maximum that is available.[13] This "diversity enhancement" makes the competition among outlets more intense and strengthens the presumption the regulation is not needed to guarantee diversity.

VCRs also can serve as substitutes for television. This happens when, for example, consumers rent or buy prerecorded tapes and view them instead of broadcast (or cable) programming.

It is likely that VCRs are used in both the substitute and the complement modes by the same household, at different times. The simple model of this paper is incapable of distinguishing the two effects. The practical consequence is that the price (and availability) coefficients are biased toward zero, since the signs for substitution and complementarity effects are opposite.

There is some a priori reason to think that, for pay television, the substitution effect is predominant. Most pay television consists of movie channels such as HBO, and each movie is shown several times per month anyway, which probably reduces the demand for time-shifting.

C. Joint Estimation

The VCR and cable equations are implicitly part of a system of demand equations. They may be interdependent in the sense that they are generated by a utility-maximization process in which first a share of income is allocated to "video services" and then that share is allocated among various particular services—VCRs and cable being two of them (movies, cassettes, and even DBS may be others). The various equations are subject to an "adding up" constraint. The econometric techniques designed to account for this constraint are not employed here.

D. The Opportunity Cost of Time

In addition to out-of-pocket expenses, the consumption of video services requires time. Time itself is a scarce resource (since it can always be used for something else), so it has an opportunity cost (price) that must be taken into account in estimating demand. The opportunity cost of time is difficult to measure. If it were assumed not to vary across states, it would drop out of the analysis entirely. However, the opportunity cost of time is often related to earnings. The intuitive idea is that a person's hourly earnings represent the amount forgone by choosing an hour of leisure. Although in the short run most people are not in a position to make such marginal choices about hours worked, this mechanism suggests a relationship between the cost of time and hourly earnings (or income). To the extent that the cost of time is correlated with household income, it is picked up by that variable in the equations estimated.

The effects of increases in income and the opportunity cost of time may, however, be offsetting. The standard income effect suggests that the demand for VCRs increases with income. On the other hand, consumers with high opportunity costs of time may devote less of it to leisure. This would reduce their demand for video services. Finally, the effect of the high opportunity cost of time may differ across media, with a smaller demand reduction for those systems that increase time flexibility (e.g., VCRs).

IV. RESULTS

This section discusses the regression results. Ordinary least squares regressions were estimated for VCR and cable dependent variables against various combinations of the independent variables suggested by the theoretical model constructed earlier. The first part presents a discussion of simple correlation coefficients for the various variables considered. The next part presents the regression equations which specify the determinants of VCR demand using the number of VCRs per household. The third part presents the regression equations specifying the determinants of cable demand. For reference, table 2.2 provides a list of variable names and definitions.

A. Simple Correlation Coefficients

Simple correlation coefficients were calculated for most pairs of variables.[14] Table 2.3 contains these results. This analysis was useful in selecting independent and dependent variables for regression analy-

Table 2.2. Variable Names

VCR79—VCR sales to dealers in 1979
VCR80—VCR sales to dealers in 1980
VCR81—VCR sales to dealers in 1981
VCR82—VCR sales to dealers in 1982
VCRTOT = VCR79 + VCR80 + VCR81 + VCR82

TVHHN—Number of television households

VCRPH = VCRTOT/TVHHN
VCRLN = ln(VCRPH/(1 − VCRPH))
PHLN = ln(VCRPH)
VTOTLN = ln(VCRTOT)

BASSUB—Number of homes subscribing to basic cable
PAYSUB — Number of subscriptions to pay cable
BASPH = BASSUB/TVHHN
PAYPH = PAYSUB/TVHHN
BASPHL = ln(BASPH/(1 − BASPH))
PAYPHL = ln(PAYPH/(1 − PAYPH))
PHPAY = ln(PAYPH)

HPASSE—Number of homes passed by cable
HPPH = HPASSE/TVHHN
HPPHLN = ln(HPPH)

DPI—Disposable personal income ($ millions)
DPIPC—Per capita disposable personal income
DPIHH = 3 · DPIPC
DPILN = ln(DPI)
DPIHLN = ln(DPIHH)

STATOT—Average total broadcast stations available per television household
STAVHF—Average VHF broadcast stations available per television household
STAUHF—Average UHF broadcast stations available per television household
STOTLN = ln(STATOT)
SVHFLN = ln(STAVHF)

BASRAT—Monthly basic cable rate ($)
PAYRAT—Monthly pay cable rate—one channel ($)
CRAT = BASRAT + PAYRAT
BASLN = ln(BASRAT)
PAYLN = ln(PAYRAT)
CRATLN = ln(CRAT)

TVHLN = ln(TVHHN)

C = the constant term

NOTE: "ln" means natural logarithm.

sis.[15] Three conclusions were reached on the basis of these correlation results and early regression equations.

First, the total sales of VCRs for 1979 through 1982, VCRTOT, was not as useful a dependent variable as the ratio of total VCR sales to the total number of television households (VCRPH). This is the case because the VCRTOT variable is so highly correlated with total disposable income (DPI) and the total number of television households (TVHHN). The correlation coefficient for VCRTOT–DPI is .954. The correlation coefficient for VCRTOT–TVHHN is .935. These high correlations might be expected to mask the effects of other independent variables on the demand for VCRs. In effect, regressions employing these variables merely reflect size differences across states. An ordinary least squares regression of VCRTOT against DPI alone gives an R^2 of .9087. (See table 2.9 in the appendix.) The VCR-per-household variable (VCRPH) is a more useful dependent variable because it is not as highly correlated with DPI (.559), TVHHN (.527), and disposable income per household, DPIHH (.508). Therefore, when analyzing the demand for VCRs, specifications using VCRPH and transformations thereof as the dependent variable were selected.

Second, table 2.3 reveals that there is a fairly high correlation between basic cable rates and pay cable rates (.483), and quite a high correlation between the pay and composite rates (.883) and between the basic and composite rates (.837). These high correlations help explain the fact that while theory might suggest otherwise, analysis of the various regression equations showed that these independent variables were rarely significant unless used alone. When two cable rates were used together, it was never the case that both were significant.

Third, the correlation coefficients suggest some other points about the appropriate independent variables to be used with the (admittedly less satisfactory) VCRTOT variable. Table 2.3 also shows that DPI is highly correlated with TVHHN (.994), while DPIHH is not as highly correlated with TVHHN (.356). A regression of VCRTOT against both DPI and TVHHN gives a high R^2, but the coefficient of the TVHHN variable is both *negative* and significant. (See table 2.9 in the appendix.)[16] That the demand for VCRs should be inversely related to the number of television households conflicts with any demand theory that is plausible. Apparently, multicollinearity is making it impossible to separate the effects of income and population. Regression of VCRTOT

Table 2.3. Selected Simple Correlation Coefficients

VCRTOT–DPI	.954
VCRTOT–DPIHH	.411
VCRTOT–TVHHN	.935
VCRTOT–HPASSE	.909
VCR82–VCR81	.991
VCR82–VCR80	.991
VCR82–VCR79	.982
VCR81–VCR80	.997
VCR81–VCR79	.993
VCR80–VCR79	.994
VCRPH–DPI	.559
VCRPH–DPIHH	.508
VCRPH–TVHHN	.527
HPASSE–DPI	.968
HPASSE–DPIHH	.353
HPASSE–TVHHN	.975
HPPH–DPI	.050
HPPH–DPIHH	.202
HPPH–TVHHN	.044
DPI–TVHHN	.994
DPI–STATOT	.499
DPI–STAVHF	.074
DPIHH–TVHHN	.356
DPIHH–STATOT	.498
DPIHH–STAVHF	.374
STATOT–TVHHN	.457
STATOT–STAVHF	.345
CRAT–PAYRAT	.883
CRAT–BASRAT	.837
PAYRAT–BASRAT	.483

against both DPIHH and TVHHN, however, produces intuitive results. Both DPIHH and TVHHN are positive and TVHHN is highly significant. (See table 2.9 in the appendix. Table 2.10 presents additional

VCRTOT results.) Table 2.3 also shows a very high correlation between TVHHN and HPASSE. This suggests that equations using DPIHH, TVHHN, and HPPH as independent variables are most appropriate.

B. The VCR Results

This subsection examines those regression equations which best explain the demand for VCRs. On the basis of the correlation coefficient analysis, it was determined that VCRPH, the VCRs-per-household variable, is preferable to VCRTOT, the total number of VCRs. Five specifications were employed: VCRPH with the independent variables in linear and log forms; VCRLN (i.e., ln[VCRPH/(1 − VCRPH)]) with the independent variables in linear and log forms; and PHLN (i.e., lnVCRPH) with the independent variables in log form. As suggested by the model, independent variables reflecting household disposable income, the share of television households passed by cable, total television station availability per household,[17] and cable subscription rates were included.

There is some ambiguity in the theory on the question of what cable rates should be included in the equation. As explained in section II.C.3., both the pay and composite rates are relevant for the choice of pay cable, and both the basic and combined rates are relevant to the basic cable choice. If basic and pay cable are distinct products, each of which could be a substitute or complement to VCRs, then all three rates should go into the VCR equation. Since the composite rate is a simple linear combination of the other two, this is clearly impossible. Furthermore, the pairwise simple correlation coefficients of the cable rates are relatively high, suggesting that it may be difficult to separate their effects in a single equation. Therefore various combinations were tried.

The results, reported in tables 2.4, 2.5, and 2.6 (and in table 2.11 in the appendix) are quite similar for all five specifications. The preferred equations appear in columns two and four of tables 2.4 and 2.5, and in column two of table 2.6. The homes-passed variable is significant at the 95 percent level and negative in all cases, the household income variable is significant and positive in all cases, while the variable of total station availability is always positive but not quite significant.[18] The cable price variables are never significant either alone or in pairs. The coefficients are sometimes positive and sometimes negative. The re-

Table 2.4. Selected VCR Regression Results with VCRPH as the Dependent Variable

Independent Variables	(1)	(2)	(3)	(4)	(5)
DPIHH	.340E05* (4.00)	.311E05* (3.25)	—	—	—
DPIHLN	—	—	—	.080* (3.14)	—
HPPH	—	−.051* (−2.44)	−.042 (−1.83)	—	—
HPPHLN	—	—	—	−.023* (−2.06)	−.020 (−1.60)
STATOT	—	.167E02 (1.54)	.334E02 (3.17)	—	—
STOTLN	—	—	—	.012 (1.42)	.023* (2.85)
PAYRAT	—	−.507E04 (−.01)	.220E02 (.51)	—	—
PAYLN	—	—	—	−.784E03 (−.02)	.024 (.62)
C	−.048* (−2.06)	−.022 (−.57)	.024 (.61)	−.801* (−3.23)	−.066 (−.75)
R^2	.2416	.3235	.1766	.2907	.1483

NOTES: See table 2.2 for variable definitions. "E" means exponent; E02 means "multiplied by .01," E04 means "multiplied by 10,000," etc.

The figures in parentheses are t statistics. R^2 is adjusted for degrees of freedom.

*Significant at the 95 percent level.

sults reported in tables 2.4 through 2.6 include the pay rate alone; this choice was made because, with the preferred set of independent variables, the station availability variable came closest to significance there in four of the five specifications.

These also show results for two other specifications. The first equation in each table indicates that the disposable-income variables alone explain a substantial portion of the total variation in the dependent variables. Equations with the income variable removed are also presented. These equations were estimated because of the relatively high simple correlation coefficient (.498) between DPIHH and STATOT, which may make it impossible to identify clearly their separate effects. The results are consistent with this interpretation, since without the

Table 2.5. Selected VCR Regression Results with VCRLN as the Dependent Variable

Independent Variables	(1)	(2)	(3)	(4)	(5)
DPIHH	.841E04*	.820E04*	—	—	—
	(4.06)	(3.52)			
DPIHLN	—	—	—	2.113*	—
				(3.45)	
HPPH	—	− 1.306*	− 1.058	—	—
		(− 2.56)	(− 1.87)		
HPPHLN	—	—	—	− 6.13*	− .519
				(− 2.26)	(− 1.72)
STATOT	—	.031	.075*	—	—
		(1.19)	(2.89)		
STOTLN	—	—	—	.226	.534*
				(1.12)	(2.63)
PAYRAT	—	− .013	.046	—	—
		(− .13)	(.43)		
PAYLN	—	—	—	− .126	.544
				(− .14)	(.56)
C	− 5.469*	− 4.761*	− 3.568*	− 25.247*	− 5.734*
	(− 9.75)	(− 5.18)	(− 3.72)	(− 4.22)	(2.63)
R^2	.2482	.3261	.1517	.3061	.1340

NOTES: See table 2.2 for variable definitions. "E" means exponent; E02 means "multiplied by .01," E04 means "multiplied by 10,000," etc.

The figures in parentheses are t statistics. R^2 is adjusted for degrees of freedom.

*Significant at the 95 percent level.

income variable in the equation the station-availability coefficient becomes significant and larger in magnitude (taking up some of the effect of the income variable). These specifications are, of course, less satisfactory over all, due to the omission of income, the reduced significance of the homes-passed variable, and the lower R^2, but they do strengthen the conclusion that the sign of the station-availability variable is positive.

The results therefore support the conclusion that VCRs and cable are substitutes, and less strongly that VCRs and broadcast television are complements. The negative sign on the homes-passed variable indicates that, as the share of homes passed rises (i.e., as the "price" of cable service *falls*) fewer homes acquire VCRs. The positive sign on the television station-availability variables indicates that as the average number of broadcast stations available rises (i.e., as the "price" of television service falls), more homes acquire VCRs. The positive signs of the income coefficients indicate that the VCR is a normal good; that is, the quantity of VCRs demanded increases when personal income increases.

C. The Cable Results

This subsection discusses the results of the estimation of basic and pay cable demand. While no interesting results were obtained for basic cable, good results were obtained for pay cable under a variety of specifications.

1. The Basic Cable Results

For basic cable, linear equations were estimated with BASPH and BASPHL as dependent variables. While the portion of variation explained is high, almost all of it is due to HPPH, which has the expected

Table 2.6. Selected VCR Regression Results with PHLN as the Dependent Variable

	(1)	(2)	(3)
Independent Variables			
DPIHLN	2.142*	2.030*	—
	(4.06)	(3.46)	
HPPHLN	—	−.589*	−.499
		(−2.26)	(−1.72)
STOTLN	—	.214	.509
		(1.10)	(2.62)
PAYLN	—	−.125	.519
		(−.15)	(.56)
C	−25.087*	−24.404*	−5.662*
	(−4.66)	(−4.26)	(−2.71)
R^2	.2478	.3058	.1328

NOTES: See table 2.2 for variable definitions.
The figures in parentheses are t statistics.
R^2 is adjusted for degrees of freedom.
*Significant at the 95 percent level.

positive sign and is always significant. This variable plus the constant term together explain 77 percent of the variation in the dependent variables. No equation explains more than 79 percent. Table 2.12 in the appendix exhibits some basic-cable demand regression results. None of the other variables is ever significant, with the exception of DPIHH, which is occasionally significant but has a negative sign, contrary to hypothesis. The station availability variables are of mixed sign, as is BASRAT. CRAT is always positive, contrary to hypothesis, but never significant.

2. The Pay Cable Results

Five specifications of the pay-cable demand equation were estimated, and the results obtained were robust with respect to all alternatives. While the homes-passed variable once again explained most of the variation in the dependent variable, the other independent variables also add substantially to the goodness of fit. (Compare columns 1, 2, and 3 of table 2.7 to columns 1, 4, and 5 of table 2.8.)

The following five specifications were estimated: PAYPH with the independent variables in linear and log forms; PAYPHL with the independent variables in linear and log form; and PHPAY with the independent variables in log form. Each equation included a household income variable, a homes-passed variable, a total broadcast station availability variable,[19] and a cable price variable or variables. The income variable is always significant and positive, as hypothesized. The homes-passed variable is also significant and positive, as hypothesized. As the share of homes passed by cable rises, the collective "price" of pay cable to the residents of a state falls, and more subscriptions are purchased. (Recall that the pay-cable dependent variables are based on subscriptions rather than on unduplicated homes subscribing). The total station-availability variable is always negative and frequently (60 percent of the time) significant. This suggests that broadcast television and pay cable are substitute services. The results indicate that as the number of television broadcast stations available increases (i.e., as the "price" of broadcast television service decreases) pay cable subscriptions decrease.

As explained in section II.C.3., theory suggests that pay cable rate *and* the composite (pay plus basic) rate belong in the equations. In every case, however, while the pay rate was significant, the combined

Table 2.7. Pay Cable Regression Results: Homes-Passed Only and Theoretically Preferred Specifications

	Dependent Variable				
	(1)	*(2)*	*(3)*	*(4)*	*(5)*
	PAYPH	*PAYPHL*	*PHPAY*	*PAYPHL*	*PHPAY*
Independent Variables					
DPIHLN	—	—	—	1.514*	1.108*
				(5.99)	(6.15)
HPPHLN	—	1.247*	.946*	1.277*	.966*
		(7.33)	(7.46)	(10.95)	(11.63)
HPPH	.420*	—	—	—	—
	(7.07)				
STOTLN	—	—	—	− .170*	− .125*
				(− 1.98)	(− 2.05)
PAYLN	—	—	—	− 2.725*	− 2.269*
	—	—	—	(− 3.51)	(− 4.10)
CRATLN	—	—	—	.316	.449
				(.33)	(.65)
C	.013	− .387*	− .862*	− 10.339*	− 8.157*
	(.38)	(− 3.66)	(− 10.97)	(− 3.87)	(− 4.29)
R²	.5100	.5287	.5379	.8048	.8247

NOTES: See table 2.2 for variable definitions.
The figures in parentheses are t statistics. R^2 is adjusted for degrees of freedom.
*Significant at the 95 percent level.

rate proved insignificant. Its sign varied. This lack of significance may be due to the relatively high simple correlation between the pay and combined rates (see table 2.3). Equations were therefore estimated using the pay rate alone and the combined rate alone. These coefficients were invariably significant and negative, as hypothesized.

Columns 4 and 5 of table 2.7 present examples of the theoretically preferred set of independent variables (i.e., including both the pay and combined cable rates). These are the only two cases in which the station availability variable is significant and the theoretically preferred set of independent variables is used. In the other three cases, the sign is negative but the coefficient is not quite significant. (See table 2.13 in the appendix.) When only the composite rate is used, the station availability variable becomes significant in all cases, and all other independent variables are significant. Table 2.8 presents these results. When

Table 2.8. Pay Cable Regression Results: Five Alternative Specifications with Composite Cable Rate Only

	Dependent Variable				
	(1)	*(2)*	*(3)*	*(4)*	*(5)*
	PAYPH	*PAYPH*	*PAYPHL*	*PAYPHL*	*PHPAY*
Independent Variables					
DPIHH	.100E-04*	—	.525E-04*	—	—
	(4.72)		(4.69)		
DPIHLN	—	.288*	—	1.508*	1.103*
		(5.13)		(5.31)	(5.23)
HPPH	.462*	—	2.579*	—	—
	(9.75)		(10.33)		
HPPHLN	—	.238*	—	1.353*	1.030*
		(9.37)		(10.51)	(10.79)
STATOT	− .523E-02*	—	− .030*	—	—
	(− 2.19)		(− 2.41)		
STOTLN	—	− .041*	—	− .234*	− .179*
		(− 2.21)		(− 2.49)	(− 2.56)
CRAT	− .029*	—	− .161*	—	—
	(− 5.12)		(− 5.43)		
CRATLN	—	− .475*	—	− 2.692*	− 2.055*
		(− 4.70)		(− 5.26)	(− 5.42)
C	.266*	− 1.097	− .942	− 7.520*	− 5.810*
	(2.78)	(− 1.94)	(− 1.87)	(− 2.63)	(− 2.74)
R^2	.7282	.7143	.7454	.7533	.7602

NOTES: See table 2.2 for variable definitions. "E" means exponent; E-04 means "multiplied by .0001," etc.

The figures in parentheses are t statistics. R^2 is adjusted for degrees of freedom.

*Significant at the 95 percent level.

only the pay rate is used, the station availability variable is significant in two of five specifications. In their basic-cable demand work, Dunmore and Bykowsky (1982) found the same pattern found here: the composite rate was significant and negative, while the basic rate was insignificant (and positive) in their equation.

V. CONCLUSIONS

This paper has presented estimates of VCR and cable demand, based on 1982 cross-section data for the 48 contiguous states. In spite of the fact that the state is not the best unit of analysis (market data would be preferable), several significant results were obtained.

VCR demand equations were estimated with the fraction of television households owning a VCR as the dependent variable. Several transformations of that variable were also used, and the independent variables were expressed in both linear and logarithmic forms. In every equation with a dependent variable based on the fraction of television households owning a VCR, the household-income coefficient had its expected positive sign and was significant. In equations with the preferred set of independent variables, the homes-passed coefficient was consistently negative and significant, lending strong support to the proposition that VCRs and cable are substitutes. The consistent positive sign on the television station-availability variable lends some support to the conclusion that VCRs and broadcast television are complements. These coefficients are not quite significant when estimated with the preferred set of independent variables, but this appears to be due to multicollinearity with the income variable. The complementary relationship is quite consistent with the survey data on use of VCRs for time-shifting. To the authors' knowledge, these results are the first to estimate statistically the VCR-cable and VCR-television relations. The R^2 values of the equations are reasonably good for cross-sectional data.

There are two fragments of evidence on VCR use that are worthy of mention. First, a survey conducted for the Motion Picture Association of America sheds some light on VCR-cable substitution (NPD Special Industry Services 1983b:78).[20] The survey indicates that .05176 (5.2 percent) of homes passed by cable owned a VCR, while .05405 (5.4 percent) of homes not passed by cable owned one. The figures, from April 1982, show that .05273 (5.3 percent) of all households owned VCRs.

Second, some international data collected by the Motion Picture Association of America, Inc. (1984c) illustrate the complexity of the relationship between VCRs and other video delivery systems. The figures are estimates of numbers of television receivers and VCRs by country for 1983. Although there is some doubt about the quality of the data, the variation in the ratio of VCRs to television receivers across countries is interesting. For the United States, the figure is 5.4 percent. The figures for France, West Germany, and Britain are 8 percent, 13.6 percent, and 30 percent, respectively. For Australia it is 18 percent. These countries have per capita incomes in the same range as the United States, but they have fewer television alternatives, and much broadcasting is on a non-commercial basis. It appears that VCRs are being used by viewers in those countries to substitute for over-the-air broadcasting. Italy, with an unusually free, heavily commercial broadcasting system, has only a 1.8 percent ratio (although this may be explained in part by relatively low income). At the other extreme, the ratios for Israel and the United Arab Emirates are 44 percent and 411 percent, respectively. The substitution effect is relevant in both cases, while high per capita income probably is important in the latter case. The case of Japan, with a 29.4 percent ratio, shows that the pattern is not uniform, since Japan has a relatively diverse menu of broadcast fare available (but Japan is the center of world VCR production and innovation). While those data are suggestive of substitution, they are by no means conclusive. In particular, there may be differences in fractions of multiple television receiver households across countries. Such differences would mean that the ratios reported here distort the picture of VCR penetration of households.

The results for pay cable demand were also good, in terms of goodness of fit and significance of coefficients. However, no meaningful results were obtained for basic cable demand. Pay-cable equations were estimated with pay-cable subscriptions divided by television households as the dependent variable, and for several transformations of that variable. Again the independent variables were included in linear and logarithmic forms. The income and homes-passed variables were positive and significant, as expected, while the cable-rate variable (when only one was included in an equation and multicollinearity problems avoided) was significant and negative, as an own price should be. The station-availability coefficient was consistently negative and frequently significant. This implies a substitution relationship between cable and broadcast television. While these results are not unfamiliar, they are useful because they provide additional empirical documentation on cable demand, and because replicating familiar results on this new data set gives some confidence that the distortions due to the less-than-optimal unit of observation are not great. Hence the cable results allow somewhat more credence to be placed in the VCR results.

While the empirical results are interesting and useful, their significance is tempered by the methodological difficulties encountered in the analysis. The primary one is the fact that the VCR can be both a substitute and a complement to other video delivery systems for the same household. In statistical terms, this biases the price and availability coefficients for other video delivery systems toward zero. This is a two-edged sword. The confidence one has in statistically significant coefficients is increased, but there may be differences in fractions of multiple television receiver households across countries. Such differences would mean that the ratios reported here distort the picture of VCR penetration of households.

The results for pay cable demand were also good, in terms of goodness of fit and significance of coefficients. However, no meaningful results were obtained for basic cable demand. Pay-cable equations wre estimated with pay-cable subscriptions divided by television households as the dependent variable, and for several transformations of that variable. Again the independent variables were included in linear and logarithmic forms. The income and homes-passed variables were positive and significant, as expected, while the cable-rate variable (when only one was included in an equation and multicollinearity problems avoided) was significant and negative, as an own price should be. The station-availability coefficient was consistently negative and frequently significant. This implies a substitution relationship between cable and broadcast television. While these results are not unfamiliar, they are useful because they provide additional empirical documentation on cable demand, and because replicating familiar results on this new data set gives some confidence that the distortions due to the less-than-optimal unit of observation are not great. Hence the cable results allow somewhat more credence to be placed in the VCR results.

While the empirical results are interesting and useful, their significance is tempered by the methodological difficulties encountered in the analysis. The primary one is the fact that the VCR can be both a substitute and a complement to other video delivery systems for the same household. In statistical terms, this biases the price and availability coefficients for other video delivery systems toward zero. This is a two-edged sword. The confidence one has in statistically significant coefficients is increased, but insignificant coefficients may mask opposing but significant effects. Indeed, even a significant coefficient may be the resultant of two bona fide effects—substitute and complement—of opposite signs and substantially different magnitudes. Hence the basis for rejecting hypotheses is weakened.

The VCR and cable results, when considered together, appear at first to exhibit a "transitivity paradox." The pay-cable results suggest that broadcast television and pay cable are substitutes. The VCR results

suggest that pay cable and VCRs are substitutes. This seems to imply that broadcast television and VCRs are substitutes. Yet the empirical results suggest that they are complements. This may be explained by the fact that VCRs provide a bundle of services, e.g., they can be used for time-shifting and for playback of prerecorded materials. Thus, VCRs may serve as a complement to broadcast television when used to time-shift broadcast programming, and serve as a substitute for cable when used to play prerecorded cassettes in place of some pay-cable programming. The dual nature of the VCR thus resolves the apparent inconsistency.[21]

Just as the dual nature of the VCR may blur the underlying economic relationships, the use of state-level data may have done the same thing. This is because the state is not likely, in general, to be a meaningful economic market.

While it would have been nice to have been able to take explicit account of disequilibrium in the VCR market, it is unlikely that doing so would have altered the basic results. As explained in section III.A., new products frequently follow an S-shaped growth curve (of penetration plotted against time). The parameters of the growth curve may differ by state. States with "faster" diffusion curves will have higher VCR penetration, aside from the static effects of price and availability of other video systems. However, it is likely that the same factors that influence that static choice among video delivery systems also influence the dynamic phenomenon of diffusion, and in the same way. Thus, if VCRs and broadcast television are complements, states with high availability of television might have faster diffusion rates. While this would bias the station-availability coefficient away from zero (in the positive direction), it would do so only because of the complementary relationship. Thus, while the coefficient may reflect both the effect of television on the diffusion rate of VCRs and on the static (at one point in time) decision to acquire a VCR, both of them are reflections of the same underlying relationship.

Thus, the statistical evidence tends to support the proposition that the video product market should be broadly defined—to include, at least, broadcast television, cable, and VCRs. This proposition has important implications in terms of the reduced need for content regulation, structural (ownership) regulation, and rate regulation for cable and other pay services. The results could be strengthened by the following improvements, which await future work: (1) the collection of better data—on a market basis and including theater movies: (2) the construction of a richer model, one that can accommodate the use of VCRs as both substitute and complement to other delivery systems and can handle disequilibrium (for this, time series data would be needed); and (3) the application of more sophisticated econometric techniques.

Appendix

This appendix provides a brief description of the VCRTOT regressions and the basic cable regressions, and provides some additional statistical results.

Linear equations were estimated with VCRTOT as the dependent variables. Selected results are presented in tables 2.9 and 2.10. Table 2.9 shows that DPI alone or DPIHH plus TVHHN explains most of the variance in VCRTOT. As suggested in section IV.A., it appears that the VCRTOT regressions are primarily picking up differences in state size. The counterintuitive negative coefficient for TVHHN in column 2 of table 2.9 probably results from the high simple correlation between DPI and TVHHN.

Table 2.10 shows additional VCRTOT results. They reflect the fact that TVHHN is negative in equations with DPI and positive (and significant) in equations with DPIHH and other variables. The homes-passed variable is always negative and never significant. The total station-availability variable is of mixed sign and never significant. As column 3 of table 2.10 indicates, the VHF variable is occasionally positive and significant. The cable service-price variables had positive coefficients most of the time. The only time they were significant was when alone; and even then they were not always significant, as table 2.10 indicates.

There were also some regressions run using the natural logarithm of VCRTOT as the dependent variable. These, like the other VCRTOT regressions, were not very useful.

Table 2.11 provides some additional VCR results with VCRPH and VCRLN as the dependent variables. Columns 1 and 2 illustrate the point

Table 2.9. VCRTOT Regression Results with VCRTOT as the
Dependent Variable and with Income and Population Variables

	(1)	*(2)*	*(3)*
Independent Variables			
DPI	3.015*	6.679*	—
	(21.65)	(5.66)	
DPIHH	—	—	4.292
			(1.64)
TVHHN	—	−.105*	.081*
		(−3.12)	(16.44)
C	−3.824E04*	−2.071E04*	−.159E06*
	(−4.10)	(−2.03)	(−2.33)
R²	.9087	.9233	.8761

NOTES: See table 2.2 for variable definitions. "E" means exponent; E04 means "multiplied by 10,000," etc.

The figures in parentheses are t statistics. R² is adjusted for degrees of freedom.

*Significant at the 95 percent level.

that the cable rate variables are not significant when more than one is included in an equation. They also allow comparison of results using the total station-availability variable and results with separate VHF and UHF variables. The latter are inferior. Columns 3 and 4 show the result of using the VHF variable instead of total stations available. (Compare with column 2 in tables 2.4 and 2.5.)

Table 2.12 displays selected basic-cable regression results. As columns 1 and 4 make clear, most of the variation in basic-cable penetration is explained by the homes-passed variable. When DPIHH is added, its sign is negative (contrary to hypothesis) and sometimes significant. The other variables are generally insignificant. The combined cable rate variable is positive (contrary to hypothesis) and sometimes significant. These results are not particularly useful.

In table 2.13 are some additional pay-cable results. Columns 1, 2, and 3 show the preferred set of independent variables in the three specifications out of five in which the total station-availability variable was *not* significant. The other two specifications are exhibited in table 2.7 (columns 4 and 5). Columns 4 and 5 of table 2.13 can be compared with columns 1 and 3 to see the effect of substituting separate VHF and UHF station-availability variables for the total station-availability variable. The total availability variable specification is better.

Table 2.10. Selected Regression Results with VCRTOT as the Dependent Variable and Alternative Homes-Passed Variables

Independent Variables	(1)	(2)	(3)	(4)	(5)	(6)
DPI	6.128* (4.04)	—	—	6.033* (4.04)	—	—
DPIHH	—	.613 (.22)	.079 (.03)	—	1.170 (.42)	.570 (.21)
HPASSE	-.014 (-.53)	-.034 (-1.08)	-.025 (-.83)	—	—	—
HPPH	—	—	—	-5.578E03 (-1.07)	-8.965E04 (-1.48)	-5.225E04 (-.84)
TVHHN	-.078 (-1.62)	.104* (5.09)	.101* (5.13)	-.084* (-2.02)	.083* (16.54)	.085* (18.51)
STATOT	-1.397E03 (-.48)	3.851E03 (1.17)	—	-1.174E03 (-.41)	3.821E03 (1.18)	—
STAVHF	—	—	1.382E04* (2.19)	—	—	1.273E04 (1.93)
CRAT	9.270E03 (1.37)	2.125E04* (2.86)	1.708E04* (2.31)	1.080E04 (1.58)	2.238E04* (3.02)	1.768E04 (2.32)
C	-.181E06 (-1.41)	-.469E06* (-3.65)	-.411E06* (-3.24)	-.177E06 (-1.46)	-.450E06* (-3.65)	-.399E06 (-3.22)
R^2	.9221	.8920	.8999	.9237	.8945	.8999

NOTES: See table 2.2 for variable definitions. "E" means exponent; E04 means "multiplied by 10,000," etc. The figures in parentheses are t statistics. R^2 is adjusted for degrees of freedom.
*Significant at the 95 percent level.

Table 2.11. Additional VCR Regression Results with VCRPH and VCRLN as Dependent Variables

Independent Variables	(1) VCRPH	(2) VCRPH	(3) VCRPH	(4) VCRLN
DPIHH	.316E05*	.310E05*	.363E05*	.927E04*
	(3.24)	(3.07)	(3.93)	(4.16)
HPPH	−.049*	−.047*	−.048*	−1.266*
	(−2.21)	(−1.99)	(−2.16)	(−2.35)
STATOT	.156E02	—	—	—
	(1.37)			
STAVHF	—	.221E02	.130E02	.018
		(.87)	(.53)	(.30)
STAUHF	—	.146E02	—	—
		(1.23)		
PAYRAT	.723E03	.374E03	−.560E03	−.019
	(.16)	(.08)	(−.13)	(−.18)
BASRAT	−.207E02	−.236E02	—	—
	(−.38)	(−.42)		
C	−.013	−.906E02	−.026	−4.863*
	(−.29)	(−.20)	(−.65)	(−5.13)
R^2	.3097	.2937	.2907	.3055

NOTES: See table 2.2 for variable definitions. "E" means exponent; E02 means "multiplied by .01," etc.

The figures in parentheses are t statistics. R^2 is adjusted for degrees of freedom.

*Significant at the 95 percent level.

Table 2.12. Selected Basic Cable Regression Results

Independent Variables	(1) BASPH	(2) BASPH	Dependent Variable (3) BASPH	(4) BASPHL	(5) BASPHL	(6) BASPHL
DPIHH	—	-.436E-05 (-1.78)	.364E-05 (-1.46)	—	-.252E-04* (-2.12)	-.223E-04 (-1.83)
HPPH	.670* (12.62)	.678* (12.22)	.656* (11.27)	3.249* (12.75)	3.301* (12.28)	3.213* (11.32)
STATOT	—	-.145E-02 (-.51)	—	—	.469E-04 (.003)	—
STAVHF	—	—	-.830E-02 (-1.33)	—	—	-.027 (-.90)
STAUHF	—	—	-.753E-03 (-.26)	—	—	.272E-02 (.19)
BASRAT	—	-.024 (-1.13)	-.025 (1.18)	—	-.061 (-.59)	-.065 (-.62)
CRAT	—	.020 (1.77)	.023* (2.02)	—	.062 (1.12)	.075 (1.33)
C	-.054 (-1.70)	-.079 (-.71)	-.115 (-1.00)	-2.609* (-17.17)	-2.536* (-4.69)	-2.675* (-4.79)
R^2	.7710	.7870	.7895	.7747	.7861	.7860

NOTES: See table 2.2 for variable definitions. "E" means exponent; E-02 means "multiplied by .01," etc.
The figures in parentheses are t statistics. R^2 is adjusted for degrees of freedom.
* Significant at the 95 percent level.

Table 2.13. Selected Pay Cable Regression Results

	(1) PAYPH	(2) PAYPH	(3) PAYPHL	(4) PAYPH	(5) PAYPHL
Independent Variables					
DPIHH	.982E-05* (4.95)	—	.511E-04* (5.22)	.976E-05* (4.74)	.515E-04* (5.08)
DPIHLN	—	.289* (5.42)	—	—	—
HPPH	.442* (9.84)	—	2.442* (11.04)	.444* (9.26)	2.430* (10.29)
HPPHLN	—	.227* (9.25)	—	—	—
STATOT	.367E-02 (−1.59)	—	−.019 (−1.71)	—	—
STOTLN	—	−.032 (−1.76)	—	—	—
STAVHF	—	—	—	−.314E-02 (−.61)	−.024 (−.94)
STAUHF	—	—	—	−.371E-02 (−1.53)	−.019 (−1.59)
PAYRAT	−.046* (−2.67)	—	−.323* (−3.79)	−.046* (−2.64)	−.323* (−3.73)
PAYLN	—	−.391* (−2.39)	—	—	—
CRAT	−.247E-02 (−.22)	—	.022 (.41)	−.265E-02 (−.23)	.024 (.43)
CRATLN	—	−.043 (−.21)	—	—	—
C	.234* (2.59)	−1.502* (−2.67)	−1.167* (−2.62)	.236* (−2.49)	−1.195* (−2.57)
R^2	.7621	.7426	.8057	.7561	.8011

NOTES: See table 2.2 for variable definitions. "E" means exponent; E-02 means "multiplied by .01," etc.

The figures in parentheses are t statistics. R^2 is adjusted for degrees of freedom.

*Significant at the 95 percent level.

Notes

1. The views expressed herein are those of the authors. They do not necessarily reflect the views of the Federal Communications Commission or other members of its staff. The authors gratefully acknowledge the comments of Jerry

Brock, Ken Gordon, John Haring, Evan Kwerel, and Florence Setzer. The authors alone are responsible for any remaining errors.

2. The assumption of a perfectly elastic supply of VCRs was also used in the Batelle study, a time series model estimated on three years' worth of monthly data (Cronin et al. 1983:32–34). This study was provided to the authors by the Motion Picture Association of America, Inc. Its public release was pending. Here the supply elasticity assumption simply implies that VCR prices are constant across the continental United States and that more can be supplied at that constant price. The availability of VCRs by mail order makes the assumption reasonable. For cable the supply will be considered perfectly elastic among homes passed by cable.

3. These data come from the *Census of Service Industries,* conducted every five years. The 1977 data are too old and the 1982 data, while scheduled for release in the spring of 1984, were not available in time for this study. The lack of data dictates that P_{movies} be eliminated as well.

4. $P_{cassettes}$ should be thought of as a vector that includes the purchase prices of blank and prerecorded cassettes as well as the rental rate for the latter. There may in fact be some variation in these prices between population centers and rural areas.

5. State data were first collected in 1979. These data were unpublished, but the Electrical Industries Association was kind enough to supply them to the authors.

6. As long as there are no systematic differences across states in the relation between VCRs in use and sales to dealers, the conclusions on whether the VCR is a substitute or a complement will not be affected.

7. The data do not allow multi-VCR households to be distinguished. The assumption of one VCR per household introduces a (small) distortion in the variable.

8. In fact, the average household had 2.72 members in 1982 (U.S. Department of Commerce 1983a:1).

9. State-level figures on household size in 1982 are not available. However, U.S. Department of Commerce (1983b) provides 1980 figures. The national average was 2.75 persons; 37 of 48 state averages were between 2.65 and 2.85 (i.e., within 3.6 percent of the average). Utah had the largest average (3.20), and Florida had the smallest (2.55).

10. The cable systems covered in the Kagan Census are those that offer pay television. Kagan estimates that the Census excludes only some small cable systems, with a total of 300,000 basic subscribers (Paul Kagan Associates, 1983d:1). By Kagan's reckoning, this amounts to 1.1 percent of cable subscribers, a negligible omission.

11. The data are for subscriptions; cable homes subscribing to more than one tier are counted twice. Kagan estimates the number of unduplicated pay homes at 17.8 million. (Paul Kagan Associates 1983d:1). On the assumption that no MDS or STV homes get more than one tier (which is not quite accurate, since late night "adult" tiers are offered in many cases), this implies that 87 percent of pay subscribers are on cable.

12. There is also an installation fee for cable. However, this one-time fee is frequently waived or reduced in promotional campaigns to sign up new subscribers. (Dunmore and Bykowsky 1982:14). Furthermore, even when it is paid it is amortized over a matter of years. Hence the per-month equivalent is probably low and can be ignored safely.

13. In a sense, the VCR functions in the same way that resellers of voice- and data-communications services do. Resellers don't change the underlying competitive conditions, but they do help insure that the maximum benefits available from the existing market structure can be obtained by all consumers.

14. The simple correlation coefficient ranges from zero to one in absolute value. It measures the association between two variables without accounting for the effects of additional variables. See Johnston (1972:32–35). Multiple regression analysis is used to separate the effects of several independent variables on a dependent variable. See Kmenta (1971:347–408).

15. In fact a variety of specifications suggested by the model were estimated before examining the correlation coefficients, which were then used to rationalize poor results as well as choose additional specifications to estimate. The correlation coefficient discussion is placed first for expositional convenience.

16. R^2 is a measure of "goodness of fit," i.e., of how much of the variation in the dependent variable is explained by the independent variables. See Kmenta (1971:364–366).

17. A few regressions were estimated with separate VHF and UHF station-availability variables. These coefficients were positive but invariably far more significant. In some of the VCRTOT regressions a VHF station variable used alone was positive and significant. However, as noted, these regressions have other fatal deficiencies.

18. In this paper, whenever coefficients are described as significant, it should be understood as significant at the 95 percent level using a two-tailed test. See Kmenta (1971:136–44, 225–27).

19. As noted earlier, some preliminary regressions were estimated using separate VHF and UHF station availability variables. This specification was rejected because the VHF variable was never significant, the UHF variable was rarely significant, and the R^2 was lower than for corresponding equations with the total station-availability variable.

20. This study was provided to the authors by the Motion Picture Association of America, Inc. before publication.

21. Fischer (1971) uses the economic theory of consumer demand to analyze the substitute and complement properties of three- and four-good systems. Using the (relatively implausible) assumption of only three goods, it is possible to show the following. If VCRs and cable are substitutes, and cable and broadcast television are complements, then VCRs and broadcast television may be either substitutes or complements. This is reassuring but of limited relevance due to the restrictiveness of the three goods only assumption and to the fact that the multiple attributes of the VCR are ignored in the theory.

3

Economies of Scale in Cable Television: A Multiproduct Analysis

ELI M. NOAM

CONTENTS

  I. Research Issue
 II. The Model
III. Data
    A. Labor Inputs
    B. Capital Inputs
    C. Programming Inputs
    D. Outputs
    E. Other Variables
 IV. Results
  V. Conclusion

I. THE RESEARCH ISSUE

This study is an investigation of the economies of scale in cable television operations. The results are intended as an empirical contribution to the question of whether competition among rival cable television operators is likely, an issue of significant interest for regulatory policy towards the new medium.

The study proceeds by specifying a multiproduct function, and incorporates the effects of regulation in the multi-equation model. The statistical estimation is based on data for all 4,800 U.S. cable systems in operation in 1981.

The U.S. television industry is presently undergoing rapid change. Where once there was a limit on viewing options imposed by the scarcity of electromagnetic spectrum, confining most viewers to a handful of channels, cable television is emerging as "the television of abundance" (Sloan Commission 1971). Yet ironically, the market structure of "abundant" cable television may be more restrictive than that of "scarce" broadcast television, since the present franchising system has led to the establishment of parallel local franchises, one for each franchise area. This raises concern about a cable operator's ability, if left unconstrained by competition or regulation to charge monopolistic prices to subscribers, and, more significantly, to control the content of a large number of program channels. A variety of policy proposals have therefore been made, seeking to reach some form of either conduct regulation, public ownership, common carrier status, or competitive market structure. The latter approach, in particular, has been taken by the Federal Communications Commission, whose philosophy it is to permit entry and encourage *inter*-media competition between cable and other video technologies.[1]

A second and distinct competitive approach is to rely on *intra*-medium competition among cable companies. In New York State, for example, a governor's bill, based on recommendations by Alfred Kahn and Irwin Stelzer had sought to open each cable franchise area to additional cable companies, thereby reducing their local economic power. The likelihood of such entry, however, is based on the assumption that more than one cable company could successfully operate in a territory. But such competition is normally not likely to be sustainable, absent collusion, if cable exhibits strong economies of scale and economies of scope, i.e., cost advantages of size and of diversified production.

The question of cable television's economies of scale also has implications on the scope of local regulation (Schmalensee 1979) and on the treatment of the medium as a "public utility," issues that have arisen in a number of court cases.[2] (In one decision, for example, the court declared that "CATV is not a natural monopoly. Thus, the scope of regulation which is necessary in the natural monopolies is not here necessary . . . (and) CATV is not a public utility . . . (*Greater Freemont, Inc. v. City of Freemont,* 1968)." Information on scale elasticities is also important in assessing the likelihood of future consolidations into regional or national cable systems, finding the economically most efficient subdivision of large cities into franchise zones,[3] and in analyzing the price structure of cable television.[4]

Despite the relevance of the question of cable television economies of scale and scope, it has not received much empirical investigation.[5] Previous studies of cable television have typically centered on questions of demand analysis and of audience diversion. Most are dated, since their impetus was the 1966 FCC rules restricting CATV (Mitre 1974; CTIC 1972; Mitchell and Smiley 1974; Crandall and Fray 1974; Noll et al. 1973; Panko et al. 1975). As pointed out in an article jointly authored by a comfortable majority of the economists engaged in cable television research (Besen et al. 1977): "All of these models are synthetic and eclectic, drawing their cost data for the specific components of a system from engineering specification and field experience; no satisfactory data set exists from which to estimate econometric cost or production functions" (p. 66).[6]

Since that observation, several empirical studies on the demand for pay-cable services were undertaken (Bloch and Wirth 1982; Dunmore and Bykowsky 1982; Smith and Gallagher 1980). However, no comparable research on the production side was undertaken, with the recent exception of Owen and Greenhalgh (1983).

The Owen and Greenhalgh study, though it also relies on a cost function approach, is empirically based on figures from the applications by competing franchise bidders in 34 cities. As the authors themselves note, these figures do not represent actual operational data, but rather promises, possibly based on some form of "gamesmanship," and including those made by losing and therefore possibly inefficient bidders. Furthermore, no capital measures are available. Nevertheless, the Owen-Greenhalgh study is a great improvement over the previous state of knowledge. Webb (1983) also includes a brief and simple estimation of economies of scale, but the magnitudes of the elasticities are so vast (in the order of 4 to 10) as to be unpersuasive.

II. THE MODEL

Economies of scale and natural monopoly are closely related but not identical concepts.[7] Baumol (1977) together with Bailey and Willig (Baumol et al., 1977), formalized the analysis of these terms for the multiproduct case, defining natural monopoly as "[a]n industry in which multifirm production is more costly than production by a monopoly (subadditivity of the cost function)." Accordingly, to establish a natural monopoly anywhere along an output ray, it is necessary and sufficient to demonstrate strict ray subadditivity, i.e., that the costs of joint production by one firm are less than the cost of separate production by several firms for any scale of output mix Q. The existence of subadditivity is difficult to prove.[8] However, a number of conditions exist that are sufficient—though not necessary—for ray subadditivity. Among these is the proposition that increasing returns to scale up to output combination Q imply decreasing ray average costs and ray subadditivity up to Q. Hence, a showing of increasing returns to scale for the output range below Q would demonstrate a natural monopoly along that output ray.[9]

For purposes of analysis and estimation, consider the multiproduct cost function of i, uniquely corresponding to the production function under duality assumptions,

(1) $C_i = f_i (P_1. \ldots .P_n; Q_1. \ldots .Q_q; M_m)$

where C_i are total costs of production, Q_q is the output vector, P_i are the prices for input factors i, assumed to be independent of output of the system, and M_m are a set of other variables that may affect cost. Under the assumption of cost-minimization, we have from Shepherd's lemma an identity of the cost-price elasticities E_{CP}; with the share of each input factor in total cost, i.e.,

(2) $S_i \equiv \dfrac{P_i X_i}{C} = \dfrac{\partial lnC}{\partial lnP_i} = E_{CPi}$

where X_i is the quantity of input i. (The estimation of these cost-share equations jointly with the cost function increases the degrees of freedom and the statistical weight of an empirical estimation.)

Furthermore, let the cost function f be given by the translog function, a second-order logarithmic approximation to an arbitrary twice-differentiable transformation surface (Griliches and Ringstad 1971; Jorgenson et al. 1971). The translog function imposes no restrictions of production such as homogeneity, homotheticity, or unitary elasticities of factor substitution, and is hence convenient for testing the existence of these properties.[10] A major problem with the application of a multiproduct specification of a cost function is that if even one of the products has the value zero, the observation's value becomes meaningless. For that reason, it is necessary to specify an alternative functional form that is well behaved. As Caves, Christensen, and Tretheway (1980), pointed out, the use of the log metric for outputs in the generalized translog function is unnecessary for a homogeneity of degree one in factor prices, a condition which is usually imposed. Instead, one can substitute the Box-Cox metric

$$(3) \ g_i(Q_q) = \frac{Q_q^w - 1}{w}$$

which is defined for zero values, and which approaches the standard natural logarithm lnO_q as $w \to O$. Using this expression, we can define the "hybrid" multiproduct translog cost function.

$$(4) \ lnC(P_i, Q_q, M_m) = a_0 + \Sigma a_i lnP_i + \Sigma a_q \left(\frac{Q_q^w - 1}{w} \right)$$

$$+ \Sigma a_m lnM_k + \frac{1}{2}\Sigma\Sigma a_{ij} lnP_i lnP_j + \frac{1}{2}\Sigma\Sigma a_{qp} \left(\frac{Q_q^w - 1}{w} \right)\left(\frac{Q_p^w - 1}{w} \right)$$

$$+ \frac{1}{2} \Sigma\Sigma (lnM)^2 + \Sigma\Sigma a_{iq} lnP_i \left(\frac{Q_q^w - 1}{w} \right)$$

$$+ \Sigma\Sigma a_{im} lnP_i lnM + \Sigma\Sigma a_{qm} \left(\frac{Q_q^w - 1}{w} \right) lnM$$

The partial elasticities of total cost are then the logarithmic partial derivatives

$$(5) \ E_{CPi} = a_i + \Sigma a_{ij} lnP_j + \Sigma a_{iq} \left(\frac{Q_q^w - 1}{w} \right) + \Sigma a_{im} lnM$$

$$(6) \ E_{CQq} = Q_q^w \left(a_q + \Sigma a_{qp} \frac{Q_p^w - 1}{w} \right) + \Sigma a_{iq} lnP_i + \Sigma a_{qm} lnM \right)$$

$$(7) \ E_{CMm} = a_m + a_{mm} lnM + \Sigma a_{im} lnP_i + \Sigma a_{qm} \left(\frac{Q_q^w - 1}{w} \right)$$

Several parametric restrictions must be put on the cost function. The cost shares must add to unity which implies that $\Sigma E_{CPi} = 1$; under symmetry conditions, the cost function must be linearly homogeneous in factor prices at all values of factor prices, output and maturity. That is,

(8) $\sum_i a_i = 1$; $\sum_i a_{ij} = \sum_i a_{iq} = \sum_i a_{im} = 0$

and, the cross partial derivatives of the translog cost function must be equal, by its second-order approximation property, i.e., the symmetry condition exists

(9) $a_{ij} = a_{ji}$ and $a_{qp} = a_{pq}$, where $i \neq j, p \neq q$

The cost function is homothetic if and only if it can be written as a separable function of factor prices and outputs (Shepherd 1970). The optimal factor share combination is then independent of output, i.e., the expansion path is linear. From equation (5), it then must be

(10) $a_{iq} = 0$

which imposes $n-1$ independent restrictions, where n is the number of inputs i. Furthermore, the function is homogeneous at the sample mean if overall cost elasticity with respect to output is constant, i.e., if the conditions hold

(11)[11] $a_{qp} = a_{iq} = a_{qm} = w = 0$

For a test of constant returns to scale to exist, we add the independent restriction,

(12) $a_q = 1$

Finally, for a neutrality of technical change, we impose the $n-1$ independent restrictions, for an M that measures time,

(13) $a_{im} = 0$

Economies of scale must be evaluated along output rather than along input-mix, since the relative composition of inputs may change over the range of output. Only when the cost function is homothetic will the two be identical (Hanoch 1975). The implication is that scale economies are better described by the relation of cost to changes in output rather than by that of outputs to changes in inputs, which makes a cost function an advantageous specification. Following Frisch (1965), the cost elasticity with respect to output E_{CQ} is the reciprocal of scale elasticity, E_S. For the multiproduct case, local overall scale economies, as shown by Fuss and Waverman (1982), are

(14) $E_S = \dfrac{1}{\sum\limits_q E_{CQq}}$

so that

$$(15)\ E_S = 1/\Sigma_q \left(Q_q^w \left(a_q + \Sigma_p a_{qp} \left(\frac{Q_p^w - 1}{w} \right) + \Sigma_i a_{iq} lnP_i + \Sigma_m a_{qm} lnM \right) \right)$$

Product specific economies of scale are, using the definition in Baumol, Panzar, and Willig (1982)

$$(16)\ E_{Sq} = \frac{IC_q}{Q_q \dfrac{\partial C}{\partial Q_q}}$$

where IC_q are the incremental costs of producing product q. This incremental cost is described by

$$(17)\ IC_q = C(Q_1, \ldots Q_N) - C(Q_1, \ldots Q_{q-1}, 0, Q_{q+1} \ldots Q_N)$$

This elasticity can be rewritten as

$$(18)\ E_{Sq} = \frac{IC_q}{C} \bigg| E_{CQq}$$

which is

$$(19)\ E_{Sq} = \frac{IC_q}{C} \bigg| Q_q^w \left(a_q + \Sigma_p a_q \frac{Q_q^w - 1}{w} \right) + \Sigma_i a_{iq} lnP_i + \Sigma_m a_{qm} lnM \right).$$

For the hybrid translog function, sample mean values are $P_i = Q_q = M = 1$; thus the cost functions simplify to

$$(20)\ C(Q_1 \ldots Q_N) = \exp(a_0)$$

so that equation (19) for the product-specific economies of scale becomes

$$(21)^{12}\ C(Q_1 \ldots Q_{q-1},\ 0,\ Q_{q+1} \ldots Q_N) = \exp\left(a_0 - \frac{a_q}{w} + \frac{a_{qq}}{2w^2} \right)$$

$$(22)\ E_{Sq} = \frac{\exp(a_0) - \exp\left(a_0 - \dfrac{a_q}{w} + \dfrac{a_{qq}}{2w^2} \right)}{\exp(a_0) \cdot a_q}$$

The degree of overall economies of *scope* is the proportion of the total cost of joint production that is saved by joint production

$$(23) \ S_C = \frac{\left(\sum_q^N C_q(Q_q)\right) - C(Q_1 \ \ldots \ Q_N)}{C(Q_1 \ \ldots \ Q_N)}$$

At the sample mean, we observe that the product-specific cost function $C_q(Q_q)$ is

$$(24) \ C_q(Q_q) = C(0, 0 \ldots, Q_q, \ldots 0) = \exp\left(a_0 - \sum_{g \neq q}^N \frac{a_g}{w} + \frac{1}{2w^2} \sum_{\substack{g \\ g,s \neq q}}^N \sum_s^N a_{gs}\right)$$

Therefore, equation (23) becomes

$$(25) \ S_C = \frac{\left(\sum_q^N \exp\left(a_0 - \sum_g^N \frac{a_g}{w} + \frac{1}{2w^2} \sum_g^N \sum_s^N a_{gs}\right)\right) - \exp(a_0)}{\exp(a_0)}$$

In order to solve this equation, it is necessary to observe, for each product, the costs of separate and independent production. Since this is not feasible in the case of cable television, a test for economies of scope must proceed differently. As Panzar and Willig (1977a) have shown, it is a sufficient condition for economies of scope for the twice differentiable multiproduct cost function to have cost complementarities of the form

$$(26) \ \frac{\partial^2 C}{\partial Q_q \partial Q_p} < 0$$

which can be expressed by

$$(27) \ \frac{\partial^2 C}{\partial Q_g Q_q} = \frac{C}{Q_q Q_g}\left(\frac{\partial \ln C}{\partial \ln Q_q} \frac{\partial \ln C}{\partial \ln Q_q} + \frac{\partial^2 \ln C}{\partial \ln Q_q \ln Q_p}\right) < 0$$

At the sample mean of the hybrid translog cost function, this condition is met when $a_q a_g < -a_{qg}$ for each combination of outputs q and g, with $q \neq g$.

If some but not all products can be observed at the zero output level, *product-specific*—rather than overall—economies of scope can also be measured. These are defined as the degree of cost reduction due to the joint rather than separate production of q together with the other $N - 1$ products.

The model for estimation is the multivariate regression system comprising the cost function (4), the behavioral equations (2) and (5)–(7), and the restrictions (8) and (9).

Several alternative models are considered. First, we estimate different multiproduct models. Model A imposes no restrictions as to homotheticity, homogeneity, constant returns to scales, or neutrality. Model B imposes homotheticity (restriction (10)). Model C imposes homogeneity (restriction (11)). Model D imposes constant returns to scale (restrictions (11) and (12)). Model E imposes neutrality (restriction (13)). All models include the linearity restrictions (8) and (9).

The form of estimation that is used to determine this system follows Zellner's (1962) iterative method. That technique is a form of generalized least squares, shown to yield maximum likelihood estimates that are invariant to which of the cost-share equations is omitted (Barten 1969). In estimating such a system, it is generally assumed that disturbances in each of the share equations are additive, and that they have a joint normal distribution. These assumptions are made here too.[13]

The testing of the hypotheses of homogeneity etc. can be accomplished by likelihood ratio tests, since the iterative Zellner method results in maximum likelihood estimates of parameters (Christensen and Greene 1976). We define the determinants of the restricted and unrestricted estimates of the disturbance covariance matrix values. We then have

(28) $\lambda = (|\Omega|_R / |\Omega|_U)^{-N/2}$

where N is the number of observations. $-2 \ln \lambda$ is distributed asymptotically as chi-squared with degrees of freedom equal to the number of independent restrictions imposed, and can be tested.

III. DATA

The empirical estimation of this study is based on an unusually good body of data for several thousand cable television systems, all producing essentially the same service,[14] operating and accounting in a single-plant mode, supplying their local market only, and reporting data according to the fairly detailed categories of a mandatory federal form.[15]

The data covers virtually all 4,800 U.S. cable systems,[16] and is composed of four disparate and extensive files for each of the years

1978 to 1981 for technical, programming, financial, local community, and employment information. The financial data includes both balance sheet and income figures.[17]

All variables are standardized around the sample mean in order to overcome the problem of arbitrary scaling that can become an issue in translog functions.[18]

A. Labor Inputs[19]

The factor quantity is the number of full-time employees (with part-timers added at half value). Its cost is the average salary of employees, weighted according to their classification by nine job categories (professionals, technicians, unskilled laborers, etc.).

B. Capital Inputs

Accounting data for different classes of assets is reported to the FCC in book value form. Although the great bulk of assets in the cable television industry have been acquired within the past decade, thus limiting the extent of inflationary distortion, it was considered prudent to re-value these assets. To do so, the study took advantage of a highly detailed engineering study, commissioned by the federal government, on the cost and pattern of investment in the construction of cable systems. In that report, the required investment flow in a medium-sized cable system over a period of ten years was calculated.[20] We assume that this time distribution of investment over the first ten years holds proportionally for all systems, with investment in the eleventh year and further years identical to that of the tenth year in real terms, and that the cost of acquiring capital assets required in a cable television system increases at the rate of a weighted index of communications and utilities equipment.[21]

For each observation, we know the first year of operation and the aggregate historical value of capital assets. It is then possible to allocate capital investments to the different years and different types of investment, and to inflate their value to the prices of the observation year. The input price P_K of this capital stock K is determined by its opportunity cost in a competitive environment, consisting of potential returns r on equity E and payments for debt D, with an allowance for the deductibility of interest expense (tax rate $= t$).[22]

$$(29) \quad P_K = r_E \cdot \frac{E}{K} + r_D(1 - t)\frac{D}{K}$$

The required return on equity is determined according to the risk premium ρ required above the return on risk-free investments, R_F; that is, $r_E = R_F + \rho$. Ibbotson and Sinquefield (1979) found ρ for the Standard & Poor 5000 to be 8.8 for the period 1926–1977. Hence, using the capital asset pricing model (Sharpe 1964; Lintner 1965), an estimate of β for a specific firm is 8.8 times β, where β is the measure of nondiversifiable (systematic) risk. The average β for cable companies listed by Moody's is, for 1980, $\beta = 1.42$, resulting in a risk premium of 12.49 percent over the treasury bill rate.[23]

For r_D, the return on long-term debt, the following method was employed: for each observation it was determined, using several financial measures, what its hypothetical bond rating would have been, based on a company's financial characteristics. These "shadow" bond ratings for each observation were then applied to the actual average interest rates existing in the observation years for different bond ratings (Moody's 1981). This procedure is novel, but is based on a series of previous studies in the finance literature of bond ratings and their relation to financial ratios.[24]

Tax rate w is defined as the corporate income tax rate (federal and average net state). Debt is defined as long term liabilities.

C. Programming Inputs

The third production factor of the model is the input of programming. A cable system that carries no communications messages would be of no interest to subscribers. Therefore, cable operators supply programs in addition to providing the communication wire. These programs are not produced or generated by the operators; with trivial exceptions,[25] programming is supplied by broadcasters and program networks.[26] Program costs are both direct and indirect. Direct costs are the outlays for program services, for example to pay-TV networks and to suppliers such as Cable News Network (CNN), which charge operators according to the number of their subscribers, plus the cost of program importation and its equipment. Direct costs, however, are only part of the programming cost; indirect costs that must also be considered are the foregone net earning from advertising. For example, CNN is able to sell some of its "air" time to advertisers. This time is in effect a compensation in kind by the cable operator to CNN for the supply of the program. Similarly, local broadcasters are carried by cable for free, and the programming cost of these "must carry" to cable operators, too, is the foregone earnings, largely in advertising revenues.[27]

Direct costs are reported to the FCC and are available. Included are also such capital cost as those of origination studios and signal importation equipment and cost to carriers. The indirect cost of foregone advertising revenue is defined as the potential minus the actual advertising revenue obtained by cable operators net of cost. Actual figures are reported to the FCC; potential revenues are estimated by reference to the average net advertising revenue in television broadcasting per household/and viewing time.[28] The unit price of programming inputs is their total divided by the number of program hours and channels.

It is one of the convenient properties of cable television that it uses very little in inputs beyond those of capital, labor, and programming. It does not use raw materials of intermediate inputs to speak of, apart from programming. Even its energy requirements are quite small, in the order of .7 percent of total expenses, if capital expenses are included (Weinberg 1972, tables C-1 and C-2). Office supplies, telephone, postage, insurance etc. add another 1.8 percent of costs that include capital inputs. For consistent treatment of inputs and outputs, this small residual input is added to the inputs K, L, and P; since one cannot determine for what the residual input is a substitute, we prorate K, L, and P.

D. Outputs

Costs and revenues in cable television are nearly entirely for subscription rather than actual use. Pay-per-view billing systems are rare, and in their absence there are only negligible marginal costs to the operator for a subscriber's actual viewing of the channels. Interactive communications services, though maybe of future importance, are very rare at present. Advertisements, similarly, are largely supplied by program providers as part of an exchange arrangement; as discussed above, they are an input. Hence, the number of actual and potential subscribers—as opposed to their viewing—are the measures of the operator's outputs.

Cable television operators' major outputs then are of the following dimensions: (a) basic service subscriptions; (b) pay-TV service subscriptions; and (c) the size of the market developed, measured by the number of *potential* subscribers that are reached. The latter is reflected by the number of "homes passed" by cable. The larger this number, the more subscribers can be potentially enrolled. Cable trunk lines or feeder lines pass their house; only drops need to be added for their inclusion as paying customers.[29]

E. Other Variables

M, maturity in operation, is one variable that is introduced to allow for the period that a cable operator had to improve operations and to establish itself in the local market. It is defined by the number of years of actual operation.

This variable may be thought of as if it were an output factor. Quite possibly, it is substitutable for the more conventional input factors of capital and labor, reflecting improvements in productivity of a firm whose experience shifts the cost function downwards. The variable also allows to reflect different technological vintages, and a possible tightening of franchise contract requirements over time. There is no clear-cut relation of time and size per se. Old systems include both the smallest backwoods operators and the largest, due to the time available for penetration.

Two additional variables are introduced in order to adjust for differences in the cable systems that may affect costs of production and ability to attract subscribers. The density of population has a role in determining cost. The further houses are from each other physically, the more capital and labor inputs must go into reaching each. To allow for density variations, we define D as the length of cable trunk lines per household passed. The resultant ratio is used as a proxy for density.[30]

A third variable is the number E of video channels offered by a cable operator. Clearly, the more channels offered, the more inputs are required. At the same time, one would expect subscription outputs to be affected positively, *ceteris paribus,* since the cable service is more varied and hence probably more attractive to potential subscribers.[31]

IV. RESULTS

Table 3.1 represents the parameter estimates for the five models (A-E), for the multiproduct specification, for the year 1982.

The system has a good fit, with system R^2 values above .97 for the models. Similarly, the coefficients are generally significant at the .05 level, and common parameters are of similar size. High R^2 values are found for the cost share equations, when these are estimated separately.[32]

Overall elasticity of scale is calculated, using equation (14), as $E_S = 1.096$. That is, a 10 percent increase in size is associated with a unit cost decrease of about 1 percent.

We are also able to calculate, using equation (19), measures for the product-specific economies of scale for the three outputs. They are:

E_S (Homes passed) $= 1.020$
E_S (Basic subscriptions) $= 1.054$
E_S (Pay subscriptions) $= 1.072$

Economies of scale are thus observed for two outputs—basic and pay subscriptions. However, for "Homes passed," these are relatively small; it may be recalled that this output description refers to a physical measure, namely the extent of the cable network in accessing a market.[33]

The implication from this result is that scale economies do not appear to exist primarily in the technical distribution aspects of cable television, as reflected by "Homes passed." Instead, they are observed for the output definitions that include a strong element of marketing success.

It is particularly interesting to observe that the overall economies of scale are larger than the product-specific economies of scale. There are then economies to joint production, or of "scope."

It is, however, one thing to observe that economies of scope must exist, and quite another to actually apply the equations of the analytical part to their estimation in order to get a specific number. As discussed above, one cannot, at least for cable television, observe zero production levels or stand-alone production for separate products except—rarely—

Table 3.1. Cost Function Parameters Output Definition: Multiproduct

Parameter	Model A: unrestricted	Model B: homotheticity	Model C: homogeneity	Model D: constant returns	Model E: neutrality
a(0)	−0.4295	−0.3551	−0.2669	−0.4353	−0.3780
	(21.0098)	(16.3044)	(14.1049)	(9.2915)	(18.4553)
a(P1)	0.3349	0.2824	0.2150	0.4507	0.2889
	(12.4595)	(9.4205)	(8.2853)	(13.3905)	(11.2621)
a(P2)	0.3417	0.2490	0.1584	0.3947	0.2831
	(10.2453)	(7.2420)	(6.3529)	(11.5193)	(8.6899)
a(P3)	0.3233	0.4685	0.6265	0.1545	0.4278
	(7.6582)	(10.1526)	(27.2923)	(4.9320)	(10.3827)
a(Qa)	0.2920	0.3219	0.5476	0.5399	0.2858
	(4.1001)	(5.4185)	(12.7492)	(12.6206)	(4.0156)
a(Qb)	0.1211	0.1629	0.1972	0.2977	0.2762
	(1.5862)	(2.0956)	(3.7183)	(2.0495)	(3.5872)
a(Qc)	0.4987	0.3622	0.1970	0.5585	0.4314
	(13.5994)	(9.2298)	(11.5557)	(22.4069)	(11.8519)
a(D)	0.1927	0.0844	−0.2019	−0.1778	0.0029
	(2.4782)	(1.0149)	(2.8993)	(0.9504)	(0.0407)
a(E)	0.4407	0.4219	0.5284	0.0204	0.4089
	(6.1587)	(5.4698)	(7.2090)	(0.1173)	(6.0793)
a(M)	−0.0092	−0.0587	−0.0296	0.0209	0.0552
	(2.0556)	(1.6472)	(0.6157)	(0.1649)	(1.1232)
a(P1)(SQ)	0.0192	0.0169	0.0653	0.1096	0.0318
	(1.2457)	(1.2603)	(5.0556)	(5.4497)	(2.1764)
a(P1)(P2)	0.1757	0.0126	−0.0996	−0.1322	0.0297
	(4.5319)	(0.5000)	(4.4764)	(3.6293)	(0.8589)

Table 3.1. (Continued)

Parameter	Model A: unrestricted	Model B: homotheticity	Model C: homogeneity	Model D: constant returns	Model E neutrality
a(P1)(P3)	−0.2142	−0.0464	−0.0309	−0.0870	−0.0935
	(5.1888)	(4.3946)	(3.4134)	(6.1643)	(2.5117)
a(P1)(Qa)	0.0814	—	—	—	0.2007
	(0.9600)				(2.7285)
a(P1)(Qb)	0.2438	—	—	—	0.0231
	(2.8283)				(0.3134)
a(P1)(Qc)	0.0094	—	—	—	−0.0807
	(0.2667)				(2.4471)
a(P1)(D)	−0.1481	−0.0095	0.1114	0.1900	—
	(1.7573)	(0.1166)	(1.7598)	(2.2280)	
a(P1)(E)	−0.4059	0.2317	−0.0369	0.0406	—
	(3.8088)	(2.3676)	(0.4621)	(0.3447)	
a(P1)(M)	−0.0478	0.1963	0.0493	0.0750	—
	(0.9377)	(4.6775)	(1.3034)	(1.2297)	
a(P2)(SQ)	0.4082	0.0332	0.0750	0.1204	0.2905
	(12.4739)	(2.4624)	(6.6422)	(6.4273)	(9.3819)
a(P2)(P3)	−0.9922	−0.0792	−0.0504	−0.1086	−0.6109
	(13.4510)	(5.9905)	(5.4034)	(7.4886)	(10.0694)
a(P2)(Qa)	−0.2334	—	—	—	0.1112
	(2.1867)				(1.1449)
a(P2)(Qb)	0.4235	—	—	—	−0.0737
	(3.7497)				(0.7668)
a(P2)(Qc)	0.7728	—	—	—	0.4742
	(12.0940)				(8.7495)

a(P2)(D)	-0.2435 (2.2640)	-0.2612 (2.7856)	-0.0077 (0.1290)	0.0252 (0.2989)	—
a(P2)(E)	-0.5717 (3.8874)	0.3377 (3.0053)	0.0485 (0.6524)	0.0625 (0.5585)	—
a(P2)(M)	0.3278 (4.7756)	0.2077 (3.3537)	-0.0280 (0.8139)	0.0314 (0.5559)	
a(P3)(SQ)	0.6032 (12.5321)	0.0628 (7.8259)	0.0406 (14.8110)	0.0314 (0.5559)	0.3522 (9.1544)
a(P3)(Qa)	0.1520 (1.1172)	—	—	—	-0.3120 (2.5455)
a(P3)(Qb)	-0.6674 (4.7819)				0.0505 (0.4287)
a(P3)(Qc)	-0.7823 (9.8163)				-0.3935 (6.0579)
a(P3)(D)	0.3916 (2.9928)	0.2708 (2.2879)	-0.1037 (3.5403)	-0.2152 (2.8686)	
a(P3)(E)	0.9776 (5.4791)	-0.5694 (3.8618)	-0.0115 (0.3923)	-0.1031 (1.3260)	—
a(P3)(M)	-0.2800 (3.7788)	-0.4041 (5.8027)	-0.0213 (1.1789)	-0.1065 (2.3104)	—
a(Qa)(SQ)	0.1509 (0.9408)	0.2967 (1.7608)	—	—	0.1634 (1.0060)
a(Qa)(Qb)	-0.5721 (1.6672)	-0.7997 (2.2508)			-0.4138 (1.2027)
a(Qa)(Qc)	-0.1156 (0.9659)	0.0691 (1.6512)			0.2345 (2.0869)
a(Qa)(D)	0.2968 (1.2781)	0.4290 (1.7567)			0.2673 (1.1416)

Table 3.1. (Continued)

Parameter	Model A: unrestricted	Model B: homotheticity	Model C: homogeneity	Model D: constant returns	Model E: neutrality
a(Qa)(E)	0.0502	−0.0498			−0.4212
	(0.1517)	(0.1501)			(1.2502)
a(Qa)(M)	0.0305	0.0410			−0.2483
	(0.1895)	(0.2419)			(1.5042)
a(Qb)(SQ)	−0.0337	0.0334			−0.3023
	(3.3132)	(0.4302)			(3.3153)
a(Qb)(Qc)	0.2981	−0.2418			−0.2545
	(2.4572)	(5.5954)			(2.3535)
a(Qb)(D)	−0.5525	−0.5936			−0.4203
	(2.2777)	(2.3360)			(1.7505)
a(Qb)(E)	−0.5389	0.2512			0.3580
	(1.6146)	(0.7674)			(1.0777)
a(Qb)(M)	−0.0251	0.0802			0.2326
	(0.1617)	(0.4982)			(1.4746)
a(Qc)(SQ)	0.0319	0.0292			0.1710
	(9.4927)	(4.1997)			(6.0260)
a(Qc)(D)	−0.2008	−0.1169			0.0794
	(1.9116)	(1.2390)			(2.1344)
a(Qc)(E)	−0.5338	0.5509			0.1880
	(3.7968)	(4.4980)			(5.1626)
a(Qc)(M)	0.2751	0.3351			0.0190
	(4.2650)	(5.3635)			(0.9946)
a(D)(SQ)	−0.0316	0.0862	0.0972	0.1290	0.0117
	(0.3699)	(0.9853)	(2.0793)	(1.0478)	(0.1594)

a(D)(E)	0.5141	0.4598	0.4015	0.9788	0.3799
	(2.0282)	(1.7958)	(2.7186)	(2.4377)	(1.6409)
a(D)(M)	0.1819	0.2374	0.1653	0.2217	0.1005
	(1.5034)	(1.8710)	(1.5121)	(0.7486)	(0.8209)
a(E)(SQ)	1.0449	−0.1151	0.1148	0.5262	0.2549
	(4.8100)	(0.5416)	(0.6843)	(1.1270)	(1.4826)
a(L)(M)	0.5639	−0.0926	0.4372	1.1679	0.6205
	(3.0229)	(0.4949)	(2.8572)	(2.8955)	(3.3830)
(M)(SQ)	0.1849	0.0779	0.1309	0.3789	0.2041
	(3.7133)	(1.4725)	(2.9945)	(3.4417)	(44.0412)
R^2	0.9771	0.9816	0.9707	0.8714	0.9772

for pay TV subscriptions, because no CATV operation is conceivable without homes passed and basic subscribers. And cable systems without TV tend to be small, outmoded, unrepresentative. If one relies solely on extrapolation, in these circumstances a method of dubious validity, the calculated overall economies of scope are 2.699. No claim of validity is attached to the scope figure.

The product-specific scale elasticity measures listed above also provide another insight. Since they are the ratios of average to marginal cost, their value being generally above unity reflects marginal costs that are below average costs. This suggests that in a hypothetical competitive environment, when subscriber prices are driven to marginal cost, total costs will not be recovered.

It is also interesting to look at the estimates for the effects of operational maturity M. This factor, it may be recalled, measures the effects of experience in operation. We find the elasticity of costs with respect to such maturity to be $E_{CM} = -.01$, suggesting a downward shift of the cost function with experience, with inputs and outputs held even.

It should be noted that the maturity effect M actually embodies two separate effects, that of experience, given a technology, and that of changes in the technology itself. Conceptually, it is the difference between a movement along a curve, and the shift of the curve. The separation of these effects is an item for further research.

A look at the other control variables is interesting, too. Here, we can observe that the coefficient for density (trunk length/homes passed) has a value of .19, with a good statistical significance. That is, costs are declining with density, which is an expected result, though its magnitude is not particularly great. Furthermore, cost savings decline with density and there are diminishing economies to density. This would confirm the observation that in highly dense inner city franchise areas costs increase again.

The number of channels, E, on the other hand, is associated with increasing cost; this, too, is as intuitively expected. Here, cost increases rise with channels, implying increasing marginal cost of channel capacity beyond the mean.

V. CONCLUSION

This study of the U.S. cable industry, using 1981 data from the more than 4,800 American cable companies, shows that economies of scale exist in the current range of production. On the other hand, fairly small returns to scale are observed for the separate output measure "Homes passed," which is largely a transmission definition of output. This suggests that the cost advantages of size are not derived primarily by the technical distribution network, but rather by a larger operator's greater ability to package and sell his services more effectively to potential basic and pay subscribers.

While this paper deals with scale economies of cable, such conditions are not the only factor pertinent to entry. Theoretically, it is for example possible that several rivals coexist in a market, even in the presence of subadditivity, if they enter into some form of oligopolistic agreement to assure their mutual survival. However, such interaction is less likely with a single incumbent, as is the case in cable television. A hostile entry,[34] on the other hand, is costly: since many of the cable companies operate multiple systems across the country, a hostile entry would under normal circumstances invite retaliation or a protective price cut (Milgrom and Roberts 1982).

The likelihood of competitive entry could also be affected by sunk cost of the incumbent cable operator. Sunk cost—the difference between the *ex ante* cost of investment and its *ex post* sale value—may permit strategic investment behavior in order to create entry barriers (Dixit 1979; Spence 1977). It differentiates the cost of incumbents from those of contestants, and imposes an exit cost on a contestant. Knieps and Vogelsang (1982) have shown that entry and a multifirm equilibrium may still be possible in a sunk cost situation under Cournot assumptions, provided demand is high relative to cost, but that under a Bertrand behavioral assumption entry can be deterred if a sufficiently high share of cost is sunk. It is not clear which of the assumptions better reflects a hypothetical oligopolistic interaction in cable television, or even if one can accept the simplistic assumption of invariable post-entry behavior.[35] As an empirical matter, it is very hard to assess the existence of sunk cost and to separate it from good will in cable television, although there are indications of its existence. In a sale of cable assets, the physical cable network may be acquired by other communication carriers as a broadband transmission facility,[36] possibly as a "by-pass" to telephone companies, but such use is only beginning, and probably not profit-generating for some time. In any event, it has been shown (Panzar and Willig 1977b) that competitive entry can be deterred where sunk costs are zero, if average cost is continuously diminishing; in the presence of sunk costs this result should hold all the more.

Beyond the theoretical arguments, there is also the reality of competitive entry, or rather the lack thereof. In practice there are no second entrants, apart from minor cream skimming instances. Competitive cable television services (known in the industry as "overbuilds") exist in less than 50 franchises out of 4,800 and are usually caused by disputes about the scope of the initial franchise award. Of these operations, only those in Allentown, Pennsylvania, and Phoenix, Arizona, are of appreciable size. (J. Smith 1984). Despite rivalry, subscriber rates in Allentown are above the national average. "Where cities have tried to spur competition during refranchising by inviting competitive bidding, they have been unable to inspire even a nibble of interest from any companies other than the incumbent operator." (Stoller 1982:36)

The rivalry among cable operators is thus primarily for the right of first entry. Being first assures a head start and thus advantages of some economies of larger size; this, together with the likely existence of sunk costs, the ability of the incumbent to cut prices fairly rapidly, and consumers' conservative adjustment to new offerings,[37] violates the criteria for actual or potential contestability.

If the estimation results are accepted, their implications are that large cable corporations have cost advantages over smaller ones when they function as more than a mere distributor. Under the results, a pure distribution network with no programming or marketing role, such as a passive common carrier, is likely to have some but not large cost advantage over potential rivals. The imposition of such a pure transmission status would therefore be doubly injurious to the cable television industry (which strenuously opposes it): it would not only eliminate operators' control over and profit from nontransmission activities such as program selection, but it would also reduce the cost-advantage protection of incumbents against entry.

On the other hand, the conclusions require a reassessment of the pro-separations argument. That position, held by institutions as disparate as the Nixon White House and the American Civil Liberties Union, is normally presented as one of protection against a vertical extension of the natural monopoly in one stage of production (transmission) upstream into other stages such as program selection. The implications of our estimation, however, do not support the view that such advantages are primarily derived from a naturally monopolistic distribution stage.

Instead, the cost advantages appear to lie in the economies of scope (of integration) which provide cable television firms with some protection against rivalry in the distribution phase of their operations by other cable entrants. There are therefore some efficiency losses in operations associated with a separation policy, which must be weighed against the greater competitiveness in program supply.

Notes

1. For example, conventional commercial television, subscription television (STV), direct broadcast satellites (DBS), or multipoint distribution (MDS) (FCC 1980f).

2. In *Community Communications Co. v. City of Boulder,* (1981), the city's moratorium on expansion had been challenged by the local cable company. "The City concluded that cable systems are natural monopolies. Consequently, the City became concerned that CCC, because of its headstart, would always be the only cable operator in Boulder if allowed to expand, even though it might not be the best operator Boulder could otherwise obtain . . ." Yet the factual issue is hotly disputed, as a dissenting judge notes: "the city's sole defense is to pretend disingeniously and contrary to the extensive, uncontradicted testimony and the findings of the trial judge, . . . that cable television is a natural monopoly."

3. An example for the present ad hoc approach to this question is the cable plan for New York City. In that two-volume report, which recommends several franchise areas, the entire analysis of economies of scale consists of the following nonsequitur: "there were only twelve—of more than 4,000 operating cable systems in the United States—which served more than 50,000 subscribers. Unquestionably, this is an acceptable minimum for the size of a franchise area. Moreover, economies of scale would also exist for smaller franchise areas." Arnold and Porter, (1982:1:135).

4. If average costs fall continuously, marginal costs are below average cost, and at a nondiscriminatory price $P = MC,$ a cable company will operate at a loss. (Scherer 1980). If prices are regulated at a uniform level $P = AC,$ there are no losses, but allocative inefficiency exists, since some consumers are left without service who would have been willing to pay above marginal cost. A set of discriminatory prices is therefore most likely.

5. Examples of research on scale economies exist for other industries; in particular, for electric generation, Christensen and Greene (1976), Gollop and

Roberts (1981), Nerlove (1968), Belinfante (1978), Dhrymes and Kurz (1964). For telephone service, the controversy over the nature of telecommunications has sparked studies in the United States and Canada, including Vinod (1972); Sudit (1973); Dobell et al. (1972); Fischelson (1977); Eldor et al. (1979). Recent noteworthy treatments have been Nadiri and Schankerman (1981), and Denny et al. (1981a, b). In a multi-product setting, such work has included Fuss and Waverman's (1981) study of telephone service, Caves et al. (1980). For a review of this and related literature, see Bailey and Friedlaender (1982).

6. More precisely, earlier attempts at cost studies of cable television have been chapters in two doctoral dissertations on the economics of Canadian television (Good 1974; Babe 1975), which include simple regressions of cost per size for several Canadian systems and which come to conclusions that are contradictory to each other.

7. The concept of natural monopoly, introduced (with a different terminology) by John Stuart Mill (1848), and refined by Richard R. Ely (1937:628), has been used as a prime argument for regulation. "Natural monopoly is traditionally the classic case for extensive regulation" (Kaysen and Turner 1959:14–18), though others disagree (Posner 1969; Lowry 1973). Kahn, in his treatise on regulation (1971:2:119–23), properly distinguishes the case of natural monopoly from one of mere duplication of facilities, an insufficient condition. He describes the "critical and—if properly defined—all-embracing characteristic of natural monopoly (as) an inherent tendency to decreasing unit cases over the entire range of the market." Kahn lists factors that make a natural monopoly likely: large fixed investments; a fixed and essentially immovable connection between suppliers and customer; a nonstorable type of service; obligation of instantaneous supply; wide fluctuations in demands for service. Of these, all but the last appear to apply to cable television. Schmalensee (1979) extends this analysis to distribution networks and shows that continually decreasing costs of transmission can be treated in the same way as Kahn's decreasing unit costs. On the regulation of natural monopolies, see Demsetz (1968), Posner (1969, 1970), and Comanor and Mitchell (1970).

8. "Unfortunately, the intuitive appeal of the subadditivity concept is counterbalanced by its analytical elusiveness . . . there apparently exist no straightforward mechanical criteria that permit us to test whether or not a particular function is subadditive." (Baumol et al. 1982:170.) One insight of the multiproduct analysis is that the multiproduct firm may enjoy economies of scope with or without economies of scale.

9. Propositions 7D2 and 7D1 (Baumol et al. 1982:175).

10. Furthermore, as Diewert (1976) has demonstrated, a Divisia index of total factor productivity that is based on a translog function is exact rather than approximate. The cost function is generally superior in allowing for an endogeneity of inputs when nonconstant returns exist; Belinfante (1978). The choice among flexible functional forms is discussed by Berndt and Khaled (1979).

11. The imposition of $w = 0$ leads to a general multiproduct cost function, and this is reasonable. For the concept of homogeneity to be meaningful, all

output quantities must be able to vary, and none can be restricted to zero, obviating the need for the transform (3).

12. Without the hybrid specification, an equation of type (21) could not be numerically expressed in translog form.

13. The parameter w is found by minimizing the residual sum of squares $0^2(w)$. (Madalla, 1977:315).

14. Reporting is according to local operations; national cable companies (Multiple Systems Operators, or MSOs) must therefore report their different operations separately.

15. These reports are likely to be fairly accurate due to cable companies' vulnerability to FCC charges of misreporting in a period in which they are actively seeking new franchises.

16. Cable franchise areas are not identical with communities, since most cities subdivide their area into different franchise zones; subscriber size for a cable operation—once one goes beyond small communities—therefore does not necessarily correlate with community size. This holds even more for the major media market-size definition of population. Variations in system size are therefore not systematically related to different forms of urban governance, regulation, or number of other media outlets.

17. Cable Bureau, (1981). To assure confidentiality, financial data had been aggregated in the publicly available FCC documents; particularly detailed subaggregations—for each state according to seven size categories, and with many such categories of financial information—had been made specially available to the author.

18. On the statistical aspects of this scaling, which is widespread in translog estimations, see Denny and Fuss (1977).

19. All input prices are assumed to be independent of production level. Furthermore, input prices are not controlled by cable operators. This seems unexceptional in light of the mobility of capital and labor. For programming, some market power will exist in the future if cable should become a dominant medium. As an advertising outlet, cable television has no particular market power. While some input prices may be lower for multiple system operators, there is no systematic relation between size and MSO status. TCI, the largest MSO in the country, consists primarily of small and medium wired systems.

20. The study looks into hundreds of items of equipment, different techniques for laying cable, etc. Its use here is for the relative distribution of capital investments over time (Weinberg 1972:128).

21. The formula employed is: Current Value $=$ Book Value $\times$ T_M; where T_M is the adjustment factor

$$T_M = \frac{\sum\limits_{i=0}^{M} T_i}{\sum\limits_{i=0}^{M} E_i / R_S + I}$$

with M = age (in years) of system; I = annual capital investment for a cable operation in year i; R = inflation adjustment factor for years $S+i$ of cable operation; S = starting year. The inflation adjustment is defined such that R_{1980} = 1.00. R inflates the investment of earlier years, i.e., reflects on how much a one-dollar investment in year X would cost in today's prices. No deflator/inflator data are directly available for cable television. We therefore use those of two related industries, communications equipment and public utilities. Both deflator series are available from survey data by the Bureau of Economic Analysis, U.S. Department of Commerce. We use Weinberg (1972) to obtain the shares in capital of, first, headend, amplifiers, and customer converters, which is the weight applied to the series of communications, and second, the share of transmission system, which is the weight applied to the utilities series. The result is a weighted aggregate index. Investment figures are available before depreciation, permitting a calculation of depreciation from asset life figures (Weinberg 1972) rather than relying on divergent company depreciation accounting procedures.

22. There is no evidence that tax rates, or investment cycles, are systematically different by subscriber size.

23. There is no reason to assume that β is functionally related to subscriber size.

24. Such models exist since 1966 (Horrigan), and have been refined by Pogue and Saldofsky (1969), Pinches and Mingo (1973, 1975) and Altman and Katz (1976). The model used here is taken from the Kaplan and Urwitz survey (1979, table 6, model 5) which determines bond rating with a fairly high explanatory power (R^2 = .79). The financial variables used in that model are: (a) "cash flow before tax/interest charges; (b) long-term debt/net worth; (c) net income/total assets; (d) total assets; (e) subordination of debt. Bond ratings ranging from AAA (model values ≥ 9) to C (≤ 1) can then be obtained for each observation point by substitution of the appropriate financial values. Bond rates are those reported by Moody's (1981). For low ratings, no interest rates are reported by the services. For the lowest rating (C), the values estimated by an investment banker specializing in cable television were used (4 percent above prime); for the next higher ratings, interest rates were reduced proportionally until the reported ratings were reached.

25. Usually restricted to a studio for a low budget public-access channel, and of an automated news/weather display.

26. It would be faulty to view the quantity of programs themselves as the outputs of a cable operator rather than as inputs. Neither are they produced by operators, as mentioned, nor are they sold on a quantity basis. Under the presently existing subscription based system of revenue generation (as opposed to the embryonic pay-per-view system), programs serve as an incentive to buy subscriptions, not as the product itself.

27. There are constraints on the operator's choice of programming; a certain number of channels are mandated ("must carry") of broadcasters; public access, leased access, and governmental channels. This may distort inputs.

28. Calculated by dividing total TV advertising billing (McCann-Erickson, as reported in *Television Digest* 1980:76a) by a number of households (Arbitron, as reported in *Television Digest* 1980:104a), and by viewing time. Nielsen figures for average weekly viewing of TV households is 42.6 hours; of cable households, 51.7 hours (A.C. Nielsen 1981). TV advertising revenues per household viewing hour is found at close to 5.5 cents. This figure is adjusted for cable subscribers' viewing hours.

29. Owen and Greenhalgh (1982) similarly used "homes passed" as an output.

30. The density variable can correct for different transmission requirements (ducts in central cities; poles in suburban and rural areas). The flexible translog specification permits a U-shaped relation of cost and density, which one would intuitively expect.

31. Channels are not outputs; they serve to generate the revenue producing subscriptions. However, the specifications of the main equation permits an interpretation of channel capacity as an output.

32. There is a possibility that some cable systems are backwards or old; the time variable "experience" can allow for the latter; to correct for the former—and to test its validity—the model was also used with all 12-channel systems (likely to be the most "backward") excluded. The results were substantially similar, alleviating the concern.

33. The definition of output-specific economies of scale is particularly important in the analysis of an industry with the technological characteristics of cable television, where outputs are not necessarily changed along a ray, i.e., by equal proportions. For example, if two cable companies serve an area that has previously been served by only one firm, their technical outputs "homes passed" or "channels provided" are, let us assume, as large for each separate firm as they had been for the monopolist. However, their outputs "basic subscribers" and "pay subscribers" are smaller than before, since they now share the market. Multifirm rivalry would normally not be substainable if product-specific economies of scale for these products existed over the range of production of the other outputs.

34. Most cable franchises are, by their terms, not exclusive.

35. Once a more realistic variable post-entry strategic behavior is introduced, the sustainability of a single firm monopoly is subject to a variety of assumptions.

36. In 1977 the Chase Manhattan Bank analyzed the cost differences between telephone and cable transmission and concluded in an intraoffice memo: "Even with the higher installation cost which is due to them (Manhattan Cable) having to run cable into both sites and cable into the buildings, the cost saving over New York Telephone for the first year is $10,000 and $15,000 every year after. There are several other advantages in using Manhattan cable: 1) fast response to service calls, 2) use of modems with up-to-date technology, 3) very low cost for installation for any additional circuits required at these sites since buildings will be cabled" (Kalba 1977).

37. For example, a study commissioned by the National Cable Television Association found that an above average proportion of customers of both subscription (i.e., pay) television (STV) and of cable television remain with the previous system after the introduction of a new one (Pottle and Bortz 1982).

4

The Broadcasters: The Future Role of Local Stations and the Three Networks

MICHAEL O. WIRTH and
HARRY BLOCH

CONTENTS

  I. Introduction
 II. The Models
     A. The Competitive Model
     B. The Oligopoly Model
III. Regression Results
 IV. The Impact of Cable on Television Broadcast Revenues
  V. Implications
 VI. Conclusions

I. INTRODUCTION

Various observers have predicted a dark future for the commercial television networks and over-the-air commercial television broadcasters as a result of the increased competition from new forms of video program delivery. Most of the prophecies of doom stem from declines in network prime-time audience shares (table 4.1) and in local-station audience shares among cable subscribers (table 4.2), and from expected increases in video market competition from new video delivery technologies.

A number of past empirical studies (Fisher, McGowan, and Evans 1980: Park 1971: Schink and Thanawala 1978: and Webster 1983) have clearly established that cable television has a significant negative impact on the audience levels achieved by over-the-air commercial television stations. There is little disagreement concerning cable's impact on

Table 4.1. Television Network Prime-Time Share Decline in Cable and Pay Cable Homes 1979–1982

Year	Three-Network Share		
	Noncable Homes	*Basic Cable Homes*	*Pay Cable Homes*
1979–80	87.0%	80.5%	64.5%
1980–81	86.0	78.8	63.3
1981–82	84.5	75.3	59.3

SOURCE: The information contained in this table is from A. C. Nielsen Co., National Television Index, *Cable TV A Status Report,* various issues, as found in Bortz, Pottle, and Wycke (1983).

the information and entertainment side of local television stations and the television networks. The impact is negative and significant, and it appears to be increasing in magnitude over time (see tables 4.1 and 4.2). As new forms of video delivery technology become available to expand the number of channels from which consumers can choose, a similar negative impact on broadcast audiences can be expected.

The impact of competition from cable and other new technologies on television station and television network audiences, however, does not necessarily mean that any stations or networks will be driven out of business. In fact, increased competition on the information/entertainment side of the video marketplace may not even cause a decrease in their profitability, because cable and other forms of pay-television delivery do not provide meaningful competition for television broadcasters on the *advertising* side of the video marketplace, at least at this time.

Table 4.2. Local Television Station, Sunday–Saturday, 7 A.M.–1 A.M. Share Decline in Cable Homes, 1979–1982

MARKETS	Local Station Average Share 1979–80		Local Station Average Share 1980–81		Local Station Average Share 1981–82	
	Noncable Homes	*Cable Homes*	*Noncable Homes*	*Cable Homes*	*Noncable Homes*	*Cable Homes*
Top 50	93.7%	80.6%	94.9%	77.0%	94.7%	73.8%
51–100	88.3	69.2	88.1	64.4	87.9	62.5
101 +	78.3	53.9	77.9	50.7	78.0	48.0

SOURCE: The information contained in this table was compiled from A. C. Nielsen Co. (1982a).

If broadcasters continue to possess significant market power in advertising, they may be able to increase the price per thousand or per rating point for which they sell their audience to advertisers, and maintain revenue levels in spite of significant audience decline. To the extent that broadcasters are viewed by advertisers as "must buys" for reaching a mass audience and to the extent that broadcasters continue to operate in oligopolistic advertising markets, their revenue levels can be expected to be relatively unaffected by cable and other new delivery technologies.

The primary focus of this study will be to determine whether broadcasters continue to operate in oligopolistic advertising markets in spite of the increased program competition they face from cable television. Our empirical focus is on local television markets owing to the availability of published data in this area. Although we are not able to test our hypotheses empirically with respect to the television networks, we can extend the results obtained from our analysis to the network television advertising market.[1]

II. THE MODELS

In this section we develop two alternative models of the value of commercial time. The first is based on the assumption that the price paid for commercial time is determined in a competitive market for exposures to viewers, with the value of a particular audience determined by the characteristics of that audience. The second model is an application of oligopoly pricing, with price determined by both the characteristics of the potential viewing audience and the intensity of competition in providing access to commercial broadcast time in the market.

A. The Competitive Model

The first type of model has been widely applied in estimation of the audience-revenue relationship for television stations. An example is the work of Fisher, McGowan, and Evans (1980). A general representation of the estimating equation is

$$(1) \quad R/H = b_0 + b_1(V/H) + \sum_{i=1}^{n} b_{i+1} X_i$$

where:

R = the revenue received from the sale of commercial time of a particular duration (e.g., one 30-second spot) or over a period of time (e.g., one year).
H = the number of households in a station's viewing area;
V = a measure of audience size for the station during the revenue period;
X_i = a vector of variables which affects the quality of the audience provided by the station (e.g., average household income);
b = estimated coefficients.

The coefficient for V/H in equation (1) provides an estimate of the price for a viewer exposure. A linear relation between R/H and V/H is used because the existence of perfect competition implies that the price charged for a viewer is independent of the number of viewers provided.[2] The elements of X_i which represent characteristics of the viewers provided by a particular station, are generally interpreted as hedonic price-function parameters which show the value of a particular audience characteristic to advertisers.

B. The Oligopoly Model

Our alternative model of the value of commercial time is derived from the theory of oligopoly pricing. Following Stigler (1964), we treat the likelihood that a firm can successfully use secret price concessions to undercut its rivals as decreasing with increases in market concentration. The particular measure of concentration used by Stigler is the Herfindahl index, which is calculated as the sum of the squares of the market shares of all firms in the market. The reduced likelihood of success with secret price concessions leads to a higher expected average price level in the market. Thus, a positive relation is expected between the value of commercial time and the Herfindahl index for concentration of stations selling time in a market.[3] We use a log-linear function to apply the oligopoly pricing model to estimating the value of commercial time. Our estimating equations are of the general form.

$$(2) \ \log(R) = b_0 + b_1\log(H) + b_2\log(V/H) + b_3\log(HI)$$

$$+ \sum_{i=1}^{n} b_{i+3}\log(X_i)$$

where HI is the Herfindahl index of market concentration (and all other variables have been defined above). The oligopoly pricing model implies that the value of b_3 in equation (2) is positive.

The difference in the dependent variable between equations (1) and (2) reflects a difference in the conception of the product being purchased by advertisers. In the competitive model the product is viewer exposures, while in the oligopoly model the product is access to a particular viewing audience. This difference is subtle but critical. If the product is viewer exposures, it is reasonable to consider television stations in different local markets to be competing for the same advertising dollars. The number of sellers in the relevant market is large, and perfect competition is a reasonable expectation. However, if the product is access to a particular viewing audience, the number of sellers in the relevant market is limited to the small number of stations that can reach the particular audience. This implies that viewer exposures in distant markets are not good substitutes for exposures in a local market, and competition in the local market may be very imperfect, although competition from other media certainly limits a station market power. Still, even the viewer exposures within a particular television market are imperfect substitutes for each other because the audience delivered differs across stations and programs.

The conception of the product as access to a particular audience in equation (2) affects the specification of the independent variables as well as the dependent variable. We use the number of households in the viewing area, H, as the measure of the potential audience to which a station is selling access. The ratio of households viewing an individual station to total households in the viewing area, V/H, then measures the station's success in reaching the potential audience. The coefficients of both $\log(H)$ and $\log(V/H)$ are expected to be positive, as both a larger potential audience and greater success in reaching that audience are valuable to advertisers.[4] The log-linear form of equation (2) means that the coefficients of the independent variables provide estimates of the elasticity of the price of commercial time with respect to each independent variable.

The concept of the product being access to a particular audience also affects the measurement of the Herfindahl index. The market shares provided by rating services are shares of the total viewing audience. Those households which are viewing noncommercial local stations, cable programming, or non-local-market stations are not reachable through advertising on local-market stations. Consequently, the relevant market share for measuring concentration in the local market is the share of viewers watching local commercial stations. The measure of the Herfindahl index used in our regressions is the sum of the squared market shares for local commercial stations where the shares are re-calculated as shares of those viewers watching only local commercial stations.

Regression equations of form (1) are not directly comparable to those of type (2). Theil (1971:544) points out that the residual variance crite-rion cannot be used to choose between alternative specifications of a relationship when the left-hand variable is not the same in each specifi-cation. We can, however, test the estimated coefficients of regressions of type (2) for consistency with either the competitive pricing model or the oligopoly pricing model.

In the competitive pricing model market concentration as measured by the Herfindahl index does not affect the price paid for commercial time, because competition from other media or markets is sufficient to keep price to the competitive level with or without concentration. This implies a value of zero for b_3 in equation (2), rather than the greater-than-zero value implied by the oligopoly pricing model. If it is possible to reject the hypothesis that b_3 is equal to zero while, at the same time, it is not possible to reject the hypothesis that b_3 is greater than zero, we have clear empirical support for the oligopoly pricing model over the competitive model. If we can reject the hypothesis that b_3 is greater than zero but not the hypothesis that b_3 equals zero, we have empirical support for preferring the competitive pricing model over the oligopoly model.

A further test for discriminating between the competitive and oligopoly pricing models involves the estimated value for b_2 in regres-sions of type (2). In the competitive pricing model, the product sold by a station is viewer exposures. An increase in the number of viewer exposures results in a proportional increase in the value of commercial time because the price received for the product is independent of the quantity supplied by a competitive seller. This implies a value of 1.0 for b_2 in equation (2), rather than merely the greater-than-zero value im-plied by the oligopoly pricing model. If we can reject either the hypoth-esis that b_2 is equal to 1.0 or the hypothesis that b_2 is greater than zero, while not rejecting the other hypothesis, we again have a clear indica-tion of consistency with one pricing model but not with the other. The only limitation to such a test is that it is clearly biased in favor of the oligopoly pricing model because any estimated value of b_2 that is consistent with the hypothesis that b_2 equals 1.0 is necessarily consistent with the hypothesis that b_2 is greater than zero.

III. REGRESSION RESULTS

The results from the application of regression equations of types (1) and (2) with data for a sample of 105 television stations are given in tables 4.4 and 4.5. The variable definitions and data sources are given in table 4.3. The sample of stations used in the regressions includes all CBS affiliated stations for which spot prices were available from *SRDS: Spot Television Rates and Data*, thereby limiting the range of factors affecting the value of commercial time on the stations.[5] We focus on the relationship between the highest rate charged by each station for a 30-second spot and the audience attracted by "MASH", the highest-rated half-hour program for the average CBS affiliate in November 1982.

The regression results in table 4.4 have low explanatory power and reliability as indicated by the low values of the corrected R^2's and t-ratios. This contrasts sharply with the results of prior studies employing the competitive model, such as those of the FCC (1980h) and Fisher, McGowan and Evans (1980). We attribute our lower explanatory power and reliability to the different nature of the regression samples. We have purposely limited the variation in network affiliation and programming, which accounts for much of the explanatory power in the prior studies. Thus, it is inappropriate to conclude that the competitive model should be rejected solely on the basis of the results in table 4.4.

Our test for choosing between the competitive and oligopoly models is based instead on the results provided in table 4.5. The coefficients of $\log(HI)$, the Herfindahl index, are all positive and significantly greater than zero at the 1 percent level, using a one-tailed t-test. A significantly positive impact on price is expected in the oligopoly pricing model, but not in the competitive model. Furthermore, the estimated coefficients of $\log(V/H)$, the ratio of viewers to households for the designated market area (DMA), are positive but significantly less than 1.0 at the 1 percent level, using a one-tailed t-test.[6] In the competitive model, increases in viewers supplied to advertisers are expected to lead to proportional increases in the value of commercial time. In contrast, the oligopoly pricing model implies only that the coefficient of V/H is greater than

Table 4.3. Variable Definitions and Data Sources

Variable	Definition	Data Source
R	List price of a 30-second spot for "M*A*S*H," or for highest-price non-special-event prime-time spot if "M*A*S*H" price was not directly available.	Standard Rate and Data Service: Spot TV Rates and Data (March 1983) (Hereinafter SRDS)
H	Number of households in the designated market area (DMA) (in thousands)	A. C. Nielsen Co. (1982a)
V	Average quarter-hour audience for "M*A*S*H" (in thousands)	A. C. Nielsen (1982a)
HI	Calculated as sum of squared market shares for all local commercial broadcast stations in the designated market area (denominator of share is total average daily viewers (7 A.M.–1 A.M., Sunday–Saturday) of local commercial stations as a group and numerator is the average daily viewers for each station). The share thus calculated differs from that provided directly in Nielsen, which includes in the denominator viewers of noncommercial local stations, stations from other designated market areas, and cable programming.	A. C. Nielsen (1982a)
SALES	Average total retail sales per DMA household (in hundreds)	SRDS
VHR	A dummy variable = 1 if station is a VHF station (= 0 otherwise)	SRDS
M	Average quarter-hour metro-area household audience for "M*A*S*H" (in thousands)	Nielsen
CAB	Households in DMA subscribing to cable services (in thousands)	Pay TV Census (December 31, 1983)
PAY	Number of subscribers to a pay programming service in the DMA (in thousands)	Pay TV Census

Table 4.4. Regression Results for Competitive Model (R/H Dependent Variable)

Constant	V/H	*Estimated Coefficients* SALES	VHF	M/H	$\bar{R}^2$
1.354	5.962*	.060			.019
	(1.84)[a]	(.73)			
1.374	3.939	.045	.712		.031
	(1.13)	(.55)	(1.48)		
1.623	1.430	.019	.693	4.325	.030
	(.33)	(.22)	(1.44)	(.97)	

[a]Figures in parentheses are t-ratios.
*Coefficient is statistically significant at 10 percent level using a two-tailed t-test.

zero. Thus we find empirical support for the oligopoly pricing model but none for the competitive pricing model.[7]

IV. THE IMPACT OF CABLE TELEVISION ON BROADCAST REVENUES

The traditional approach to estimating the impact of cable television on the revenues of commercial broadcast stations involves two steps. First, the impact of a station's audience on its revenues is estimated using equations of type (1). Second, the impact of cable on the size and characteristics of the audience obtained by commercial stations is estimated using regressions with audience site or characteristics as the dependent variable. A study which nicely illustrates the two-step approach is that of Liebowitz (1982).

Our regression results suggest a critical flaw in this traditional approach. The audience-revenue relationship in equations of type (1) is based on an explicit or implicit assumption that viewer exposures are sold in a perfectly competitive market. Our results are inconsistent with the existence of a perfectly competitive market, and instead support the interpretation that commercial broadcast time is sold in oligopolistic markets.

In our oligopolistic pricing model, competition affects a station's revenues through two variables, the station's audience share, V/H, and the level of concentration in the market for selling viewer exposures to advertisers as measured by the Herfindahl index, HI. Since most cable systems do not currently provide significant competition for sales to

Table 4.5. Regression Results for Oligopoly Model [Log(R) Dependent Variable]

Constant	log(H)	log(V/H)	Estimated Coefficients log(HI)	log(SALES)	VHF	log(M/V)	R̄²
1.889	1.028* (13.52)[a]	.238 (1.55)	.647* (3.41)				.720
1.094	1.054* (13.18)	.229 (1.49)	.700* (3.56)	.281 (1.03)			.720
1.022	1.039* (12.96)	.113 (.65)	.673* (3.42)	.222 (.81)	.167 (1.40)		.723
1.364	1.041* (13.00)	.137 (.79)	.677* (3.45)	.123 (.43)	.167 (1.40)	.165 (1.19)	.724

[a]Figures in parentheses are t-ratios.

*Indicates coefficient is statistically significant at 1 percent level using a two-tailed t-test.

advertisers, their competition extends only to the first variable, audience share. Treating the competition associated with cable offerings of distant signals and pay programming as equivalent to the competition from rival local broadcasters is therefore inappropriate. Yet, this is exactly the treatment used in the traditional approach.

The impact of both cable and other competition on broadcast revenues in the traditional approach is equal in percentage terms to their impact on the broadcast audience. In contrast, the coefficients of log (V/H) in table 4.5 provide estimates of between 0.11 percent and 0.24 percent for the effect on revenues of a 1.0 percent change in audience. Thus, we estimate that the impact of cable on broadcast revenues is only one-ninth to one-fourth as large as that assumed in the traditional approach.

Liebowitz (1982) argues that cable does not reduce the advertising revenues of commercial broadcast stations, even though he uses the two-step approach for estimating cable's impact. He finds that while cable reduces the audience of broadcast stations, it also improves the characteristics of the audience provided. He estimates the net effect on advertising revenues as approximately zero.

Our rejection of the competitive assumption implicit in the two-step approach leads us to question the validity of Liebowitz's result. Nonetheless, the argument that cable has a revenue-increasing impact on the characteristics of the audience offered by broadcast stations is plausible. This would imply that even our low estimates of the impact of cable on broadcast revenues obtained from the regressions in table 4.5 are biased upward because we do not take account of the possible impact of cable on the characteristics of the remaining broadcast audience.

We therefore allow for a possible influence of cable on audience characteristics by adding cable-penetration variables to the oligopoly pricing model regressions in table 4.5. The cable penetration variables measure the ratio of pay programming subscribers to households in the DMA, CAB/H, and the ratio of pay programming subscribers to households in the DMA, PAY/H. The results of these regressions are given in table 4.6. None of the estimated coefficients of the cable penetration variables is significantly different from zero at the 10 percent level using a two-tailed t-test.[8] Thus, we find no support for the hypothesis that cable penetration affects broadcast station revenue through audience characteristics.

Table 4.6. Regression Results for Oligopoly Model with Cable-Penetration Variable [log(R) Dependent Variable]

Constant				Estimated Coefficients					$\bar{R}^2$
	log(H)	log(V/H)	log(HI)	log(SALES)	VHF	log(M/V)	log(CAB/H)	log(PAY/H)	
1.956	1.028*	.237	.666*				−.011	.046	.715
	(12.94)a	(1.50)	(3.32)				(.09)	(.41)	
1.115	1.052*	.226	.705*	.278			−.011	.007	.714
	(12.63)	(1.42)	(3.44)	(.84)			(.09)	(.06)	
1.023	1.038*	.111	.676*	.223	.167		−.007	.001	.717
	(12.45)	(.62)	(3.29)	(.75)	(1.38)		(.06)	(.01)	
1.349	1.041*	.137	.676*	.126	.167	.165	.001	−.004	.718
	(12.50)	(.76)	(3.30)	(.41)	(1.38)	(1.18)	(.01)	(.03)	

aFigures in parentheses are t-ratios.
*Coefficient is significant at 1 percent using a two-tailed t-test.

Table 4.7. Further Regression Results for Oligopoly Model with Cable-Penetration Variables [log(R) Dependent Variable]

Constant			Estimated Coefficients					$\bar{R}^2$
	log(H)	log(HI)	log(SALES)	VHF	log(M/V)	log(CAB/H)	log(PAY/H)	
1.761	1.021*	.722*				−.047	.049	.711
	(12.80)a	(3.64)				(.41)	(.43)	
.835	1.047*	.763*	.309			−.045	.006	.711
	(12.53)	(3.77)	(1.04)			(.39)	(.05)	
.896	1.034*	.692*	.224	.202**		−.020	−.000	.719
	(12.48)	(3.41)	(.76)	(1.90)		(.17)	(.00)	
1.168	1.035*	.695*	.135	.209**	.152	−.015	−.006	.719
	(12.51)	(3.43)	(.44)	(1.96)	(1.09)	(.13)	(.05)	

aFigures in parentheses are t-ratios.
*Coefficient is significant at 1 percent level using a two-tailed t-test.
**Coefficient is significant at 5 percent level using a two-tailed t-test.

Our final test for an effect of cable on broadcast revenues involves removing the audience variable, V/H, from the regressions in table 4.6. By omitting the audience variable, we are allowing the cable-penetration variables to pick up the effect of cable on revenues that occurs either through a change in audience characteristics or through a change in audience size. The results for these regressions are given in table 4.7. None of the estimated coefficients of the cable-penetration variables in table 4.7 is significantly different from zero at the 10 percent level using a two-tailed t-test. Thus, when we measure the impact of cable and pay penetration on broadcast revenues directly, we find no evidence of a significant negative impact.[9]

V. IMPLICATIONS

The empirical results presented in the preceding section suggest that the increased competition television broadcasters are facing from new delivery technologies such as cable and pay television on the program side of the video marketplace has had little impact on the market power possessed by television broadcasters on the advertiser side. This suggests that television station (and by extension television network) revenues have not been negatively affected by cable and various forms of pay program delivery. It is our belief that local television stations and the television networks will be able to maintain their revenues (in real dollar terms) even as their audience declines, as long as new forms of video program delivery do not provide meaningful competition for television broadcasters on the advertising side of the video market. Various pieces of descriptive information gleaned from the trade press and from research reports provide support for this notion. Data provided in Bortz, Pottle, and Wyche (1983) and in "Broadcasters Show Profit Margin Drop" (1984), for instance, indicate that television network and television station revenues have continued to increase even in the face of declines in audience shares.

Our results suggest that increased competition from new forms of video delivery technology is not affecting broadcast advertising revenues. However, this does not necessarily mean that cable and various forms of pay program delivery have not had an impact on broadcast-television profits. To the extent that the increased competition for the television audience from various new video delivery technologies has caused the television networks and local television stations to spend an increasingly large percentage of each dollar of revenue on programming or promotion, television broadcast profit margins may well decline as a result of this increased competition.

Veronis, Shuler, and Associates (VS&A) ("Broadcasters Show Profit Margin Drop," 1984) provide descriptive data supportive of this hypothesis. Specifically, VS&A found that "pre-tax operating profit margins among 'typical' publicly traded broadcasting companies shrunk nearly 20% between 1978 and 1981" in spite of the fact that revenue growth averaged 13% during this same period. VS&A suggest that increasing costs, especially those in the programming area, were responsible for at least part of the decline in profit margins. Information provided in Bortz, Pottle, and Wyche (1983) provides support for the theory that increased competition from new technologies and/or independent television stations on the information/ entertainment side of the video market is largely responsible for the decline in network profit margins discovered by the VS&A report. FCC data contained in Bortz, Pottle, and Wyche (1983) indicate that the television networks experienced an average annual compound increase in advertising revenues of 13.7 percent from 1978 to 1980, while program expenses increased at an average annual compound rate of 17 percent over this same period. This finding is in sharp contrast to the "pre-audience decline" in the average annual compound growth rates of revenue and program costs experienced by the television networks from 1973 to 1977 (15.1 percent and 15.0 percent, respectively). Additional information provided by Bortz, Pottle, and Wyche (1983) for ABC-TV prime-time gross revenues and prime-time program costs from 1973 to 1981 is even more supportive of the theory that increased competition from cable or independent television stations has caused the television networks to increase their program expenditures, thus lowering profit margins. From 1978 to 1981, ABC increased its prime-time gross advertising revenues at an average compound rate of 7.9 percent. Over this same period, prime-time program expenditures increased at an average compound rate of 16.6 percent. Comparable figures for average annual compound growth in revenue and program expense from 1973 to 1977 are 18.2 percent and 15.5 percent, respectively.

VI. CONCLUSIONS

Local television stations and the television networks face increasingly complex competition for audience attention. As a result, television broadcasters have increased their program expenditures by a disproportionate amount in an attempt to reduce loss of audience share. Such an expenditure strategy is less risky than it might otherwise be since television broadcasters and the networks are not facing any significant increase in competition for advertiser revenues. The short-run result of the "program expenditure" strategy being employed by television broadcasters has been to reduce broadcaster profit margins. However, television broadcasters continue to earn above-normal returns on average (see "Broadcasters Show Profit Margin Drop" 1984). Future declines in broadcast profit margins are bounded by what entrepreneurs consider to be a normal economic return for television broadcasting.

The information in this article leads us to the conclusion that the television networks and local advertiser-supported television stations are far from moribund. As long as advertisers view television broadcast audiences as "must buys" for reaching a mass television audience, the broadcast television business continues to be a viable one. However, broadcast profit margins can be expected to continue their decline as television broadcasters spend an increasingly large amount of each dollar they take in attempting to maintain their audience share.[10]

Notes

1. Helpful suggestions on earlier versions of this paper were received from Pam Weidler, Mark Nadel, and Doug Webbink. Nancy Kuehl provided invaluable research assistance.

2. Some past studies employ the square of (V/H) as an explanatory variable. However, this term is not interpreted as implying a lack of competition in the sense that stations face downward-sloping demand curves for viewer exposures. In the Fisher, McGowan, and Evans (1980) study, the estimated coefficient of the

squared (*V/H*) term is uniformly positive, suggesting the implausible, i.e., that the stations face upward-sloping demand curves.

3. Stigler cites evidence closely related to our hypothesis in support of his theory. He cites a negative estimated relationship between the number of newspapers or radio stations in a market and the list price for advertising space or commercial broadcast time, respectively.

4. If the coefficient of log(*H*) exceeds the coefficient of log(*V/H*), the cost-per-thousand of reaching viewers in larger markets exceeds that in smaller markets. The competitive model does not allow for the possibility that the cost per thousand viewers depends on market size. This can lead to bias in the estimated coefficient of log (*HI*) because market size and market concentration are highly correlated.

5. The reader is referred to earlier studies of the audience-revenue relationship for commercial television stations for results on the influence on the value of commercial time of factors such as network affiliation and time of day. See, for example, FCC (1980h); Fisher, McGowan, and Evans (1980), and Park (1979). Limiting our sample to CBS affiliates and to one of the highest-rated programs on these affiliates reduces the number of variables that enter the statistical analysis while still providing a sample large enough to limit the influence of sampling error.

While our conclusions are specific to a particular network and program, this is an advantage rather than a limitation. Studies that include a wider sample are subject to bias if the influence of competition varies across categories of affiliation and programming. In contrast, our approach can be used on alternative samples to test for constancy in the estimated coefficients without introducing the possibility of bias.

6. The t-ratios for the difference between 1.0 and the estimated coefficients of *V/H* in table 4.5 range from 4.94 to 5.11.

7. These findings contrast sharply with those of Fournier and Martin (1983). Fournier and Martin estimate an OLS regression similar to our regressions of form (2) and find a coefficient for the Herfindahl index which is negative and not statistically significant. The Herfindahl index in the regression is apparently calculated from market shares which have not been adjusted to eliminate the viewers of noncommercial local stations, cable programming, and non-local-market stations. We reestimated the regressions in table 4.5 substituting a Herfindahl index based on unadjusted market shares, and found that the coefficient of the Herfindahl index was consistently negative and generally statistically significant at the 1% level using a two-tailed t-test. Thus, we suspect that the failure to find a positive and significant coefficient of the Herfindahl index in the Fournier and Martin study results from inappropriate measurement of the Herfindahl index.

8. An attempt was also made to explicitly include the impact of subscription television (STV) and of multipoint distribution service (MDS) competition on local station revenues by including the number of STV and the number of MDS

subscribers in our pay-penetration variable. The results obtained were virtually identical to those contained herein.

9. This result is in contrast to Wirth and Wollert (1984) who find cable penetration had a significant negative impact on local television news prices in 1978. These different results are from regressions focused on local-news advertising rates rather than prime-time entertainment advertising rates.

10. Note that this conclusion is not directly related to the circumstances of marginal broadcasters (small market, independent UHF, LPTV) because average returns are dominated by large-market network-affiliated VHF stations. The fact that cable's impact on audience improves the relative position of UHF stations (Park 1979) suggests that this group of marginal stations may not be as adversely impacted by competition.

5

The Impact of Competing Technologies on Cable Television

KENNETH THORPE

CONTENTS

I. Introduction
II. Growth in Alternate Video Distribution Sources
III. Detecting the Impact of Competition on Cable Operators
    A. Multiproduct Learner Index
    B. Determinants of Price-Cost Margins
IV. Nonprice Competition
V. Explaining Variations in Price-Cost Margins
    A. Characteristics of the Basic and Expanded Basic Service Package
    B. Signal Quality
    C. Income
    D. Rate Regulation
    E. Number of Pay Services Offered by the Cable System
    F. Ownership Characteristics
    G. Age of the System
VI. Data
    A. The Sample
    B. Empirical Results
    C. Supply-Side Results
    D. Impact of Competition on Program Selection
VII. Conclusions and Policy Implications

I. INTRODUCTION

Cable television systems distribute both video and nonvideo services to local subscribers through coaxial cables.[1] Like other physical distribution services, cable television is characterized by relatively high fixed capital costs and low marginal operating costs. Indeed, it is the high fixed cost of providing cable service that has led a number of observers to believe that it displays elements of a natural monopoly.[2] Empirical studies of these cost conditions tend to give some support to this belief (Owen and Greenhalgh 1982; Noam 1982a). Because of common perception that cable television is a natural monopoly, franchises are usually awarded on an exclusive basis.

Much of the recent policy debate over future regulation in the cable television industry has focused on the connection between cable's natural monopoly and market power (U.S. Congress 1983e,f). Those favoring the maintenance of a regulatory presence note that market power— generated from cable's natural monopoly—may adversely affect stated governmental goals in the communications industry (National League of Cities 1981). Others disagree with this assessment, noting the recent explosion in new video competitors to cable. They favor a more relaxed regulatory atmosphere. Although cable may be a natural monopoly for distributing video over cable, it still must compete with a number of noncable sources of video programming. Competition from noncable programming sources, it is argued, is an effective check on any market power cable operators might attempt to exert (Gordon, et al. 1981).

One of the more notable aspects of the recent debate over the regulation of cable television is the lack of empirical data. Although the recent "explosion" of new video technologies has been widely heralded and discussed (Stern, et al. 1983), little is currently known about their competitive impact on the cable television industry. Indeed, to date there have been no empirical studies documenting this impact.[3] My goal here, therefore, is to provide empirical information regarding the impact of noncable distribution sources on the market power of cable operators. I shall discuss this impact in two ways: first I shall examine how competition affects the ability of cable operators to raise prices significantly without losing a significant number of their customers; second, I shall examine how competition affects the programs cable firms decide to select.

My discussion of the impact of competition on cable television firms will be broken into six sections. Section I will document the growth in the technologies competing with cable television. Section II will discuss the methodology employed to detect market power in the cable television industry. Section III will discuss competitive responses by cable firms in their selection of programming (i.e., nonprice competition). Section IV will provide a description of variables affecting the market power of cable operators, including penetration by STV.[4] Section V will outline the empirical results of the study, while section VI will draw policy implications from the analysis.

II. GROWTH IN ALTERNATIVE VIDEO DISTRIBUTION SOURCES

Cable television is only one of a number of methods for distributing video sources which have recently become available. Indeed, an alphabet soup of new competition has recently evolved, including, for example, subscription television (STV), multipoint distribution service (MDS), direct broadcast satellites (DBS), subscription master antenna TV (SMATV), videocassette recorders (VCR) and low-power television (LPTV). Table 5.1 documents the recent growth in popularity of these different video programmers.

Although cable television remains the largest provider of pay television, other technologies continue to grow in importance. In 1977, cable television accounted for over 98 percent of all pay television subscribers, but by 1983 cable's share fell to under 90 percent. (Of course, the aggregate total increased dramatically during that period.)

Although interesting, national comparisons may be misleading. Such comparisons, for example, are too aggregated for us to infer much about the performance of video technologies in individual markets. Indeed, the interesting factor to examine is the performance of competing video technologies in the same video market. Consider penetration data in table 5.2.

When examining some of the media markets where cable and noncable firms are rivals, these markets appear to be rather competitive. Indeed, as of 1983, over 25 percent of all video subscribers purchased noncable sources of video programming in Los Angeles, Detroit, Washington–Baltimore, and Phoenix. However, the market shares presented

Table 5.1. Video Subscribers by Source[a] (in millions)

End of Year	Transmission Source			
	Cable	STV	MDS	VCR
1975	1.98	0.0	0.0	n.a.
1976	4.37	0.0	0.04	n.a.
1977	6.48	0.02	0.07	n.a.
1978	9.40	0.14	0.15	n.a.
1979	13.87	0.40	0.28	0.50
1980	18.07	0.79	0.45	0.80
1981	22.53	1.54	0.53	1.40
1982	27.20	1.82	0.57	2.00
1983	31.40	1.20	0.49	4.10

SOURCES: Paul Kagan Associates (1983c); Waterman (1984).
[a]DBS was not available until 1983, historical data on SMATV were also not available.

in table 5.2 overstate the importance of the competitors to cable. Much of the problem results from the lack of data documenting the performance of competing video technologies in individual submarkets where cable television is also available. For example, table 5.2 reveals that competitive video technologies account for over 35 percent of total subscribers in the Washington–Baltimore area. The Washington–Baltimore metropolitan area, however, like other large media markets, is composed of dozens of smaller, autonomous jurisdictions. Local and county governments within the larger metropolitan area determine both

Table 5.2. Video Subscribers by Market and Type, 1983 (in thousands)

Market[a]	Cable	STV	MDS	SMATV	Total	% Cable
New York	1666	105	55	n.a.	1826	91
Los Angeles	864	458	4	n.a.	1326	65
Chicago	365	84	14	62	525	70
Miami	346	41	12	n.a.	399	87
Dallas	305	74	11	5	395	77
Detroit	240	63	26	n.a.	329	73
Washington-Baltimore	192	72	35	n.a.	299	64
Phoenix	145	32	24	n.a.	201	72

SOURCES: Paul Kagan Associates (1983c); Television Digest (1983).
[a]Area of Dominant Influence

the existence and characteristics of cable systems. Thus, it would be fallacious to assume that these figures accurately portray the penetration by competing technologies where cable television is also available. In this market, for example, STV has probably performed well in the District of Columbia, where cable television is not available. Further, until very recently, most of the cities of Los Angeles, Detroit, and Phoenix areas did not have cable television services available. Therefore, the actual competitive impact of competing technologies, based on information presented in table 5.2, may be illusory. At best, only general statements regarding competition in the industry should be made.

III. DETECTING THE IMPACT OF COMPETITION ON CABLE OPERATORS

A number of approaches have been used to measure market power, including firm profitability, structural measures (i.e., n firm concentration ratio), Tobin's Q, and price-cost margins (Scherer 1980), but as discussed below, the first three measures will not be used in this study.

The existence of positive economic profits is not by itself a measure of market power. Positive profits may reflect a number of conditions, including scarcity rents created by government franchise agreements, a risky venture, or simply that a company is a "superior" firm (Lintner 1965; Demsetz 1969, 1973). Indeed, even competitive firms may earn economic rents simply because they are superior enterprises. Further, one would have to rely on accounting rates of return as a proxy for the variable of interest, the economic rate of return. The use of accounting data, however, to infer market power may be quite inaccurate (Fisher 1979; Fisher and McGowen 1983).

Use of structural measures, like concentration ratios or the Herfindahl index, are also problematic. These measures ignore possible entry and exit barriers and are complicated by problems involved in defining the relevant product market (Fisher 1979). Finally, highly concentrated industries characterized by significant barriers to entry still may not display elements of monopoly welfare losses. Indeed, even with a small number of firms, monopolistic outcomes could be precluded depending on the degree and type of pricing interdependence in the industry.[5]

Tobin's Q, which is the ratio of the market value of a firm to the replacement value of its physical assets, is a useful measure of long-run market power (Salinger 1984). Its use stems from the fact that a firm's market value reflects the present value of all expected profits. On the other hand, Tobin's Q ignores the important role existing tax laws have on the market value of a firm. Indeed, high market selling prices may reflect high expected future profits as well as tax benefits resulting from the sale. The importance of tax laws in bidding up selling prices in media industries appears substantial (Dertouzos and Thorpe 1982). Hence, what may appear to be long-term market power by the Q measure may, in part, reflect high market prices caused by current federal tax laws. Since in practice it may be very difficult to separate these two determinants of market value, this approach will not be employed.

A. Multiproduct Lerner Index

One indicator of market power is the ability to raise prices significantly above costs without total loss of customers. This indicator of market power is useful for two reasons. First, higher cable prices reduce the number of cable subscribers served and increase the welfare losses in the industry.[6] Second, the ability to set high subscriber prices implies an increased ability to set high access fees to potential programmers.[7] Hence, market power by this definition adversely affects two stated federal policy goals in the communications industry.

The most elementary measure employing this definition of market power is the Lerner Index.[8] According to this index, the ability of any firm to increase prices above marginal costs is constrained by the elasticity of demand for the product. That is, a monopolist with entry into the industry blocked, through some combination of entry or exit barriers, maximizes profits in the following manner.

$$\frac{P - MC}{P} = \frac{1}{\eta}$$

Where P represents the product price,
MC is the firm's marginal cost and
η is the own-price elasticity of demand facing the firm.

The greater the elasticity of demand (i.e., more elastic) for cable services, the lower the price-cost margin. Here, the monopolist cannot increase price as much above marginal cost as another firm facing a more inelastic demand for cable service. Hence, the firm facing the more elastic demand would, ceteris paribus, be constrained in its ability to set higher prices for cable services or higher access fees to potential programmers.

Given appropriate knowledge of prices and the own-price elasticity of demand, one could—through inferring marginal costs—indirectly calculate price-cost margins. This approach is often useful, especially in industries where marginal cost data are very difficult to identify (Rosse 1970; Dertouzos and Thorpe 1982). The actual calculation of price-cost margins in the cable industry, however, is somewhat more difficult, because cable operators are multiproduct firms. Therefore, the price-cost margin that the profit-maximizing cable operator would set for any product depends on a series of complex relationships between the relevant own- and cross-price elasticities of the products produced.[9]

Entry conditions in the industry will also affect the price-cost margins of cable operators. If, for example, there exists a competitive fringe of firms supplying similar video programming, pricing decisions by the cable operator would be constrained by the residual demand curve rather than the market demand curve.[10] Further, pricing behavior of the cable operator will also be a function of how the operator expects its competitors to compete along both price and product selection dimensions.[11]

To assess the impact of competition on price-cost margins, a single, summary price-cost margin for each cable operator will be constructed. This indexing approach will be used for a number of reasons. It is especially significant that cable operators have a great deal of freedom in choosing pricing strategies in response to competition. Indeed, these pricing responses for individual services (e.g., basic, expanded basic, and pay packages) will vary according to a number of factors that we may or may not be able to measure. As the first-order conditions for profit maximization for a multiproduct firm indicate, price-cost margins for any particular product depends crucially on the cross-price elasticities between the goods sold.[12] In the cable industry, for example, one would expect to see different price-cost margins, ceteris paribus, for cable operators offering HBO and the Disney Channel compared with one offering Showtime and the Movie Channel. This difference in price-cost margin for each of these services—under the ceteris paribus assumptions—occurs since the cross-price elasticity of HBO with respect to the Disney Channel is probably lower than the cross-price elasticity of Showtime with respect to the Movie Channel. Hence, low or high price-cost margins for individual program services may reflect a number of factors, including the own- and all relevant cross-price elasticities as well as the programs contribution to total system revenues. Therefore, the examination of a single price-cost margin may be misleading unless special care is taken to control the composition of pay program packages. To facilitate comparison across cable firms, I will create a single price-cost margin. The price-cost margin will represent a weighted average (weighted by its share of total revenue) of each of the program specific price-cost margins. The dependent variable I will use appears below.[13]

$$PCM = ln\left[\sum_{i=1}^{J} \left(\frac{Pi - MCi}{Pi} \right) \cdot \left(\frac{Pi \cdot Qi}{Pz \; Qz} \right) \right].$$

Where $P_z Q_z$ is total revenue, Pi is the price of the particular service offered by the cable operator, MCi is the marginal programming cost for the ith service, summed over all j services.

B. Determinants of Price-Cost Margins

Demand and cost conditions in the cable industry will affect the relative magnitude of their price-cost margins. Relevant demand-side factors are those affecting the own-price elasticity of demand for cable television, including the availability of substitute products such as STV and good television reception. In addition, regulatory interventions, especially rate regulation, could affect the price-cost divergence.

Cost conditions in the industry also affect the relative size of price-cost margins. The most important marginal cost incurred when a new subscriber initially purchases cable, or simply purchases more cable services, is the marginal license fee paid to programmers.[14] That is, most major programmers offering either advertiser supported or pay programming charge cable operators a certain monthly license fee per subscriber per month. Some examples of these license fees appear below (see table 5.3).

Table 5.3. License Fees for Basic Television Services, 1983

Basic service	Fee (per subscriber per month)
Arts	Free
Christian Broadcast Network (CBN)	Free
Cable Health Network	Free
Cable News Network (CNN)	0.20, 0.15 if take WTBS
CNN Headline News	0.05, free if with CNN
C-Span	0.03
Daytime	Free
ESPN	0.10
Music Television (MTV)	Free
Nashville Network	Free
Nickelodeon	0.10–.15
Spanish Info. Network	
USA	0.07–.13[a]
WGN	0.10
WOR	0.0–.10
WTBS	0.10 for first 18,000 subscribers zero for additional
Pay TV service	
HBO	3.20–5.00[b]
Showtime	3.08–5.00[b]
The Movie Channel	3.75–4.60[c]
Prism	5.25–6.75[d]
Cinemax	2.66–4.25[b]

SOURCE: Paul Kagan (1983e), plus conversations with relevant basic pay cable program representatives.

[a] .07 if USA is on Basic Service, up to .13 if on Expanded Basic

[b] Price varies depending on the number of subscribers and the price charged to subscribers.

[c] Price varies depending on the number of subscribers.

[d] Price varies depending on the price charged to subscribers.

In general, license fees that cable operators remit to program packagers depends on the total number of subscribers served by the operator. If the cable firm is a member of a group (multiple system operator), the price would depend on the total number of subscribers purchasing program type x at the *group level*. Cable firms that are not members of groups may also receive volume discounts—based on the number of subscribers served in the franchise area—or they may receive performance discounts when available. Performance discounts depend, in general, on the total number of cable subscribers purchasing a particular program. As table 5.3 illustrates, the prices cable operators are charged by HBO, Showtime, Prism, and Cinemax depend on the prices the cable operator charges subscribers for access to the programming. For example, suppose a cable firm is owned by a group that has 100,000 HBO subscribers. Now assume that the cable operator—who currently charges subscribers $9.00 for HBO—decides to increase the price to $10.00. The price the cable operator pays HBO would increase from $3.76 to $3.84 per subscriber. Showtime has a similar pricing strategy. The Movie Channel, however, charges cable operators only according to the number of subscribers served.

Vertical integration of cable operators with program packagers will also affect the firms' price-cost margin. Vertically integrated firms, if they are profit maximizing, would internally transfer programming inputs at their true social opportunity costs. Due to the public good nature of programming, the marginal social costs are zero. Hence, the price-cost margins of vertically integrated cable firms *may* be larger than other cable systems.[15]

Given that both demand and cost conditions in the industry affect price-cost margins, it is important for purposes of this study to isolate empirically the demand-side effects.

IV. NONPRICE COMPETITION

The competitiveness of media markets will also affect the number and variety of programs a cable firm offers. However, we cannot make an unambiguous a priori prediction of which market structure will lead to a greater number of programs or more program diversity. Cable firms that do not currently face competition from pay programmers could offer either more or a similar amount of programming than cable firms that do face competition.

Cable television firms will add an additional program source if the marginal program revenues exceed the marginal programming costs. Marginal revenues can be received from three sources: new cable subscribers, existing cable subscribers who purchase more (or fewer cable services),[16] and new subscribers switching from STV—or other competing technologies—to cable television. Of course, cable firms not currently facing competition from any other sources of pay television would only view marginal revenues coming from the first two sources.

As a result of these differences in perceived marginal revenues across different markets, both the number and diversity of programming would be greater in the monopolistically competitive market than in the isolated monopoly market. Indeed, it is these differences in perceived marginal revenues that has led some observers to note that monopolistically competitive industries will offer more product variety than isolated monopolists (Spence 1976).

Cable firms that deter entry through program-selection decisions could offer more programming than other cable firms. Under these assumptions, cable firms could proliferate programming in an attempt to preclude any advantages in product differentiation among potential competitors.[17] These entry-deterring strategies are given added credibility if the cable operator maintains excess channel capacity. Even if entry by a competitor were successful, the cable operator maintains post-entry flexibility to duplicate the program selection of competitors who generally have smaller channel capacities.

Finally, there are strong reasons to presume that the order of entry into a particular media market will also affect penetration. That is, cable penetration would be lower, ceteris paribus, when STV firms entered a media market before cable television. Lower penetration by cable firms in these situations could be due to product differentiation advantages of STV as the "pioneering" firm in a media market (Schmalensee 1982). This advantage of incumbent STV firms results from the relative uncertainty regarding the product (programming) quality of cable television firms.[18] Because of these asymmetries in product information, one would expect to see slower growth in cable penetration in areas where STV had originally entered.

V. EXPLAINING VARIATIONS IN PRICE-COST MARGINS

I shall use a number of variables to explain both the variation in price-cost margins and the program-selection decisions of cable television firms facing different competitive situations. These variables will measure factors affecting both demand and supply conditions in each cable market. The unit of observation will be the market area where cable television is available. As such, I have matched—as best as possible—penetration by competing technologies in each area where cable service is available.

The demand for cable television services results from a two-part process: the initial decision to purchase cable, followed by the decision about how many cable services to purchase. Factors affecting this decision process will include the following:

A. Characteristics of the Basic and Expanded Basic Service Package.

Cable operators offer a number of services on the so-called basic service package over and above what is available from over-the-air television. These networks—which are delivered either by satellite or microwave service—include those devoted primarily to sports (ESPN), children's programming (Nickelodeon), news (CNN), and a variety of other specialty programs (e.g., Weather Channel, Silent Network, Black Entertainment Network, and MTV). As one would expect, a number of past studies have revealed that the demand for basic cable service is very sensitive to the number and type of over-the-air broadcasts available on cable compared with those available over the air without cable. Indeed, the number of network, independent, and educational stations available on cable compared with that offered over the air has a strong impact on cable penetration (Park 1971; Noll et al. 1973; Charles River Associates 1978; Bloch and Wirth 1982).

B. Signal Quality

Historically, one of the more important reasons that viewers subscribed to cable television was to improve the visual quality of the television signals they received (Park 1971). Although the role of the cable operator has changed over time, the technical quality of the signals available over-the-air remains an important determinant of cable penetration.

C. Income

Past studies have revealed that cable television is a normal good. Hence, ceteris paribus, cable penetration appears to increase with income.

D. Rate Regulation

If rate regulation resulted in lower prices for basic cable service, one would expect to see lower basic price-cost margins. Overall, however, price-cost margins may not be reduced. Indeed, whether rate regulation of only the basic cable price lowers the firm's overall price-cost margin depends on how the cable operator—as a multiproduct firm—responds to the imposition of the regulatory constraint. Lower basic prices may, for example, simply result in higher pay cable prices, or the development of expanded basic service offerings which are not subject to rate regulation. Indeed, given the flexibility of cable firms to change prices for services that are not regulated, one would expect to see a reduced impact on the price-cost margins of cable operators. This study allows for such a test.

E. Number of Pay Services Offered by the Cable System

Clearly, an increase in the number of pay television services offered by the cable system will increase the total price-cost margin. Hence, one needs to control for this. Unfortunately, as the previous discussion illustrates, the service offerings by cable operators are clearly not exogenous in this model. To correct for this, two-stage least squares regressions will be run to determine the impact of endogeneity on this variable as well as other variables of interest.

F. Ownership Characteristics

There are strong incentives for vertical integration in the cable television industry.[19] Vertically integrated firms may increase profits if they internally transfer inputs (i.e., programming) at the competitive marginal cost (Vernon and Graham 1971). Given the public-good element of such programming, the social marginal cost is zero. Hence, the price-cost margins of vertically integrated firms are likely to exceed those of other firms. In addition, the marginal programming costs paid by cable firms depend crucially on total number of subscribers served. In general, group-owned cable systems serve more subscribers than independently owned systems. Hence, the marginal programming costs for all cable firms within a group are lower, ceteris paribus, than they would be if independently owned. On the other hand, if marginal costs decrease one would expect that the product price would also decrease. Hence, the net effect on the price-cost margin depends on the relative magnitude of these two effects.

G. Age of the Cable System

Observed price-cost margins will also depend on the age of the cable system. The inclusion of an age variable recognizes that both penetration and prices depend on the rate that cable systems mature. Linear splines will be employed to allow for flexibility in the functional form.

VI. DATA

Any serious study attempting to document the competitive impact of the new video technologies on cable television needs very refined data. In particular, one would need to know the performance of these technologies in areas that currently have cable television available. As part of this study, I have compiled a unique data set. A number of STV operators throughout the country agreed to provide—on a confidential basis—the location of their subscribers by zip code. This information is unique in two respects. First, it will allow a direct comparison of the penetration of a major competitor to cable—STV—in cabled areas. Second, it provides an opportunity to detect empirically the economic impact of this competition on the cable industry.

In addition to the unique information regarding the location of STV subscribers, a telephone survey of nearly 175 cable firms was used to gather more detailed information on actual pricing patterns in the cable industry.[20] The survey was undertaken because there was no systematic published information available documenting either the actual pricing patterns of cable firms (e.g., bundling practices) or how programming has been packaged. Both pieces of information are crucial in determining the competitive impact of new technologies on the cable industry.[21]

A. The Sample

On average, the sample used for the study represented slightly larger cable systems than the national average (see table 5.4). The difference, although not very large, reflected in part the attempt to match the sample. Since most cable firms facing competition from STV are larger systems located in major metropolitan areas, an attempt was made to pick urban and suburban systems that do not face STV competition for comparison. The estimation of the impact of competition on the price-

Table 5.4. Comparison of 175 Firm Sample to National Averages, 1983

Variable	Sample Average	National Average
Basic subscribers	10,250	8,243
Homes passed	17,675	15,779
Price basic	8.56	8.45

SOURCE: Sample and Paul Kagan Associates (1983c).

cost margins of cable operators requires some assumptions about the functional form of the model. Specifically, the general expression of the model(s) estimated appears below. The definitions of the variables, including their sources, are displayed in table 5.5.

$$LPCM = \alpha_0 + \alpha_1(COMNET) + \alpha_2(COMIND) + \alpha_3(COMED)$$
$$+ \alpha_4(TOP100) + \alpha_5(TOP200) + \alpha_6(OUTSIDE)$$
$$+ \alpha_7(LYR) + \alpha_8(SPLINE1) + \alpha_9(SPLINE2)$$
$$+ \alpha_{10}(PION) + \alpha_{11}(PION1) + \alpha_{12}(PION2) + \alpha_{13}(SIG)$$
$$+ \alpha_{14}(LARGE) + \alpha_{15}(INDEP) + \alpha_{16}(MID)$$
$$+ \alpha_{17}(VI) + \alpha_{18}(INIT) + \alpha_{19}(LSERV) + \alpha_{20}(LAHI)$$
$$+ \alpha_{21}(REG) + \alpha_{22}(LSTV) + \alpha_{23}(SAT) + \alpha_{24}(XSAT)$$
$$+ \alpha_{25}(C1) + \alpha_{26}(C2) + \alpha_{27}(C3) + \alpha_{28}(C4).$$

Table 5.5. Variable Definition

Name	Definition	Data Source
LPCM	Log of the cable firms price-cost margin + 1 where each service offered was weighted by its share of total revenue.	Paul Kagan Associates 1983c. Phone survey to determine how program services were bundled together and how they were priced.
LSTV	Log of the number of STV subscribers in a cable area + 1.	Data received directly from STV operators throughout the U.S.
SAT	Log of number of satellite services available on the basic service package + 1.	*Television Digest* (1983) and direct phone survey to cable operators.
XSAT	Log of number of satellite services on the expanded basic service package + 1.	Same as SAT.

Table 5.5. (Continued)

Name	Definition	Data Source
COMNET	Log (number of network services on cable/number of network station in the Grade B contour area).[a]	*Television Digest* (1983).
COMIND	Log (number of independent stations on cable/number of educational stations within the Grade B contour on the cabled area).	Same as COMNET.
COMED	Log (number of educational stations on cable/number of educational stations within the Grade B contour of cable area).	Same as COMNET.
LSERV	Log (number of pay television services not available on basic or expanded basic service).	Paul Kagan Associates 1983c.
LAHI	Log of average household income in county where cable was available.	*Circulation* (1983).
TOP100	Dummy variable for existence of cable system in TV market between 51 and 100.	*Television Digest* (1983).
TOP200	Dummy variable for existence of cable system in TV market between 101 and 200.	Same as TOP100.
OUTSIDE	Dummy variable for existence of cable system outside all TV markets.	Same as TOP100.
SIG	Variable ranging from 1 to 5 to denote physical obstructions of television signals.	Department of Interior, (1970).
C1	Dummy variable for cable system in the South region.	U.S. Department of Commerce (1977).
C2	Dummy variable for cable system in the North Central region.	U.S. Department of Commerce (1977).
C3	Dummy variable for cable system in the West region.	U.S. Department of Commerce (1977).
C4	Dummy variable for cable in the Plains region.	U.S. Department of Commerce (1977).
C5	Dummy variable for cable system in the East region.	U.S. Department of Commerce (1977).
INIT	Dummy variable equal to 1 if STV operator entered market before the cable firm.	Paul Kagan Associates, *Census of Pay TV, 1983*.
LCAP	Log of total channel capacity of the cable system.	Same as INIT
LPOP	Log of population in cable franchise area.	Same as INIT

Table 5.5. (Continued)

Name	Definition	Data Source
REG	Dummy variable equal to 1 if cable firm's rates are regulated.	National Cable Television Assoc.
INDEP	Cable firms not owned by a multiple system operator.	
LYR	Log of the cable system age (in years).	Paul Kagan Associates (1983).
SPLINE1	Allows for a separate coefficient to be estimated for cable systems that are less than or equal to three years old. That is, it is $\min(0, \log(YR) - \log(3))$.	
SPLINE2	Allows for a separate coefficient to be estimated for cable systems greater than or equal to ten years old. Hence, it is defined as $\max(0, \log(YR) - \log(10))$.	
PION1	Is an interaction term between spline 1 and init.	
PION2	Is an interaction term between spline 2 and init.	
VI	Dummy variable equal to 1 if cable firm was commonly owned with a major pay television programmer. These included:	*Television Digest* (1983).

Pay Programmer	MSO
Home Box Office (HBO), Cinemax	ATC
The Movie Channel (TMC)	Warner Amex
Showtime	Viacom

Name	Definition	Data Source
PION	Is an interaction term between age of system and cabled areas where STV was available before cable.	
LARGE	Identifies cable firms owned by one of the top 20 cable multiple system operators.	Paul Kagan Associates (1983f).
MID	Identifies cable firms owned by the next 30 largest multiple system operators.	
SMALL	Identifies all remaining cable firms owned by multiple systems operators.	

[a]Grade B contour area is a technical measure indicating the quality of the television picture received. Within a given Grade B contour, the quality of the reception should be satisfactory to the median observer at least 90 percent of the time, for at least 50 percent of the receiving locations.

B. Empirical Results

A number of different models were evaluated to assess the effect of existing models of video competition, primarily over-the-air television and STV, on the price-cost margins of cable firms. The results across these models were remarkably consistent.[22] A number of interesting results emerged from the study (see table 5.6). Perhaps the most notable was the impact STV had on the ability of cable firms to raise prices above costs. This impact differed appreciably depending on which technology was available first. In cable franchise areas where cable preceded STV, STV had a negative, although *very minor* impact on cable price-cost margins. In these markets, a 1 percent increase in STV penetration was associated with approximately a .004 to .007 percent decrease in the price-cost margin. The competitive impact of STV on cable operators was more pronounced, however, when STV was the first video technology available. In these video markets, the price-cost margins on cable operators were an additional 9 percent lower.[23] Hence, STV appears to have a significant impact on the price-cost margins of cable operators, but this impact occurs only in certain markets where STV was available before cable.

Price-cost margins of cable television firms outside the top 50 television markets were approximately 2 to 3 percent larger. This result seems plausible for a number of reasons. Most importantly, these variables were included to capture a number of potential competitors to cable and television viewing in general, such as other sources of entertainment, that are not easily measured. Cable firms outside the top media markets have fewer sources of competition for cable viewing, and therefore appear to have more market power.

Price-cost margins increase with the age of the cable system. This result is consistent with past studies examining the demand for cable television where the final system's penetration was time dependent (Comanor and Mitchell 1966). To allow for flexibility in estimating the functional form of the age variable, a series of linear splines was employed. When a log linear relationship between the system's age and the price-cost margin is assumed, the price-cost margins of cable operators increased approximately 3 percent each year. Subsequent models using the splines, however, indicate that this relationship is not linear. Using this more flexible functional form, the relevant elasticities range from .05 to .08 over the first ten years of operation. Hence, cable systems

Table 5.6. Factors Affecting Price-Cost Margins of Cable Operators: Ordinary Least Squares Estimates and Standard Errors

MODEL	CONSTANT	COMNET	COMIND	COMED	TOP100	TOP200	OUTSIDE	1YR	SPLINE1	SPLINE2	PION	PION1	PION2	SIG
1	.833*	-.0007	.0004	.011	.016	.0009	.013	.028*	—	—	.075*	—	—	.008
	(.280)	(.009)	(.008)	(.011)	(.013)	(.012)	(.013)	(.008)			(.017)			(.011)
2	.809*	—	—	—	.021**	.007	.001	.052*	.038	-.049*	.044*	—	—	—
	(.246)				(.012)	(.011)	(.013)	(.014)	(.033)	(.023)	(.019)			
3	.871	—	—	—	.025*	.011	.019**	.038*	.079	-.031	.128*	-.097	-.203*	—
	(.244)				(.012)	(.011)	(.011)	(.017)	(.065)	(.025)	(.042)	(.081)	(.087)	

MODEL	LARGE	INDEP	MID	VI	INIT	LSERV	LAHI	REG	LSTV	SAT	XSAT	C1	C2	C3	C4	R²
1	.030*	.009	.013	.006	-.169*	.005	-.109*	.009	-.004*	-.005	.001	.007	.005	.024	-.021	.70
	(.009)	(.014)	(.012)	(.013)	(.034)	(.015)	(.027)	(.012)	(.002)	(.006)	(.005)	(.015)	(.015)	(.015)	(.019)	—
2	.033*	.017	.016	—	-.102*	—	-.111*	—	-.004	—	—	—	—	.020*	—	.69
	(.008)	(.013)	(.011)		(.039)		(.023)		(.002)					(.010)		—
3	.033*	.011	.014	—	-.240*	—	-.116*	.023*	-.004*	—	—	—	—	.025*	—	.71
	(.008)	(.013)	(.011)		(.075)		(.023)	(.011)	(.002)					(.011)		—

*Significantly different from zero, P ≤ .05 (two-tailed test).

**Significantly different from zero, P ≤ .10 (two-tailed test).

appear to mature within the 10-year time period. Beyond this time, price-cost margins appeared lower. Of course, this relationship could again be partially explained by the positive correlation between the system's age, channel capacity, and number of program offerings.

The price-cost margins of cable systems facing rate regulation by either state or local governments did not differ appreciably from other systems. In fact, in one specification, rate regulation, appeared positively related. As previously noted, the fact that rate regulation did not have a discernible negative effect on price-cost margins may not be surprising given the pricing flexibility which remains on expanded basic and pay television tiers. Further, rate regulation in the cable industry is more ad hoc than other industries. Indeed, there is rarely any formal rate of return decision; instead local regulators appear to use external references such as the rate of inflation to guide their decisions (Kalba 1980).

Other competition related variables, such as the comparative service offerings of over-the-air television and signal quality, did not add to the explanatory power of the model.

One final demand-side factor that was examined, average household income, produced the only seemingly anomolous result. The results imply that the price-cost margins of cable operators were negatively associated with higher income. This result runs counter to the expectation that higher income would, through demand-side effects, lead to higher price-cost margins. One potential explanation of this result is that it is driven by supply- and not demand-side factors. In particular, the negative relationship between income and price-cost margins could be an artifact of the correlation between large cable groups, who have relatively lower programming costs and television market size (see table 5.7). Because of the programming cost advantage these groups enjoy, price-cost margins would be larger due to both demand-side (since there is less video competition) and supply-side factors resulting from lower

Table 5.7. Cross-Tabulation of Market Size by Group Ownership

MSO Size	Group Ownership			
Market Size	*Large*	*Mid*	*Small*	*Independent*
Top 50	23	12	14	5
Top 100	8	0	12	2
Top 200	22	5	13	0
Outside	27	8	10	8

programming cost. Hence, the observed relationship may be driven by supply rather than any perverse demand-side responses.

C. Supply-Side Results

Price-cost margins of cable systems owned by the top 20 multiple system operators were 3 percent higher than other cable firms.[24] Other ownership characteristics explained little of the cross-sectional variation in price-cost margins.[25]

D. Impact of Competition on Program Selection

Two different models were used to explore the factors affecting programming decisions. The first model explained variations in the total number of cable channels programmed, while the second model examined the number of pay television programs offered (see table 5.8).

Table 5.8A. Log Number of Cable Channels Programmed: Estimated Coefficients and Standard Errors

DEP VAR: LPROGS

Variable	Estimated Coefficient	Standard Error
INTERCEPT	12.19	2.47
LCAP*	0.28	0.11
LPOP*	0.09	0.03
LSTV	−0.0055	0.01
TOP100	−0.31	0.12
TOP200	−0.20	0.12
OUTSIDE	−0.25	0.12
INIT	−0.04	0.15
LYR*	−0.42	0.15
SPLINE1	0.11	0.30
SPLINE2**	0.44	0.23
VI	0.08	0.13
LARGE	0.06	0.09
MID	0.12	0.11
INDEP	−0.02	0.14
SIG	−0.006	0.08
REG	−0.12	0.11
LAHI*	−1.10	0.24

*Statistically different from zero, $P \leq .05$ (two-tailed test).
**Statistically different from zero, $P \leq .10$ (two-tailed test).

Table 5.8B. Log Number of Pay Television Programs Offered:
Estimated Coefficients and Standard Errors

Dependent Variable: LSERV

Variable	Estimated Coefficient	Standard Error
INTERCEPT	1.67	1.33
LCAP**	0.10	0.06
LPOP	0.02	0.02
LSTV	.00002	0.01
TOP100	−0.08	0.06
TOP200	−0.08	0.06
OUTSIDE	−0.08	0.06
INIT	0.004	0.08
LYR*	−0.20	0.08
SPLINE1	0.11	0.16
SPLINE2**	0.30	0.12
VI	−0.08	0.07
LARGE	0.02	0.05
MID	−0.008	0.06
INDEP	−0.08	0.07
SIG	−0.02	0.04
REG	0.06	0.06
LAHI	−0.11	0.13

*Statistically different from zero, $P \leq .05$ (two-tailed test).
**Statistically different from zero, $P \leq .10$ (two-tailed test).

Demand-side influences included the population of the cable franchise area. The estimated elasticity of the number of programs offered with respect to population was .09. Hence, a 10 percent increase in population was associated with nearly a 1 percent increase in the number of channels programmed. Not surprisingly, the channel capacity of the system also affected the number of channels programmed. The estimates suggest that a 10 percent increase in the number of channels offered is associated with approximately a 3 percent increase in the number of cable programs.

Competition from STV firms did not appear to influence the number of cable programs offered. This result was consistent across both models. Hence, at least in this particular sample, cable firms did not respond to competition by proliferating more programming. This is not to say, of course, that cable operators do not attempt to duplicate the program offerings of STV operators. Instead, there appears no substantial evidence that cable operators have attempted to deter entry through program proliferation.

The age of the cable system was also associated with the number of programs offered. Once again, the relationship between the system's age and the number of programs was nonlinear. In particular, newer cable systems tended to offer more cable programming. The relationship between age and number of programs offered was negative up to a threshold of 10 years; beyond that time, there was no apparent relationship between age and the number of programs.

The particular television market where the cable firm was located also influenced the number of programs offered. Cable systems located outside the top 50 television markets offered anywhere from 25 to 30 percent fewer programs. This result may or may not have resulted from competition between cable operators and over-the-air television. Alternatively, the result could simply be an artifact of the larger channel capacity of cable systems in larger metropolitan markets that have resulted from local franchising proceedings. Based on the information presented, we cannot separate these competing explanations.

The average household income in the county where the cable franchise is located appears negatively related to the number of programs offered. Again, this result runs counter to the maintained hypothesis that higher income should, through demand-side effects, lead to more cable programs.[26]

Finally, there is no evidence from the data supporting the proposition that vertically integrated firms discriminate against other programmers and therefore provide fewer services.

VII. CONCLUSIONS AND POLICY IMPLICATIONS

Much of the recent debate over the structure of regulation in the cable television industry has focused on the competitiveness of video media markets. One point of contention is that cable operators are natural monopolists with monopoly pricing powers which thwart federal policy goals promoting source and program diversity, access to the media, and economic efficiency. As part of this policy debate, Congress has recently passed legislation which alters the current regulatory structure, most notably by restricting the regulatory powers of state and local governments in the cable franchising process. Much of the rationale for the movement toward "deregulation" stems from the growth in competitive alternatives to cable television. Because of this influx of new technology, it is argued, most media markets are "workably" competitive, thus warranting a more relaxed regulatory atmosphere. Policy prescriptions that follow have usually included loosened cross-ownership restrictions between cable systems and broadcasters, eliminating rate regulation and access requirements.

Much of the policy discussion appears to lead to a simple dichotomy: if cable firms have market power then regulate; otherwise do not. This framework is too narrow, however, since it neglects the role of long term contracts as a form of regulation (Goldberg 1976; Thorpe 1984a). Given the specialized technology employed by the cable industry, some form of regulation will always be required. Long-term contracts are required to initially attract the specialized capital to build a cable television system. Because of the legal entry barriers created by local governments, as well as those resulting from the "sunk" cost nature of cable technology, cable firms are able to exercise monopoly powers (Baumol et al. 1982). Hence, the interesting policy question is not whether to regulate cable systems if they price above costs—surely they all do. Rather, the question is how to structure and administer long-term cable franchise agreements to further stated federal policy goals.

Within this broader regulatory context, there are a number of important decisions regulators must undertake. These decisions include tradeoffs that are important to highlight. Potential bidders for the cable franchise base their bids on expectations concerning the profitability of the franchise. Larger expected profits increase the likelihood that potential bidders will install cable systems of higher "quality" (i.e., larger channel capacity, two-way interactive systems, and more channels programmed). Of course, the converse is also true. Local regulators have substantial influence over a number of factors influencing the profitability of a cable system. This power stems from the regulator's influence over the regulation of competitors to cable, contract length, renewal expectations, franchise fees, and rate regulation. More profitable cable contracts, in part influenced by the terms of the contract, may provide greater cable "quality" but may also entail costs such as short-run monopoly pricing, and inhibiting consumers from adopting newer, potentially cheaper substitutes to cable. Hence, the "appropriate" tradeoffs between prices and quality are difficult, *a priori,* to prescribe.

Within the broader context of long-term cable franchise agreements, a number of "short" run allocation decisions are required. That is, cable regulators must administer the contract by choosing among numerous mechanisms to allow for short-run price and quality adjustments. It is for these short-run allocation decisions that the analysis presented above is most useful. In particular, my empirical analysis provides information for policymakers regarding the impact of rate regulation, and video competition on the short-run price and quality decisions of cable firms.

Given the current method of rate regulation, which covers only the basic cable rates, there was no discernible difference between cable price-cost margins, or the number of programs offered over cable in regulated or non-rate-regulated systems. Hence, recent legislation proposing to restrict the ability of local regulators to use rate regulation as a short-run policy tool may not, on average, significantly affect consumers, cable operators, or federal policy goals. In contrast, competition from other video media did have a competitive impact on cable operators. In areas where STV firms entered a market before cable was available, cable price-cost margins were nearly 10 percent lower than in other markets. Where STV entered after cable was available, however, there was a negligible impact on the price-cost margins of cable firms. Although the finding that competition from even a single-channel competitor to cable may reduce overall price-cost margins is interesting, it may not be a useful guide for public policy. Many areas of the country already have cable available. Indeed, most of the growth in the industry has already been completed. Hence, new competitive technologies, such as multichannel MDS and DBS, will usually face competition from an entrenched cable operator. Although these technologies are multichannel, they generally have fewer channels available than cable. Hence, unless the new technologies are able to enter cabled areas through differentiating their program offerings from cable, the competitive role of these outlets may be limited.[27] Indeed, some DBS firms have already focused on areas of the country that will never have cable for their marketing efforts.

The rapid growth in videocassette recorders (VCRs), however, may have a greater impact on cable firms than other technologies. The extent of this impact is yet to be fully realized and should be monitored carefully. It is not clear, however, whether VCRs are substitutes for or merely complementary to purchasing cable television.

Cable television firms in the top 50 television markets have lower price-cost margins than other cable firms. In fact, the analysis suggested that the price-cost margins in these markets were approximately 3 percent lower than elsewhere. This result seems reasonable given the large number of competing sources of entertainment to cable in the largest media markets.

Competition from either STV or over-the-air television did not appear to influence the number of programs offered by the cable operator. Indeed, it appears that these decisions are influenced primarily by local cable regulators through the initial franchise bidding process, the renewal process, as well as the population size of the cable franchise market.

Finally, whether the competitive impacts of STV observed in the study are "adequate" for the short-run allocation goals of local regulators cannot be easily determined. One can say, however, that existing rate regulation of basic cable rates does not have a discernible negative impact on price-cost margins. Hence, existing rate regulation is not an effective short-run allocation tool. If local cable regulators want to achieve short-run resource allocation results similar to those cable firms in the top 50 markets, or those facing competition from an entrenched STV firm, other policy instruments need to be explored.

Notes

1. Although in the near future, because of technological advances, cable services will be provided by other types of cable.

2. Strictly, for a multiproduct firm such as cable television, two conditions must be met before a firm can be considered naturally monopolistic. First, cost conditions must produce economies of scale in the production of each good, and second, the firm must exhibit economies of scope. See, Sharkey (1982).

3. One study examining the "competitiveness" of the industry simply examined penetration by subscription television in two cabled areas. See Pottle and Bortz (1982).

4. The focus of the study on over-the-air television and STV, to the apparent exclusion of other forms of video programming outlets, is quite deliberate. First, detailed data on MDS penetration were not available. However, even a cursory examination of the relevant penetration data reveals that MDS and SMATV rarely compete directly with cable. With respect to MDS, the reason is rather simple. Of the 570,000 subscribers currently taking MDS services, 66 percent receive programming from HBO. Another 11 percent of MDS subscribers receive their programming from either Showtime or the Movie Channel (Paul Kagan Associates, 1983c). Hence, less than one-quarter of all MDS subscribers receive programming other than that provided by the three largest pay programmers. Thus, in areas which could technically receive either MDS or cable, incentives for direct competition are either reduced, or contractually prohibited. Of course, there are important exceptions. Cable firms in Dallas and Milwaukee, for example, face direct competition from both STV and MDS. Here, the MDS programming provided is not available over cable television. Although SMATV alone competes against cable in other markets there was insufficient subscriber data available to analyze properly.

5. Indeed, if conjectures are made in quantity space, outcomes ranging from either monopoly or competition emerge. Further, if conjectures are made in prices, competitive outcomes could also result under Bertrand assumptions.

6. Assuming that the cable operator does not price discriminate, and using linear demand curves, the welfare loss (w) associated with monopoly pricing can be approximated by the following (assuming changes in price and output are relatively small). The Harberger welfare loss measure is as follows:

$$W = \frac{1}{2} \, \Delta P \Delta Q$$

This can be rearranged to yield the following

$$W = (\tfrac{1}{2}P) \cdot Qnd^2$$

where d is the price-cost margin ($(P - MC)/P$), n is the own-price elasticity of demand, Q is the product output and P is the final product price. Hence, welfare losses increase quadratically with the relative price distortion away from competitive (marginal cost) pricing, and as a linear function of the own-price demand elasticity. See Harberger (1954).

7. In general there are two problems stemming from monopoly: resource allocation and income distribution. Assuming the cable operator has some market power, and does not price discriminate, higher deviations of price from cost implies larger welfare losses, and a larger redistribution of income from consumers to the cable operator. Further, greater price-cost margins imply an increased ability to set high access fees to the cable system. On the other hand, there are a number of methods the cable operator can employ to price discriminate. Most

cable operators, for example, provide volume discounts when purchasing more channels of programming. In some cases, when these discounts are used, the welfare losses associated with monopoly may be reduced, but the distributional implications of monopoly remain. For a discussion of the regulatory implications of cable pricing practices, see Thorpe (1984a).

8. The Lerner Index has been used on a number of occasions to measure market power. Although the Lerner Index provides useful information about the extent of resource misallocation and pricing flexibility, it is limited as a normative tool for prescribing regulatory interventions. Firms with significant fixed costs, for example, may have large price-cost margins yet in the long run make zero economic profits. For a general discussion, see Scherer (1980).

9. Specifically, it can be shown that price-cost margins for a multiproduct firm are determined in the following manner.

$$\frac{P_i - MC_i}{P_i} = \frac{1}{N_i} + \frac{1}{\displaystyle\sum_{i=1}^{J} S_i/S_j} (CE_{ij})$$

Where P is the specific product price, MC is the marginal cost associated with the individual product, N is the own-price elasticity of demand, CE is the cross-price elasticity of demand and S indicates the share of total revenue (j) received from product (program) i. See Needham (1978).

10. That is, the elasticity of demand facing a single seller is . . . .

$$\eta_i = \left(\frac{Q_D}{qi}\right)\eta + \left(\frac{Q_S}{qi}\right)E$$

where η is the market demand elasticity, E represents the elasticity of supply of potential competitors with respect to the market price, Q_D is the total quantity demanded, Q_S is the total quantity supplied by all firms, and qi is the amount supplied by firm i. For its derivation, see McCloskey (1982).

11. Cowling and Waterson (1976), Dickson (1981), and Applebaum (1982). In general, these indexes note that firms will equate marginal costs with *perceived* marginal revenues. Hence, the degree of monopoly, or oligopoly power will be a function of both the relevant own-price demand elasticities and the firm's conjectural elasticity of total industry output with respect to the output of the firm.

12. Phillips (1980), also see note 9.

13. Although I could have directly estimated the equation suggested in note 9, the revenue shares are endogenous. Hence, through simple algebraic rearrangement, I have placed all endogenous variables on the left-hand side resulting in each individual price-cost margin weighted by its share of total system revenues.

14. Other factors to consider could include drop lines—which include installation charges, splitters, traps, and amplifiers—and converters. These were not considered for a variety of reasons. First, all of the marginal costs cited here are one-time charges. Once amortized over the expected length of time a subscriber is expected to have cable service, they are not very important. Second,

except for labor costs, there is little cross-sectional variation in these charges (although converter prices do vary as a function of the size of the cable group, or total subscriber base). Finally, once the initial hookup has been completed, and either the subscriber decides to upgrade his services or a new subscriber moves into the premises, marginal costs are substantially less. Given the data at hand, it would be impossible to distinguish between these latter two types of customers.

15. Both cable operators and program suppliers face downward sloping demand curves—that is, they are serial monopolies. In general, one may not easily determine whether the price-cost margins of serial monopolists are smaller than vertically integrated firms. Serial monopolists charge higher prices than vertically integrated firms. However, vertically integrated firms have lower marginal programming costs. The ultimate outcome depends whether the lower final product price resulting from integration is less than the reduction in marginal cost. Given the large pay programming markups over marginal costs (anywhere from $3 to $5), one would expect the reduction in marginal programming costs would swamp the reduction on final product price. Even a cursory examination of the relevant data provides strong support for this assumption.

16. Monopoly firms must also consider changes in revenue that could result if existing subscribers drop other services the firm offers.

17. The argument presented here is very similar to the one presented by Schmalensee and by Scherer in their discussions of the ready-to-eat breakfast cereal case. There, it was suggested that existing cereal companies had deterred entry by proliferating cereal brands, which reduced the profitability of entry. See, for example, Schmalensee (1979) and Scherer (1979). For a general discussion of the role of product selection as an entry deterrent strategy, see Eaton and Lipsey (1979), and Wildman (1980).

18. In addition to the advantages associated with being the pioneering firm, STV firms have traditionally had an advertising advantage over most cable operators. That is, STV—thanks to its larger relevant market—has made great use of television as a method to reach its audience. Cable, on the other hand, because of the franchising process, faces a much smaller market area. For the most part, the relatively small market areas have made advertising on television impractical. This trend has recently been reversed, however, because of the recent growth in chain ownership of clusters of adjacent cable systems. This clustering has allowed chains to further exploit scale economies.

19. Given that the competitive marginal cost of pay programming is zero, total revenues available to both the cable firm and the pay programmer are maximized when the cable firm uses the zero marginal cost to guide pricing decisions. Any positive price charged by the pay programmer will reduce total revenues available.

20. Cable systems used in the analysis were drawn from Paul Kagan's publication *Pay Cable TV by Households, 1983*. In this publication, relatively detailed information regarding the number of households receiving multiple pay programming was provided. Kagan reports this information for 392 of 2,562 systems in their annual survey. Of the 392 first reported in this publication, I

randomly selected 175 firms for analysis. All 175 firms provided the requisite information on pricing and bundling decisions.

21. The welfare implications of these pricing schemes are discussed in Thorpe (1984a).

22. A number of different model specifications were used. For example, the sample was stratified by group and market size where separate regressions were run to detect whether the results were robust. Coefficient estimates for the variables of interest (i.e., rate regulation, competition) were remarkably consistent across these different models. Further, there was some initial concern regarding the likely endogeneity of the variables characterizing the number of channels programmed. A number of different models were used to assess the sensitivity of the coefficient estimates, including two-stage least squares, as well as separate models estimating price-cost margins for cable firms offering two three, four, or five pay programs. Results were very similar across these widely different specifications. Finally, to test for the possible influential effect that individual observations could have on the coefficient estimates, statistics suggested by Cook (1977) and Belsley, et al. (1980) were calculated. In general, the Cook test allows one to detect the change in each parameter estimate by deleting the observation. Of the 175 observations, four were found to have an especially influential impact in the estimated coefficients. Although the deletion of these observations did change some coefficient estimates, resulting policy conclusions were not affected.

23. This effect, of course, includes all relevant interaction terms.

24. This result was not particularly sensitive to the definition of "large" group. In particular, redefining the variable to include only the largest 10 cable multiple system operators yielded similar results.

25. In order to test for the sensitivity of the results to the maintained hypothesis that vertically integrated firms internally transfer programming at its true social marginal cost, another series of regressions was run using positive marginal costs for these firms. That is, I assumed that the marginal programming costs paid by vertically integrated firms were calculated in exactly the same manner as nonintegrated firms. This assumption did little to change the underlying relationships of interest.

26. One of the problems with this line of analysis is that the initial size of the cable system is determined by the local cable regulatory body. There has been a clear trend over time for new cable systems to have much larger channel capacity and program offerings than older systems. For a quick analysis of these trends over time, see *Television Digest* (1983).

27. Again, it is important to point out that through existing licensing regulation by the FCC and local cable regulatory authorities, there is generally *not* free entry into cabled areas. These procedures give cable operators who have larger channel capacities time to "react" through changing their pricing or programming decisions.

Comment: Empirical Studies of Media Competition

Douglas W. Webbink

In 1980, the FCC finally decided to allow the unlimited carriage of distant signals on cable TV and to repeal its syndicated exclusivity rules, in part because it believed that the adverse impact on local stations would be minimal and that local UHF stations might be helped by cable TV carriage (Federal Communications Commission, 1980e). Of course, the lack of significant economic impact on existing stations may have been a good legal argument for deregulation, but it certainly was a poor economic policy reason for repealing cable TV restrictions. The economic argument for repeal would have been far stronger if the econometric studies had suggested that the consumer demand for cable TV was so intense that deregulating cable TV would have caused a much larger decline in the audience for local television stations, and indeed that widespread bankruptcy among local TV stations would follow cable TV deregulation. We can be grateful that the present FCC is no longer so concerned with protecting the profits of existing TV stations. As a result of FCC deregulation and the provision of new cable network services, cable TV has been growing rapidly. Ironically, it may well be that the new video outlets such as MDS, DBS, and SMATV, as well as local franchise regulation and possibly Copyright Tribunal regulation, may place limits on the growth of cable TV, even though the FCC has repealed most of its major restrictions on cable TV.

All three articles deal with the feasibility or likelihood of competition and substitutability of one video media for another. Moreover, all three of them actually run regressions and statistically test hypotheses using real data. The contribution by Jonathan Levy and Peter Pitsch is particularly interesting because it is the first research I have seen that estimates the demand for video cassette recorders. It is also an excellent model of how to write a research paper because it is open and explicit about the assumptions and methodology used and about the limitations of its models and data.

One such significant limitation on the study was imposed by the fact that the unit of observation was the state, rather than the local television or cable TV viewing market. While many earlier studies of cable TV used a local market as the unit of observation (Besen et al. 1977), the only data available to Levy and Pitsch on video cassette recorders (VCRs) was state data. Because of the problems with using aggregate state data, their cable TV equations did not include many of the separate independent variables included in earlier studies, such as the number of network and independent VHF and UHF stations and the number of noncommercial VHF and UHF stations in each market (Besen et al. 1977). For that reason, the results for the cable TV demand equations are not as satisfactory as some of the earlier studies.

Of course, many of the most interesting questions concerning VCR demand remain unanswered pending the availability of more disaggregated data and a more complex model. In particular, it would be very interesting to see not only the extent to which VCRs substitute for movie viewing in theaters, but also the extent to which the substitute and complementary effects of VCRs, with respect to commercial television, can be separated. In addition, it will also be interesting to observe the impact of VCRs on other media after the percent of homes owning VCRs has risen significantly. It is entirely possible that some of the nonsignificant results in Levy and Pitsch's regressions would then become significant. It would be interesting to compare data at the end of 1984 with the 1982 data which L & P used. It would also be revealing to run similar regressions on data for European countries where the number of commercial television choices are far fewer, and the penetration of VCRs is much greater than in the U.S.

Eli Noam's study represents the first major attempt to measure economies of scale and scope in cable TV systems, and continues earlier work by Noam (1983) to the next stage. The only other recent estimates of economies of scale in cable are by Owen and Greenhalgh (1983). In his study, Noam has tried to consider carefully what the major factors are that would affect a production function and hence a cost function for cable TV.

Noam's conclusion that there are only small economies of scale in homes passed is an important conclusion. If the major economies really are in packaging and sale of services, there would appear, I believe, to be little reason to support the traditional arguments for natural monopoly regulation such as price regulation of cable TV systems. The fact that the economies appear to be modest may also suggest, in my view, that many other video outlets will be capable of competing with cable TV, particularly if it is true that there is little or no consumer demand for more than 20 or 30 channels of video, a conclusion that data from the Warner Amex QUBE systems apparently support (Kahn 1983a).

A number of questions for further research suggest themselves. For example, would the estimated economies of scale and scope be smaller or larger if cable systems were not constrained by many municipal franchise requirements to provide such services as extra channel capacity and the provision of "free" local access studios and institutional cable TV networks? A recent report by William Shew (1984) estimates that those municipal requirements substantially raise the costs of providing cable TV service above what the costs would be for an unregulated consumer surplus maximizing cable system. An interesting and possibly unanswerable question (since the FCC has stopped collecting this information) is how the results would change if regressions were run using 1984 data, since many of the newer systems tend to have far more channel capacity and other add-on requirements than the older systems.

Michael Wirth and Harry Bloch suggest that (1) television stations have oligopoly power and are not perfect competitors; (2) competitive sources of video such as cable TV and pay TV will have little or no impact on the market power of television stations in the sale of advertising time; (3) as local television station audience declines in response to increased viewing options, broadcasters will simply raise the price per thousand viewers which they charge advertisers; (4) because of broadcasters' ability to raise the price of time to advertisers, competitive video systems will not affect television station advertising revenues; (5) but stations may react to the loss of audience to competitive systems by increasing their expenditures on programming; (6) increased program expenditures will decrease the profit margins of television stations; but (7) station owners can suffer significant declines in their profit margins and still be viable.

Wirth and Bloch certainly are correct in arguing that if one wants to measure the impact of new video distribution media on television stations, studying the impact on audience size or share alone is not enough. However, the really interesting question is the impact on station *profits*, not revenues; but it is revenues which W & B study.

Stations may have oligopoly power in certain television advertising markets, but W & B have not proven their case, and there is counter evidence available (Fournier and Martin 1983). Wirth and Bloch have not provided an adequate test to prove the counterintuitive result of hypothesis (2) that cable TV and pay TV will not affect a station's market power in the sale of advertising time. Hypotheses (3) and (4) seem unconvincing and W & B certainly have not demonstrated such an effect. Assumptions (5), (6), and (7) seem quite believable if not obvious, but again W & B have not adequately tested that those effects are really taking place.

Wirth and Bloch admit that cable TV in the same market has a significant effect (usually negative) on local station viewing audience. But they claim that this negative effect will not have any effect on advertising revenues since advertisers consider television to be a "must buy" and therefore cable TV and pay TV are not substitutes to advertisers; hence stations will have the ability to raise the price per thousand viewers which they charge to advertisers. It is difficult to accept this logic. First, they discuss but never define what it means to say that local stations represent a "must buy" situation for advertisers. Surely, they do not mean that advertisers will buy station time at *any* price. Hence advertisers must be sensitive to some price differential between television advertising and cable TV advertising.

If television stations behave as profit maximizing oligopolists in the sale of advertising time, one would assume they are already setting prices to maximize their profits. If some viewers now shift to other media so total station viewing declines, the remaining number of viewers will surely be less valuable to advertisers, especially since people who purchase cable TV and pay TV services are likely on average to be higher income than those who do not, and hence more valuable per viewer to advertisers than viewers who continue to watch only the local stations. In other words, the demand for television advertising time should decline, not remain constant or increase, which suggests that station advertising prices and revenues should also decline. How much it will decline is, of course, an empirical question.

This then leads to the question of whether or not the authors are correctly and adequately testing whether advertising revenue is affected by the existence of video alternatives. For one thing, the study uses as its dependent variable the log of the *list* price of a 30-second advertising spot on M.A.S.H. or the highest 30-second nonspecial event prime-time spot rate as the dependent variable. Others have pointed out the problems in using list price as a market price, especially because there is substantial discounting of advertising list prices (Besen 1976; Fournier and Martin 1983). Moreover, some measure of total advertising revenue or average revenue per 30 seconds would seem a better measure of the possible impact of new media than would the list price from one particular very popular show. It may (or may not) be true that substitute media affect the price of advertising on some (less popular) shows far more than on other (very popular) shows.

In their regression, Wirth and Bloch use the Herfindahl Index (HI), a measure of market concentration, as one of their independent variables to test for the existence of market power.[1] It is not clear precisely what the use of this variable demonstrates. Most studies have used concentration as an independent variable to "explain" profits or price-cost margins, and even then it is unclear whether the apparent positive relationship between concentration and profitability can be explained by market power of firms in concentrated industries or whether it is explained by the lower costs or more efficient operation of firms in concentrated industries (Scherer 1980: 267–295). In any case, by using cross-section data for prices, not profits or price-cost margins, and only including a few other variables that might affect prices across markets, and therefore ought to be held constant, Wirth and Bloch appear to have left out many other possibly significant variables which possibly cause price to vary across markets.

Other studies (Ferguson 1983) have found that there is a significant cross elasticity between the advertising prices in one media and availability of other media in the same market. Indeed, an earlier study by Wirth and Allen (1979) found that cable TV penetration did have a negative effect on television revenues in the top 50 markets and a positive effect in 74 smaller markets. This contradicts the present study, and needs to be reconciled.

Notes

The views expressed in this comment are my own and not necessarily those of the Federal Trade Commission or its staff.

1. It should also be noted that early in their paper, W & B indicate that they are testing whether a competitive or an oligopoly market better describes the television advertising market. They report much better regression fits with the oligopoly model, but admit that the two equations can not be directly compared since they use different specifications of the dependent variables. In fact, many studies have shown that the results of a regression can depend significantly upon the specification of the demand model chosen, and of course there ought to be *a priori* reasons from preferring one specification over another (Webbink 1977). However, the authors do not explain their choice of a log-linear demand equation in one case, and a linear form in the other case.

Comment: Multichannel Video Competition

Mark S. Nadel

Exactly where do video cassette recorders (VCRs) fit into the competitive video media picture? When Levy and Setzer (1982) examined media competition and measured the number of video channels available in each local television market they did not spend much time considering VCRs, and treated their presence as numerically equivalent to a single broadcast station. On careful examination, however, a VCR outlet is much more significant.

The video industry comprises four groups: video producers, video consumers, and the two groups of distributors in between: wholesale distribution networks and local retail outlets. Most discussions of media competition, like those in this volume, are concerned primarily with competition among retail distributors of video programming—those who sell directly to consumers. Where does a VCR fit in? It does not seem to be comparable to only a single channel retail outlet like a single screen movie theater or a single channel television or STV broadcaster, for a VCR gives a viewer several simultaneous viewing options. Nor is it comparable to multichannel retailers like multiple screen theaters, MMDS, or cable systems. Rather than being limited to the offerings that some retailer/editor selects, a VCR enables a consumer to bypass retailers completely.

The VCR enables a consumer to choose from among any of the programs recorded on video cassettes (VCs) and distributed over time via a variety of channels. While most consumers get access to VC software via local retail outlets—some are even located at movie theaters (Karp 1984)—viewers are not limited to any retailer's selection; they may deal directly with a wholesaler or even a producer.

Monroe Price (1984), observing the recent release of Fassbinder's 15-hour film *Berlin Alexanderplatz* as a $400 VC, noted that such minority interest material would ordinarily remain inaccessible to most consumers; it is doubtful that it would be shown outside the few cities that have movie theaters catering to such very specialized audiences. VCRs, however, permit small groups to gain easy access to such programs no matter how small a minority they represent.

Rather than being comparable to any of the other retail video distribution technologies, VCRs and VCs suggest comparison to the *book* industry and—if Levy and Pitsch are correct in foreseeing the possibility that VCs may be used to disseminate news as well as entertainment—the entire, highly competitive print industry. VCRs increase diversity of content unlike any media except print and while cable television may or may not provide narrowcasting for live material or material of strictly local interest, VCRs permit the kind of national narrowcasting pursued by book and magazine publishers.

How will this whole industry affect the other video media? The present growth trend of VCRs is comparable to the path that color TVs took in their early days (Carey and Moss 1984); the continuing rapid decline of costs (VCR Sales to Dealers 1983) suggests that this trend will continue. Meanwhile, as the cost of machines declines and VCRs proliferate, additional software continues to be made available at a low price, due to the proliferation of cassette rentals and clubs for sharing cassettes (Harmetz 1984). If VCR penetration continues to rise swiftly, the substitution effect that Levy and Pitsch found between VCRs and pay cable could have dramatic effects. Consumers who desire access to movies at home may find it more attractive to see exactly what they want and when they want it on VCRs rather than settling for the time schedule and selections of pay TV movie services. Yet this also suggests how competing media owners might respond to competition from VCRs.

Although consumers may enjoy having the freedom to select exactly which video titles to watch, many may not have the time to carefully search for the most desirable combination of programs. They are probably willing to pay for an editing service to make expert selections for them. In fact, consumers pay print media editors precisely for that service rather than sorting through the reams of news stories produced daily (Nadel 1984). Cable and other new media owners may seek to follow this lead and shape channels to particular consumer groups the way that radio and independent television stations do now. Consumers can buy their own records, but often they prefer to take advantage of the services of a radio disk jockey/editor, who monitors both new and old music and selects a combination to satisfy their tastes. Wholesale cable networks like Cable News Network (CNN) and Music Television (MTV) are already specializing to serve particular groups of viewers.

It would be desirable if VCR competition forces many retail media technologies to act this way—as value-added carriers of video programming—serving as video editors on individual channels or even groups of channels, rather than serving merely as electronic newsstands. Those operating the new media are certainly uniquely qualified to assess and serve their subscribers' needs and desires by vertically integrating into editing individuals or groups of video channels. Thus, in addition to providing the useful transmission service (similar to broadcast station network affiliates) for specially edited wholesale networks, they could also perform the valuable editorial service that independent broadcast stations do on their channels. Cable operators will probably continue to approach this "broadcast station" model as they get more involved in the type of advertising efforts that broadcast stations perform, efforts discussed by Wirth and Bloch.

Wirth and Bloch's results indicate that broadcast television advertising revenues have not suffered very much from the introduction of cable television. The authors dispute the widely shared belief that the decline in broadcast audiences translates into a similar decrease in advertising revenues. Wirth and Bloch find that the decline is substantially smaller.

On first blush their conclusions appear very surprising. They suggest that stations can make up for lost audience by exercising oligopoly power to increase the per capita amount that they charge advertisers (CPM). But if stations have such oligopoly power, why do they not exercise it when there is no cable? It is possible—though unlikely—that stations are simply apathetic, but why only those in cable markets?

Wirth and Bloch's results may be biased because they are based on data for the highest rated prime time program on CBS. Basic cable (advertising) networks would presumably have their smallest audiences when competing against the most popular (and expensive) network programs (although pay TV services are gaining growing audiences during this period). Cable networks probably have a considerably greater effect on station audiences and advertising revenues during daytime or late night viewing.

The results may also suffer from premature obsolescence, and there are a number of reasons why their conclusions are probably not applicable today.

Not very long ago, neither cable networks nor their affiliate cable systems were very significant players in the advertising market. Networks faced a number of obstacles. They were handicapped by their inability to document the size of their audiences with the sacred Nielsen ratings that advertising agencies demand. Agencies were generally unwilling to spend much on cable unless cable could document the results of that spending in the only terms that agency clients found understandable (Kaatz 1982). The cable industry quickly discovered how "frightfully important" Nielsen numbers are (Hausman 1984a; I. Smith 1984).

A second problem was that the cable network audiences were simply too small overall to attract the interest of advertisers looking to reach large mass national audiences. All of the available cable networks combined did not even reach the audience of one of the three major television networks, and it was much easier to negotiate with one large network than with many smaller ones. Advertisers also desired more detailed information about the audiences that cable reached (Hausman 1984a; I.V. Smith 1984).

Finally, cable networks were as concerned with securing channels on cable systems as they were with attracting advertising, and maybe more so. They realized that it was necessary to reach a critical mass of audience before they could get Nielsen ratings and thereby become a reasonable purchase for national advertisers; thus their efforts focused on reaching such a critical mass. Access was the foundation that had to be laid before significant advertising revenues could be earned.

Meanwhile, cable systems operators faced their own roadblocks. First and foremost was the cost of equipment to insert ads into the programming feeds. High-quality equipment cost in the neighborhood of $200,000 and operators felt that its purchase was not justified unless they could realize $500,000 in annual gross billings (Rosenthal 1984). This made it impractical for smaller systems to sell advertising time. In addition, under the terms of the 1982 actors union contract, a talent compensation fee of $300 was set for each performer who appeared on camera in a commercial that was cablecast (New Union Pact 1984). Many advertisers in small markets found this amount to be prohibitively high.

Additionally operators felt that their first priority was to build their system and then market their services to consumers. Most early system managers were experts at local government relations, technical aspects of cable, and marketing. Advertising sales were treated as a secondary priority (Moozakis 1983).

Today things have changed dramatically. A number of cable networks are finally being measured by Nielsen and other rating services, partly because cable networks are serving larger audiences—on an aggregated basis they match the approximate 19 percent audience share of the television networks (Hausman 1984a; Ziegler 1984). By selling commercial time across all the cable networks they carry, cable operators can offer a cable "cross buy" on the same terms as television network time. Advertising agencies are therefore more willing to buy time on cable networks (Taub 1984).

Finally, cable networks had long stressed the advantages of using their specialized channels to reach targeted audiences in new ways, such as through five-minute commercials or "infomercials." Most advertising agencies wanted to see how well such tactics worked in practice before committing any significant portion of their budget on such new ventures. As the results of early experiments are being analyzed, the advertising community has begun to feel more comfortable with the medium. In one example, Warner Amex has released the results of a test use of the Columbus, Ohio interactive QUBE system for Ralph Lauren cosmetics (Dougherty 1984), in order to demonstrate the effectiveness of specialized advertising on cable.

Similarly, things continue to improve on the affiliate front. Multiple systems operators (MSOs) are seeking to trade local systems with each other to establish more economical regional clusters of systems. Such clusters increase the subscriber base over which systems can spread the cost of advertising sales equipment and staff (Marks 1983). And even where clusters are not possible, systems cooperate with each other to facilitate interconnections that permit ad sales to become economical (Rosenthal 1984). Finally, a new union pact has decreased the minimum on-camera fee for performers from $300 to $12.70 for systems of 10,000 or fewer basic subscribers (New Union Pact 1984).

MSOs are also beginning to treat advertising sales as a high priority. They are now hiring more advertising professionals on staff and soliciting reluctant buyers. For example, Group W Cable offered free time to advertisers on its Detroit system (Moozakis 1983; Rosenthal 1984). Meanwhile, a Times Mirror system in Louisville, Kentucky is being sued for breach of contract by its advertising sales representative, who charges that "when the ultimate profitability of the advertising sales became apparent, the cable company wanted that business for itself." (Cable Ad Network 1984).

And as operators concentrate more on advertising they seem to be finding significant demand, permitting them to charge hefty ad rates, which may, at times, even surpass television broadcasters' rates (Hausman 1984b). In summary, despite Bloch and Wirth's results, cable systems appear likely to provide a competitive outlet for local advertising and force advertising rates to decline to competitive market levels.

Comment: Analyzing the Critical, Unknown Factor

Stuart N. Brotman

The cable television industry, in recent years, has been broadening its view to encompass a full range of spectrum-based media. At an earlier stage, the focus was on the potential pay programming competition from subscription television (STV) and multipoint distribution service (MDS). In retrospect, the predictions of fierce competition by them has proven to be way off the mark. STV and MDS will be recorded in the annals of electronic media development as transitional technologies that only attracted and retained subscribers until a cable service was franchised and constructed in the same geographic area. Once direct competition with cable arose, these single-channel pay programming systems lost their subscribers because cable could offer more programming services at a comparable or lower price.

The advent of multichannel technologies, however, will present the cable industry with what many industry observers deem a much tougher competitive challenge. Already, the industry has fought a number of battles in the video marketplace with entrepreneurs operating satellite master antenna television (SMATV) systems and SMATV has proven to be a feisty competitor. Well after cable service becomes available, SMATV operators have managed to retain subscribers—displaying staying power that STV and MDS have failed to establish. SMATV has succeeded—albeit on a modest scale—largely because of its ability to offer a minimum of four to six channels of programming, typically a mix of pay movies, sports, news, and superstations.

And SMATV represents merely the beginning; the cable industry increasingly will be forced by the realities of competition to formulate and implement aggressive strategies to maintain its leadership position in an expanding pay media universe. Emerging in the near distance will be two new competitive threats—direct broadcast satellites (DBS) and multichannel multipoint distribution service (MMDS).

Like SMATV, these technologies offer attractive costs, in comparison with urban cable, for both construction and maintenance. Moreover, the financial, management and marketing resources behind them are significantly more formidable. The SMATV industry has developed as a series of largely independent local or regional businesses backed by modest financing of individual investors or newly organized limited partnerships. In contrast, industry giants such as CBS, Comsat, The New York Times Company, Prudential Insurance, ABC, and dozens of other major companies are casting their lot with DBS, MMDS, or both. Even the big names of cable, among them American Television & Communications (ATC), Cox Cable and Daniels & Associates, are jumping on the multichannel bandwagon to ensure that their investments will be sufficiently diversified to capture viewers who turn away from cable to more available or attractive competitors.

The rush to become involved with the DBS industry or to apply for an MMDS license to date has been predicated on little more than a defensive instinct by cable to deal with new competitors at an early stage, and by others who envision large financial rewards from newer exotic technologies.

There is also some sketchy evidence that viewers will freely substitute cable for another technology if a core of comparable programming is available on each, but it lacks the level of precision necessary to justify anything more than an educated guess. In November 1983, for example, Television Audience Assessment, Inc. (TAA) released a report entitled *The Multichannel Environment: A Study of Television Viewing in Two Cable Markets*. The research it reported involved 3,000 randomly selected individuals living in cable franchise areas in New Britain, Connecticut and Kansas City, Missouri, and encompassed both subscribers and nonsubscribers. One of the study's primary objectives was to gain insights into the effect that cable is having on viewers' reactions to television programs and on the way viewers use the medium.

A clear message that emerged was that cable subscribers, although having a more positive attitude toward television than nonsubscribers, did not find specific programming to be more enjoyable or compelling. "It's not the method of delivery that makes the difference," explained the study's director, "but the program itself." In other words, data indicated that enjoyment of television programming was not necessarily a function of how many channels were available.

Viewers are becoming increasingly comfortable with, and therefore oblivious to, new communication technologies. The medium, contrary to the teachings of Marshall McLuhan, is *not* the message. Rather, all that seems to matter for viewers is the message itself—namely, what programming can the viewer receive and enjoy on a television screen? DBS, MMDS and all the other acronyms are to the average viewer just letters in an alphabet soup. As Gertrude Stein might say if she were alive today, "Television is television is television."

The TAA report is an interesting, though unintended, complement to a 1982 contract research study released by the National Cable Television Association (NCTA), entitled *The Impact of Competitive Distribution Technologies on Cable Television* (Pottle and Bortz 1982). No empirical data were available which could have provided reliable subscriber penetration estimates or pricing structures. A number of indicators were presented, however, to suggest that relatively few premium and non-premium channels could satisfy most expressed demand for nonbroadcast services by any individual viewer. These indicators included data from *The Pay TV Census* (Paul Kagan Associates 1983c) which showed the decrease in demand for each additional premium TV services after the first in both typical and new build cable systems, and Nielsen data which showed that although viewing of premium cable channels was comparatively high, viewership of other cable program services was relatively low.

"Taken together," the NCTA study summarized, "these data imply that a large portion of consumer demand for nonbroadcast program services can probably be met by a four- or five-channel service, suggesting multichannel [technologies such as DBS or MMDS] can capture a significant market share" (Pottle and Bortz 1982).

Random experience in the field seems to underscore further the implications suggested by these studies. Both cable industry insiders and outsiders have begun to realize that the initial honeymoon with viewers has ended. The technological razzle-dazzle of interactivity and enhanced services is giving way to a revived emphasis on marketing, product differentiation, and customer service. The cable industry is now confronting the real bottom line: maximizing subscriber units.

These activities, however, may be implemented too late to prevent the cable industry from losing a substantial number of viewers to DBS or MMDS, both of which will be able to offer multichannel packages on a national basis comparable with the four or five most popular nonbroadcast channels on cable television.

DBS has the ability to aggregate substantially more subscribers than any multiple group of cable systems, and MMDS can underprice its service because of lower capital costs. Both represent potential barriers to increased cable revenues and higher profit margins.

Moreover, DBS and MMDS will not be hampered by the layers of local and state regulations that govern the cable industry, regulations that frequently have generated substantial financial commitments to secure franchises rather than to promote profitable operation of the system. Backed by substantial corporate resources, DBS and MMDS may have a superior ability to focus on the most profitable services and thus lower their cost vis-à-vis cable to acquire and retain subscribers.

Historically, those who conjure up projections of market growth in a competitive media environment have often been proven wrong because of an inability to project one or more critical, unknown factors that have the power to skew underlying assumptions. What at first seemed like a potential rivalry frequently evolved into parallel searches for separate positions in the marketplace. For example, an ongoing debate for many years dealt with how cable television systems would siphon viewers from conventional television stations. The critical, unknown factor that demonstrated the fallacy of this assumption was the development of satellite pay services, which provided the financial basis for cable's growth. Advertiser-supported television and pay-supported television were transformed rather rapidly into bushels of apples and oranges that defied the simple comparisons of old.

Similarly, the developers of the videodisc staked much of their business on an ability to underprice the same movies available for purchase by videocassette owners. But again, the marketplace was unexpectedly turned upside down: the videocassette industry's sales-only strategy was abandoned in favor of low-cost rentals from local retail stores. Those remaining in the videodisc business now search for new market possibilities in instructional and arcade game programming, having conceded feature films largely to the videocassette market.

The list could continue. Long-playing records vs. audio cassettes. Radio vs. television. Television vs. motion pictures. Each time, a critical, unknown factor has demonstrated that something that seemed like a direct competitor turned out not to be one at all. In these cases, the critical, unknown factors were respectively, the rising popularity of automobile and personal stereo units; the development of rock and other music formats; and increased budgets for theatrical films. Given this brief litany, any projections for DBS or MMDS growth should at least be tempered with a reminder that, again, the unexpected may emerge.

Although it is possible to speculate on a virtually infinite number of situations that could generate the unexpected, my discussion here will be limited briefly to several key questions whose answers are likely to produce dramatically changed perceptions of the multichannel video marketplace.

First, to what extent will DBS or MMDS pursue business opportunities in heavily cabled areas? At least for DBS, the original business plans of the initial two entrants—Satellite Television Corporation and United Satellite Communications Incorporated—indicated a strategy favoring homes in areas without access to cable. If such a strategy is in fact implemented, there may be little direct competition between cable and the other multichannel technologies, since they will be pursuing separate market niches. But given the increased costs of urban wiring, and the growing trend of cable operators to scale down the elaborate construction plans promised in franchise agreements, the opportunity to pursue lucrative cable markets seems too good for DBS and MMDS to maintain a separatist business plan.

Second, will DBS and MMDS emphasize pay programming, or will they move to a hybrid system of pay and advertiser-supported channels, thus resembling a conventional cable system on a much smaller scale? The original thinking among DBS and MMDS planners was to "cream skim" the pay cable audience by offering a comparable package of pay services at a lower price. Yet with Microband Corporation of America's plan to launch a twelve-channel MMDS hybrid system in cities such as New Orleans, Philadelphia, and San Francisco, it appears that one original premise for multichannel competition—pay channels—may become rapidly diluted. With basic cable rates in newly constructed urban markets such as Boston and Denver in the two to four dollar range for 35 to 54 channels, it is difficult to imagine how DBS and MMDS will be able to underprice cable if all that is offered is a combination of basic and pay services.

Price sensitivity, as suggested above, looms as a critical, unknown factor. The 1982 NCTA study was premised on the notion that a DBS or

MMDS service could attract price-sensitive viewers away from cable by charging half of what cable subscribers were billed. Although that may have been a valid assumption upon which to establish an initial level of price sensitivity, it is unlikely that in the marketplace DBS or MMDS will be able to reach those benchmarks. How attractive will DBS or MMDS be if they are able to reduce the price of their service only slightly below that of cable; further along the continuum, how competitive will they be if they offer a more limited quantity of service (namely, fewer channels) at the same price as cable, or even in excess of it?

Most of the upbeat talk about DBS and MMDS has unfortunately focused on the hardware and its capital costs, while ironically justifying their future growth on research indicating that software, not hardware, is the real point of differentiation to attract viewers. When DBS and MMDS are actually in the market, if they cannot underprice cable yet still choose to compete directly against it, they will have to offer programming or services that are somehow unique. Will it be something on the order of pay-per-view or high-definition television? So far, demand for these types of enhanced services is barely existent, and thus does not seem likely to represent the primary financial basis for other multichannel video entrants. Unless a new type of programming service emerges, a budding one develops a substantial market, or current program sources utilize DBS and MMDS as distribution windows before selling to cable, there seems to be little on the horizon to make cable television appear as yesterday's news.

Even if DBS and MMDS can erode cable penetration to some significant extent—on the order of five to twenty percent—it remains to be seen how long such erosion can be sustained, and how successful the cable industry will be in launching a counterattack. On the first point, there has been no real experience with disconnects for DBS or MMDS, hence no data to compare it with disconnects for cable service. This is a critical, unknown factor that will have a direct bearing on the depth and length of cable audience erosion.

Finally, like all vigorous competitors, the cable industry can be expected to move forcefully to stem market-share erosion, and to expand its overall share as well. With a newly organized Council for Cable Information, the industry will be committing substantial resources to build viewer loyalty to the cable medium itself, thereby sharpening the distinction between cable and other multichannel technologies in the minds of consumers. If this marketing campaign is successful—and that is a big "if" indeed—the premise that DBS and MMDS would be able to capitalize on viewers' not distinguishing among delivery modes could be all but destroyed.

The foregoing analysis underscores my central theme: be prepared for a major turn of events to change current perceptions about multi-channel video market entry and long-term success. History and the rapid flow of events in the field of electronic media suggest that today's seers have skipped too lightly over areas that lead to the unknown, perhaps fearful of discovering that beyond the beyond may be just a slightly altered version of the status quo.

6

Telephone and Cable Companies: Rivals or Partners in Video Distribution?

WALTER S. BAER

CONTENTS

I. Introduction
II. Technological Considerations for Wired Video Distribution
    A. Tree-and-Branch vs. Switched System Architectures
    B. Analog vs. Digital Transmission
    C. Coaxial Cables vs. Optical Fibers
    D. Mini-Hubs and Other Transitional Steps
III. Current Telco Roles in Video Distribution
    A. Cable Service Outside Telco Franchises
    B. Rural Telephone/Video Services
    C. Regional Video Interconnection of Cable Systems
    D. Video Distribution Within Local Area Networks
    E. Construction and Leaseback of Video Distribution Facilities
IV. Proposed Telco Video Distribution Projects
    A. Pacific Bell's Palo Alto Proposal
    B. Video Distribution Systems in the United Kingdom
V. Telco/Cable Hybrids for Interactive Services
VI. The Future of Wired Video Distribution
    A. Telco Scenarios
    B. Cable Scenarios
    C. Integration or Competition?

I. INTRODUCTION

In October 1983, only a few weeks before the breakup of the Bell System, Pacific Telephone formally proposed to build a fiber optic and coaxial cable network to serve Palo Alto and several neighboring communities in Northern California.[1] Pacific's proposal trumpeted:

A New Approach . . . Entertainment and Two-Way Information Services in One System

YOU HAVE AN OPPORTUNITY to be served by the first telecommunications system of its kind anywhere in the nation. It combines several types of systems in one: traditional cable TV, high speed data transfer, and a teleconferencing and video network. (Pacific Telephone 1983)

Pacific's Palo Alto proposal spotlights the intent of the Bell Regional Holding Companies and other telephone carriers to leverage their technological and financial assets in new markets. Local video distribution presents one such attractive market opportunity, particularly in cities that have not yet awarded franchises to cable television companies.

Quite naturally, cable companies view actions such as Pacific's as a major competitive threat. More than DBS, MDS, SMATV or other video distribution technologies, the cable industry sees the telephone companies (telcos) as their longstanding past and chief future adversaries. Irving Kahn, a cable industry pioneer, now president of Broadband Communications, called Pacific's proposal an attempt "to get a telco foot—a *big* telco foot—into cable television's front door." Citing the telco interest in cable as "the stirrings of a dinosaur," Kahn continued, "Once one of them gets this kind of project off the ground, what we will have is a dinosaur up on all fours, breathing fire. And it is the status quo cable television industry that is going to get burned" (Kahn 1983b). The California Cable Television Association has vowed to fight Pacific's attempt to displace cable companies as owners and operators of video distribution networks (Schley 1984).

Yet while aggressively pursuing its Palo Alto proposal, Pacific has also sought to offer an olive branch to cable operators. At the Western Cable Show in December 1983, Pacific Vice President Al Boschulte called for partnerships with cable operators:

We're seeking alliances, not adversary relationships . . . . Sometimes from very bad beginnings great friendships have sprung, and I want to pursue that very vigorously. (Paul Kagan Associates 1983a)

Pacific's Manager of CATV/Wideband Services, Kare Anderson, has met with cable companies to reiterate that theme. Ms. Anderson suggests that Pacific and cable operators work together to develop "hybrid" approaches to pay-per-view and other interactive services, using telephone lines for upstream signaling and cable for downstream video distribution. Pacific also proposes to use its regional video transmission facilities to interconnect cable systems "for joint marketing efforts."

Telephone and cable companies thus see each other as likely competitors as well as potential partners (Pepper 1983; Yankee Group 1983). Both views are probably correct. This paper explores the evolving relationships between them in light of changes in underlying video distribution technologies, costs, and regulatory rules. It begins by describing the technological requirements for multichannel video transmission and the alternatives offered by coaxial cable and fiber optic systems.[2] The next two sections deal with current plans and likely strategies of the telephone companies for local and regional video distribution. Prospects for hybrid cable/telco services are then discussed. The final section offers possible scenarios in the next ten years for competition and/ or cooperation between telephone companies and cable system operators for video distribution systems in the United States.

II. TECHNOLOGICAL CONSIDERATIONS FOR WIRED VIDEO DISTRIBUTION

Technologically, the future of wired video distribution is clear: it will be all-switched, all-digital, and all-fiber. Today, however, cable systems transmit video to the home over tree-and-branch, analog, coaxial cable networks. The evolutionary paths and trade-offs among these three aspects of video distribution technology are discussed below.

A. Tree-and-Branch vs. Switched System Architectures

Cable television systems in the United States are basically broadcast distribution networks using coaxial cables. They distribute video signals to subscribers one-way from a central headend through trunk, feeder, and drop cables (figure 6.1a). Large urban systems (figure 6.1b) have several interconnected subheadends, or hubs, and each hub may serve multiple trunks, but the basic system architecture remains the same. All video channels are sent simultaneously to each subscriber, who then chooses which one to watch.[3]

In contrast, the switched telephone network provides each subscriber with a dedicated wire pair (loop) running to the local telephone central office (figure 6.1c). A switched or "star" system offers each subscriber access to any signal coming to the switching center, but only one signal at a time is transmitted on the dedicated subscriber loop. Two-way, point-to-point voice and data communications require a switched network architecture.

Even for one-way distribution, switched systems often appear esthetically more pleasing and "efficient" to the nonengineer. It seems inherently wasteful to distribute 50 or more video channels to each television receiver, when a viewer can watch only one at a time. A similar argument sometimes is heard about information and advertising in a large daily newspaper. Delivering 100 pages of newsprint to the door may appear wasteful when a typical reader scans less than 10 percent of the paper's articles, features, and ads. Yet publishing economics make it far more efficient to print and distribute a large general-purpose newspaper than a smaller, special edition for each subscriber.

A tree-and-branch video distribution network is less costly today than a switched network for distributing 100 or fewer program sources to a large number of subscribers. Estimates of the cost differential range from under 35 percent—United Cable's estimate for Alameda, California—to more than 100 percent—Bell of Pennsylvania's estimate for Philadelphia (Yankee Group 1983). But over the long term, cost and performance trends will likely favor a switched network for video as well as for voice and data. As Israel Switzer, a leading designer of cable

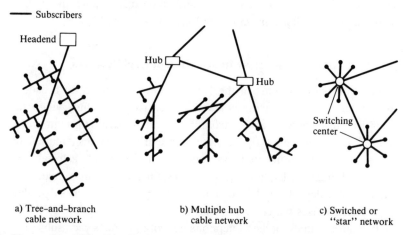

a) Tree-and-branch
cable network

b) Multiple hub
cable network

c) Switched or
"star" network

Figure 6.1. Video Distribution Network Architectures

systems in the United States and Canada, stated in a speech to the British Society of Television Engineers:

The cable systems we build today will never be able to provide "television on demand"—the provision of the "program of choice" to every individual subscriber. Such a capability will ultimately be provided by an advanced version of the "star configured" telephone system. A future upgrading of telephone system bandwidth will ultimately provide individual, switchable video pathways into each home and office. In my view this capability is still some years away (probably the end of this decade). (Switzer 1983)

Technical field trials of switched video systems have been under way since about 1980 in North America, Europe, and Japan (Asatani et al. 1982; Fox et al. 1982; Chang and Hara 1983).

B. Analog vs. Digital Transmission

Television distribution systems, as well as the voice telephone network, have been designed for continuous wave, analog transmission. Analog transmission of television in the U.S. standard (NTSC) format requires a 6 Megahertz (MHz) channel bandwidth, some 1500 times greater than the bandwidth needed to transmit a telephone voice conversation. From a communications bandwidth perspective, then, one picture is worth considerably more than a thousand words.

Computers have brought digital transmission concepts to commercial telecommunications networks. Digital transmission results in less distortion, greater security, and more flexibility than analog transmission. These advantages come at the cost of greater bandwidth requirements, however. For digital transmission, computers sample the analog wave at a rapid rate and send the resulting information as a series of digital bits over the network. Using straightforward digital encoding techniques, voice transmission requires 64,000 bits per second (64 *K*bps), while NTSC television demands 90 million bits per second (90 *M*bps). Most other communications services to the home require much less than the 64 Kbps data rate for voice (table 6.1).

Additional processing of the source information can reduce the data transmission rate—a process known as data compression. By eliminating redundant elements of voice and video signals, data compression factors of 2–4 are technically feasible today without noticeable sound or picture degradation. Pictures that do not move rapidly can be compressed significantly more. Head and shoulder video shots, where lip

Table 6.1. Digital Data Requirements for Home Communications Services

Service	Uncompressed data rate (kbps)
Telephone	64
Alarms	0.1
Utility metering	0.1–1
Energy management	0.1–1
Videotex	
1984	1.2
late 1980s	4.8–64
Electronic mail	1.2–64
Home computer networks	
1984	0.3–1.2
late 1980s	1.2–64
Slow scan video	1.2–64
Video teleconferencing	1,500–6,300
Television (NTSC)	90,000
High definition television (HDTV)	200,000 and up

movement is the most prominent moving feature, can be compressed from a nominal 90 Mbps to standard telephone transmission rates of 6.3 or even 1.5 Mbps. Such compression may be perfectly acceptable for teleconferencing, but not for fast-moving entertainment television such as sports events. Transmitting a touchdown pass at 6.3 Mbps would either blur the receiver's hands out of focus or show a jerky series of movements, like a parody of old-time movies. Even with continuing technical improvements, compression to rates much below about 20 Mbps seems unlikely for NTSC entertainment television (Koga et al. 1981). The data rates necessary for high definition television (HDTV) are, of course, several times greater.

C. Coaxial Cables vs. Optical Fibers

Technology has steadily increased the effective video bandwidth of coaxial cable systems. In the past thirty years, state-of-the-art systems have progressively moved from carrying 3 to 12, then 20, 36, 54, and now more than 70, 6 MHz channels on each cable (table 6.2). Although cable is considered a mature technology, there is every reason to expect further technical improvements. Systems capable of carrying 90 or more 6 MHz video channels per cable seem likely by 1990.

Table 6.2.   Video Channel Capacity Trends in Coaxial Cable Systems

Year	Number of 6MHz Video Channels Per Cable in State-of-the-Art Cable Systems
1950	3
1960	12
1970	20
1980	54
1990	90 (est.)

Today's fiber optic systems generally carry one digital video channel per fiber. Although analog fiber optic links have been designed to carry up to twelve video channels per fiber, the medium is inherently better suited for digital transmission. Optical fiber links being installed today in the telephone distribution plant carry 90 or 135 Mbps, enough for only one uncompressed NTSC video signal. The Olympic Games were televised in the summer of 1984 over a 90 Mbps, one-channel-per-fiber Digital Television Lightwave System installed in Southern California by AT&T, Pacific Bell, and GTE.

Fiber optic performance continues to advance impressively. AT&T is now installing fiber pairs for intercity transmission with 180 and 270 Mbps capacities. A 432 Mbps link is planned for commercial introduction by the end of 1985, and fibers capable of carrying more than a billion bits per second (1 Gbps) appear almost certain by 1990. AT&T has already successfully tested a 1 Gbps fiber system at Bell Laboratories (Rubin 1984).

At a billion bits per second, a single fiber could carry 11 NTSC television channels without compression, or some 25 to 50 channels with data compression. Multiple fibers can be bundled together to distribute larger numbers of channels. But for tree-and-branch distribution systems, installing several optical fibers directly to the home does not appear to be economically competitive with one coaxial cable. Fiber optics are much more likely to enter the home as part of a switched system.

D. Mini-Hubs and Other Transitional Steps

Video distribution systems incorporating elements of both tree-and-branch and switched architectures have been available from Rediffu-

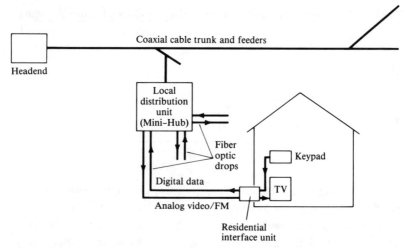

Figure 6.2. Schematic of Times Fiber Mini-Hub System

sion, Ltd., a U.K. company, for more than a decade. Two years ago, Times Fiber Communications, Inc., introduced a similar architecture using both coaxial cable and fiber optic elements. The Times Fiber Mini-Hub system distributes up to 54 video channels over conventional tree-and-branch coaxial cables to "local distribution units" (Mini-Hubs) serving up to 24 subscribers (figure 6.2). A pair of optical fibers runs from the Mini-Hub to each subscriber. The downlink fiber can carry two analog video channels or one video channel plus FM audio. The uplink fibers transmits digital signals from the subscriber's keypad to the Mini-Hub to select the program desired.

Mini-Hub systems were designed for high density "vertical" applications such as large apartment buildings with relatively short subscriber drops. Optical fibers are particularly attractive for these applications since they take up less space than coaxial cables and can often be installed in places where building codes do not permit cables or wires carrying electrical signals. Cable industry interest intensified when United Cable won the Alameda, California, franchise with a Mini-Hub design for the entire community of 24,000 households. United Cable is currently installing the system, and while some technical problems have arisen, the company expects it to be fully operational in 1984.

The Jerrold Omnitel™ system offers a different approach to video distribution with some switching capability (figure 6.3). Originally developed by the Manitoba Telephone System for its "Project Ida" field

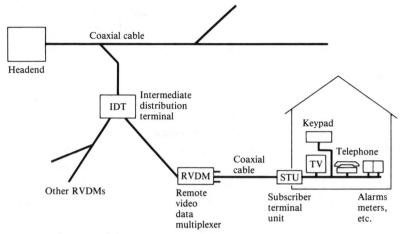

Figure 6.3. Schematic of Jerrold Omnitel System

trial in 1980-1981, the Omnitel system combines analog video with digital voice and data on a single coaxial cable. Television program selection is controlled from a "remote video data multiplexer" outside the home. Equipment at the headend and at "intermediate distribution terminals" assigns digital voice and data circuits to subscribers on a shared 2 Mbps data stream. Manitoba Telephone has licensed the technology to the Jerrold Division of General Instrument Company, which plans to market it principally in Europe.

The Mini-Hub and Omnitel technologies are sophisticated examples of "off-premises converter" systems designed to provide more secure and reliable television service to cable subscribers. They are primarily television distribution systems, although they have some two-way transmission and switching capacity for other services. Both technologies have been field tested in relatively small systems serving a few hundred subscribers. Their performance and cost for carrying interactive, non-video services among large numbers of subscribers have not yet been operationally determined. Nevertheless, they represent first steps toward "distributed intelligence" and switching in television distribution networks, a trend likely to accelerate later in this decade.

III. CURRENT TELCO ROLES IN VIDEO DISTRIBUTION

The telephone and cable industries have locked horns over most of the past twenty-five years. In the 1940s and early 1950s, telephone companies largely ignored the small-town CATV operators who distributed two or three television channels on coaxial cables. Although policies differed from telco to telco, most permitted fledgling cable companies to lease space on telephone company poles for annual rates of one or two dollars.

In the late 1950s, as cable's technical capacity increased to 12 video channels, telcos became aware of the expanding television distribution business and of CATV companies as potential competitors. The Bell System Operating Companies introduced the concept of "channel service," in which the telephone company built the cable distribution plant and leased it back to an independent CATV operator. By the mid-1960s, 18 of the 22 Bell Operating Companies had filed tariffs for channel service (NCTV 1983).

But the cost of channel service leaseback was high. The telephone companies built cable distribution systems to telco standards and used conventional telco accounting and revenue requirements to set rates. Cable operators preferred to build their own distribution plant, using telephone company poles or underground conduits. Battles between cable operators and the telcos for pole attachment rights heated up, with cable operators charging that the telcos refused access to their poles in order to extend their telephone monopolies to video distribution.

In 1967, the FCC began an investigation into telephone company channel leasing policies, pole attachment rights, and related cable service issues. Three years later the commission adopted an order prohibiting telephone companies from directly or indirectly providing cable service in their telephone franchise areas. The Commission concluded that the public interest would be best served

by preserving, to the extent practical, a competitive environment for the development and use of broadband cable facilities and services and thereby avoid undue and unnecessary concentration of control over communications media by existing carriers. (FCC 1970)

Although this cross-ownership ban has been in effect since 1970, telcos are still very much involved in video distribution. This section describes their current roles, including:

— Telco operation of cable systems outside their telephone franchises
— Rural telephone/video distribution systems
— Regional video interconnection of cable systems
— Video distribution within local area networks
— Construction and leaseback of video distribution facilities.

The following section discusses Pacific Bell's ambitious video distribution plan for Palo Alto. It also outlines the recent proposals for cable systems in the United Kingdom, which move in the direction of combining television distribution with other switched services.

A. Cable Service Outside Telco Franchises

A few telephone companies have diversified by acquiring cable systems outside their telephone franchise areas, which is permissable under the FCC cross-ownership rules. Centel Corp. (formerly Central Telephone and Utilities Corp.), for example, has purchased 120 cable systems with 235,000 subscribers and continues to seek additional cable acquisitions. Centel owns conventional cable systems in small towns and suburban areas. The company has not sought to push the technical state-of-the-art in its systems, nor has it bid for large urban cable franchises. However, Centel has pioneered in developing a regional video interconnect system (see below), as well as participating in one of the first commercial U.S. videotex services.

Pacific Telecom owns 94 percent of the cable system serving Anchorage, Alaska, in addition to several smaller systems in Alaska, Minnesota, and Wisconsin. The company's principal business is operating small telephone companies in the Pacific Northwest and Alaska, as well as providing long-distance telephone services in Alaska. Pacific Telecom's cable acquisitions are part of its strategy to diversity into other communications businesses.

With these and a few other exceptions, telcos generally have stayed away from cable operations since the FCC adopted its cross-ownership rules in 1970. The Bell Regional Holding Companies (RHCs) undoubtedly have considered buying cable systems outside their telephone territories, but none have made overt moves as yet. With competing demands for capital and their lack of conventional cable operating experience, it seems doubtful that the RHCs have their sights set on acquiring existing cable systems as the route toward becoming major factors in local video distribution.

B. Rural Telephone/Video Services

The FCC rules expressly provide for waivers of the telco/cable cross-ownership prohibitions upon showing "(1) that cable service demonstrably cannot exist except through a CATV system related to or affiliated with the local telephone common carrier; or (2) that other 'good cause' for waiver exists" (Fogarty 1980). The commission has taken the position that independent cable operation is infeasible in rural areas with densities of fewer than 30 households per mile. More than 50 such waivers have been filed since 1979, most of them unopposed by cable interests (Wheeler 1981).

Telephone and Data Systems, Inc. (TDS), a company with telephone interests in 22 states, has sought authority to provide video as well as telephone service in its small-town and rural franchises (Burrill 1981). TDS serves its more than 12,000 video subscribers via conventional cable systems, not physically linked with its telephone facilities.

During the 1970s, the 3M Company developed equipment to provide both telephone and video distribution over a common, coaxial cable facility. 3M aggressively marketed its "Total Communications" package to REA-financed and other rural telephone companies. Costs remained high, however, and after the first trial installations failed to bring large-scale orders, 3M quietly abandoned the project. The company remains actively interested in regional video interconnection among cable systems in major markets (see below).

Although the rapid development of fiber optic systems has rekindled interest in combining telephone and video distribution in rural areas, it already may be too late. Direct broadcast satellite (DBS) systems soon will offer several additional channels of movies, sports, and other popular video programming to rural households. Although DBS may find rough going in the major markets, it should be very cost competitive with other video distribution technologies in low-density areas. For rural America, integrated telecommunications services on optical fibers may be another example of a future technology whose time is past.

C. Regional Video Interconnection Of Cable Systems

Several telephone companies have shown interest in providing video transmission facilities to link cable systems within a metropolitan area or region. Cable systems seek interconnection for two principal reasons: to aggregate audiences for regional sports events and other programming not available by satellite and to sell advertising on a regional basis.

Cable system fragmentation places cable companies at a competitive disadvantage with broadcast stations and newspapers for national and regional advertising. Advertisers much prefer to make a single placement that reaches most target households within the market than to deal separately with multiple cable operators. A regional interconnect among cable headends permits advertisers to make one buy and to deliver one tape that can be shown simultaneously to subscribers in all participating systems.[4]

Centel Videopath, Inc., a subsidiary of Centel Corp., is completing a microwave network interconnecting cable systems in the Chicago metropolitan area. The 3M Company has similar plans for cable interconnection in the New York metropolitan area and in other cities.

Cable operators themselves can join forces to interconnect regionally, as Viacom and Gill Cable have done to establish the Bay Area Interconnect around San Francisco. However, it may be easier for an independent third party—whether a telephone carrier or another company—to build the regional interconnect and to offer services to individual cable operators.

D. Video Distribution Within Local Area Networks

Among the first applications for integrated video, voice, and data services will be new office buildings, hotels, and commercial centers. More and more developers recognize the importance of building an advanced telecommunications infrastructure in their new projects in order to attract tenants and to generate additional revenues. A building owner can offer tenants such services as video security monitoring, teleconferencing, high speed data channels, shared word processing, and satellite television distribution—all carried on a coaxial cable or fiber optic local area network.

Some developers are joint venturing with communications companies to design and operate local area networks. Olympia and York, one of the largest developers in North America, recently formed such a joint venture with United Telecommunications. Satellite Business Systems, itself a joint venture between IBM and Aetna, has formed SBS Real Estate Communications Corp. (RealCom) to provide advanced communications services to office space developers and owners. Ameritech will provide communications equipment and services to RealCom.

AT&T and United Technologies have also announced a joint venture to offer communications services to commercial building owners and tenants. Other similar joint ventures are likely to be announced this year.

Spurred by the threat of "bypass" by AT&T and other long distance carriers, the RHCs, GTE, and other telcos are moving quickly to serve new commercial facilities with high-speed digital lines. Optical fibers are now the technology of choice for many new business installations. By 1990, a substantial fraction of large business customers will have direct fiber optic connections to telco switching centers for integrated voice, data, and video communications.

E. Construction and Leaseback of Video Distribution Facilities

The current FCC cross-ownership rules do not bar telcos from building video distribution plant and then selling or leasing it back to a cable operator. Several Bell Operating Companies, including Wisconsin Telephone, Michigan Bell, Illinois Bell, Bell of Pennsylvania, and Chesapeake and Potomac (C&P) have announced their interest in seeking out such arrangements.

Wisconsin Bell has entered into a construction/leaseback arrangement with TeleNational Communications, a relatively small cable operator, for the cable system serving Brookfield, Wisconsin. The telco will build a 54 channel coaxial cable system with two-way data capability and addressable, off-premises converters. Wisconsin Bell will keep control of the bandwidth for two-way services but has announced no plans to integrate these cable services with its telephone operations.

In 1983, Michigan Bell contacted city officials in Detroit about building a $150 million cable system for the city. The company also joined with Bloomfield Associates, a local group, to bid for two suburban cable franchises outside Detroit. Michigan Bell proposed to construct a conventional tree-and-branch system with dual cables providing more than 100 video channels plus two-way interactive capacity. The telco planned to lease the video channels back to its cable partner, but would maintain control over the two-way services. The franchises, however, were awarded to other applicants.

In February 1984, C&P Telephone agreed to construct and maintain a cable transport system for District Cablevision, Inc. (DCI), in the event

DCI is awarded a cable television franchise by the District of Columbia government. DCI is one of three applicants for the District of Columbia cable franchise. C&P proposes to construct a tree-and-branch dual coaxial cable distribution system with eight interconnected hubs. The first cable will employ newly developed 550 MHz cable amplifiers providing more than 70 downstream video channels. The second cable will be held in reserve for future growth. The proposed system represents state-of-the-art coaxial cable technology, but its design does not seem easily upgradable to switched video service, nor does it appear to be a step toward integration of voice, data, and video communications on a single telco facility.

IV. PROPOSED TELCO VIDEO DISTRIBUTION PROJECTS

A. Pacific Bell's Palo Alto Proposal

Pacific Bell's plan to build a wideband distribution network in northern California differs from other telco construction/leaseback proposals in several key respects:

— It includes substantial fiber optic facilities, as well as coaxial cable for video distribution.
— The sytem includes a switched fiber optic institutional network that integrates video, voice, and data services.
— The distribution system is linked with Pacific's regional network.
— Pacific will not lease the entire network capacity to others but will retain substantial bandwidth for current and future services.

1. Fiber Optics for Video Distribution

Pacific proposes to build a fiber optic supertrunk from the headend on Stanford University property to the two hubs serving Palo Alto subscribers. The supertrunk bundles 40 separate optical fibers, each carrying one digital television signal. At the hubs, the television signals are converted from digital to analog and inserted onto coaxial cables for distribution to subscribers.

The Pacific proposal does not extend optical fibers to the home, nor does it integrate video with voice and data services for residential subscribers. Subscribers would still have two separate wire facilities—

coaxial cable for video and a standard telephone wire pair for voice and data. Not by coincidence, however, the video distribution hubs are located at the telco central offices serving Palo Alto. Pacific Bell would thus have the basic system architecture in place to integrate all residential services on fiber optic loops when technology and costs permit.

2. Integrated Services on the Institutional Network

Pacific's plan for the institutional network serving Palo Alto and surrounding communities does integrate services over switched fiber optic facilities. Pacific proposes to install three fiber optic pairs, each with digital data capacity of 135 Mbps, to Stanford University and more than 60 other businesses, government offices, and schools. The institutional network could handle 250 video teleconferencing channels at the 1.5 Mbps (T1) data rate, as well as digital voice and data services.

Pacific sees the institutional network as a natural extension of its present services to business and government customers. The Palo Alto video proposal provides Pacific with an opportunity to upgrade existing facilities and market new services such as video teleconferencing to its institutional subscribers.

3. Regional Interconnection

Pacific's proposal also calls for direct interconnection of the video distribution and institutional networks to the company's regional facilities. Technically, this is readily accomplished by co-locating the cable distribution hubs at the telco central offices. Like other telcos, Pacific has a substantial fiber optic interexchange network in place that can carry communications to and from the Palo Alto system.

The regional interconnect could be used, for example, to transmit educational video programs from Stanford University to homes, businesses, and schools throughout the Bay Area. Pacific also emphasizes its use for regional advertising sales on cable systems—an application that would compete directly with the microwave Bay Area Interconnect run by cable companies. But voice, data, and other nonvideo business services constitute the chief interconnect applications. By tying the institutional network with Pacific's other facilities, the telco can offer its business and institutional customers a complete range of services fully interconnected with the outside world.

4. Telco Control of Bandwidth

Perhaps the most important distinction between Pacific's proposal and other telco construction/leaseback arrangements is the carrier's ongoing control of system bandwidth. In other proposals, the telcos have leased the full capacity of the system to a cable operator. Pacific has no such idea in mind. It will make available 80 channels to the city of Palo Alto and other local governments so that they can seek "competitive bids from organizations wishing to manage the 80 channel system. Then the group they choose will sublease channels to competing service providers" (Pacific Telephone 1983). Pacific, however, will retain control over capacity beyond these 80 channels, specifically including the institutional network and any interactive services offered on the subscriber network.

Pacific thus would maintain control over any two-way services offered to business and residential customers. Moreover, it would control the video bandwidth over and above the 80 leased channels. Although the FCC cross-ownership rules now prohibit telcos from providing video programming services, the current climate of deregulation has spawned proposals to relax these rules and permit telcos to compete directly with cable operators (Noam 1982b). While Pacific has not indicated any intent to do so, the system it has proposed for Palo Alto gives it the technical capability to offer competitive program services if the regulatory rules change.

B. Video Distribution Systems in the United Kingdom

Many of the newly planned video distribution systems in the United Kingdom include some degree of telco participation and consequently deserve mention here. In December 1983, after years of government study commissions, "white papers," and false starts, the British Department of Trade and Industry awarded eleven cable franchises covering more than one million homes (table 6.3). British Telecom (BT), the government telecommunications authority slated to be privatized in late 1984, holds equity in five of the eleven winning applicants. Two U.S. cable companies (Time Inc.'s American Television & Communications subsidiary and Comcast Corp.) and three U.S. equipment suppliers (Jerrold, Scientific-Atlanta, and Oak) are also involved in winning proposals.

Table 6.3. Cable Systems in the United Kingdom

Area	Households	Cable Operator	Type of System Proposed (Supplier)
Aberdeen	75,000	Aberdeen Cable Services (British Telecom and American TV & Communications (ATC) are major shareholders)	tree-and-branch upgradable to star (BT)
Belfast	100,000	Ulster Cablevision (20% owned by BT; 20% owned by Thorn-EMI)	switched star (BT)
Coventry	100,000	Coventry Cable (100% owned by Thorn-EMI)	tree-and-branch upgradable to star (BT)
Croydon (London)	98,000	Croydon & Cable TV (20% owned by Racal-Oak)	switched star (Plessy-Scientific Atlanta (SA))
Ealing (London)	100,000	Cabletel Communications (20% owned by Comcast)	switched star (Plessy-SA)
Guilford	22,000	Rediffusion Consumer Electronics	switched star (Rediffusion)
North Glasgow	100,000	Clyde Cablevision	switched star (Plessy-SA)
South Liverpool	100,000	Merseyside Cablevision (30% owned by BT)	switched star (BT)
Swindon	53,000	Swindon Cable Service (majority owned by Thorn-EMI)	tree-and-branch upgradable to star
Westminster (London)	73,000	Westminster Cable (BT, Plessy and ATC major shareholders)	switched star (BT)
Windsor, Slough, and Maidenhead (London)	84,000	Windsor Television (GEC is major shareholder)	switched star (GEC-Jerrold)

The U.K. proposals appear technically more advanced and more adventurous than their U.S. counterparts. Eight of the eleven winning applicants proposed switched video systems of new design. Most called for fiber optic/coaxial cable hybrids. Most proposals also discussed integrating data and other interactive services with video distribution.

The proposed U.K. systems carry with them substantial technical risk, however. Israel Switzer, in a speech to the British Society of Cable Television Engineers, commented:

If you are willing to wait a few years, and if organizations exist willing to invest several hundred million dollars in developing and proving brand new technologies, you can have radically new and improved telecommunications systems truly fulfilling all of the promises that have been spewing from the publicists' word processors for the last year or so.

I am not against new technology development. I ask that such development be regarded realistically in terms of its cost and time scale. If Britain wants new cable services now, it will have to use modest extensions of existing technologies. If it is prepared to wait a while, Britain can have a completely new generation technology.

I have the impression that the task—time and money—involved in the widespread construction and commissioning of radically new cable systems in this country is being seriously underestimated. (Switzer 1983)

In most countries outside the United States and Canada, government Post, Telephone, and Telegraph (PTT) administrations will play major if not dominant roles in the development of video distribution systems. The PTTs may prefer to wait for switched video systems and all-digital integration of services rather than build today's state-of-the-art cable systems. As a government agency scheduled to go private, British Telecom occupies an interesting middle position between PTTs and U.S. telcos. If the switched systems designed by BT and others prove successful in the United Kingdom, they will provide both technical and business models to U.S. telcos considering active roles in video distribution.

V. TELCO/CABLE HYBRIDS FOR INTERACTIVE SERVICES

Despite enthusiasm for interactive services on cable, fewer than two percent of U.S. cable subscribers have access to operating two-way cable services. Warner Amex's Qube systems, the most visible of interactive cable projects, have failed to generate substantial revenues and no longer serve as models for two-way cable development. Yet service such as pay-per-view (PPV) movies, sports, and special events appear attractive to cable operators if subscribers can order them easily, on impulse, and at the last minute before the program begins. Without two-way cable, the most obvious way for a subscriber to request a pay-per-view program is to place a telephone call.

The hybrid cable/telephone concept involves using the cable system for downstream television program distribution and the telephone network for upstream data requests (figure 6.4). The concept is particularly attractive because the technical requirements are so asymmetric in the two directions. Delivery of the television program downstream requires a full 6 MHz channel, while the upstream request can easily be accommodated within the normal telephone bandwidth. Moreover, since virtually every household has telephone service, there is no need to develop two-way cable communications for pay-per-view or other services with low upstream data requirements. Alarm services, transactions, videotex—essentially all the services listed in table 6.1 except those requiring two-way video—can in principle use a hybrid approach.

Hybrid telco/cable services thus appear attractive for both partners. For the cable operator, they provide a relatively inexpensive return link for interactive services such as pay-per-view. The cable operator need not invest substantial capital in two-way cable communications that

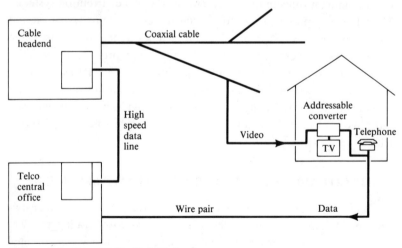

Figure 6.4. Telco/Cable Hybrid Services

hold at best marginal profit potential. For the telephone companies, hybrid services provide additional revenue from existing plant, as well as opportunities to form constructive partnerships with cable companies. A recent report by The Yankee Group discusses these opportunities in detail (Yankee Group 1983).

If the hybrid concept has such great appeal, why have telephone and cable companies not yet eagerly embraced it? Several obstacles presently stand in the way of successful partnerships:

— *Subscriber equipment.* Hybrid services require a touch-key telephone or a modular link from the cable converter to the phone. Systems designed to accommodate dial pulse phones are generally more expensive and cumbersome. Today only about half of U.S. households have touch-key telephones. Other households would have to purchase one for about $20. Cable converters with modular links to the telephone line have been designed by Zenith and other companies, but very few are actually in place.

— *Central office and headend equipment.* Although the hybrid concept is technically straightforward, equipment to implement it has not yet been installed in telco central offices or cable system headends. Hybrid pay-per-view systems must handle large numbers of incoming calls in the final half hour before a premium program begins. Equipment at the telco central office must receive the subscriber's call, record the necessary information, and pass it on to the cable headend, which will then signal the subscriber's converter to receive the requested program. Several prototype systems of this kind have been developed, but few are yet in operation.

— *Uncertain revenues from pay-per-view.* Although pay-per-view appeals to subscribers in concept, cable operators have had mixed results from their early experience with it. Some PPV programs, such as the movie version of "Pirates of Penzance," have drawn few paying customers and consequently have taken some of the luster from the PPV star. This may be due in part to a lack of marketing commitment by cable operators to PPV or to a dearth of programming attractive enough to command continued subscriber interest. Better marketing and programming may well make PPV an important source of cable revenues in future years. Today, however, PPV remains an attractive possibility for cable systems that has not yet turned into a clearly profitable reality.

— *Cable's suspicion of telco partnerships.* Some cable industry leaders still question the wisdom of forging alliances with telephone companies which may represent their principal future competitors. This attitude is by no means universal among cable operators, but it certainly acts today to restrain enthusiasm for hybrid joint ventures.

Still, with the telcos now actively seeking new businesses, we may expect to see several hybrid telco/cable ventures in the next several years. The Bell Regional Holding Companies are actively considering hybrids as part of their near-term marketing plans. And although cable companies are their most logical partners, telcos can also contemplate hybrid arrangements with DBS, MDS, or other video suppliers. DBS systems in particular will need to make arrangements for subscriber sales, installation, service, and billing, all of which the telephone companies are well-positioned to provide. The prospects for telco hybrids with these video distributors depend, of course, on their economic viability, a topic treated in other contributions to this volume. The possibility of such partnerships, however, will clearly influence negotiations between telcos and cable operators for hybrid services.

VI. THE FUTURE OF WIRED VIDEO DISTRIBUTION

A. Telco Scenarios

We are still some years away from the all-switched, all-digital, and all-fiber video distribution systems of the future. The telephone companies do not have video switches or distribution plant in place to deliver video programming to the home. Despite advances in data compression and related digital technologies, engineers do not expect to be able to deliver television-quality video over telephone wire pairs from telco central offices.[5]

If the telcos are to compete directly for video distribution, the key question is how quickly and under what circumstances they can justify installation of fiber optic local loops to the home. This can come about either through continued cost reduction of fiber optic distribution systems or by new consumer demand for high speed data or switched video services. Increased demand for electronic banking, videotex, and similar data services is not enough to justify fiber optics, nor is the planned evolution toward digital voice communications. These services can still be carried on copper wires.

Although fiber optic links to business customers are increasingly common, they are still too expensive today for residential installation. Most observers expect them to be cost justified for new residential customers within five years. Southern Bell reportedly will begin installing fiber optic loops to all new customers in 1985 (Baker 1983). However, it may be well into the next decade before telcos can justify replacing existing wire pairs for residential subscribers.

Nevertheless, many telephone companies appear to be positioning themselves to offer integrated voice, data, and video services to the home by the early 1990s. Their likely steps along this evolutionary path include the following:

— Telcos will move quickly to serve their major commercial customers with digital (principally fiber optic) links. Once in place, telcos can offer wide-band digital services such as video teleconferencing to these subscribers. In most metropolitan areas the telcos will have built switched, digital, fiber optic networks serving their large institutional customers before the end of the decade.

— Telcos will vigorously oppose attempts by cable operators to offer voice and two-way data services over cable. Every indication exists that telcos will seek to force cable companies to provide such services under state PUC regulations. Regulatory proceedings on this topic have been under way in New York, New Jersey, Connecticut, and Nebraska (Lloyd 1983). Even if the telcos are not ultimately successful in placing two-way cable services under state PUC jurisdiction, these tactics add delays and costs to cable efforts to develop interactive services.

— At the same time, telcos will offer agreements to cable operators for hybrid two-way services. Hybrid services add to telco revenues in the short term and keep cable companies from developing their own two-way facilities.

— Telcos will offer regional video interconnection of local cable systems, largely through the fiber optic interexchange facilities they are installing in metropolitan areas.

— Telcos will try to remove or relax the cross-ownership rules that prohibit them from owning cable systems within their service areas. The independent telephone companies have already petitioned the FCC to abandon these cross-ownership restrictions. If successful, this would permit the large independent telcos such as GTE to move aggressively into cable system operation.

— Many telcos will seek to gain experience in the video distribution business via leasebacks or through ambitious projects such as Pacific Bell's plan for Palo Alto. At this time, these projects seem more like targets of opportunity than steps in a well thought through strategy to compete with cable. The telcos are still defining their strategies in the postdivestiture era and have more urgent business priorities, such as protecting their commercial customer base against bypass carriers and moving toward usage-sensitive pricing. However, telcos want to position themselves to play a larger role in video distribution technology when and if regulatory rules allow them to do so.

— The telephone companies will seek to maintain their dominance over switched services to the home by upgrading the voice network to handle data as well. Local Area Data Transport (LADT), developed by Bell Laboratories, provides low-cost packet switching for videotex, networking among personal computers, and other residential data services. Bell South's LADT network in Miami is the first of many such installations planned by the RHCs.

— Installing fiber optic loops partway to residential customers represents the next step in the technical evolution of the telco subscriber network (Bohn, Buchen, and Rao 1983). The SLC™-96 system developed by AT&T Bell Laboratories handles up to ninety-six subscribers on an optical fiber transmission line running from the central office to a remote terminal closer to the customer. The last links to the home remain copper wires. Originally developed for rural applications, the Fiber-SLC systems are now less expensive than copper wires for many new urban and suburban installations.

— As planned at least through 1990, Fiber-SLC systems will carry digital voice and data, but not video, to the home. They fit into the overall telco strategic concept of an Integrated Services Digital Network or ISDN (Kostas 1984; Bhursi 1984; Wienski 1984). The ISDN goal in this decade is to provide every residential and business subscriber with digital capacity up to 144 kbps—enough for all the voice and data services listed in table 6.1, but still insufficient for television-quality video.

— Sometime after 1990 it will prove economically feasible to upgrade the remote terminal to a "remote switching unit" (RSU) capable of handling television-quality video and to install the final fiber link to the home. At that point, the telephone network will have all the technical pieces in place to provide switched, digital video on demand to any home or business customer.

B. Cable Scenarios

Despite some well-publicized financial problems within the cable television industry, cable's basic business of providing video entertainment to the home remains a healthy one. Cable systems in 1983 passed 55 million of the nation's 85 million households and served more than 30 million subscribers (Paul Kagan Associates 1983b). Forecasts for 1990 project cable passing more than 75 million homes and serving more than 48 million subscribers (Paul Kagan Associates 1983b; Yankee Group 1983). Cable's increasing presence makes building a second wired video distribution system to the home less attractive to the telcos or to anyone else.[6]

On the other hand, even after more than ten years of experimentation with two-way communications, cable companies have yet to develop successful businesses from interactive services. Revenues from the institutional cable networks serving New York City, Portland, Oregon, and a few other cities totaled less than $5 million in 1983. Most institutional cable networks are still developmental (Hanneman and LaRose 1983). Nevertheless, some likely technological and regulatory developments should enable cable systems to compete more effectively for non-video services in the years ahead:

— New technology for two-way, packet switched data and voice communication on cable will be commercially available in 1985. Two such systems are under development by the Jerrold Division of General Instrument Corp., a leading equipment supplier to the cable industry, and by PacketCable, Inc., a new company in Silicon Valley, California. These systems promise to be far more cost effective for interactive services on cable than were the Qube-like systems of the past.

— Cable operators can profit from the usage-sensitive pricing (USP) plans of the telephone companies. The RHCs and other telcos expect state PUC approval of some form of USP in their franchise areas within the next three years. Residential telco customers will then pay by the call or by the minute for services they now use on flat monthly rates. New data services such as videotex and networking among personal computers could be especially impacted by USP. The cable industry thus may see a real demand for data services on cable once the telcos put usage-sensitive pricing into effect.

— If regulations permit, cable systems can offer bandwidth to long distance carriers to bypass the local telco network. MCI and GTE Sprint have already sought to lease some two-way cable channels for the voice and data services they provide to their customers. Channel leasing represents a tiny business to cable operators today. But as packet switching technology lowers the cost of these services on cable and as the telcos move to USP or otherwise increase their prices, more substantial business opoortunities may open up in the mid- to late-1980s.

— Cable systems will install more fiber optic supertrunks linking their satellite receivers, headends, and hubs.

— Improved technical performance and cost will make cable operators take a closer look at Mini-Hub and similar switched systems employing optical fiber links to the home. By the end of this decade, these systems may well prove cost-competitive with tree-and-branch coaxial cable networks.

C. Integration or Competition?

Cable systems and telcos operate distinctly different businesses today, with different technical facilities. Cable systems have the video distribution links without the switches. Telcos have the switches without the video links. However, it is clear that the technologies supporting both businesses are quickly converging. Certainly by the end of the century video distribution technology will have evolved to switched, fiber optic systems. But this does not necessarily demand a single integrated telecommunications link to the home. There are no technical reasons why two separate systems cannot coexist and compete for services.

Economies of scale appeal strongly to regulators and engineers, but the argument for them is by no means compelling. The principal economy lies in using the same ducts or poles for all video, voice, and data services. The additional cost savings from integrating services on a single switched, fiber optic system seem relatively small for newly built systems and even less if a well-functioning video distribution system is already in place.[7]

The emergence of high definition television (TDTV) in the 1990s does not materially improve the economy of scale argument or change the competitive equation between telcos and cable systems. HDTV requires much greater bandwidth than conventional NTSC television signals and represents an ideal service for digital transmission over optical fiber loops. However, coaxial cable technology is advancing as well (table 6.2) and should be capable of carrying HDTV channels along with conventional video channels in cable distribution systems planned for the late 1980s and 1990s.

The real battle between telcos and cable companies will probably focus on metropolitan area refranchising (and any remaining new builds) toward the end of this decade. By then, the telephone companies will have adjusted to the Bell System breakup, will have begun to implement their new business strategies, and will have gained some experience in video distribution. The cable industry will have wired most of the major cities and will have access to 75 percent or more of the nation's households. Fiber optic technology will be available to both.

In the end, the choice between one or two wideband links to the home will most likely be made on social and political rather than on technical and economic grounds. We may well conclude that the advantages of maintaining competitive systems outweigh whatever costs might be saved by integrating all services on a single fiber. On the other hand, financial problems of cable companies, or telephone companies, or both, may require consolidation under a single organizational entity. It is possible, too, that after years of chaos resulting from the Bell System breakup, society might demand a return to a single regulated carrier (Oettinger and Weinhaus 1983). What is critical to understand is that the technology and costs of wired video distribution support either an integrated or a competitive solution.

Notes

1. On January 1, 1984, Pacific Telephone became Pacific Bell, part of the Pacific Telesis Group, a Bell Regional Holding Company.

2. This paper focuses on "wired" video distribution technologies such as coaxial cable and fiber optics. Over-the-air video distribution via satellite, terrestrial microwave, and other broadcasting technologies is discussed in other papers.

3. State-of-the-art cable systems provide subscribers with addressable converters that can be controlled from the headend to pass or reject individual channels or tiers. Subscribers can then choose among the video channels or other services for which they have paid.

4. Satellite programmers eventually will be able to offer regional buys to advertisers through increased use of satellite spot beams covering smaller geographic areas. This would remove part of the economic incentive for terrestrial interconnects.

5. Single-channel television distribution over telephone wire pairs is feasible over short distances and can serve specialized applications such as some hotel, motel, and apartment installations.

6. A recent report by a well-respected consulting firm concludes that fiber optic installations by electric power utilities could seriously challenge both telcos and cable companies for video distribution (IRD 1983). Although possible, this scenario seems unlikely, given the current financial problems, regulatory constraints, and management styles of U.S. electric power companies.

7. The cost of video switching represents the principal uncertainty in estimating economies of scale for integrated video, voice, and data services. Although very expensive today, video switching equipment costs are declining and could drop markedly through advances in integrated optics and optoelectronics. A full discussion of these costs is beyond the scope of this paper.

Comment: Telephone and Cable Issues

John K. Hopley

Cable systems and telephone companies operate distinctly different businesses today with different technical facilities; cable systems have video distribution links to homes without switching capabilities, and telephone companies have local loops to homes and businesses on a switched basis but without video capability. But Walter Baer notes that the technologies supporting both enterprises are quickly converging and that it is an important question whether the cable companies and telephone companies will become rivals or partners in video distribution.

My central comment on Baer's article concerns its final conclusion that the principal factors that will influence the cable and telephone industries in the post-divestiture era are market definition, efficient technology, and the economics of efficient pricing structures. These factors will carry greater influence in creating new telecommunications services and delivery techniques than social and political factors; however, in regulated industries, social and political considerations often dominate the manner in which new markets are established and the extent to which existing markets are managed. Telephone companies are mindful of their new roles as communicators in the post-divestiture era. Greater energy and more astute planning will dominate the way they create new markets in the future.

The focus of telephone expertise will be to address three principal activities over the next five years: the need to reevaluate traditional switched and dedicated narrowband voice and data networks employing upgraded technologies of digital switching and fiber interoffice trunk plant; the need to plan new switched and dedicated wideband voice, data, and video networks; and the need to move as rapidly as possible, in the context of the social and political realities of existing regulation, to reorient the present pricing structures from those based on large cross-subsidies to those that place greater emphasis on cost-based pricing. To a large extent, the ability of the telephone companies and regulatory agencies to accomplish this last goal will determine the success of the companies to enter new markets—with or without participation by cable companies.

Existing voice and data network prices are now set well in excess of embedded, fully allocated costs, thereby generating revenues to subsidize the basic exchange loop connections to the central office. Interstate long distance prices are set at artificially high levels through the transfer of a portion of local exchange plant costs to the interstate enterprise via the separation and division of the revenue process. Similarly, intrastate long distance and local network prices are set artifically above traffic-sensitive costs through a similar but less formal process whereby state regulatory agencies have priced these network services above cost largely on a judgment basis in order to hold local exchange prices to affordable levels.

To the extent that large institutional customers and residential customers with high network usage are faced with prices that exceed the costs of telephone networks and competitors' prices, they will move their voice and data requirements to lower-priced bypass systems. As greater amounts of traffic are displaced from the established networks to those employing wideband fiber transmission, a growing source of revenue will be developed by competitors, enabling them to undertake wider penetration in video markets.

Uneconomic bypass of the telephone companies' networks is harmful because it results in the misallocation of society's resources by establishing wasteful and duplicative networks which require large amounts of capital that could be used more productively elsewhere in society. Uneconomic bypass can also lead to the stranding of existing costly telephone company plant which has not been fully depreciated and which requires a continuing stream of revenue to provide for capital recovery.

The contribution from network rates, which were designed historically to keep local telephone rates at affordable levels, would also be lost to the bypass systems. Competitive bypass systems and cable companies recognize no obligation to provide a contribution to hold basic exchange rates of telephone customers at affordable levels, although many state regulatory agencies and legislative bodies around the country are reviewing this situation.

The presence of uneconomic bypass thus stifles healthy competition, and telephone companies ought to be allowed to establish fair, cost-based, and where appropriate, market-driven prices so that they may compete on equal terms with other suppliers of telecommunications services. The deployment of the newest technology to create lower operational costs is also inhibited because, under the present pricing scheme, the telephone companies are severely hampered in recovering the capital investment in new technology when faced with competition from uneconomic bypass. The established telephone companies must continuously modernize their plant. When their hands are in a sense tied, they are precluded from taking reasonable and responsive pricing actions to compete fairly in the new environment.

Greater overall economic benefits would result from a system where fair and equal competition is permitted. When the telephone companies are not constrained from making technological and operational improvements in the design and marketing of their services, their rates reflect true economic value. Telephone companies must offer subscribers new options, including a wide array of wideband value-added services, at rates which are consistent with costs. If permitted by regulators, fair and equal competition by all parties in the marketplace will drive the prices of telecommunications to their proper levels.

The president of New York Telephone Company, William C. Ferguson, recently raised these issues with the New York State Public Service Commission, and outlined two approaches for the commission's consideration: It could decide not to allow bypass of the established telephone network, or it could establish a course of action that would permit the orderly restructuring of existing network prices and access charges applicable to other carriers to permit fair competition among all carriers.

The New York Telephone Company does not believe that maintaining monopoly control is either manageable over the long run or desirable in light of the speed with which new technologies of ever decreasing costs are being developed for the transport of information. The very nature of the rapidly expanding market for telecommunications—with service provided by the established telephone companies, by companies employing their own bypass systems, and by cable companies emerging into the fields of data and video transmission—will bring high-volume transmission systems employing new technology at lower costs within the reach of many business customers.

The massive extent of internal cross-subsidies within New York Telephone's pricing system, which distort network costs of toll and local calling, is shown in table C6.1. Although these data apply only to New York Telephone, most other telephone companies around the country have similar required subsidies. New York Telephone has recommended a five-point plan which provides the basic framework for a workable and competitive pricing structure. It allows adequate time for all parties to adopt their respective budgets and capital programs devoted to tele-communications services and precludes disruptive rate impacts on basic subscriber rates while providing a fair and equitable pricing structure to all of the carriers in the state. Most important, the plan provides for the long-term continuation of universal basic telephone service and for the benefits of programmed rate reductions in most usage rates and carrier access charges at specified intervals. The key elements of such a policy follow:

1. Maintenance of Universal Service

The longstanding policy of regulatory commissions and telephone companies has been to make access to the telephone network available to as many people as possible by keeping the price of basic access as low as possible. This objective is achieved first by offering some form of low-priced telephone service to people with modest incomes. After the recent restructuring of the telecommunications industry resulting from divestiture, the New York Telephone Company was the first telephone company in the nation to come forward with a sound and work-able proposal that recognizes its responsibility for the continuance of a low-priced service option. This proposed service, known as Life Line, is targeted specifically to customers with low incomes. With highly subsidized monthly rates and low connection charges, it will ensure the continuation of universal telephone service in New York State.

Table C6.1. Required Subsidy from Existing Network Prices to Subsidize Basic Telephone Exchange Services (Millions)

Service Category		
—Local coin telephone (10¢)	$	85
—Directory assistance calling		35
—Business connection charges		5
—Business message rate local line		225
—Residence connection charges		60
—Residence flat rate local line		545
—Residence message rate local line		720
—Residence basic budget local line		115
Total		$1,790

Source: New York Telephone, 1983.

2. Orderly Transition in Network Rates
3. Orderly Transition in Access Charge Tariffs
4. Repricing of Usage and Access Charge Contribution
5. Pricing Flexibility To Meet the Changing Marketplace Demands

The large established regional telephone companies and the smaller independent companies, while considering the possibilities of joint ventures with cable companies, are hesitant and even skeptical of such contractual arrangements in the video marketplace. Services such as pay-per-view have not proven themselves to be widely marketable. Although little capital would be required for upstream signaling requirements over telephone company local loops, the fundamental question remains as to the long-term possibility of sustaining the home video market on a switched basis. The telephone companies require more research to ascertain the desirability of entering residential markets, although hybrid telephone-cable systems require little new capital on their part.

The telephone companies are focusing their attention on significant market research oriented toward the large commercial and industrial sectors where the transport of wideband data and video is envisioned to be a vast market. It is here that telephone companies see the possibility of profitably deploying their own wideband fiber transmission systems with switchable capabilities. Undoubtedly, cable companies also sense the vast scope of the market and are conducting similar research and engineering studies pursuant to entry. Inevitably, the two industries will compete head on because neither presently has fiber links directly to the customer's premises. Large amounts of capital will be required to upgrade the local loop plant; consequently both industries will gear their market approach to well-defined services and carefully placed facilities which promise the greatest return. Initially the wide band commercial markets will develop slowly on a customer by customer basis in the large metropolitan regions and in selected high-density suburban industrial parks.

The telephone companies, operating under present regulatory ground rules, run greater risks in these new emerging markets than unregulated cable companies do. Prices for wideband services furnished by telephone companies on a fiber basis would ordinarily be established on the basis of statewide average cost factors employing fully allocated loadings for common and joint access costs. Under these ground rules, the telephone industry will be hindered economically in their pricing efforts and will have to carry the day in the open market relying on their reputation as a quality provider of service. The new entrants, however, are not known for poor service, and their pricing structures, set on direct costs without social pricing loadings, underprice established telephone tariffs by significant amounts.

This raises the issue of the "level playing field" in the new competitive era of telecommunications. Telephone companies want regulatory forebearance in order to compete equally. The cable companies want no regulatory controls beyond those necessary to obtain franchises to place cables. In this context, Baer's conclusion is correct that social and political factors will influence the outcome. Telephone companies will attempt to influence regulatory agencies and will seek changed ground rules to price according to the market. Some evidence exists that the state commissions are beginning to see the problems of traditional regulation in a competitive environment because of the growing record of bypass of the established networks.

In the main, whether by legislation or by regulatory reform, the social factors to be considered in the context of emerging competitive technologies and wideband services will be resolved by the underlying forces of the market and economic pressures. Most telephone companies will plan for the deployment of their own wideband networks, believing this to be a natural evolution of their mission in contrast to approaching the market on a partnership basis with cable companies. I predict that following a period of three to five years of regulatory revision, during which cable companies will have an advantage in the market unless blocked by legislation, they will basically continue to provide entertainment video distribution to the home market with some limited successes in business data and video conferencing. Telephone companies will become aggressive suppliers of wideband data and video on a switched basis in commercial markets. More development of new, low-cost technologies and greater market definition are required, however, before telephone companies address the residence market in the fields of interactive data. It is doubtful that the residential market will be greatly developed in the near term for interactive video services by either telephone companies or cable companies. While some telephone companies have opposed congressional adoption of cable legislation, that opposition is not expressed as intentionally barring cable companies from handling voice and data servcies. It reflects the need for fairness in the marketplace where both industries can meet the potential customer on equal pricing terms. Two sets of costing and pricing rules cannot be applied to a common marketplace, nor can one industry be held to inflexible tariffs while the other industry has greater freedom in addressing changing market conditions.

The market pie is now expanding at a rapid rate, and both telephone and cable industries will search for their independent markets.

7

Prerecorded Home Video and the Distribution of Theatrical Feature Films

DAVID WATERMAN

CONTENTS

  I. Introduction
 II. Prerecorded Home Video Software Distribution
    A. Consumer Demand for Hardware and Software
    B. Market Structure of Software Distribution
    C. Pricing and Product Diversity
III. Competition of Prerecorded Home Video with Other Media
    A. The Theatrical Film Release Sequence
    B. Prerecorded Home Video in the Price Tiering Sequence
 IV. Prospects for Prerecorded Home Video
  V. The Effects of Prerecorded Home Video

1. INTRODUCTION

In 1982 and 1983 prerecorded videocassettes began taking their turn as the fastest growing of the new media for video program distribution. The "home video" industries of videocassettes and videodiscs are important to understand because they are not only changing the economic system by which media products are delivered but they are also disrupting the framework of copyright law governing that system. Prevailing industry forecasts maintain that household penetration of videocassette recorders (VCRs) alone will reach at least 25–30 percent by 1990, with some predicting as much as 50 percent penetration (*Videoweek*, October 10, 1983, p. 6) While RCA's decision to stop production of the CED videodisc player in 1984 was a setback for program distributors, discs represented a relatively minor portion of the market.

This chapter deals with the distribution process of prerecorded videocassettes and videodiscs and how these media compete with alternative delivery systems. Understanding the competition among video media greatly benefits from attention to the process of theatrical feature film distribution. Theatrical features are by far the dominant product on prerecorded software as well as on pay-TV systems, and remain among the most important programming ingredients of advertiser-supported television. Consumer demand for all the video media, as well as movies shown in theaters, are closely related.

The thesis of this chapter is that prerecorded home video successfully competes as a delivery system by offering distributors more efficient, "unbundled" methods of pricing programs to consumers. This direct, unbundled pricing is far superior to that of advertiser-supported broadcasting and, in important respects, is superior to the "bundled" pricing of the subscription-supported pay-TV systems. Home video's better pricing can significantly increase the revenues a distributor earns from a given supply of programs. As a result, its main impact on advertiser-supported broadcasting is likely to be not only the direct diversion of viewers' time but also the indirect effect of increased competition and inflation in the program supply market.

A handicap to home video's ability to compete with other pay media has been the First Sale Doctrine of the 1976 Copyright Act, which constrains the distributor's ability to control the pricing of prerecorded software. Congress may modify the doctrine before this article appears, but comments on this issue are offered, if only for posterity's sake.

II. PRERECORDED HOME VIDEO SOFTWARE DISTRIBUTION

A. Consumer Demand for Hardware and Software

Table 7.1 documents the explosive growth of home video hardware and software. By early fall 1984, videocassette and videodisc hardware had reached into about 16 percent of U.S. TV households, with about half of that growth in the previous twelve months alone. Especially in the case of VCRs, the demand has been fueled by steadily dropping hardware

Table 7.1. Growth of Home Video Hardware and Software (Wholesale to Dealers), 1979–1983 (in millions)

	1979	1980	1981	1982	1983
Hardware					
Videocassette recorders					
units	0.5	0.8	1.4	2.0	4.1
$	N/A	N/A	$1,300	$1,550	$2,150
Videodisc players[a]					
units	—	—	N/A	0.2	0.3
$	—	—	N/A	$65	$75
Software					
Blank cassettes					
units	10	15.0	23.0	34.0	57.0
$	N/A	N/A	$304	$384	$485
Prerecorded cassettes					
units	2.6	3.8	5.0	5.5	9.5
$	$75	$120	$270	$344	$400
Videodiscs[a]					
units	—	—	N/A	5.0	8.0
$	—	—	N/A	N/A	$150

SOURCES: Knowledge Industry Publications, Inc., Electronic Industries Association.
[a]The CED videodisc, which has dominated the market, was introduced in 1981.

prices in the last few years. In 1984, VCRs ranged in price from about $300 to about $1200 for high fidelity models.[1] Videodisc players ranged from about $200 for the lower-priced CED machines to about $700 for the more sophisticated and generally superior laser disc models. In spite of their higher prices, VCR sales have dominated disc player sales by more than a ten to one margin. With the demise of the CED player, the disc has become a negligible market element; only about 100,000 laser disc players have been sold in the United States, compared to over 500,000 for the CED player.

The greater popularity of VCRs is due to their ability to record programs off the air. This is suggested by the higher sales of blank tape in contrast to prerecorded tapes, as shown in table 7.1. Surveys, in fact, consistently show that the main consumer use of VCRs is time-shift viewing—the recording of programs from broadcast and pay television for watching at a more convenient time (U.S. Congress 1983d). Nevertheless, prerecorded home video programming is emerging as a major domestic industry. Analysts placed total retail volume of domestic sales and rentals of prerecorded tapes and discs at the $1 billion-plus level in

1983, about one-third to one-half of current consumer expenditures on pay cable TV subscriptions (*Videoweek,* January 23, 1984, p. 7).

An important advantage for home video's ability to compete with other media is the great product diversity it offers. As of early 1984, about 6,000 titles were reported to be available on tape (*Videoweek,* January 2, 1984, p. 8), though only about 1,200 appeared on the CED videodisc and much fewer than that on laser disc (*Videoweek,* October 10, 1983, p. 6). Theatrical feature films, which are usually made available four to nine months after their initial theatrical release, dominate the program fare of both cassettes and discs; table 7.2 demonstrates this fact for videocassettes. A small proportion of exercise and "how to" tapes included in the "Instructional and Informational" category make up the majority of all programming that is now originally produced for videocassettes. A rapidly growing category has been music video, an outgrowth of MTV's success on cable television. The available feature films on cassette include the majority of all Hollywood movies released in the past few years and hundreds of old Hollywood, foreign, and cult features. Home video brings you not only *Star Wars* but *Casablanca* and *I Walked with a Zombie.*

Prices for prerecorded software are extremely varied and are changing rapidly. Prerecorded cassettes are both sold and rented to consumers. Rentals overwhelm sales; retailer surveys indicate that rentals usually make up 80 to 99 percent of all their transactions. This is not surprising in light of relative prices. Cassettes can usually be rented for $1 to $5 for a 24- to 48-hour period, while sales prices, generally $24.95 to $79.95, are exceedingly high by electronic media standards. Unlike cassettes, a high proportion of videodiscs are sold rather than rented. One explanation is certainly that sales prices have been lower

Table 7.2. Prerecorded Videocassette Software by Type of Programming (Wholesale Volume, 1983)

Theatrical features	67%
Adult films	14
Instructional and informational	7
Children's	7
Music	4
Other	1
TOTAL	100%

SOURCE: *Videoweek,* January 23, 1984; F. Eberstadt & Co., Inc. data.

for discs, generally $19.95 to $34.95, while rental prices (where rentals are available) have been in the same $1 to $5 range. As a result, owners of disc players have a far greater tendency to build libraries of pre-recorded programming than do VCR owners. Table 7.1—which shows unit sales of discs at nearly as high a level as prerecorded cassettes, despite the much smaller number of disc players in use—underscores this trend.

How do the home video software industries create such great diversity at these radically different prices?

B. Market Structure of Software Distribution

Even though the industry's structure remains unsettled, outlines are emerging. As illustrated in figure 7.1, five stages to the videocassette production-distribution process can be identified. Program producers for videocassettes are mostly the same as for the movie industry because the main product is movies. In addition, hundreds of other entities produce music videos, instructional and other programming. Distributors (often referred to as "distributors/manufacturers") are mainly the theatrical movie distributors because they own the rights to the best-selling movies. Table 7.3 shows their identities and 1983 market shares. Most of the movie studios have simply formed a home video division.

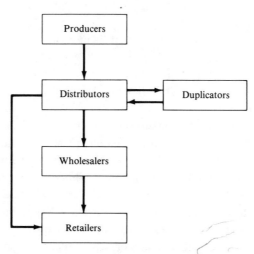

Figure 7.1. The Prerecorded Videocassette Distribution Process

Table 7.3. Distributor Market Shares of Prerecorded Videocassette Shipments, 1983

Distributor	% Share, Prerecorded Units[a]
CBS/Fox	18%
Paramount	18
RCA/Columbia	12
Warner	10
MGM/UA	10
MCA	8
Vestron	6
Disney	6
Thorn EMI	5
Embassy	3
Others	4
TOTAL	100%

SOURCE: *Videoweek*, January 2, 1984.
[a]Not including adult titles.

Two of the major firms, CBS/Fox and RCA/Columbia, are joint ventures managed separately from the film studios involved. All these distributors actively compete to buy the home video rights to independently produced and distributed theatrical features and to nontheatrical programming. As a result, the larger distributors offer several hundred titles, including many the movie studios have retrieved from their film libraries. Virtually all revenues, however, are derived from recent major theatrical features during the period immediately following their release on cassettes. Consumer acceptance of them varies as drastically as their popularity with theatergoers. In the duplication stage hundreds of videocassette recorders simultaneously copy the original tape. The duplicator then ships the tapes in bulk under instruction from the distributor to wholesaler warehouses.

The wholesalers negotiate advance orders with retailers and deliver the tapes by reshipping them in smaller quantities. Although wholesalers usually concentrate their activities within geographic regions, they do not retain exclusive geographic rights or dominate local areas. Most important, distributors do not grant exclusive selling rights to a wholesaler for major films. The result is that wholesaling is a free-for-all; firms compete intensely for orders from widely dispersed retailers. Various reports put the number of wholesalers now operating on a national basis at 20 to 30 and steadily declining.

Some of the major distributors avoid the wholesale stage altogether by direct sale and shipment to retail outlets, but to date, such distribution has accounted for a small share of volume. Independent wholesalers have been at an advantage because of the large number of different titles they have to offer. Direct distribution has therefore been primarily to large chain stores and department stores for which transactional economies of scale for individual titles are sufficiently high to compensate for the low number of titles available. Most of the thousands of retailers across the country are specialty stores, some of which also sell audio records and tapes. Growth of nonspecialty outlets has been occurring very rapidly, notably among supermarket chains, department stores and movie theaters.

Videodisc distribution mostly piggybacks on cassette distribution. The main difference is that RCA, the primary manufacturer of CED discs, and Pioneer, the primary manufacturer of laser discs, also distribute discs through their own hardware outlets as well as through other retailers. Usually, however, the disc manufacturers do "custom pressings" for the cassette distributors, which relegates them to a role like that of videotape duplicators.

C. Pricing and Product Diversity

The diversity in the home video industries is based on the fact that economies of scale in manufacturing and physical distribution are reached at very low output levels. The most popular movie titles enjoy a distribution of 100,000 or more videotape units—*Flashdance* (225,000), *Star Trek II* (150,000), and *Raiders of the Lost Ark* (550,000) are examples (*Videoweek*, September 5, 1983, p. 2; *Videoweek*, November 22, 1983, p. 2). More typical movie titles are in the 10,000 to 25,000 unit range. But major distributors interviewed indicate that titles with expected wholesale shipments of as low as 3,000 units are economical to distribute. Many programs, especially those of the smaller distributors, sell fewer than 1,000 units, which is fewer than 1 per 10,000 videocassette machines in the market. High plant costs characterize tape duplication and particularly disc pressing, but most production economies are realized at these low levels, as they are in the distribution process. Each firm acts as a "common carrier" to all program suppliers, which permits physical distribution economies to be quickly reached.

Prerecorded software prices are determined by both economic and legal factors. First, the cost of the physical process of distributing individual cassette and disc units is high. The prevailing allocations of revenues for typically priced units are shown in table 7.4. Manufacturing costs alone are in the $7.50 to $10 range for both cassettes and discs. The large shares to the distributor include inventory and operating expenses and apparently escalating budgets for advertising and promotion. The large variations of retail sales prices for cassettes of $24.95 to $79.95 and for discs $19.95 to $34.95 are partly the result of price experimentation by distributors and a generally downward current price movement[2]. Of greatest interest is the relationship between cassette retail sale prices and their dramatically lower rental prices. This relationship, and that of videocassette to videodisc sale prices, is partly determined by copyright law, a topic we return to below.

III. COMPETITION OF PRERECORDED HOME VIDEO WITH OTHER MEDIA

The competitive role of videocassettes and videodiscs as program delivery systems is best understood in the context of the time release sequence for their dominant programming of theatrical features; the age of the film product is the most important way prerecorded software is differentiated from other media.

Table 7.4. Distribution of Revenues by Industry Branch in Prerecorded Software Sales, 1984

	Videocassettes @ $50 Retail		Videodiscs @ $30 Retail	
	%	$	%	$
Producer/copyright holder	12	5.80	12	3.48
Distributor	28	14.20	21	6.42
Duplicator	18	9.00	25	7.50
Wholesaler	12	6.00	12	3.60
Retailer	30	15.00	30	9.00
	100%	$50.00	100%	$30.00

SOURCE: Waterman and Associates.

A. The Theatrical Film Release Sequence

1. The Film Distribution Process

The first step in the film distribution process is the acquisition of film rights by distributors, for there is little actual vertical integration of theatrical distribution into film production. In most cases, distributors finance films made by independent producers or purchase distribution rights to completed films. There are about twenty national distributors, but six of them, the "majors," consistently earn 80 to 90 percent of domestic theatrical rentals, as shown in table 7.5. The year to year fluctuation in their market shares reflects the notoriously high risk of film production, but the same six or seven firms have nevertheless dominated the industry for over forty years (Waterman 1979).

It is significant that for major films, the distributor usually obtains the rights not only to domestic theater distribution but also to foreign and all domestic video markets including pay TV, broadcast TV, and home video. By purchasing the rights to all theatrical and ancillary markets, distributors gain the opportunity to choose the "windows," the number of exhibitions within each window, the timing and amount of advertising, and, to the extent allowed by technology and the law, retail prices.

The prevailing sequence of theatrical movie distribution is shown in figure 7.2. There are many variations, but this is a representative pattern. After a movie is released to theaters, it is distributed shortly

Table 7.5. Distributor Market Shares of Domestic Theatrical Rentals, United States and Canada, 1977–1983

	1977	1978	1979	1980	1981	1982	1983	Averages 1977–83
Columbia	12%	11%	11%	14%	13%	10%	14%	12%
MGM/UA	18	11	15	7	9	11	10	12
Paramount	10	24	15	16	15	14	14	15
Twentieth Century Fox	20	13	9	16	13	14	21	15
Universal	12	17	15	20	14	30	13	17
Warner Brothers	14	13	20	14	18	10	17	15
All Others	14	11	15	13	18	11	11	13

SOURCE: *Daily Variety*, January 12, 1984.

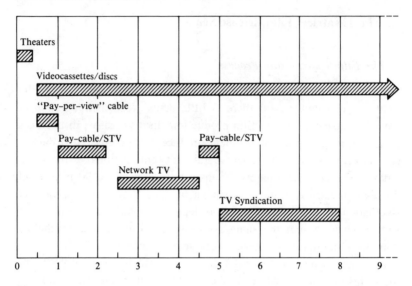

Figure 7.2. Representative Release Sequence for a Major Theatrical Feature, 1984. Source: Waterman and Associates (1984).

thereafter as home video. It then appears on pay-television systems, network television, and then on pay-television again and is finally syndicated to independent TV stations where contracts for films not reclaimed by cable may be renewed for decades. "Pay-per-view" exhibition roughly coincides with home video release but has been a negligible part of total revenues because few cable systems have the required technology.

Although theaters are still the dominant source of distributor income, the distribution process has become increasingly oriented toward this motley collection of downstream video markets; they now account for 40 to 50 percent of domestic net revenues from theatrical features, including about 5 percent from prerecorded home video (Waterman and Associates 1984; "Cablecasting" 1983). The process of exclusive first-run theater showings followed by progressively wider release to "subrun" theaters has declined. Simultaneous nationwide releases to 500 to 1,000 or even more theaters including as many as 40 to 60 within a single urban area, are increasingly common for major films. A very successful feature may stay in theaters for six months or more, but others are withdrawn much sooner to maximize their value in ancillary markets.

2. Price Tiering

The release sequence is essentially a method of price discrimination by theatrical distributors, or to use a less incriminating term, "price tiering." The value of a movie declines with its age. Movies are first released in theaters at highest prices to "high value" consumers who are most eager to see them. Others who are less eager, but will pay something, may wait to see them a year or more later on pay-TV. Those unwilling to pay anything, "low value" consumers, wait three years or more until the movies are released to the free television market. These "high value" and "low value" consumer markets are segmented by means of the time lags between release to each successive medium.

The pre-television theater distribution system represented the classic example of price tiering. As illustrated by the system used in Chicago in the 1930s (table 7.6), "Class A" films were successively priced in major cities at 75¢, 50¢, 40¢, etc., to as low as 10¢ in a series of twelve or more separate theater runs over a period of several months (Conant 1960). Common knowledge of the elapsed time before the movie would appear at later run theaters separated the "high value" from the "low value" patrons because the former were less willing to wait for lower prices.

Broadcast television and the new video delivery systems have taken the place of subrun theaters in the price tiering sequence. Price tiering at the retail level is harder to identify in the differentiated collection of new technologies, but the outlines are evident. Single pay-per-view exhibitions of movies on the QUBE cable system, for example, are usually priced at $3 to $4 per household, compared to only $10 for a monthly menu of sixteen to twenty new features appearing several weeks later on pay cable.

Achieving the optimal release strategy for an individual theatrical feature is as much an art as a science;[3] underlying the art, however, the role of each delivery system in the modern release sequence is determined by its usefulness to the distributor as a price tiering tool. The distributor's ultimate interest is not retail price, of course, but the net revenue per viewer which the delivery system can earn. This will depend on the delivery system's costs, on its attractiveness to consumers, and, in particular, on the technology's pricing mechanism. In trading subrun theaters for electronic media, the distributor achieved lower delivery costs but sacrificed the pricing efficiency of the theater turnstile.

Table 7.6. The Chicago System of Release for "Class A" Feature Films, 1939

(1) Run Stage	(2) Number of Theaters Classified as Eligible	(3) Admission Price	(4) Run Length	(5) Temporal Clearance[a]
Loop First Run	7	75¢	1 week or longer	3 weeks
A Pre-Release	9	50¢	1 week	1 week
B Pre-Release	20	40¢	½ week	0–1½ weeks
C Pre-Release	49	30¢	2–4 days	0–5 days
1st week, general release	81	25¢	2–3 days	0–5 days
2d week, general release	115	20¢	2–3 days	0–5 days
3d week, general release	40	N/A	2–3 days	0–5 days
4th week, general release	⎫	N/A	2–3 days	0–5 days
5th week, general release	23	N/A	2–3 days	0–5 days
6th week, general release	in	N/A	2–3 days	0–5 days
7th week, general release	⎭ total	N/A	2–3 days	0–5 days
TOTALS	310		approx. 17 weeks	

SOURCE: Conant (1960). Compiled by the author from text discussion.

[a] A temporal clearance is a guarantee to a prior run theater that a certain film will not be released to any subrun theater within a certain time interval following the end of the film's run at the prior run theater. For a third through eleventh run, the theater had a choice for the clearance time within the indicated range. In First Week General Release, for example, the theater could exhibit the film for any 2 or 3 day period within an assigned one week interval. Any remainder of the week at the end of the run was clearance time.

Distributors can be expected to place delivery systems with direct unbundled pricing toward the front of the release sequence because those media can more effectively skim the surplus from high value consumers and therefore return higher net revenues per viewer to them. Contrast, for example, broadcast television, pay cable, and pay-per-view cable. The hapless pricing mechanism of advertiser-supported broadcasting offers no possibility of segmenting high value from low value consumers, banishing them to the end of the sequence. Monthly pay cable is more efficient, but the bundling of sixteen to twenty movies together for a single monthly subscription price—of about $10—cannot take advantage of high intensities of demand for individual movies within the group. Pay-per-view cable is direct, unbundled pricing; it permits the same kind of self-selection of high value consumers for individual movies as the theater turnstile does.

The available data is illustrative. Distributors have typically received about 50 percent of gross revenues from pay-per-view cable exhibitions, or about $1.50 to $2.00 per household when applied to the QUBE system's price levels. This compares to net revenues of approximately 20¢ per subscribing household which distributors are reported to collect from the pay television services. Assuming typical ratings, prevailing license terms for theatrical features on network television yield only about 8¢ per household to the distributor, or about 4¢ per viewer .[4]

It is hard to imagine an invention which could bring more havoc to this economic system than the videocassette recorder. Commercial piracy and home taping have been the subjects of highly publicized legal battles and apparently continue to drain distributors' income.[5] Prerecorded programming is also constrained by technology and the law of copyright, but is an evident net addition to the distributor's earning capacity.

B. Prerecorded Home Video in the Price Tiering Sequence

Both rental and sales of prerecorded software offer new opportunities for the distributor to tier prices and earn higher revenues from each movie. In this respect, retail sales are a bonanza to the distributor. Surplus revenue can be skimmed from consumers with such high value demand that they want to own the whole movie. Distributors heavily promote tape sales and have long expressed an interest in advancing the release of movies on cassette into an overlapping or perhaps even co-incident position with theatrical release. One indication of these inter-ests is that the royalty fee which accrues to the copyright holder (usually the distributor, for major films) for a typically priced $49.95 cassette is about $5.80 (table 7.4 above). Movie theaters are otherwise the most lucrative component of the price tiering sequence; net revenue per pa-tron is about 10 to 15 percent of box office gross, which based on the MPAA 1983 average admission price of $3.14, is approximately 30¢ to 50¢ per individual.[6]

Comparison with the high royalty for tape sales can be misleading, however, without taking into account the distributor's peculiar problem that once sold by the retailer, all control of the tape's use is lost; other individuals besides the purchaser may see it or copies made from it. Data about the extent of this grapevine of viewers is elusive, but dis-tributors apparently believe that its undercutting effect on theater atten-dance is slight. At least one company, Paramount, has encouraged theater owners to set up videocassette stores in theater lobbies by pub-licizing survey data that theater attendance and cassette sales are actu-ally complementary; that is, Paramount reported, large percentages of cassette buyers prefer to see the movie in a theater before purchasing a tape of it (Sutherland 1984).

Distributor enthusiasm for cassette rentals has been markedly less because of restraints of copyright law discussed below. But like cassette sales, rentals offer an unbundled method of pricing which is better able to skim revenues from higher-value consumers than the unbundled pric-ing of pay-TV services downstream in the release sequence. Technology constrains cassette release of movies to be in advance of their pay-TV release; otherwise, the VCR's ability to record programs off the air would undermine the market for prerecorded programming. The un-bundled pricing of both cassette sales and rentals, however, is an eco-nomic rationale for why they would precede pay-TV regardless of this problem.

1. Effects of the First Sale Doctrine

The distributor's flexibility in the pricing and timing of home video software release has been restrained by the First Sale Doctrine of the Copyright Act, which prevents the distributor of a copyrighted product from controlling its disposition by a retailer. Under the doctrine, retailers have been able to either rent or sell prerecorded videocassettes or discs obtained from distributors at their own discretion. As physical objects, cassettes are very durable and can be rented out almost indefinitely. The distributor has still been able to at least crudely control rental prices that competing retailers set, and thus the number of times each tape is rented, by controlling the wholesale price of the tape. The First Sale Doctrine has simply forced the distributor to use the same wholesale price to control both the retail sale and rental prices of the cassette.

It would be a complete accident if the relevant elasticities of demand were such that the distributor's optimal wholesale price for rentals and for sales were identical. The available evidence is that the price elasticity of demand for tape sales at prevailing retail prices has been very high, above the distributor's profit-maximizing level, and that conversely, the price elasticity of demand for tape rentals has been very low, below the distributor's profit-maximizing level. An executive of one distribution company presented consumer survey data to this effect in 1983 congressional hearings and testified that if the First Sale Doctrine were repealed, his company's strategy would be to raise wholesale prices of videocassettes earmarked to retailers for rental and lower wholesale prices of tapes earmarked for sale. The pricing experiments of some distributors seem to have confirmed the high price elasticity of sales demand. The discounted $39.95 prices for *Flashdance* and *Raiders of the Lost Ark* in 1983 produced much greater sales than higher-priced but similarly successful theatrical films, such as *Tootsie* ($79.95) (*Home Video and Cable TV Report,* February 13, 1984, p. 1).

A main reason that videodisc sale prices have been lower than cassette sale prices also follows from this agreement; videodiscs are subject to physical damage, and player penetration has been too low for a rental market to be successful. Distributors have therefore set wholesale disc prices at optimal levels for retail sale.

The First Sale Doctrine has also necessarily constrained the timing of sale and rental release to be the same as well. It is likely that the doctrine has inhibited the distributor from moving software release of feature films, at least for retail sales, forward to an earlier date.[7] Release for sale prior to rental release is consistent with the price tiering model since sales appeal to high-value consumers more than do rentals.

From the distributor's point of view, it is evident that software sales and software rentals are essentially two different media which require different decisions as to timing and pricing in order for total revenues from the full release sequence to be maximized. From a public policy point of view, the need to modify the First Sale Doctrine is clear. Because it inhibits efficient pricing by distributors, the doctrine lowers the supply of programming that can profitably be produced. In this respect, it is little more than a quirk in the Copyright Act, another example of the inability of legislation to anticipate technological and marketing developments in communications.

2. Summary

The fact that distributors have chosen to release movies on prerecorded software in spite of the doctrine is evidence that they increase their net revenues by doing so. Because of the doctrine distributors lose control of relative sales and rental prices, but not absolute price levels. By setting wholesale prices high enough, the distributor can ensure that prerecorded software release contributes more revenues than it subtracts from other media in the release sequence. The First Sale Doctrine constrains the distributor, but the end result is a more efficient price tiering system.

IV. PROSPECTS FOR PRERECORDED HOME VIDEO

Eventually, pay-per-view or some other electronic system will no doubt take its turn in the progress of technology toward more efficient video pricing and delivery systems. Until then, there is at least more than just extrapolation from last year's trend behind the high expectations for prerecorded software distribution. We can expect to see these developments:

1. Lower hardware and software prices
    Higher volume and improved technology should continue the trend in the last few years of dropping VCR prices. Reports of VCRs to come in the $200 to $300 suggested retail price range have appeared in the trade press (e.g., *Videoweek,* September 12, 1983, p. 3).

Several factors should contribute to lower costs for prerecorded cassette manufacturing and distribution. Tape manufacturing costs are widely predicted to fall as the technology becomes more efficient, including the prospect for "compressed time" rather than "real time" methods of duplication. VHS seems likely to win the videocassette compatibility war, which will put downward pressure on retailer margins by decreasing their inventory costs.[8] The major impetus toward lower software prices will probably be increased hardware penetration. As software volume rises with it, the distribution system will become cheaper because of greater economies in physical handling and transactions. Direct distribution, rather than the shipping and reshipping process now in practice at the wholesale level, will benefit from a proliferation of nonspecialty outlets.

The relationship of lower software costs to lower software prices must be qualified. Repeal of the First Sale Doctrine may still result in a net increase in rental prices. The overall price trend for software sales and rentals, however, will be downward.

2. Greater program diversity

As hardware penetration rises, it will become increasingly profitable to manufacture and distribute obscure program materials. The film studios, for example, will be able to reach into more and more remote corners of their libraries.

Higher penetration will widen the economic base to support original programming for home video. While the audience base needed to support fictional drama for cassette release alone is very large, there is no reason that original programming for cassettes cannot be price tiered just as made-for-pay TV movies are now sold downstream to independent broadcast stations. Sale and rental of music videos along with their cable TV exhibition on MTV also shows the possibility of price tiering outside the theatrical film category.

Lower prices and greater diversity will increase the competitive edge of home video as a delivery system. What can compete against it? Other unbundled pricing media like pay-per-view cable are the best prospects. The greatest handicap of prerecorded cassette distribution is the inconvenience of traveling to and from rental locations for tapes, a problem solved by pay-per-view systems.

The survival of the laser disc as a significant entertainment medium, faced as it is with the prospect of still lower VCR prices, appears to rest on its use as a read-only-memory (ROM) device for personal computers, a function which some believe will be important. In the meantime, the laser disc will make only very minor contributions to the prerecorded software industry.

V. THE EFFECTS OF PRERECORDED HOME VIDEO

Some fragmentation of theater audiences is inevitable if higher VCR penetration occurs or if software release moves closer to theatrical release. The main impact on video media is likely to be on its downstream neighbor in the release sequence, pay-TV; because of its unbundled pricing, home video rentals and sales can undermine pay-TV's revenue base by skimming off its higher-value subscribers. Still, because cassette rentals and sales offer products differentiated from both theaters and pay-TV, their role as a complementary source of distributor income is ensured.

Of particular interest is the impact of prerecorded home video on the still dominant competitor in the video marketplace, broadcast television. The degree to which prerecorded programming actually diverts viewers' time from broadcasting appears minor. The 1982 Nielsen diary study showed that during the four-week survey period, VCR owners watched an average of only 1.8 prerecorded tapes, a very small proportion of total household viewing. The 1983–84 Nielsen Update reportedly shows little change.[9] However, there is likely to be a greater indirect impact via the program supply market. Along with pay-TV, home video is part of a process by which more efficient program pricing is shifting a vast pool of consumer surplus away from viewers of advertiser-supported broadcast television to the producers and distributors of that programming (see Noll, Peck, and McGowan 1973 for a general discussion). The higher revenues that suppliers can earn from a given supply of programming encourages entry into the market and bids up production factor costs.

Consider the effects to date of all the pay media on the demand for theatrical features. In sharp contrast to broadcast television's decimation of theater attendance in the 1950s, table 7.7 shows that the wear and tear of the new video revolution on domestic theater demand has been slight. Both real box office revenues and theater admissions have remained roughly constant since 1977, in spite of the rapid growth through 1983 of VCRs (1 to 10 percent penetration) and pay-TV services (2 to 22 percent penetration) ("Cable Stats" 1984, p. 5). Theatrical film revenues from the broadcast networks have apparently declined during this period, but not nearly as much as pay-TV and home video income has increased; since 1977, the contribution of all domestic ancillary

Table 7.7. Motion Picture Theater Admissions and Box Office
Revenues, 1977–1983 (Millions)

	1977	*1978*	*1979*	*1980*	*1981*	*1982*	*1983*
Number of admissions	1063	1128	1120	1021	1067	1175	1197
Box office revenues							
current $	$2372	$2643	$2821	$2749	$2960	$3452	$3766
1977 $, CPI-deflated	$2372	$2454	$2353	$2020	$1971	$2162	$2250

SOURCE: Motion Picture Association of America.

markets to theatrical film revenues has risen from about 20 percent to its
present 40 or 50 percent level (Waterman and Associates 1984;
Cablecasting, 1983), mostly because of growth in pay cable television.[10]

A similar expansion has occurred in foreign markets for theatrical
features, where the respective position of pay-cable and home video in
the domestic market are reversed; while pay-TV is almost nonexistent
in most countries outside North America, home video has boomed even
faster overseas than in the United States. In spite of heavy losses from
piracy, foreign sales of home video software were reported to account
for about $2 billion in gross revenues for 1983 (Terry, 1984). This has
been at significant expense to foreign theatrical rentals, but the result
has evidently been positive for U.S. distributors.

The result of this market expansion has been as expected—increased
theatrical production. The number of theatrical features released since
1977 has steadily risen, as shown in Table 7.8. Meanwhile, inflation in
production factor costs is suggested by a reported rise in the average
feature budget of MPAA member companies from $5.6 million in 1977
to $11.9 million in 1983, a 29 percent increase in 1977 constant dollar
terms (*Millimeter,* 1984).

Theatrical production is accelerating. Based on 1983 production activity, another 12 to 20 percent increase in theatrical features by the
major distributors should have occurred by the end of 1984. *Daily
Variety* reports theatrical production investment planned by the nine
major distributors to be $1.7 billion in 1984, an increase by 36 percent
over 1983 expenditures (Cohn 1984). If history is a lesson, the 1983–84
frenzy of theatrical production may be part of the perennial boom and
bust cycles the film industry is famous for. The general trend skyward,
however, is clear.

Table 7.8. U.S. Theatrical Motion Picture Releases (not including reissues), 1977–1983

	1977	1978	1979	1980	1981	1982	1983
Nine largest distributors[a]	112	121	133	136	145	149	165
All national distributors[b]	167	171	188	193	208	222	265
All distributors[c]	N/A	N/A	N/A	N/A	N/A	379	429

SOURCE: Motion Picture Association of America.

[a]MPAA Member Companies: Columbia, MGM/UA, Paramount, Twentieth Century Fox, Universal, Warner, Embassy, Orion, Buena Vista (Walt Disney). These data do not include releases by the "classics" divisions which five of these companies formed in 1981 and later; these accounted for 8 new releases in 1981, 14 in 1982, 33 in 1983.

[b]Eighteen to twenty companies; also includes releases by the "classics" divisions of the major distributors.

[c]Includes approximately ninety distributors for which data has been tracked by the MPAA since 1982; includes releases by the "classics" divisions of the major distributors.

The role which home video alone has played in building these high expectations for theatrical features cannot be isolated, but it certainly has been important. Foreign home video markets are widely expected to continue growing (Terry 1984). If expectations for VCR penetration in the United States materialize, net domestic revenues to distributors from prerecorded home video could approach the income from subscription-supported pay-cable by the end of the decade.[11]

Theatrical films are themselves a relatively minor ingredient on broadcast television, but the higher costs of making them inevitably spill over and raise television production costs since both media draw on essentially the same factor markets. Substantial investment in original programming by the pay-TV networks contributes to this. The 21 to 35 percent constant dollar increases reported for various network TV program types since 1976–77 (table 7.9) suggest the extent of these inflationary pressures to date.

A key question for the future is the elasticity that the film and program supply markets will show in the face of this increased demand. Will there be more and better programming, or just higher costs for the same programming? To the extent that inflation is the determining factor, how will the broadcast networks be affected? To the degree that network advertising demand is inelastic, higher prices can presumably be passed along to advertisers without damage to programming appeal and audience sizes. To the degree advertising demand is absorbed by substitute media, however, the direct diversion of network audiences by

Table 7.9. TV Program Production Cost Trends,
1976/7–1983/4 Seasons

	1976/7 (current $)	1983/4 (current $)	% Increase (current $)	% Increase 1977 (constant $)
60-minute action/ adventure	$330,000	$672,000	103%	24%
30-minute situation comedy	$168,000	$336,000	100%	21%
Made-for-TV movies	$850,000	$2,000,000	122%	35%

SOURCE: *Millimeter,* Anniversary Issue, 1984; *Daily Variety* data.

home video and other pay media will be exacerbated by lower program values. In spite of current efforts by the networks to differentiate their programming from pay-TV and home video with more of their own "made-for" material, broadcast television may eventually be forced to increasingly rely on leftover programming, originating, if not in theaters, then on pay-TV, pay-per-view, or, perhaps, prerecorded home video.

Notes

1. Like videodisc players, VCRs are manufactured using two incompatible technologies. The advantages of one VCR format over the other (called Beta and VHS) are fairly minor, but VHS is becoming more dominant; the percentage of VHS hardware sales has risen from 55% in 1979 to 70% in 1983 (*Home Video and Cable TV Report,* January 21, 1983:3; *Home Video Yearbook,* 1982:146). The dual format problem has some effects on distribution costs and software availability, but we will generally not distinguish between them.

2. Judgments are difficult to make in this rapidly changing industry, but it appears that a dual pricing structure may be developing in which the lower grossing theatrical features are priced relatively high—$79.95 is a predominant benchmark—and the higher grossing films such as *Flashdance* and *Raiders of the Lost Ark* are priced low—$24.95 or $39.95 are the current standards. An economic explanation is that the low grossing films tend to be minority taste

films with relatively inelastic sales demands and the high grossing films popular taste programming with elastic price demand. See Spence and Owen 1977.

3. Word-of-mouth from the theatrical release, potential appeal of the film on alternative media, and the prospects for repeat viewing are among the numerous factors which enter in. The advertising campaign is also a key component of all release strategies. In general, time periods before the "windows" of each medium must be long enough to encourage early patronage but not so long that the impact of the advertising and publicity from the theatrical release is lost.

4. Theatrical feature prime time ratings are usually in the 14 to 18 range. Reports of transactions compiled from the trade press indicate prices for major features (typically allowing two to three exhibitions), have generally been in the $2 to $4 million range since 1979. (See, for example, *Weekly Variety,* March 21, 1979; December 19, 1979; March 12, 1980; March 21, 1980.) Transactions in the past two years have apparently been very few. A 16 rating and a $1 million per exhibition license fee yields approximately 8¢ per viewing household.

5. Commercial piracy, at least in the United States, has been greatly contained through tighter security and stiffer penalties (Tusher 1984). Surveys show that there is a significant amount of home taping from pay-TV and trading of these tapes among friends (U.S. Congress, 1983d; A. C. Nielsen Co., 1982b). In early 1984 the U.S. Supreme Court (*Sony v. Universal Studios* 1984) held that the sale of VCRs did not violate the copyright law.

6. About 55 percent of box office revenues remains with the theaters to cover their utilities, labor, capital depreciation, and a share of local advertising expenditures. Another 10 percent is accounted for by the distributor's overhead and operating expenses for an elaborate process of negotiating license terms with theaters and making and shipping film prints to them (Waterman 1979, Londoner 1980). The major expense of theatrical distribution is advertising, which accounted for an average of 24 percent of all box office revenues from 1980 to 1982 (Motion Picture Association of America 1984b).

7. A major obstacle to any home video release during a movie's theatrical run or to sales of any cassettes at movie theaters has been the opposition of theater owners. This seems to be crumbling rapidly and one distributor, at least, recently released a major feature on home video software before the end of the film's theatrical release (Sutherland 1984).

8. Retail stores compete on the basis of title availability, and a major expense is inventory. Larger retailers often stock 3,000 to 4,000 titles. Although some stores have now dropped Beta tapes and others carry them in more limited quantities, most retailers carry the majority of titles in both VHS and Beta formats.

9. The 1982 calculation uses all owners of VCRs, renters, and nonrenters as a base. *Cablevision* reports that the November 1983 to January 1984 update of the Nielsen diary study shows an average of 5 prerecorded tapes rented by the 38 percent of respondents who rented any tapes (Capuzzi 1984). Again taking all VCR owners as a base, this translates into an average number of rental tapes viewed by VCR owners as approximately two per month.

10. Assuming that the producer-distributors earned, net of all expenses, 25 percent of the approximately $368 million in 1983 domestic wholesale volume for theatrical feature cassettes and discs (67 percent of $550 million, the wholesale volume for all program categories), net theatrical distributor revenues from domestic cassette and disc release were in the $100 million range. Distributor revenues from pay cable license fees were reported to be about $425 million in 1983.

11. If pay cable revenues double by 1990, as is generally expected, and domestic home video revenues quadruple, domestic home video's contribution will be about 40 percent of pay cable's (see note 10 above). Scenarios assuming substantial substitution effects or faster home video revenue growth predict that home video will contribute a significantly higher percentage of total revenues to distributors.

8

Program Competition, Diversity, and Multichannel Bundling in the New Video Industry

STEVEN S. WILDMAN and

BRUCE M. OWEN

CONTENTS

 I. Introduction
 II. Access Diversity
III. Content Diversity and Competition
    A. Welfare Effects of Competition Among Technologies
    B. Competition Within a Given Broadcast Technology
    C. Competition Among Multichannel Broadcasters
IV. Conclusion
    Appendix 8.1
    Appendix 8.2

I. INTRODUCTION

In the days when the Federal Communications Commission severely limited the number of local video outlets, the analysis of diversity and viewer welfare in the television industry was focused on channel scarcity. Today new technologies and the movement toward regulatory reform have acted to reduce or remove artificial sources of resource scarcity in broadcasting, and the analysis of competition and policy in the new video industry must address fresh issues. One of these questions is the effect of the competitive process on diversity and economic welfare when it involves competing multichannel broadcasters with both viewer and advertiser-supported programming. This paper is a first step in the analysis of this problem.

Maintainance of a responsive and flexible political process in a pluralistic and democratic society requires the existence of some reasonable (though hard to determine) number of independent media vehicles available for the dissemination of divergent viewpoints. The operative words in the preceding sentence are "reasonable number" and "independent." The concern here is that if control over the means of access to individual decision makers is concentrated in too few hands, political debate will be unduly restricted. In this context diversity refers to diversity of access to media vehicles.[1] In an economy in which transactions are based largely on private property, diversity of access or of "sources" implies either diversity of ownership or governmentally imposed standards for deciding who has access if ownership is not diverse, although these two options are not necessarily mutually exclusive. In any case it is necessary to define access or source diversity with respect to a particular audience—local, regional, or national. While First Amendment values may suggest unlimited source diversity, this may come at a cost both in resources and in content diversity.

Content diversity, as distinguished from access diversity, refers to the variety of programming offered to viewers. Programming is the industry's product and, just as the range of product characteristics must be considered in evaluating the economic performance of any industry, diversity of this type must be considered in evaluating the efficiency with which the industry that supplies programming creates value.

Programming may be a source of two types of value. The first concerns the economic surplus created as a direct consequence of individual consumption—the difference between consumers' valuations of the product and the costs of production and distribution. It is a familiar exercise in welfare economics to determine whether value of this type is maximized by a given industry structure. Because media products are public goods and the technology of distribution is particularly limited, the outcomes may differ radically from what one would observe in nonbroadcast industries with similar structures. The models of viewer choice discussed in this paper offer one means of assessing the efficiency with which the video industry produces the direct consumption benefits associated with its programming.

The second source of value is political. Some argue that the level of content diversity that maximizes direct consumption benefits is still too little. The social benefits of having a citizenry exposed to a variety of political and cultural ideas is ignored in the usual economic welfare calculus. While this perspective undoubtedly has some merit, there is no objective way to quantify those benefits and so we will ignore the social externality aspects of content diversity in the remainder of this paper. Any standard devised to permit welfare evaluations of this type of externality must of necessity embody personal value judgments on the relative merits of various types of programming which we are unwilling to make. In addition, we suspect that a video industry that meets reasonable standards for access diversity and effectively provides programming in response to a wide range of tastes will also perform adequately when the social benefits of content diversity are considered.

In the next two sections we explore the implications of the emerging structure of the new video industry for diversity in the specific senses described above. We argue in section II that a video industry that meets current antitrust standards will also satisfy reasonable criteria for access diversity. Models of programming choice are examined in section III. With their aid we explore the implications of different industry structures for viewer welfare.

II. ACCESS DIVERSITY

Concern with access diversity presumes that for purposes of participation in public debate and political decision-making the power of the individual voice or pen (or word processor) is not sufficient.[2] Individuals must have access to the mass media to participate effectively.

Clearly, as a practical matter, access to the media cannot be unrestricted. The range of differing viewpoints is enormous on most issues of public concern. With finite resources to allocate among all activities, including participation in the political process, it is unreasonable to expect any individual to weigh all opinions on all topics, and it is undesirable that the attempt be made. Thus it is both natural and appropriate that institutions serve as filters or gatekeepers to reduce the number of voices that are actually heard. This also means that gatekeepers may fail by providing either too much or too little diversity. There seems to be general (although by no means unanimous) agreement, however, that the social dangers of too little diversity far outweigh the problems of too much. Still, when commercial gatekeepers must compete in the marketplace, either error can be fatal.

If access diversity is a legitimate policy concern, then the focus of that concern must be on the effectiveness of competition in the industry of gatekeepers. Gatekeepers may be either public or private agents. Western countries have opted for systems of private gatekeepers for print media, presumably from concern that publicly controlled gatekeepers would be too responsive to established political interests. In contrast, broadcast gatekeepers have been publicly owned or regulated. The most important gatekeepers in this country are profit-motivated media enterprises whose financial viability is only indirectly related to their performance in this social or political role. This is the source of the frequently expressed fear that the performance of media firms as gatekeeepers is inadequate and the basis for occasional attempts at corrective intervention such as the fairness doctrine. But the commercial orientation of media firms has advantages in this regard as well. Competitors have economic incentives to seek out and serve unsatisfied demands for social and political as well as other content.

A sufficiency of competing gatekeepers is the usual solution to failure evidenced by any single gatekeeper. The owner of any single outlet may seek (indeed, must seek) to restrain free debate; but the chance of responsible parties being denied media access becomes increasingly remote as the number of independently owned media outlets is increased. Assuming that we are still in a situation where an increase in access diversity is beneficial, it is hard to see how diversity in this sense can help but improve in the emerging video industry. The number of actual and potential sources of programming and gatekeepers has grown substantially with the development of cable and newer distribution technologies and continues to do so. In addition, the development of high quality, relatively inexpensive video recorders has opened up the possibility of direct sales to viewers. This permits the existence and distribution of material which, for a variety of reasons, might not be marketed to mass audiences.

Of course, if the owners of new multichannel distribution systems such as cable, DBS, or MDS control access to these respective systems, then the diversity of content may exceed the diversity of access. However, economies of scale in programming and distribution dictate that most material be widely distributed, and this attentuates the control of the local system owner. In addition, media markets are largely local in character, while viewers are mobile and frequently cross media market boundaries, thus exposing themselves to the products of other gate-keepers. Even within a geographical market, access diversity could decrease given the growth of new technologies only if competing media firms merged or if, as a consequence of competition from new technologies, traditional broadcasters were forced out of the market, to be replaced by a lesser number of multichannel distribution services.

The current Justice Department Merger Guidelines (1982) seems to us to be an adequate safeguard in the case of the first eventuality. While there is no magic number of independent voices that ensures adequate diversity of access, it would be hard to argue for standards stricter than those already applied in evaluating the economic consequences of mergers (Baseman and Owen 1982). A proposed merger attracts attention if the initial Herfindahl index is 1000 and will almost certainly be challenged if the index exceeds 1800, although there are exceptions (see White paper in this book). The minimum number of firms required for an index of 1000 is 10, and 1800 allows for no fewer than 6.

III. CONTENT DIVERSITY AND COMPETITION

The rapid and continuing increase in the number of video offerings is a direct consequence of a revolution in the regulation, technology, and costs of program delivery. Loosening of regulatory restrictions on older technologies, as with MMDS, cable, and LPTV, and cost reducing technological developments, such as DBS and the new video recorder-players, have made feasible the provision of programming in addition to that provided by the traditional broadcasting sources. An extremely complex industry is emerging with competition among and within technologies and between products with different sources of finance (advertising and viewer payments). No existing models of competition in the industry appear to be both sufficiently comprehensive to capture this complexity and be analytically tractable at the same time.

Economic models of program patterns in broadcasting have in the past assumed that all broadcasters used the same technology (or at least had the same costs) and that all were supported in the same way, either by advertisers or by payment from viewers. In the discussion below we explore the implications of relaxing these assumptions. We also explore what may be the most interesting and relevant form of competition in the future—competition among multichannel broadcasters.

A. Welfare Effects of Competition Among Technologies

An increase in the number of alternative sources of content and of gatekeepers and thus of video content diversity is almost unanimously presumed to be beneficial. We tend to agree. Increased content diversity implies a closer matching of video products with consumer tastes, which usually improves consumer welfare. However, a cautionary note must be injected. The emergence and adoption of the new delivery technologies do not necessarily lead to a welfare improvement for everyone, even if available programming alternatives do increase. The means by which an increase in content diversity is brought about are also important.

Imagine there is some program (#1) valued by some consumers, but with too few potential viewers to make the program viable on an advertiser-supported broadcast medium. Those viewers who would prefer this program watch instead some alternative program (#2) that is actually broadcast. The advent of a new technology—say video cassette players—which permits the sale of program #1 directly to consumers increases the welfare of those who now buy the program. But because the audience for program #2 has been reduced, its quality will probably be reduced, and it may even go off the air. Those who prefer program #2 are worse off, and their loss may be as great or greater than the gain to those who prefer program #1. (See appendix 8.1 for an example.) Even if it could be shown that the result of introducing new technologies with effects such as this were always welfare-enhancing in the sense that total surplus increased, there may be significant groups of viewers who are winners or losers. Alfred Kahn (1966) made a similar point concerning the abandonment of passenger rail services when he pointed out that the actual revenues of a railroad fail to reflect an important benefit to consumers: the *option* to use the service.

Programming newly available through cable, video recordings, or DBS has not led so far to the disappearance of particular types of programs from more traditional sources. However, a number of major sporting events—major boxing matches, for example—that would almost certainly have been carried by advertiser-supported broadcasters have recently been available only through pay television.

B. Competition Within a Given Broadcast Technology

Competition among over-the-air broadcasters or among programmers that depend upon and utilize cable channels (e.g., pay-TV networks) takes place within a common technological environment in which each competitor faces the same or a similar cost function. In this section we review the existing literature on such competition, ignoring the competition that exists among different technologies. We also examine some of the implications of competition between pay- and advertiser-supported programming services, a topic not covered in the earlier literature.

1. Competition Among Media with a Single Source of Financing

Programming choice models are of two distinct types: Steiner's model (Steiner 1952) and variants on his approach that were developed later (Rothenberg 1962; Wiles 1963; Beebe 1977) and the Spence-Owen model (Spence and Owen 1977). While the formal structures of the two approaches are quite different, analyses with both have reached similar conclusions. Both the Steiner-type models and the Spence-Owen model show that television markets exhibit various "biases" that depend on their structural characteristics. These biases result from inconsistencies between the set of programs and prices that optimize consumer welfare and those that can be sustained by producers in a competitive equilibrium.

The most important determinants of the performance of a television market besides the number of channels are the distribution of ownership among the channels and whether programs are financed with advertising revenues or direct viewer payments. If channel owners are competitive and advertiser supported, then programming decisions exhibit a strong tendency toward wasteful duplication. This is illustrated most vividly in the Steiner models where programs must belong to one of a number of well-defined types, and programs of a given type are perfect substitutes for each other and thus share the audience for that type. Programmer revenue is primarily a function of audience size because advertisers are paying for exposure to viewers. Thus programmers will offer duplicates of programming types that have large audiences if fractions of these audiences are larger than the audience of a single program for a minority taste audience. Different programs of a given type are perfect substitutes for one another, so the expenditure on duplicate programming produces no increase in viewer welfare. As is shown in Beebe and the third chapter of Owen, Beebe, and Manning (1974), expansion of the number of channels will eventually result in the production of programming for each program type with an audience large enough to generate advertising revenues sufficient to cover the costs of the programming. The problem of wasteful duplication still remains, but there is reason to doubt the validity of the assumption that all programs of a given type are perfect substitutes.

Unnecessary duplication in an advertiser-supported Steiner model does not occur if all channels are controlled by a monopolist. The monopolist will minimize costs by producing only one version of each programming type that is produced. Programming will be provided on additional channels, if available, as long as the increase in total audience size generates ad revenues sufficient to cover the costs of programming and operating the channels. It is this property of monopoly control in combination with the elimination of wasteful duplication that leads Steiner to conclude that with advertiser support the broadcasting industry might perform more efficiently if monopolized than if competitive. This conclusion is valid, however, only if there is no program with less audience appeal that all viewers would watch if the alternative was not viewing at all. Given the existence of a common denominator inferior choice program, a monopolist would program only a single channel with that common denominator program. Depending on the strengths of preferences for first choice over common denominator programming, viewer welfare may well be reduced by more than the savings from reduced programming costs.

Welfare comparisons are difficult within the Steiner framework because viewer preferences are described only in terms of rankings. Actual consumer valuations in terms of willingness to pay play no role in the analysis. For this reason the usual surplus measures cannot be employed to compare the economic welfare implications of various outcomes. What can be said is that viewer welfare cannot decline in either a monopolized or competitive TV market as a result of increased channel availability. (Note, however, that individual consumers can be worse off.) If available channels increase a Steiner monopolist will not respond by providing fewer programs and will provide more programs if capacity restrictions had prevented what would otherwise have been a profitable increase in the number of programs offered. With a sufficient increase in the number of channels it is certain that a competitive industry will offer all types of programming that would attract audiences large enough to cover costs with advertising revenues, though perhaps with excessive duplication. Given that only relative preferences are taken into account in the Steiner framework, the most that can be said about the welfare consequences of increasing channels is that viewer welfare cannot be reduced and will probably increase. With competition there is the possibility that increased viewer welfare will not be sufficient to justify the costs of increased duplicative programming. However, if the value of advertising is at least equal to advertiser payments, then in both cases the marginal program produces value at least equal to its costs if it is not duplicative.

The inability to make welfare comparisons in many cases because of a lack of quantifiable viewer preferences is a serious drawback of Steiner models. It also makes any analysis of pay-television extremely ad hoc. The Spence-Owen model explicitly incorporates viewer demand functions and so avoids these problems.[3] Even so, while the conditions for making welfare comparisons can be described explicitly within the Spence-Owen framework, in most cases actual welfare conclusions require difficult empirical analysis.

Spence and Owen identify the same types of biases for advertiser-supported systems as does the Steiner framework. While no firm produces an exact duplicate of another's programming in a model with continuous variation in product space, a tendency exists for competitive programmers to crowd together in those segments of the market with the most viewers. More differentiation than is optimal occurs in these market segments because producers find it more profitable to cannibalize the surplus of other producers than to establish new products in less densely populated regions of the program space. Relative to the theoretical optimum, the market solution in a competitive, *advertiser-*supported industry is "biased" against programs with small audiences, programs with steep inverse demand functions (high preference intensities), and costly programs (holding net welfare contributions constant).[4] Competitive *pay* programmers often exhibit the same tendency toward excessive cannibalization in heavily populated audience segments.[5] However, these tendencies are greatly reduced relative to an advertiser-supported system because the price mechanism takes account of preference intensity. If the number of channels is allowed to increase indefinitely, the Spence-Owen model predicts that a competitive pay system will probably, although not necessarily, perform more efficiently than a competitive advertiser-supported system.

Spence and Owen do not evaluate the performance of an advertiser-supported monopolist. However, they show that a monopolist of pay services displays some of the same tendencies of a Steiner monopolist. A pay monopolist will be concerned with the internalized costs of cannibalization. For this reason the pay monopolist will tend to offer too little diversity. Some programs for which the increase in viewer plus producer surplus would exceed costs will not be provided because the firm is concerned only with the change in producer surplus.

Steiner models of an advertiser-supported monopolist and the Spence-Owen analysis of a pay monopolist agree in predicting a tendency toward too little diversity. Spence and Owen show that in a pay system the competitive solution is generally preferable to the monopolistic solution if the number of financially viable channels is not constrained by the number of actual channels. They also demonstrate that pay programming is more likely to lead to welfare enhancement than advertiser support under the same conditions. Expanding channel capacities on various broadcast media in recent years may have produced a state in which an artificial constraint on channel availability no longer exists. Moreover, policy has ceased to penalize the development of viewer-supported programming. However, whether at any point the marginal increase in diversity remains beneficial is an empirical question. It is a matter of measuring a new service's contribution to surplus and comparing this with its programming and distribution costs. Surplus measurement is bound to be difficult, especially for advertiser-supported services.[6]

2. Mixed Systems

Steiner models and the Spence-Owen model fail to analyze competition in a mixed market of pay and advertiser-supported programming services. Another problem with both models is that they assume that viewers make exclusive choices among programs. This makes sense in the context of the single programming period which these models assume, but in actuality individual viewers have preferences for more than a single channel of programming.

In the models presented in appendix 8.2, we take a step toward the analysis of competition between advertiser-supported and pay-supported broadcasters. If viewers are confined to choosing between one or the other on an exclusive basis, it is straightforward to show that the profitability of pay-TV relative to advertiser-supported TV is greater the more sensitive viewers are to the presence of advertising and the lower the price advertisers are willing to pay per viewer. The profitability of pay relative to advertiser support will be greater the less elastic is consumer demand for pay programs.

Welfare results are somewhat clouded by the traditional difficulties in dealing with advertising. But if one assumes that a dollar paid for advertising is welfare equivalent to a dollar paid by a viewer for pay-TV, then it can be shown that in the competitive equilibrium, choices by broadcasters as to which type of support to utilize will be in themselves consistent with welfare optimization. There remain, of course, "biases" in program selection compared to the global welfare optimum.

Describing (and modeling) competition among pay- and advertiser-supported broadcasters in a world where viewers patronize multiple services is much more difficult. Complications arise from the fact that pay services and advertiser-supported services are concerned with different measures of viewer response. Because they sell exposure to audience members, ad-supported services focus on actual audience size. Pay services, on the other hand, care only about the number of viewers willing to pay for the right to view their programming on an intermittent basis. For any individual program presented by a pay service the actual audience may be much smaller than subscribership.

Central to the demonstration that when viewers are restricted to exclusive choices, broadcasters choose the welfare-maximizing alternative between pay and advertiser support is a proof that under these conditions the audiences (and potential viewership, which in this case are the same) of pay services and advertiser-supported services are equal in size. Therefore direct consumer benefits (consumer surplus) associated with the two sources of support are the same. The simulation exercise reported in appendix 8.2 shows that demand elasticity and viewer sensitivity to advertising play much the same role in determining the relative profitability of pay- and ad-supported programmers when viewers watch the product of several programmers as when their viewing choices are exclusive. However, when viewers patronize multiple services, advertiser-supported services generate much larger potential audiences, and thus greater consumer benefits, than pay services. Because consumer benefits are ignored in the profit calculus, the number of pay services in market equilibrium is likely to exceed the number that maximizes welfare.

An important caveat attends this conclusion. The models developed in appendix 8.2 assume symmetry in the demands for different types of programming. These models do not allow for minority tastes. Because prices can reflect preference intensity, pay services have a much greater incentive to program to minority audiences than do advertiser-supported services. This beneficial tendency of pay programmers must be kept in mind when judging the relative merits of pay- and ad-supported services.

C. Competition Among Multichannel Broadcasters

1. The Economics of Multichannel Bundles

Multichannel service began with cable systems retransmitting distant broadcast signals. The cable industry has since developed more complicated packages of programs, some retransmitted, others produced solely for cable audiences. Regardless of the programming mix, the cable product is a bundled one. The cable subscriber is faced with an all or nothing choice of a group of programs packaged together (commonly referred to as the basic package) and, if he subscribes to these, the further option of subscribing to additional services either singly or in bundles. New multichannel services are just beginning to emerge in the form of DBS and MMDS, but it is already clear that they too are packaged or bundled. However, for reasons that appear to be purely technological, DBS and MMDS programmers currently offer a single bundle of programs with no options for additional services.

Both demand and cost relationships may influence the decision to bundle. For example, a recent econometric study by Owen and Greenhalgh (1983) shows economies with respect to both the number of channels and subscribers; similar relationships appear to hold for other multichannel technologies.[7] Therefore it is possible to offer a multichannel cable bundle at a lower price per channel than a single-channel service. Cost savings from transacting in program bundles relative to selling many programs on an individual basis may also be a powerful incentive to bundling. Economies of scale, whatever the source, however, do not necessarily make a bundle more profitable than services priced individually. Demand conditions must also be considered. In the remainder of this section we develop an analytical framework with which to analyze these demand relationships. We employ this structure to analyze the pricing and bundling strategies of a multichannel monopolist and the probable outcomes of competition among multichannel firms.[8]

Stigler (1963) was the first to suggest that bundling may be a device by which sellers can extract more buyer surplus than would be possible if the bundled goods were sold individually, thus increasing revenue. Adams and Yellen (1976) elaborated on Stigler's work and showed by means of other examples that under various circumstances seller profits may be increased even more by giving buyers the choice of purchasing the bundle or one or more of the bundled products singly. Both Stigler and Adams and Yellen worked with two product examples and assumed the bundled goods were demand independent. Below we add an additional good (program) to illustrate the possibilities of competition among multichannel services.[9]

Stigler's basic insight is easily illustrated with a two good, two consumer example. Consider a two-channel cable system offering programs A and B to viewers 1 and 2. The maximum prices that consumers are willing to pay (reservation prices) are given in table 8.1.[10]

If programs A and B are sold separately, revenue-maximizing prices are $6 and $9 respectively. Total revenue would be $21. By selling the two programs as a bundle, the seller could set a price of $13 for the bundle and receive a total revenue of $26. Revenue increased with bundling because, due to the negative correlation between the reservation prices of viewers 1 and 2 for the two programs, the seller was charging less than 1's reservation price for program A with simple monopoly pricing. Addition of program B enables him to extract more revenue from 1 than his reservation price for program B alone. This more than offsets a reduction of $2 in receipts from viewer 2.

Table 8.1

Viewer		1	2
Program	A	$10	$6
	B	$ 3	$9

It is easy to show that bundling may make possible the provision of programs that could not generate revenue sufficient to cover cost otherwise. For example, if programs A and B cost $14 and $6 respectively, A would never be produced if the two programs were sold individually, in spite of the fact that it produces value in excess of cost.

Welfare is increasing by bundling in this case. However, it is also true that a *monopolist* selling bundled products is subject to the same inefficiencies as a single-product monopoly—a tendency to produce too little output at too high a price. Unfortunately, employment of the more sophisticated bundling schemes which we discuss momentarily does not necessarily result in a welfare improvement over simple bundling, and simple monopoly bundling does not necessarily increase welfare relative to a monopolist selling the same programs individually.

The inefficiencies associated with simple monopoly bundling are most easily stated with formulas. We will index viewers by capital letters and programs by lower case subscripts. Define RPN_i to be the reservation price of the Nth viewer for the ith program and RBN to be the reservation price of the Nth consumer for the firm's bundle. RBN is the sum of the RPN_i over all i in the bundle.

For a given bundle and given group of subscribers, the maximum price for the bundle is the minimum RB among those who become group members. For a group of K subscribers designate the minimum RB by $MRBK$. Let F_j be the cost of a program not in the bundle and D_j be the change in the minimum RB due to the inclusion of program j. Then for the bundle to be the profit-maximizing bundle, it must be the case that $D_j < F_j$, all j not in the bundle.

Profit maximization also requires that for any potential viewer, M, who is not a subscriber and with $MRBK$ the minimum RB among K subscribers, $RBM < (MRBK\text{-}RBM)K$.

The latter condition is a restatement of the marginal revenue-marginal cost relation that must be satisfied for profit maximization for a single product firm. A monopolist of a product bundle produces the same type of inefficiency that is associated with single product monop-

Table 8.2

Viewers		1	2	3	4
Programs	A	$10	$6	$ 6	$4
	B	$ 3	$9	$10	$2
	C	$ 7	$3	$ 2	$9

oly, that is, treating the reduction in price on sales to existing customers as a cost of adding a new one.

Adams and Yellen have shown that, depending on the distribution of preferences, more sophisticated bundling schemes may allow for a finer discrimination among buyers. We illustrate this by expanding on the above example. We add one more program and two more viewers with reservation prices distributed as in table 8.2. Priced individually programs A, B, and C would yield maximum revenues of $18, $18, and $14, respectively, for a total of $50. If all three are offered as a bundle, the bundle could be priced at $15 and total revenue would be $60. However, if viewers were given the option of purchasing A, B, and C as a bundle at $18 or C alone at $9, viewers 1, 2, and 3 would purchase the bundle, and 4 would buy just C. Total revenue would be $63.

Is the mixed bundling scheme more efficient than the simple bundling, and is simple bundling more efficient than pricing individually? No unambiguous answer exists in either case, although just as with single product monopoly, a perfectly price discriminating monopolist will produce the socially efficient level of output. The last bundling scheme described with C sold separately from the bundle sacrifices consumer surplus of $6 relative to simple bundling because viewer 4 does not receive programs A or B. On the other hand, if programs cost more than $20 to produce, none would be produced if not for the more sophisticated bundling arrangement.

Refer back to the example based on table 8.1 with costs of $14 and $6 for programs A and B and just two viewers. Program A would not have been produced without bundling. Imagine the existence of a third viewer with a reservation price of $5 for program 1 and $0 for program 2. The monopolist would still prefer simple bundling which would exclude the third viewer. However, both programs could be produced with individual pricing, and total surplus would be higher by $2 ($5 from the new viewer minus $3 due to viewer 1's loss of program B).

2. Multichannel Competition

Until recently a discussion of the economies of video bundling could have stopped at this point. Because cable was the only multichannel distribution technology in use for most of the past thirty years, a monopoly bundling model would have been sufficient. However, due to a combination of relaxed regulatory constraints and technological improvements, new multichannel services employing either MDS or DBS distribution technology have recently emerged as potential multichannel competitors to cable.

It is still too early to tell what, if any, economic niches the new services will occupy in the long run. Several services with 4–8 channels of programming employing both technologies have either been started recently or are scheduled to come on line in the near future.[11] Because the first of new multichannel MDS and DBS services plan to carry fewer channels than all but the smallest cable systems, it is widely speculated that the true multichannel competition will be between MDS and DBS services for the right to serve those areas in which the economics are not favorable for cable, primarily areas with low population densities in which the cost of laying cable is high relative to the number of homes passed. If this is the case, the majority of viewers reached by multichannel services will not be much affected by multichannel competition. On the other hand, the emergence of MDS or DBS "wireless cable" (12–18+ channels) is seen by many as a distinct possibility in the future.

Multichannel competition can take at least two possible forms. If competing services offer similar bundles, competition would depress price, possibly as low as average cost, even if only a single firm remained in equilibrium. The extent to which revenue could exceed cost would depend on the costs of entry and exit (Baumol, Panzar and Willig 1982). Multichannel competition may also take the form of multichannel services offering different program packages in the same markets. This becomes more likely the greater the differences in tastes among viewers. Below we explore, again by examples, the character of this type of competition. The extent of multichannel competition is dependent on the structure of demand and on cost conditions. One factor is the extent to which economies of scale with respect to channel capacity extend beyond a single channel. These may reverse before a single distribution system could produce all, or even a significant fraction, of the potentially viable program types. In the absence of economies of scale with respect to channel capacity over some initial range, demand complementarity might provide a multichannel operator with pricing options not available to competitive single channel firms. But eventually increasing costs would still be necessary to ensure the viability of more than one multichannel service.

First we examine competition between two multichannel services when the number of types of programming desired by viewers exceeds the channel capacity of a single service. Assume a market is served by two 2-channel distribution services, one (AC) offering programs A and C, the other (AB) offering programs A and B, with viewer preferences as shown in table 8.2. Assume also that the cost of programming a single channel is $8, independent of the number of viewers served. If the two services price their bundles cooperatively, joint revenue would be maximized with AC selling to viewers 1 and 4 at a price of $13 and AB selling to viewers 2 and 3 at a price of $15. Note that with cooperative pricing and only two services the BC combination would not be offered.

The extent to which price competition may reduce prices is a function of the degree to which viewers perceive the bundles as substitutes and the costs of producing and delivering a channel of programming. From the initial levels of $13 for AC and $15 for AB, AB has no incentive to cut price. If AB reduced the price of its bundle to slightly less than $9 it could pick up viewer 1 because viewer 1 would now realize more surplus from A and B ($4 +) than from A and C ($4). But AB's revenue would be reduced to less than $27. The price of AB would have to be cut to $6 to pick up both 1 and 4. Then revenue would be $24. AC does have an incentive to cut price. By reducing the price of its bundle to just under $7 it could pick up viewers 2 and 3 and have revenue of nearly $28. AB is secure against price competition from AC if it prices its bundle just below $14.5. AC would then have to set a price of less than $6.5, and it would earn less than $26. AB has no incentive to cut price further because the price reduction required to pick up an additional viewer would lower its revenue. In this example price competition between two differentiated services leads to a slight reduction in one of the prices, but both firms still earn substantial profits. If the differences between viewers' reservation prices for the two bundles were less, price competition would lower prices more. However, with this type of differentiation price competition cannot be expected to eliminate all seller profits unless there is the threat of entry by duplicative services. If positive profits attracted entry by firms offering similar packages, equilibrium industry structure would be either two firms, one selling A and C at a price of $8 to viewers 1 and 4, the other selling A and B, each at the same price to 2 and 3, or a single 2-channel service offering either the AB or AC combination to all viewers at a price of $4 per viewer.

The importance of economies of scale with respect to the number of channels is clear if we consider the possibility of simultaneous competition by single-channel firms. If a single-channel service could still deliver programming at a cost of $8 per channel, then three single-channel services, each selling at a price of $2 per viewer would displace any 2-channel competitors. If there were no diseconomies of scale associated with a third channel, a 3-channel service could do the same thing.

Generalizing from this example suggests that the factors affecting the number of multichannel media competitors will include, on the demand side, the overall extent of the video market, the marketing advantages to be gained from bundling channels, and the degree of specialization of tastes among the viewing public. On the supply side, the factors to consider are the structure of costs with respect to number of channels and the extent, if any, of continuing capacity limitations due to spectrum constraints. Our empirical knowledge of these factors is very limited; there is no reason to suppose, for example, that they will not work out to be the same or similar to those in the print media. It should be noted in this connection that the print media consist of a number of technologically similar products. Books, magazines, and newspapers, for example, are produced and delivered in relatively similar ways. But these media coexist in equilibrium because of relatively slight differentiating features that are important to customers. Video delivery technologies may similarly coexist in a competitive environment. It is not inevitable that one or another will win the race to be the dominant technology.

IV. CONCLUSION

The models that we have been exploring in this paper represent only a first step to an understanding of the future of video competition and diversity. We need better models and better data on the cost characteristics of the new media technologies. At the moment we are mostly reliant on guesses and analogies. One useful analogy is the print media. Print media are, in a sense, each made up of several "channels." For example, a newspaper of general circulation or a weekly magazine has several departments or sections. Such channels are related by demand interdependencies or by cost interdependencies, or both. To the extent the print analogues have cost and demand characteristics that are comparable to video technologies, we can expect to see video competition and diversity similar to that in today's print media.

Among the policy issues that arise as one thinks about the possible shapes of future video competition is the problem of media that are constrained to continue to provide single-channel service. It may well be the case, for example, that as cable, MMDS, and DBS penetrate significantly into the marketplace, local broadcasters will be more efficient competitors if they can coordinate their programming and advertising policy. If so, there will come a point where consumers will be better off if the FCC's duopoly rule were eliminated. It is easy to see that this will be a controversial proposal when it is first made and that harm might arise either from too early or from too tardy a relaxation of the regulation.

The other major policy issue, of course, is the necessity for licensing, content regulation, and structural reactions to the presence of transmission bottlenecks, such as a separations policy. The burgeoning new technologies and the withdrawal by the FCC of most of its entry restrictions have created an environment in which there is little if any basis for any form of licensing or content regulation. Moreover, the once widespread view that cable would eventually replace competing local broadcasters with a single local video transmission "bottleneck" looks today increasingly doubtful. In short, it is difficult to see much, if any, consumer benefit in continued FCC regulation of either the new or the old video media.

Appendix 8.1

Demand and cost conditions for two types of programming, 1 and 2, are shown in figure 8.1. Viewers in the community are divided into two groups, A and B, based on their demands for the two types of programming. We assume, as is typical in models of viewer choice, that given a choice of programs or channels each viewer watches only one. (We examine some of the consequences of relaxing this assumption in the simulation study reported in appendix 8.2.) Type A viewers prefer type 2 programming, although most of them are willing to watch type 1 programs if type 2 is not available, or if it is priced too high. Group A's inverse demand function for type 1 programming (in the absence of type 2) is DA1, and its inverse demand function for type 2 programming is DA2. DA1 and DA2 are drawn parallel to simplify the exposition. Members of group A will take type 2 programming as long as its price does not exceed the price of type 1 programming by more than the

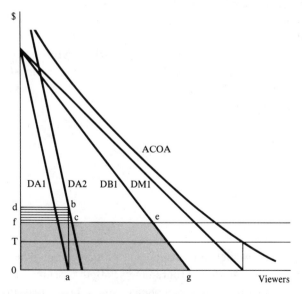

Figure 8.1. Welfare Changes Due to Competition from a New Technology

difference in the heights of the demand curves and will select type 1 otherwise. Group B viewers watch only type 1 programs. Their inverse demand function is DB1. If type 2 programming is not available, the market inverse demand function for type 1 is DM1, the horizontal sum of DA1 and DB1.

Let ACOA be the average cost per viewer for supplying programming via over-the-air broadcasts and assume that advertisers are willing to pay T per audience member. A station broadcasting type 1 programming would just break even if its audience consisted of both groups. Suppose that originally broadcasting was the only means of program distribution, but technical advances in video recordings now make it possible to distribute recorded programs at retail at constant average cost, f. Further, suppose that the supply of video recordings is competitive, b is located vertically above a. Because DA2 and DA1 are parallel, the consumer surplus area under DA2 above db is equal to the consumer surplus area under DA1; f is less than d, so group A viewers will switch to type 2 programming where they receive more surplus.

Advertising revenue from the sale of a group B audience is not sufficient to cover broadcasting costs. Therefore the broadcast services would be dropped, and type 1 programming would be available only through video recordings at price f. In this example it is clear that the benefits of the newly available type 2 programming to group A are more than offset by the reduced surplus of group B. Group A's surplus has increased by the area of trapezoid dbcf, while surplus from group B consumption is reduced by trapezoid fego, which is obviously larger. A similar example could be constructed with the broadcast service supported by viewer payments.

Appendix 8.2

In this appendix we develop two models with competition between pay- and advertiser-supported programmers. Both assume a monopolistically competitive market modeled similarly to that in Spence-

Owen. In the first we maintain the standard assumption of exclusive choices by viewers; in the second we allow for viewers to choose multiple program sources.

For both models we assume a market with n firms producing imperfect substitutes. For $i, j = 1,. . . ., n$ the demand function for the ith firm is given by

(1) $\quad q_i = V - c\,(bA_i + P_i)^r + f,$

where:

P_i = the price of the ith program

$f = f(A_1, . . .A_{i-1}, A_{i+1}, . . .A_n; P_1, . . .,P_{i-1}, P_{i+1}, . . .P_n);$
$\quad \partial f/\partial A_j, \partial f/\partial P_j > 0$

A_i = advertising on the ith program

q_i = the number of viewers on the ith program

T = advertiser payment per viewer per unit time

F_i = cost of programming and distribution for ith channel.

V, b, c and r are positive constants.

Note that we are assuming advertising reduces viewer valuation of a program. If the ith program is ad-supported, $P_i = 0$ and $A_i > 0$. If the ith program is supported by viewer payments, $P_i > 0$ and $A_i = 0$. Profits for the ith firm would be

(2) $PRp_i = P_i q_i - F_i$ if it is a pay service, and

(3) $PRa_i = TA_i q_i - F_i$ if it is ad supported.

We assume firms are Nash competitors in prices and advertising; that is, each firm sets the level of its own price or advertising on the assumption that the advertising or prices of other firms will not change. The system of equations given by (1) has a unique solution if f is quasi-convex in the A_j's and P_j's. Substituting from (1) for q_i in (2) or (3) and differentiating with respect to P_i or A_i as appropriate, we get first order conditions

(4) $V - (r+1)cP_i^r + f = 0$

if the ith service is subscriber supported, and

(5) $V - (r+1)b^r cA_i^r + f = 0$

if the ith service is advertiser supported. Profit-maximizing values of P_i and A_i are

$P_i^* = [(v+f)/(r+1)c]^{1/r}$, and

$A_i^* = [(v+f)/(r+1)b^r c]^{1/r}.$

Substituting back into (1) we get

$q_i = r(V+f)/(1+r)$

in either case. Alternative profits with pay and advertiser support are
$PRp_i = (r/(1+r))((1+r)c)^{-2/r} (V+f)^{((1+r)/r)}$, and
$PRa_i = T/b (r/(1+r))((1+r)c)^{-2/r} (V+f)^{((1+r)/r)}$.

With advertiser support the ith service would be more profitable than with pay support if $T/b > 1$, less profitable if $T/b < 1$, and equally profitable if $T/b = 1$. This relationship is as one would expect. From (1) we see that an increase in A of b units has the same effect on viewer demand as a unit increase in price. So the profitability of pay- relative to ad-supported programming is greater the greater the sensitivity of viewers to advertising relative to their sensitivity to price, and the lower the price of advertising.

Because a profit-maximizing firm has the same value for q_i with either advertiser or pay support, $bA_i^* = P_i^*$.
Designate this value by L^*, and let L' be the value of $bA_i + P_i$ for which $q_i = 0$. Consumer surplus for both pay and ad-supported services is given by

$$CS_i = \int_{L^*}^{L'} q_i(\cdot)dP,$$

where the functional form represented by $q(\cdot)$ is that given by equation (1).

The equivalence of consumer surplus with advertiser and viewer support is easily demonstrated graphically for linear demand functions $(r=1)$. This relationship is evident in figure 8.2. The upper inverse demand function, $D1$, assumes $A_i = 0$. With direct viewer support P_i is set at its revenue-maximizing level, producing the audience size for which $MR1 = 0$. The lower demand function, $D2$, assumes A_i is set at the level which maximizes profits for $P_i = 0$. Because q_i is the same in either case, $D2$ intersects the horizontal axis at the same audience size as $MR1$. $D1$ and $D2$ are parallel; therefore consumer surplus is the same with advertiser or pay support.

Because consumer surplus is the same with either advertiser or pay support, any difference in the welfare benefits associated with the two sources of support is due entirely to differences in producer benefits. As long as a dollar of revenue to a programming service is accorded the same weight regardless of whether it is contributed by subscribers or advertisers, then for the equilibrium configuration of services, firm choices with respect to advertiser support or viewer payments as a source of revenue maximize both profits and welfare.

To bring the model closer to reality we must permit viewers to patronize more than a single programming service. Implicitly this means

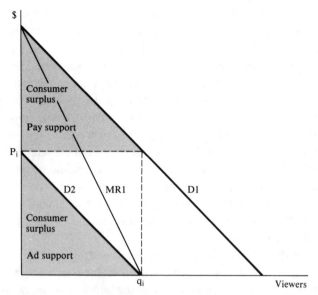

Figure 8.2. Equivalence of Consumer Surplus with Pay and Advertiser Support

extending the time dimension of the model beyond a single programming period. A programming service is now interpreted as a firm programming a single channel for all periods. A service is assumed to strive for a unique identity for its product, but as there are many uncertainties associated with matching video product to viewer tastes, its programming may not always be on the mark. In addition, viewers may themselves desire programming diversity. For both reasons viewers may prefer to have available more services than they can watch at one time. We assume this to be the case. A viewer may have a preferred programmer, but substitutes still have a positive value at the margin.

As we showed above, the formal analysis of competition between pay- and advertiser-supported services is fairly straightforward if viewers make exclusive choices among services. Allowing viewers the option of viewing more than a single service (not simultaneously, of course) brings the analysis much closer to the actual state of competition between services. Unfortunately, the required modifications to the mathematical structure complicate the formal analysis to the point that simulation methods must be employed.

The complications arise from the fact that we can no longer assume that the number of potential viewers and the actual audience for a program are the same at a given time. Divergence between the two measures requires that we develop functional expressions for both. Pay services are concerned with the number of viewers willing to pay for the right to watch their programming on an occasional basis. The size of the actual viewing audience is more important to ad-supported services.

The fact that pay- and ad-supported services are concerned with different magnitudes necessitates that, to keep the problem manageable, we restrict the total number of viewers to be invariant with respect to the number of programming services. If we had to account explicitly for the number of viewers that watch multiple services and the relative frequencies with which they watched each, the problem would be too complex to model. At any rate, this assumption does not seem to be too much at variance with available evidence. Thus we have ad-supported services trying to affect their shares of the viewing audience while pay services worry about subscriber counts.

Much of the structure of the model developed above is still useful for examining the efficiency of competitive outcomes in a more complex environment in which viewers watch the product of more than one programmer. In particular, the demand functions (advertising and price) given by (1) can be reinterpreted as giving the relationship between price and advertising and the number of people who will watch a service at least part of the time instead of the instantaneous viewer count. With this change in interpretation the profit function for a pay service is unchanged as is its first order condition (equation (4)). It is also still valid to employ these relationships to derive and compare measures of surplus since these are still demand functions for the services of TV programmers.

It is the profit expression for an advertiser-supported service (equation (3)) that must be modified. As q_i is now interpreted as the number of viewers potentially in a service's audience, not the instantaneous viewer count, it must be replaced by the service's share of the total audience that is divided among all services. Let N be the total number of TV viewers and assume for convenience that N is invariant with respect to the number and financing of programming services. Define SH_i as the ith service's share of the N viewers. NSH_i is the number of viewers in the ith service's audience. In a market in which viewers watch more than one service, $NSH_i < q_i$, and the profit function for an advertiser-supported service is

(6) $PRa_i = TNA_iSH_i.$

(1′) is the version of (1) used in the simulation. It is linear in both A and P (i.e., $r = 1$). Note that $k = bc/f$ is the linear combination of P_j's and A_j's.

(1′) $q_i = V - kA_i - cP_i + g\Sigma_j P_j + h\Sigma_j A_j, \ i \neq j; \ g, h > 0.$

With (1′) the first order condition for a pay service (equation (4)) becomes

(4′) $V - 2cP_i + g\Sigma_j P_j + h\Sigma_j A_j = 0, \ i \neq j.$

The audience share of an ad-supported service should be an increasing function of the prices of pay services and the levels of advertising of other ad-supported services and a decreasing function of its own advertising. A potentially large number of functional forms could satisfy these conditions, but few are analytically tractable. We chose a measure based on the relative valuations viewers would place on services if competing services were not available. Thus we are comparing viewers' gross valuations of different services, not benefits after netting out the effects of substitute services. Define $S_i(A_i, P_i)$ to be the area under the demand function for values of A_i and P_i if no other programming services are available. Given (1′)

$S_i(0, P_i) = (V^2/c - cP_i^2)/2$, and

$$S_i(A_i, 0) = \frac{V^2 - 2kA_i + k^2 A_i^2}{2c}$$

the functional form employed for SH_i is

$$SH_i = \frac{S_i}{S_i + \Sigma S_j}, \qquad i \neq j.$$

This expression for SH_i has the properties described as necessary above. This form of SH_i is also intuitively appealing in that programming services receive audiences in proportion to their gross valuations.

Market equilibrium properties were explored with a computer simulation for a market of 20 firms. Results reported in table 8.3 are for a market with 10 ad-supported services and 10 pay services. Because the values of T and N do not influence profit maximizing choices of P and A (although, through their influence on relative profitability they affect the numbers of pay and ad services), their values are arbitrary within this framework and were set equal to 1 for convenience. Each firm

Table 8.3. Market Equilibrium Properties for 20 Television Firms–Simulation Results

	$c=1$ $k=1$ $g=.02$	$c=1$ $k=1$ $g=.01$	$c=1$ $k=1$ $g=.03$	$c=1$ $k=.5$ $g=.02$	$c=1$ $k=1.5$ $g=.02$	$c=.5$ $k=1$ $g=.02$	$c=1.5$ $k=1$ $g=.02$
A	.36	.36	.36	.68	.24	.36	.36
P	.66	.57	.77	.79	.64	1.67	.42
$\frac{PR_p}{PR_a}$	23.08	21.64	23.06	13.64	33.15	40.42	15.88
q_a	.84	.73	.97	1.06	.80	1.01	.82
q_p	.53	.52	.54	.63	.51	.50	.55

A = Amount of advertising.

P = Price of subscriber supported service.

PR_p/PR_q = Ratio of profits of subscriber supported service to advertiser supported service.

q_a = number of potential viewers for advertiser supported service.

q_p = number of potential viewers for subscriber supported service.

c, k, g = demand function parameters appearing in equations (1) and (1').

determines the value of its own advertising or price on the assumption that the advertising and prices of its competitors will not change.

The usual symmetry conditions were employed to simplify the analysis. Thus we could solve for a single value of P for all pay services and a single value of A for all ad-supported services. Given the symmetry assumption and equation (4'), the common price, P, charged by pay services is

$$P = \frac{V + 10hA}{2c - 9g}.$$

The complexity of the profit expression for an ad-supported service necessitated employment of a simulation technique to determine profit-maximizing values of A. Profits for an ad-supported firm were calculated using equation (6) for A varying from 0 to values high enough to drive PRa_i to 0. The S_j's that are held constant in the expression for SH_i were calculated for an initially arbitrary value of advertising A_o. The value of A that maximized PRa_i then became the Ao used to calculate new values for P and the S_j's which were employed to determine new values for maximum PRa_i and the associated A. This procedure was repeated until stable values of A and P were achieved.

This simulation exercise was performed for varying values of the model's parameters.[12] Results of the standard comparative statistics exercises performed by varying model parameters were along the lines economic intuition would lead one to expect. Profits of pay services decline relative to the profits of ad-supported services the more price sensitive are viewers (the larger c is). The relative profits of pay programmers increase with increasing sensitivity of viewers to advertising (increasing k).[13]

The magnitudes of greatest policy interest are the values of q_a and q_p, the numbers of potential viewers of advertiser-supported and pay services. For all combinations of model parameters tried q_a is greater than q_p. This result appears to be a consequence of ad-supported programmers compensating for the fact that actual audience is smaller than potential audience by reducing advertising to increase their shares of total viewers.

As we showed with the first model in this appendix, advertiser-supported services and pay services generate equal amounts of consumers' surplus if q_a and q_p are equal; $q_a > q_p$ implies greater consumers' surplus for ad-supported services. If we weight producer profits equally regardless of the revenue source, an advertiser-supported service produces greater total benefits than an equally profitable pay service. Therefore, free competition between the two types of programming services is likely to produce a mix with a larger than optimal proportion of pay services. This property of competition between the two types of services must be weighed against the desirable tendency of pay services to program to minority taste audiences, which ad-supported services tend to ignore.

Notes

The authors would like to thank Peter Greenhalgh for numerous helpful comments and suggestions, and Paul Gottlieb, who did the programming for the simulation exercise reported in appendix 2.

1. For an alternative discussion of the meanings of diversity see Crandall, Noll, and Owen (1983).

2. For a discussion of diversity in the context of First Amendment concerns see Owen (1975, pp. 20–21).

3. The Spence and Owen paper was presented to an audience of professional economists. For this reason the analysis relies heavily on mathematical techniques with which the average noneconomist interested in video diversity is unlikely to be familiar. For an excellent interpretive review of the Spence-Owen article see Lence (1978). The Lence paper was written as an undergraduate project and is available on request through the Department of Economics at Stanford University.

4. "Bias" is used as a way of characterizing the differences between the optimum and the equilibrium sets of offerings.

5. Scherer (1979) provides an excellent graphical analysis of the economics of this type of cannibilization in a market with differentiated products. See also Wildman (1984) for an elaboration on Scherer's diagrams.

6. See Wildman, note 5 above, for a discussion of surplus measures for differentiated products.

7. See Eli Noam's paper in this volume for other evidence of economies of scale.

8. For a different approach to modeling the packaging of cable programming see Besen and Johnson (1982).

9. An excellent condensation of the bundling analysis is presented in the eleventh chapter of Phlips' (1983) book on price discrimination. Phlips argues that because bundling is a form of nonlinear pricing and because for any uniform price greater than marginal cost there exists a nonlinear schedule of prices that produces greater total welfare, economic welfare is greater with bundling than for simple monopoly pricing. We demonstrate below by counterexample that, while welfare may improve with bundling, the reverse is also possible.

10. For advertiser-supported channels the reservation prices would be the values advertisers place on gaining exposure to the particular viewers.

11. For example, USCI launched a 5-channel DBS service in Indianapolis in 1983 and later expanded to Chicago and some East Coast markets.

12. From equation (1') it is evident that a unit increase in advertising and a C/K increase in P have the same effect on q_i. For the purposes of the simulation this relationship was assumed to hold for the effects of substitutes in the demand function as well. Thus we set $h = gc/k$.

13. It should be remembered that because the values of N and T are arbitrary, only changes in the ratio of profits of ad-supported to pay services, not their absolute values, are of interest.

Comment: Welfare Analysis and the Video Marketplace

John R. Woodbury

Wildman and Owen present four conundrums: Will competition produce enough access diversity? Will competition between ad-supported and viewer-supported services result in a welfare maximum? What is the effect of channel-packaging on welfare and diversity? What will determine the number of multichannel competitors? Equally important is a question implied throughout: What can economic analysis say about the appropriate role for public policy in this brand new video world?

In assessing the welfare implications of video competition, economists are perhaps handicapped by second- (or nth-) best considerations to a greater extent than in, for example, the textile or automobile industries. First, programming is distinct by virtue of its heavy dose of public-good characteristics. Unlike the purchase of a sweater or a car, one person's viewing of a particular program in no way limits any other consumer from viewing exactly the same program. Economic theory advises that the optimal production of programs will occur if the marginal cost of program production is equated to the sum of prices individual consumers are willing to pay for programs. Those consumers who value the programs at less than the marginal production costs should nonetheless be allowed to view the programs at a zero price. This is true because once a program is produced, the same program can be distributed at near zero marginal cost to all viewers.

Such a scheme would require that some entity (e.g., the government) determine the demand for programs by each consumer, extract the necessary payment from those consumers, and then distribute those funds to program producers. I doubt that any economist believes that the tremendous costs of implementing such a scheme would be worth the benefits. Nonetheless, the ideal production-distribution system provides us with a benchmark for assessing the private supply of these public goods. Advertiser-supported over-the-air broadcast services approximates program distribution at zero marginal cost, but program production depends not on intensity of preferences but rather the number of viewers. Viewer-supported services take into account intensity of preferences, but do not distribute programming at zero marginal cost.

In addition to the public-good aspects of programming, welfare analysis is complicated by the nature of the FCC's spectrum allocation scheme. The Commission does not rely on any market test to allocate spectrum, but rather makes its decisions administratively on the basis of some vague "public interest" standard. Thus there is no guarantee that the spectrum allocated to, e.g., over-the-air broadcasting versus LPTV versus MDS versus satellites is "just right" or even in the right ball park. Moreover, as Botein and Geller point out in papers 9 and 10 of this book, the crazy quilt of regulations regarding the ownership and operation of the various video delivery systems has and will continue to bias the development of these systems in ways that the Commission could not have foreseen.

Wildman and Owen are understandably reluctant to draw any policy conclusions from this result. The assumption of asymmetrical demands for pay- and ad-supported programs, the authors note, preclude pro-only ad-supported services, the latter deals with both types individually but not simultaneously. Wildman and Owen extend the Spence-Owen model to encompass patronage of more than one channel simultaneously by viewers and competition between ad-supported and viewer-supported channels. Unable to derive analytically the comparative static results, Wildman and Owen rely on simulations. Over a wide range of parameters, the authors conclude that competition will produce too few ad-supported services.

Wildman and Owen are understandably reluctant to draw any policy conclusions from this result. The assumption of asymmetrical demands for pay- and ad-supported programs, the authors note, preclude programming for minority tastes. Even if one were to ignore this aspect of the model, the proliferation of ad-supported service on cable make it less than obvious what appropriate public policy ought to be.

The Wildman and Owen type of effort can, over the long term, prove productive in understanding the welfare consequences of the expanded video environment. Aside from relaxing the assumption of symmetrical demands, useful extensions of the model would include permitting programming services to be supported by a mix of advertising and viewer payments. In any event, it is clear that economists are now able to say very little about the welfare consequences of the new competition.

Wildman and Owen assess the effects of a monopolist offering to consumers channels tied together in a bundle or a package. As in cases of third-degree price discrimination, and compared to pricing each channel individually, channel packaging may permit the monopolist to more finely price discriminate and possibly improve welfare. Programs or channels of programming that might not be produced under a single price-per-channel scheme may be produced with channel packages.

Of course, price discrimination is not the only possible explanation for "all-or-nothing" channel offers. For example, Wildman and Owen characterize basic cable service as a typical "all-or-nothing" offer. You either subscribe to basic cable with all channels on basic or you do not subscribe to cable. An alternative explanation for basic cable packaging is cost minimization rather than monopolistic price discrimination. For many so-called basic services (Cable News Network, WTBS, Christian Broadcasting Network, for example), the price per subscriber would be so small that a requirement that these channels be priced individually might result in their disappearance from the market. This is because the monitoring and billing costs on a per-channel, per-subscriber basis may be considerably more than any revenues obtained from subscribers. Addressable converters, however, may lower these costs substantially. While they still may not permit per-channel, per-subscriber monitoring and billing for all individual channels, addressable converters may make it profitable to offer small bundles and more channel combinations. Interestingly, some addressable cable systems have begun "unbundling" basic services, charging a fee for "good reception" services and then additional fees for smaller basic channel bundles.

Even if finer price discrimination were the motive for packaging channels, once again there are no hard and fast policy conclusions that can be drawn. In some circumstances, monopolistic bundling may improve consumer welfare; in other instances, bundling may generate a welfare loss.

If the monopolist in the previous analysis is replaced by a number of multichannel competitors, Wildman and Owen conclude that bundling may or may not occur and single-channel firms may or may not be driven out of the market by multichannel firms. Importantly, Wildman and Owen are able to point to factors affecting the extent of multichannel competition, such as the degree of specialized tastes on the demand side and scale economies in channel provision on the cost side. They conclude that "empirical knowledge of these factors is very limited; there is no reason to suppose for example that they will not work out to be the same or similar to those in the print media." Wildman and Owen could have added that there is also no reason to believe that they will.

In addition to these caveats regarding the difficulty of welfare assessments of video competition, economic analysis is further complicated by "First Amendment" concerns, usually addressed in terms of diversity. Wildman and Owen discuss whether competition is sufficient to insure diversity of access (or voices) to the new video media, and conclude that access diversity depends upon ownership diversity. With respect to the latter, the authors assert that "it would be hard to argue for [ownership] standards stricter than those already applied in evaluating the economic consequences of mergers [as described in the Justice Department's merger guidelines]." Yet, if a range of competitive ownership configurations yielded the same level of consumer welfare conventionally calculated, I suspect that advocates of First Amendment concerns might not be indifferent as to which ownership configuration prevailed.

Wildman and Owen have absolutely no analytical basis for their conclusion, but "faith" in competition, a faith that I share. The fundamental difficulty economists have in dealing with diversity issues is our inability to incorporate those concerns into our welfare calculus. The problem, as Besen and Johnson point out in discussing the FCC's ownership policies, is that those who are concerned about diversity in the new environment will not provide anything remotely resembling a quantifiable performance standard against which different ownership configurations can be appraised. With the only standard being "I'll know it when I see it," economists will continue to have problems in determining the compatability of competition and diversity.

This discourse is not meant to be a counsel of despair, but rather a more realistic assessment of what economists can and cannot say about the welfare consequences of emerging video rivalry. But economists are clearly limited in what they can say based upon sound analysis. For example, I share Wildman and Owen's concluding sentiment that it is difficult to see how consumer welfare could be improved by a new array of FCC or legislative regulations imposed on the new video systems. As should be apparent by now, that sentiment cannot be derived from careful analysis of the emerging rivalry, but in my case, it is based on the failure of past regulatory efforts to rectify perceived ills, ills which in many cases were not even present. Moreover, in an industry undergoing as much flux as video, regulation's inflexibility may do irreparable harm to consumers. Put simply, the costs of past video regulation appear to have outweighed any benefits gained, and I have no reason to believe that any new regulations will achieve a more favorable cost-benefit ratio. But that is faith, not analysis.

Economists, however, can contribute hard analysis to the current debate. For example, Wildman and Owen suggest that economic analysis can indicate the costs of seeking more ownership diversity than might be compatible with competition. While there is no way economists can currently judge the additional benefits, policymakers will at least be aware of the costs of their actions. In a similar vein, the FCC's Network Inquiry Special Staff (FCC 1980f) defined three types of diversity (content, access, and the number of options confronting viewers at any one time) and advised the FCC that reducing artificial constraints on the number of options is likely to advance all three forms of diversity.

At the National Cable Television Association, we commissioned the National Economic Research Associates (NERA) (Shew 1984) to assess the welfare loss (conventionally calculated) of various franchising requirements imposed on cable systems. While NERA could not estimate the benefits of, e.g., public access channels (for reasons that should by now be clear), the study did indicate the likely consumer cost of those requirements. Occasionally, one can find a study that is more conclusive. For example at NCTA, the Research and Policy Analysis Department estimated that the deregulation of basic cable prices and the elimination of the delay in awarding cable franchises would result in nine to fourteen new programming services comparable in cost to Nickelodeon. In this instance, deregulation would foster all three forms of diversity.

Given the First Amendment concerns and the second-best considerations surrounding video competition, economists will not have all the answers to pressing regulatory questions. Economics can reduce the degree of guesswork in rendering policy judgments such as the apparently almost wholly arbitrary judgment by the Justice Department's Antitrust Division regarding the Showtime–Movie Channel merger (see

White in paper 11 of this book). Put simply, solid economic analysis can help reduce the extent of future policy failures.

Note

The views of the author do not necessarily reflect those of the National Cable Television Association or any of its members.

PART TWO

The Regulatory Issues in Media Competition

9

The Role of Future Regulation: Licensing, Spectrum Allocation, Content, Access, Common Carrier, and Rates

HENRY GELLER

CONTENTS

  I. Introduction
 II. Governmental Entry Barriers
     A. Licensing
     B. Spectrum Allocation, Assignment, and Authorization
        1. Spectrum Allocation
        2. Spectrum Assignment
        3. Spectrum Authorization
        4. Cable Authorization
III. The Regulatory Scheme: Content and Access
     A. The Three Main Regulatory Models—Broadcast, Print, Common Carrier
     B. Application to the Nonlicensee or Nonbroadcast Licensee
     C. Application to the Broadcast Licensee
        1. Constitutionality of the Public Trustee Scheme
        2. The Public Trustee Scheme from a Policy Viewpoint
        3. The Preferred Approach; Possible Transitional Steps
        4. Application to Cable TV
           a. The Present Status
           b. Constitutionality of These Regulatory Schemes for Cable TV

        c. Policy Considerations
        d. The "Level Playing Field"
IV. Conclusion

I. INTRODUCTION

The regulatory scheme for broadcasting goes back over half a century, but since the early seventies, we have seen the emergence of a whole series of new video delivery systems. Some face the traditional regulatory pattern of television broadcasting; some come under a different or hybrid regulatory scheme; and some essentially escape all regulation. Yet all are engaged in essentially the same process—the delivery of entertainment/information to the home for commercial gain (e.g., advertiser-based; pay-TV; "pray-TV") (Channels 1983). As Stern et al. (1983) shows, the consequence of this turmoil in the video landscape has been regulatory confusion, cries of "foul" because of the absence of a "level playing field," and attempts to fashion a new regulatory pattern for video.

The discussion below treats several important aspects of the problem—governmental entry barriers such as licensing, spectrum allocation, and authorization; the basic regulatory mode such as public trustee; public or leased access; multiple ownership or similar restrictions; and the emerging trends. In view of the broad scope, the discussion is necessarily oversimplified.

II. GOVERNMENTAL ENTRY BARRIERS

A. Licensing

The largest barrier of entry to the new media is the need to obtain governmental authorization. There is no such barrier for cassette distribution. (Where the scheme weds the broadcast station to specially adapted VCRs, as had been the case for ABC's Telefirst project [*Broadcasting,* December 5, 1983, p. 40] FCC authorization is required.) A videotext entrepreneur also needs no license; however, transmission facilities into the home or business are required, for which the provider of these facilities—the telephone company or cable TV system—has obtained government authorization. Note, however, that there is no licensing barrier to the videotext operator: the telephone system exists, is ubiquitous (94 percent penetration), and is available on a common carrier (nondiscriminatory) basis.

Some other video operators face similar situations but perhaps more difficult practical problems. Thus, Satellite Master Antenna Television (SMATV) operators can obtain service from any common carrier satellite carrier to distribute its TV programming to the rooftops of the apartment building. With the FCC's "open skies" policies, there is no shortage of satellite capacity. But a substantial legal problem has arisen: cities more and more are seeking to license SMATV because they see it as a threat to the development of cable TV. Cable TV represents a "golden goose" to the cities in light of the promises made to obtain the franchise, as discussed below. But if SMATV "cream skims" the market by making quick deals with large apartment owners, cable's ability to deliver on its promises may be undermined. Hence the cities have made an effort to bring SMATV within their franchising ambit.

SMATV operators have sought to block this "protectionist" move by the cities and in late 1983 they succeeded in convincing the FCC to preempt local regulation of SMATV (FCC 1983i). So far, the courts have gone along with the FCC.

There are other video entities that escape licensing because they use common carrier facilities. Thus, a Multipoint Distribution Service (MDS) licensee—a common carrier—can provide an outlet for a pay service operator; and there are now multichannel video service proposals (MMDS) that use both MDS and Instructional Television Fixed-Frequency Service (ITFS) channels. Similarly, a Direct Broadcast Satellite (DBS) programmer can provide service directly to the public through facilities and frequencies licensed to a common carrier; the customers of common carriers are not licensed or regulated (FCC 1982a).

The Commission allowed DBS to proceed under a "pick 'em" concept: that is, the applicant can pick its niche by applying as a common carrier, broadcaster, private radio operator, or a combination of these. But if broadcaster status is chosen, in whole or in part, the applicant will be licensed and regulated to that extent as a broadcaster under Title III of the Communications Act. And of course broadcast licensing is required in the case of the commercial TV or STV (Subscription Television) applicant or the low power TV (LPTV) operator.

Finally, licensing is required in the case of cable TV, even though there is no use of the spectrum. Cable requires a franchise from a local (or state) governmental body in order to string its wires over the streets or in the ducts beneath the streets. Arguments have been advanced in several California suits that such franchising should be open-ended and largely ministerial in light of First Amendment and antitrust considerations, but these suits are unlikely to be successful. (*Century Federal, Inc. v. Palo Alto* 1983; *Pacific West Cable Co. v. Sacramento* 1983; *Preferred Communicators v. Los Angeles* 1983).

In sum, the states or localities will continue to license but in one area only—franchising for cable and telephone. They will most likely be precluded from playing "protectionist" games to hinder rivals like SMATV. All other video transmission will continue to require an FCC license under Title III of the Communications Act of 1934 (U.S. Congress (1976): 47§301 et seq.). If the programmer desires to own its own transmission facilities (e.g., a commercial TV or LPTV station or DBS), it will obtain a broadcast license or proceed on a private radio basis, e.g., private operational-fixed microwave service (OFS) (FCC 1981c; 1983l). The other important route is for the video programmer to obtain facilities from a licensed common carrier, e.g., in DBS or MDS, or to enter into a contract with the broadcaster (usually UHF), e.g., STV. Finally hybrid operations will increase; for example, a DBS licensee can be both broadcaster and common carrier, as can the regular TV operator, by using subcarriers for data transmission. While, as we will see, there are greatly different regulatory consequences, the programmer's choice is most often dictated by practical considerations (e.g., less need for start-up capital; reduced risk; earlier entry to obtain entrenchment against rivals). The FCC's laissez-faire, "pick 'em" policy of licensing will undoubtedly continue.

B. Spectrum Allocation, Assignment, and Authorization

1. Spectrum Allocation

The FCC needs to make spectrum available for licensing in all these fields. The FCC's recent record in this respect has been generally commendable and, in light of its trend and congressional prescription, will in all likelihood continue to reflect a "letting in" process. Thus, the

Commission acted promptly to implement the 1979 World Administrative Radio Conference allocation in 12 GHz for DBS. Further, it rejected arguments that Fixed Satellites (FS) could not be used for video programs seeking common carrier facilities for an early DBS start (FCC 1982b, 1983e). In its *DBS* decision (FCC 1982a), it permitted parties to go forward with high definition TV (HDTV) DBS operation, if they so chose. It reallocated frequency so that ITFS channels could also be used for the MDS service, thus facilitating multichannel MDS operation—a necessity if MDS is to compete effectively with cable (FCC 1983:119–20). It authorized LPTV operation on any unused TV channel and specified vertical blanking intervals for teletext service (FCC 1983c, 1982d).

There is controversy as to some facets of FCC spectrum policies. For VHF drop-ins (FCC 1980c), the agency will follow the same pattern as it did in the 9 KHz AM rulemaking (FCC 1981f)—namely, to reject the notion of widespread additional VHF "drop-in" assignments on engineering and service disruption grounds, but the VHF drop-in issue is a difficult one, with strong arguments on both sides.

The agency's overall thrust to allow each service its chance in the marketplace is clear and commendable, and it has received congressional ratification. In the FCC's 1985 authorization legislation (U.S. Congress 1983a), Congress included a provision stating:

Sec. 7. (a) It shall be the policy of the United States to encourage the provision of new technologies and services to the public. Any person or party (other than the Commission) who opposes a new technology or service proposed to be permitted under this Act shall have the burden to demonstrate that such proposal is inconsistent with the public interest.

(b) The Commission shall determine whether any new technology or service proposed in a petition or application is in the public interest within one year after such petition or application is filed or twelve months after the date of the enactment of this section, if later. If the Commission initiates its own proceeding for a new technology or service, such proceeding shall be completed within 12 months after it is initiated or twelve months after the date of the enactment of this section, if later.

2. Spectrum Assignment

In addition to the allocation of spectrum, the assignment rules can be of major importance, as was illustrated by the VHF "drop-in" example. It appears most unlikely that the Commission will make any changes in the near future in the height and power rules for over-the-air TV, LPTV, or MDS. Thus, LPTV will continue to be "beltway" in nature and, equally important, will not be required to be carried by local cable TV systems—carriage that would make the weak LPTV station the equivalent of the most powerful VHF station in cable homes. MDS will continue to be limited in power (100 watts). And of course the over-the-air TV service will continue under the various zone limitations as to antenna height and power, with increasing sharing between UHF and land mobile.

An interesting development in the field is the FCC's increasing tendency to allow a spectrum allocated for one purpose to be used for other purposes—for example, DBS for broadcasting, common carrier, or private radio; FS (fixed satellites) for broadcasting purposes as well as common carrier; television auxiliary stations to transmit over their excess capacity broadcast or nonbroadcast materials to other entities; or subsidiary communications authorization (SCA) for any purpose (FCC 1983a, 1983d, 1983n). The Commission is thus allowing licensees to determine the best or most efficient use of their channels.

There is one other assignment development that merits attention—the determination of the Fowler Commission to use the marketplace to establish the technical standards for new communications services. Thus, the Commission declined to adopt technical standards for DBS systems or teletext on the grounds that an open market approach will allow firms to tailor services to specific demands or situations and to respond to changes (FCC 1982a:716–17; 1983c:1327–28).

Again this is a close issue with substantial arguments on both sides. The market did sort out 33 1/3 versus 45 RPM in record players and seems to be working in determining the VCR standard among Beta and VHS. On the other hand, the Commission's handling of AM stereo (FCC 1982c) including its decision to let all five competing systems simply fight it out in the marketplace, has been, so far, a disaster: no service has been able to establish itself, and it is not clear that a reasonably priced, all-service receiver will be feasible. AM Stereo should have been available to AM stations years ago; it has long been fully developed and is much needed to combat FM's superior sound. Virtually *any* system adopted by the FCC would have served the industry and public better than what has in fact occurred. Now, there is a clear and well-warranted fear that teletext also will be held back and perhaps fail because the FCC abdicated responsibility for adopting technical standards. If that should be the case, future Commissions are likely to eschew the open market approach.

3.Spectrum Authorization

There is the final aspect of the spectrum process—authorization. In the commercial and STV full power service, the FCC continues its regular processing procedures, including the stultifying comparative hearing. As has been unanimously found by critics (e.g., Jones, 1962; Friendly, 1962; Leventhal 1969; Anthony, 1971), this comparative process is time-consuming, wasteful, and almost wholly without merit.

Because it has been inundated by thousands of applications in new fields like LPTV and multichannel MDS, the Commission has sought and obtained from Congress the right to use lotteries (U.S. Congress 1976:47§309i(3)(A)). And it is employing them now in LPTV and proposing to do so in specified markets in the common carrier cellular field (FCC 1983t). It seems clear that the Commission will turn more and more to the lottery as the way out of the authorization logjam it faces in the new services.

In my view, this is poor policy on several grounds. First, if it is desirable to take into account public interest factors like diversification or promotion of minority ownership—and the statute so requires by weighting the applicants in the mass media lottery accordingly (U.S. Congress 1976:47§309i(3)(A);1982:40–47)—a lottery is a poor way to accomplish this. A lottery attracts even the most disadvantaged applicants since, despite the adverse weighting, they may still win. More important, it does not take into account the public interest. Just to give one example, a nonprofit station seeking a low power permit to assist in educating a substantial minority population (e.g., Hispanics in Miami) would have the same chance as an absentee multiple owner. It would be better policy to let a board of experienced civil service employees examine the applications under standards set by Congress and the Commission, and then simply choose the best applicant, without a hearing or review by the Commission itself or the courts. Congress, however, seems unlikely to follow this United Kingdom-type process, so the use of the lottery will persist and increase.

Yet there is a fundamental objection to this process—the availability of a better alternative, the auction. In common carrier fields like MDS or cellular radio, the use of comparative criteria makes even less sense than in the broadcast area, so there is a natural desire to turn to other means like the lottery. An auction has marked advantages: the license goes to the user who will pay the most and for whom the license is most valuable. *It is thus the most direct way to encourage the most efficient and highly valued use of the license, and this in turn greatly benefits the consumer.* As Webbink (1980) demonstrates, an auction is the marketplace approach which produces the most efficient MDS or cellular service. The auction process does not mean that the wealthy will garner all the spectrum, any more than the existence of a marketplace means that the wealthy will purchase all the land or similar scarce "goods": the bidder willing to pay the most must justify the high bid in terms of value to its enterprise. Moreover, no matter how the license is given out (i.e., comparative hearing; lot) the wealthy can always purchase the license subsequently if they value it highly enough.

Meanwhile an auction would provide the agency with feedback on the value of the spectrum involved. For the first time, the FCC would begin to obtain "hard" data on the value of spectrum to users, and as Robinson (1979:389–90) states, they could make good use of this information in allocation proceedings. And, the auction accomplishes this goal while avoiding the lengthy comparative hearing process, with its delays of service to the public and high costs to applicants. Finally, the auction insures that at least a part of the value of the spectrum will be collected by the public, rather than the lottery winner upon the transfer or assignment of the license at a later time.

While noting the advantages of the auction (Robinson 1979:389–90) the Commission has declined to use it because it believes that it is lacking in legal authority (FCC 1980d). Although the matter is not free from doubt, I believe that the FCC can legally proceed with auction, and it should do so in light of the small chance that Congress will expressly authorize the use of auction (FCC 1983s:par. 30).

Thus, as matters stand, the authorization process, while improved with the use of lotteries, remains quite flawed and is unlikely to improve in the near future without the adoption of the auction alternative in the circumstances where it is appropriate. The ultimate solution as proposed by Mueller (U.S. Congress 1982:53)—an open market in spectrum—is an even more remote possibility.

4. Cable Authorization

As noted, a cable television operator must obtain a franchise. The franchise is awarded upon the basis of public service promises—channel capacity, most services offered at lowest rates, a large number of public, governmental, and educational access channels with supporting studios, facilities, funding, etc. The process parallels that of the FCC in dealing with many applicants for prized VHF channels after its 1952 freeze: the applicant made extravagant promises (e.g., on average, 36 percent of programming would be local and live), and then reneged (i.e., 11 percent on the average) (FCC 1971). The motto in the cable field is: "Promise anything to get the franchise, renege later" (*New York Times,* March 4, 1984, F1) and both the cities and the cable companies are at fault.

The cable companies sought relief from Congress, and in the 1984 Cable Act (Congress 1984) they obtained guidelines dealing with revision of services in light of changed circumstances. There is, however, no reason for the federal government to intervene in this essentially local controversy. Solutions would simply be worked out over time in deals and compromises between city and cable.

The present franchising situation not only is stultifying in that it results in awards based on phony public service promises, but also it often greatly delays the institution of service. Thus, in cities like Baltimore, Washington, and Philadelphia, the franchising process has been near interminable. These new cable operators may face entrenched DBS or multichannel MDS, and will be in a very different position from a cable owner invading virgin territory. The window of opportunity may be narrowed or indeed closed if too much time elapses.

A ready solution to this problem of cable franchising is an auction system (Nadel 1983). Regulatory policy should follow a scheme that works for fulfillment of goals—not against them. If the goal of public service is accepted, the cities' scheme—public service bidding—is clearly a poor one for obtaining that goal; as both FCC and cable experience shows, it simply results in broken promises. If, on the other hand, an auction process were adopted, the franchise would be speedily awarded, and the sums obtained could then be used for public service (e.g., funding public, educational, and governmental use of cable).

It is too late now for this sensible resolution of cable entry problems;

auction is out of place in refranchising. Instead we shall see a "muddling through" of both the franchising and refranchising processes.

III. THE REGULATORY SCHEME: CONTENT AND ACCESS

Given the entry process discussed above, the next issue is the applicable regulatory scheme. There are three main regulatory models that may be applied to the video services.

A. The Three Main Regulatory Models—Broadcast, Print, Common Carrier

Three main regulatory models are considered in this analysis. The first, broadcasting, involves close governmental supervision. The TV broadcaster is a short-term (five-year) licensee which must demonstrate to the government (FCC) that it has served the public interest to insure a five-year renewal of its license (U.S. Code: 47§307(d)). Under the Act, the broadcaster is a public trustee, with the obligation to render reasonable local and informational service to its service areas (U.S. Code: 47§§307(b), 315(a); *Red Lion Broadcasting Co. v. FCC* 1969). Not only must it provide adequate coverage of public affairs, but it must do so fairly (U.S. Code: 47§315(a)). Other statutory provisions prohibit indecent or obscene programming, lottery information, rigged contests, and the failure to disclose consideration for material broadcast (U.S. Code: 18§§1304, 1464; 47§§317, 509). Further, the broadcaster must afford equal opportunities to all qualified candidates and reasonable access to those seeking federal office (U.S. Code: 47§§312(a)(7), 315(a)). In addition to these statutory requirements, the FCC has adopted rules and policies setting forth how the TV broadcaster is to ascertain the needs, problems, and interests of its area and minimal processing guidelines in the local and informational programming categories (FCC 1976, 1982i: 47§§73,4010).

In contrast, the print model cannot constitutionally be subjected to licensing, a fairness doctrine, and access requirements. The only governmental interference permitted for content is quite limited: libel or obscenity, and even in these areas, the dice are loaded in favor of the publishers (*New York Times v. Sullivan* 1964). The print model is often allied with the third model—common carrier (e.g., distribution of magazines by the Postal Service).

A common carrier serves the public indifferently, that is, on a first-come first-served basis, without discrimination, and without editorial control over the intelligence transmitted (*NARUC v. FCC,* 1976a:640–42). Title II of the Communications Act (U.S. Code: 47§201 et seq.) requires interstate communications common carriers to file tariffs and bestows on the FCC the power to determine whether they are just and reasonable. But it does not follow that every common carrier *must* be subject to rate regulation or other practices: this is simply a statutory choice. And the FCC is moving away from rate regulation as much as possible, asserting that it has the power to forbear from imposing the full panoply of Title II regulations where the carrier has no market dominance (i.e., virtually all carriers other than AT&T and its partners) (FCC 1982f:189).

B. Application to the Nonlicensee or Nonbroadcast Licensee

A video programmer that does not obtain a broadcast license escapes all of the public trustee obligations discussed above (e.g., the need for local/informational programming; fairness; equal time). Thus, the entrepreneur that utilizes common carrier facilities (MDS, FS, DBS), private radio (OFS), or, of course, cassettes, comes under the print model and is liable only for obscenity or libel. The same is true of the videotext operator employing the facilities of the telephone company and, in all likelihood, a cable system. Under the FCC policy, now under attack in court, customers do not face content regulation.[1]

This has raised the obvious argument: why should the STV operator come under public trustee regulation when it provides a pay service? Why does Satellite Television Corporation (STC) come under broadcast regulation when it provides its pay DBS service, because it also owns its broadcast satellite, when a rival, presenting exactly the same service over common carrier satellites, entirely escapes such regulation? The answer is that the statute imposes certain requirements on broadcasters, and the FCC cannot waive them; accordingly, it imposes on these new "broadcasters," like DBS or LPTV, only statutory requirements (i.e., equal time; fairness; reasonable access). Realistically, it makes little sense to impose these behavioral (content) requirements on an HBO-type operation, and there is a strong theoretical basis for not doing so— namely, the assurance of diversity through the availability of common carrier access. But clearly this area needs reexamination,[2] and the FCC has proposed an overall study (FCC 1983p:par. 32).

Significantly, the Commission has decided upon a deregulatory course for STV, concluding that the service is really hybrid, having qualities of both broadcasting and point-to-point, and exempting it from broadcast requirements on this basis (e.g., ascertainment; reasonable access) (FCC 1982j, 1978a: 1093). The FCC was influenced by the consideration that STV competes directly with other pay services which are not within the broadcast regulatory ambit. The same consideration clearly should apply to an STV operator on LPTV or using "graveyard hour" transmissions to specially adapted VCRs.

It would seem that this trend will continue—that there will be increased focus on *function:* do these video operations carry out the same function—for example, distribution of pay programming—and therefore merit the same kind of regulation? Since important and growing media (e.g., cassettes, MMDS) escape behavioral regulation like equal time and fairness, there will be an increasing tendency to relieve others carrying out the same function (e.g., pay TV) with "broadcast" licensed facilities (e.g., DBS, STV, LPTV). There may be temporary obstacles in light of statutory prescriptions or court rulings, but the result— avoidance of behavioral regulation—seems clear in the long run.

C. Application to the Broadcast Licensee

1. Constitutionality of the Public Trustee Scheme

It has been argued by the present FCC and others (e.g., Stern et al. 1983) that the broadcast model of public trustee/fairness regulation is no longer constitutional since its basis, scarcity, has now eroded in light of the growth in the number of broadcast stations and the new video alternatives. There is no sound basis for this argument, and therefore little if any likelihood that the public trustee concept will fall under judicial assault.

First, the scarcity basis was never a *relative* one—to be compared to other media or even growing numbers in the broadcast medium. Rather, it is based simply on the fact that radio is inherently not open to all; that more people wish to broadcast than there are available frequencies; and that the government must therefore choose and, in choosing, may adopt a public trustee approach (*Red Lion v. FCC* 1969; *NBC v. U.S.* 1943). Everything in the foregoing proposition is equally valid today.

Thus, there are no open TV channels in the top 25 markets, where roughly 50 percent of the U.S. population reside, and only a few vacant

UHF channels in the top 100 markets. If a VHF channel opened in any of the large markets, the FCC would be swamped with applications. Nor is it any answer to say that the TV assignment system could have been better engineered to avoid the present scarcity. Whatever the merits of this proposition (and I believe it to have considerable substance), we are stuck with the existing system, and its constitutionality will accordingly be judged on that pragmatic basis—not some hypothetical one.

Further corroboration of scarcity is provided by the source in which the FCC and its allies seem to place the most trust: the marketplace. *Broadcasting Magazine*'s wrap-up of 1983 station sales (January 9, 1984, pp. 74–82), refers to the "$342-million record-setting purchase of KHOU-TV Houston, $245-million purchase of KTLA-TV Los Angeles: [excluding these two sales] the average price of the 37 VHF sales in 1983 was $24,024,714, bettering by 37 percent the previous high set in 1980 . . . " The physical assets of KHOU-TV probably do not even come to $42 million: the $300 million represent the "scarcity rents" for the license.

In any event, the issue is a legal one. The law has not changed significantly since the 1969 *Red Lion* case. Of course, *Miami Herald Publishing Co. v. Tornillo* (1974) and *Red Lion* are inconsistent. In *Red Lion,* the Court found no chilling effects from a broadcast personal attack rule; it found that the Commission could take remedial action if such effects were to develop, and that the rule promoted First Amendment values (*Red Lion v. FCC* 1969: 256–58). In *Tornillo,* the court found that a personal attack law applicable to print had chilling effects (with no more evidence than in *Red Lion*), and that in any event, the law contravened the First Amendment because it interfered with editorial autonomy (*Miami Herald v. Tornillo* 1974: 256–58).

But the FCC and others are being naive, indeed, if they think that this conflict calls into question the constitutionality of the *Red Lion* rules. The Court, which gave not the slightest indication in *Tornillo* that it was overruling *Red Lion,* knows full well what it is doing—and it clearly regards broadcasting as sui generis from a First Amendment point of view because of the licensing scheme based on engineering scarcity. Thus, in the latest opinion dealing with this general area (*FCC v. NCCB* 1978: 799–800), the Court again stated that "in light of this physical scarcity, government allocation and regulation of broadcast frequencies are essential, as we have often recognized," and further that, as Buckley [*Buckley v. Valeo,* 424 U.S. 1 (1976)] also recognized, however, "'the broadcast media pose unique and special problems not present in the traditional free speech case.'" *Id.,* at 50 n. 55, quoting *Columbia Broadcasting System v. Democratic National Committee, supra,* 412 U.S. at 101. Thus efforts to " 'enhanc[e] the volume and quality of coverage' of public issues" through regulation of broadcasting may be permissible where similar efforts to regulate the print media would not be. 424 U.S., at 50–51, and n. 55, quoting *Red Lion Broadcasting Co. v. FCC, supra,* 395 U.S. at 303; compare *Miami Herald Publishing Co. v. Tornillo,* 418 U.S. 241 (1974). Requiring those who wish to obtain a broadcast license to demonstrate that such would serve the "public interest," does not restrict the interest of those who are denied licenses; rather, it preserves the speech of those who are the "people as a whole . . . in free speech." *Red Lion Broadcasting Co.,* at 390. . . .

The issue is therefore not one of law or constitutionality but rather of *policy.*

2. The Public Trustee Scheme from a Policy Viewpoint

In my view, the public trustee scheme has failed. It has not been effective in achieving its goals and has engendered serious First Amendment strains. The goals have been to promote reasonable local and informational service, serving the needs and interest of the station's areas. The record shows a dismal failure by the Commission over a half century. There has been no enforcement of these public service requirements, despite operations with little or no local/informational programming. The renewal process, whether regular or comparative, has been a joke, with the incumbent renewed irrespective of its public service record. And this botched agency performance has been accompanied by serious First Amendment problems (Geller 1978: 2–23).

The problem is again that the structure works *against* fulfillment of statutory goals. The statute calls the broadcaster a public trustee, but the broadcaster is a business entity in a very competitive milieu, motivated like any entrepreneur to be highly profitable; therefore, once the license is obtained, the broadcaster seeks to maximize its audience and thus collect the greatest amount of advertising revenues. It will thus serve children in the same manner as it does adults—by seeking to attract the maximum child audience (for toy manufacturers) with the cheapest popular program, that is "Sabrina the Witch" rather than a "Sesame Street"-type show. The same holds true for any and all public service programming that does not meet the critical "cost per thousand," advertiser-directed criterion.

3. The Preferred Approach; Possible Transitional Steps

The preferred approach is again to adopt a structure that will facilitate the pursuit of desired goals, as set by the legislature. Subject to periodic review, they might include worthwhile instructional/informational fare for children, cultural programming, in-depth informational programs, programming for the deaf, support for minority-owned broadcast facilities, etc. It is no longer feasible to adopt an auction approach, in light of the private auctions that have already been conducted (e.g., KHOU-TV). But it would be practical to end the public trustee regulatory regime, thus bringing broadcast under the print model, and in its place take a modest spectrum usage fee—say 1–2 percent of gross revenues. After all, the broadcaster not only volunteered to be a public trustee, and is now freed of that obligation, but it retains the valuable privilege that motivated its volunteering: the government gives it the exclusive right to operate on a valuable frequency, and will enjoin all others from interfering with the right. It is really akin to grazing sheep exclusively on federal land.

The sums obtained from usage fees could then be used directly to accomplish the noted goals—through a Corporation for Public Telecommunications much better insulated from potential political interference than the present Corporation for Public Broadcasting. This approach has been advanced by the Executive Branch (Geller 1978: 22–31), one industry trade association, and Chairman Wirth of the House Subcommittee on Telecommunications, Consumer Protection, and Finance. However, it is opposed by the powerful National Association of Broadcasters (NAB) and the three networks. Its adoption in the near term is most unlikely.

This means that while the move to the print model will take place eventually, there will be a gradual transition (perhaps radio first, then television). An appropriate interim scenario might be along the following lines:

(i) The comparative renewal would be eliminated, and the process of the ordinary renewal would be made more objective and certain by adopting percentage guidelines in the two broad programming categories—local and informational (including children's TV)—with stations appropriately grouped (e.g., top 50, 51–100, 101-on, VHF or UHF, affiliate or independent). Under the public trustee scheme, the licensee is, in any event, to be judged on its overall programming effort; it makes no sense to leave the licensee or public uncertain and subject to unbridled administrative fiat in this most sensitive area.

(ii) Reduce the constraints now imposed by behavioral regulation: apply equal opportunities only to paid time; reasonable access only on an overall, not case-by-case basis (Geller and Yurow 1982); and replace fairness with an access (e.g., "op-ed") approach, reviewed only at renewal under a *New York Times v. Sullivan* standard (i.e., governmental intervention only if there is malice, bad faith, or a pattern of reckless disregard of the access request).

The above is clearly not a panacea and falls far short of the preferred approach described earlier, but it is a marked improvement over the flawed present structure and thus an affirmative transitional step. Note, however, that only Congress can activate this transition, and that congressional movement here is by no means certain, in light of the politicians' great interest in, and concern for, the impact of television. Television faces a slow, painful transition to its final goal—video publishing (the print model).

In the meantime, the FCC, along with its "letting in" process, is "letting go" as much as it can, consistent with the statute. Thus, it has acted to deregulate radio and television (eliminating all processing and ascertainment guidelines and requiring only reasonable devotion of time to issues oriented to the community [FCC 1981b; 1984b]); it has a simplified renewal process, "postcard renewal" (FCC 1981d), and is proposing to eliminate its own corollaries to the general fairness obligation—the personal attack and political editorializing rules (FCC 1983o). And, it has sought to relax television multiple ownership policies (FCC 1984c), a poorly conceived move in my view.

But these efforts cannot result in effective deregulation—in the print model. The broadcaster remains a public trustee who can be challenged at renewal, both by petitions to deny and competing applications. It remains subject to equal time, fairness, and reasonable access requirements. Only Congress can deal with these essential issues.

In this respect, one other regulatory effort by the FCC should be noted. In its Report and Order on teletext, the Commission referred to this new transmission as "ancillary" and analogous to the "print medium," and therefore made broadcast requirements such as equal time and fairness inapplicable (FCC 1983c: 1322–24). This is commendable policy but dubious law. The teletext VBI cannot exist without the rest of the signal; it is merely an increment of time which uses the same spectrum as the main part of the signal. Teletext is thus broadcasting, "the dissemination of radio communications intended to be received by the public." (U.S. Code: 47§153(o)). And it does not matter that the signal on the screen is textual: in regular TV there can be a textual scroll. In any event, the definition of "radio communication" (U.S. Code: 47§153(b)) is "the transmission of writing, signs, signals, pictures and sounds of all kinds, including all . . . services . . . incidental to such transmissions." Thus a person engaged in teletext is broadcasting, and the broadcast regulatory provisions come into play.

Suppose a candidate contracts for a five-minute presentation, and runs a ribbon (or announces) that for more "facts," or to make contributions, the viewer should use the keypad for a teletext presentation. The candidate's rivals seek equal opportunities to use the station's teletext facilities in connection with their presentations and are denied such use. Is the Commission really saying that an equal opportunities complaint would not be entertained? And it is quite probable that, to a significant degree, the teletext service will have a tie-in to the programming on the main channel and will enhance or expand upon that programming. In these circumstances, the reasonable access provision of Section 312(a) (7) can also come into play for candidates for federal office. While it is unlikely that any legal challenge will be brought unless or until teletext achieves significant penetration, this again appears to be an area warranting congressional action.

4. Application to Cable TV

a. The Present Status. Cable TV merits special attention in light of its growing importance—large channel capacity and 40 percent penetration of U.S. TV homes with 50 percent projected in the near future. From a regulatory standpoint, cable is particularly puzzling because of its hybrid nature. It closely resembles the broadcaster when it is carrying distant TV signals; when it presents its own programming it is a video publisher; and when it carries data, it resembles the telephone company. The cable operator claims that it is a video publisher, and that, since it makes no use of the spectrum, cable should come under the print model. Dictum in some cases supports this position (*Midwest*

Video v. FCC 1978; *Home Box Office v. FCC* 1977; *Community Commu-nications Co. v. Boulder* 1981; *Omega Satellite Products v. Indianapolis* 1982).

But cable today does not escape broadcast regulation. Because of its close tie-in with the broadcast system, equal opportunities and fairness are applicable to cable. These requirements were adopted in 1969 under the FCC's general authority in the cable area (FCC 1969: 220). They now appear to have statutory backing. For in 1972, in connection with a reform making the lowest unit advertising rate available to candidates, Congress amended Section 315 of the Communications Act to provide that for the purposes of the Section, "the term 'broadcasting station' includes a community antenna system" (U.S. Congress 1972 U.S. Code: 47§315(c)). Since Section 315 specifies equal opportunities and fairness in subsection (a), these broadcast concepts are made applicable to cable. There is no explanation or reference to this in the legislative history.

There is also a substantial issue whether the reasonable access provi-sion of Section 312 (a) (7) of the Communications Act applies to cable. In this 1972 reform, Congress also amended the Communications Act to require that broadcasting stations give candidates for federal elective office reasonable access to their stations. This law also stated (in Sec-tion 102) that the term "broadcasting station" has the same meaning as in Section 315 of the Communications Act. This cross-reference would appear to make the reasonable access provision, which was a part of the 1971 Federal Election Campaign Act, applicable to cable, and the Com-mission so held in its 1972 primer (FCC 1972). However, the Commis-sion has never enforced the access requirement against cable operators and now appears to question whether it can be enforced (FCC 1981g: 24–26).

This tendency to lump cable with broadcasting is further illustrated by the ban on cigarette advertising. That ban would seem to apply to cable as well as to broadcasting since cable is a "medium of electronic communication" (U.S. Code: 15§1335). Again there is no consideration or discussion of this facet in the legislative history.

There are no ascertainment requirements or percentage guidelines (as to local or nonentertainment programming) for cable as there are for broadcast television. And today there are no federal access require-ments for cable (*FCC v. Midwest Video* 1979). Cities, however, have imposed public and, less often, leased access channel requirements. The latter is a common carrier requirement of nondiscriminatory service for hire, while the former is also made available without discrimination but on a free basis.

b. Constitutionality of These Regulatory Schemes for Cable TV. It is necessary to consider first the constitutional issues, because unlike the broadcast field, they are not settled and may well be controlling as to the regulatory approach to be adopted. Is the cable industry correct in its assertion that since it does not use the spectrum, it is a video publisher on its channels and comes within the print model?

I believe that the cable television industry will lose this argument because, unlike the newspaper, it must obtain a government franchise to conduct its business (*Community Communications Co. v. Boulder* 1981: 1378), and this franchise is given out only to a few. Actually, like telephone, it is bestowed as a de facto monopoly—that is, while usually specified as nonexclusive, only one award is given. But this monopoly aspect is not critical. What is crucial is that no franchising authority will give out an unlimited number of permits to string wires through or under the streets; it is simply too disruptive and, in any event, space on poles or in ducts is limited.

The problem with cable's position can be understood by considering the analogy to the telephone company. Suppose a telephone company applied for a franchise to use the streets for its wires, but insisted that it had a First Amendment right to pass on the content of intelligence carried on these wires. The city would obviously demur, stating that it was its policy to bestow telephone franchises only when there was a separation of content and conduit (and note that this would be true even if there were several local phone companies); if the applicant did not want to comply with this sound policy, it should step aside and allow others willing to accede to it to come forward. Clearly the city would be sustained in this position. Why then can the city not insist on some reasonable separation of content and conduit in the case of the similarly placed cable applicant?

Could governmental authority go further and apply a public trustee/fairness concept to cable, based on its licensing aspect (as akin to licensing in broadcasting)? While the matter is not settled, in my view the answer is no. *Red Lion* is uniquely limited and based now on long established tradition (Geller and Lampert 1983). The government does have a substantial purpose or interest in regulating the new cable in the major markets—namely, to deal with the unhealthy First Amendment situation that exists where one entity has the ability to control the content of 80 to 100 or more TV channels into homes because of a limited governmental franchise. The public interest standard in the communications field "necessarily invites reference to First Amendment principles . . . and, in particular, to the First Amendment goal of achieving 'the widest possible dissemination of information from diverse and antagonistic sources'" (*FCC v. NCCB* 1978: 795).

Yet, it does not follow that regulation as a public trustee (with all it embodies, such as fairness, equal time, etc.) is permissible. It is well settled that such regulation, even when in support of a compelling government purpose, must intrude on First Amendment freedoms in the narrowest possible way. (*Hymes v. Mayor of Oradell* 1976; *NAACP v. Button* 1963; *CCC v. Boulder* 1981: 1379). If public trustee regulation were relied upon to further this important governmental purpose, we would be repeating the same mistake that was made without forethought in 1927 as to broadcasting, going down the same slippery slope.

Regulation here should be structural rather than behavioral. There is an alternative that accomplishes the government purpose—diversifying the *sources* of information—and does so in a structural, content-neutral manner. The alternative is to require that some significant number of cable channels be available on a public or leased channel basis—that is, the common carrier model of nondiscriminatory service. Government intervention then is not keyed to the content of any cable programming. It is not triggered by *what* the speaker (cable operator or other user) is saying. Because this alternative is much less likely to lead to undue governmental interference with editorial decisions, it—and not the public trustee approach—must be used to deal with the substantial legitimate problem involved here. As stated, the legal issue is not yet settled, but there are cases now proceeding through the courts that could supply a definitive answer.[3]

Similarly, it is not yet clear whether cable will come within a lax or strict standard on obscene or indecent programming material. In *FCC v. Pacifica* (1978) the Supreme Court upheld the FCC's power to regulate "indecent" speech in broadcasting—to bar the use of "seven dirty words." Such speech is clearly protected by the First Amendment in other contexts. The plurality relied on two factors, both of which relate to the special impact of broadcasting: broadcasting is pervasive and it is uniquely accessible to children. Because of the fact that broadcasting intrudes upon the privacy of the home, the Court found the Commission's interpretation of 18 U.S.C. Section 1464 (to prohibit the indecent—as well as the obscene—from being broadcast) to be constitutional.

In my view (Geller and Lampert 1983), this is a most flawed holding, and appears to reflect a determination by a majority of the Court to "protect" the broadcast audience, whatever the constitutional costs. The issue is whether it will be confined to broadcasting or extended to cablecasts of "offensive" material. So far the attempts to do so have been wisely struck down on the grounds that cable is different from broadcasting and comes within *Miller v. California* (1973), requiring that all three elements of obscenity be established.[4]

c. Policy Considerations. If the foregoing legal analysis is correct, the policy issue left is whether or not government shall impose public and/or leased access requirements on cable. The cable industry does not oppose public access: the new multichannel cable systems in the large markets have ample capacity, and thus dedicating some channels to public (or educational and governmental) access, while it can have nuisance consequences in terms of possibly obscene programming, does not greatly trouble the cable industry as a practical matter. But the industry strongly opposes the leased channel requirement. Its policy arguments can be stated in the following terms:

Cable is not a monopoly in the delivery of video services, since it has several competitors (e.g., commercial TV; STV; MDS; etc); in the circumstances, it is not a necessity, as shown by its tendency to level off at a 50–55 percent penetration rate even though the homes-passed figure is much higher; and finally, it is conceded to be a high-risk business in the major markets. To achieve penetration and success in these markets, the cable entrepreneur carefully puts together its package of tiers combining various services. All this careful planning can be set at naught if it must lease channels to cable programmers who can put together their own tier or combinations. Further, this constitutes an "unfair ride" on the risk-taking and heavy investment of the cable operator.

These arguments have considerable substance. Nevertheless, it seems to me that there is a stronger policy argument in favor of the requirement of some leased channels. First and foremost, there is the *Associated Press* principle discussed earlier: it is simply wrong for one entity to control the content of so many channels (50–100, or more) on an important medium based on a governmental grant. We do not allow one entity to own all, or indeed even more than one, of the TV stations in a community. Further, while cable's penetration does seem to end up at about 55 percent of TV homes in the community (with considerable "churn"), for that 55 percent, cable is the means of entry for video programming such as pay-TV. Failure to gain access to the cable simply cuts off the programmer from the substantial cable audience. And vertical integration here can exacerbate this problem, as shown by some prior incidents.[5]

The requirement of some reasonable provision of leased channels does not mean that rate of return regulation is automatically required. As Homet (1984) argues, it is perfectly feasible to have a common carriage (nondiscriminatory) requirement without rate of return regulation, the latter being appropriate for monopoly situations like the local telephone company. The critical consideration is nondiscriminatory access—not limiting the return of the cable company. The terms and conditions of nondiscriminatory access would be fixed by the cable systems, and if controversy developed, as might be the case in light of cable's aversion to leased access, this could be handled in a number of ways. Homet (1984) suggests that the courts resolve the issue, as they have done in the past. The drawbacks here may be delay: the programmer rarely can afford to wait out a perhaps lengthy court proceeding; it must usually gain quick access for its service; compulsory arbitration may therefore be a better solution. The programmer is immediately given access, and any dispute on terms is then resolved through the arbitration process, perhaps using the "last offer" variation (i.e., the arbitrator must select from the last offers made by each side). Significantly, the cable industry has endorsed the concept of arbitration when it works in its favor (U.S. Congress 1983b: §613(d) (2)).

One suggestion to meet the arguments of the cable industry is to delay the introduction of this regulatory scheme until cable has "turned the corner" in the major markets. This approach parallels the FCC's present trend of not adopting regulatory restraints, such as multiple ownership rules for DBS, unless and until the service blossoms; if it never succeeds, there is no need for regulation. The 1974 Cabinet Committee Report on Cable Television in effect adopted this approach: it called for the separation of content and conduit on cable (with the exception of two channels) when cable penetration reached 50 percent of U.S. TV homes.

The difficulty with the approach is that the industry becomes entrenched after years of operation without the regulatory scheme and is thus in an excellent position to fend it off. Cable is now at 40 percent penetration and is rapidly approaching 50 percent—yet the industry is so entrenched and powerful that the issue is not separation of virtually all channels from the operator's control but rather whether even a few channels will be open for leasing. At present the FCC has no access provisions; cities usually require public access but not leasing (or if the latter, it is on a phony basis left to the cable system's full discretion and therefore not really utilized); and the federal legislation recently enacted (U.S. Congress 1984) appears ineffectual. For the new law preempts the area and then imposes a leasing requirement for video programming that is not likely to be of much use to a cable programmer in need of prompt access (e.g., the cable system can set terms assuring that the lease "will not adversely affect the operation, financial condition, or market development of the cable system"; the system's terms are to be considered reasonable, and a complaint must make a "clear and convincing" case to the contrary to the court) (U.S. Congress 1984: §612 (c)(1), (d), (f)).

In these circumstances, there is little likelihood of real progress in the near future. I continue to believe that eventually some separation of content and conduit will be imposed in cable. It may be that this will only arise after flagrant abuses, such as the system operator's exercise of its own prejudice to rule off some programming or issues (e.g., an operator stated its intention not to carry the antinuclear holocaust show, "The Day After," to the great embarrassment of the industry, *Broadcasting*, November 21, 1983, p. 88). This might be termed "waiting for thalidomide" as a prescription for the passage of needed effective legislation.

In the meantime, the FCC has sought to "let go" in this area also. It is therefore considering ending the application of the fairness doctrine (and its corollary rules) to cable systems with access channels, on the ground that such channels serve the purpose of the doctrine without the need for governmental intervention (FCC 1983m). That is a commendable step, but once again there is a much better solution ignored by the Commission: that is to proscribe any censorship by cable of the individual programs carried on the system (other than on local origination channels). This would not interfere with the system's operation, since the cable operator would still select the signals to be carried; how they are presented (e.g., tiers, charges); and when they are to be dropped or shifted. The operator would only be prohibited from censoring or dropping an individual program on CNN or HBO or USA and, realistically speaking, the operator usually does not know what is being presented over the many channels on the modern system.

By proceeding in this fashion, the operator would be freed not just of fairness but of all content regulation: equal opportunities, reasonable access, libel or slander, obscenity or indecency. The remedy would be to proceed against the programmer, as in the case of messages carried by the telephone company or the postal service. This is an obvious step to be taken; it is again resisted by the cable industry, which insists that it is a "telepublisher" on all 50 to 100 channels. Over time, this short-sighted opposition will be overcome.

d. The "Level Playing Field." The problems with the stultifying bidding process in the major markets has been noted. There is one other aspect that merits some discussion: cable's basic service package (access, local and distant signals, and usually some cablecasting signals like Christian Broadcasting Network or USA or CNN) is often subject to rate regulation by the local franchising entity. While the FCC preempted all regulation of pay channels and expanded this preemption to include tiers with pay or advertiser-based cable services (FCC 1975b, 1983q; *Brookhaven v. Kelley* 1978), the 1984 Cable Act will free basic rates from regulation in those markets where cable systems are subject to effective competition over a two-year transition period (U.S. Congress 1984: §623).

The policy seems to have worked well in the several states where it has been employed. Further, the cities appear to use rate regulation of basic service more as leverage to get cable to carry out promises than as a serious effort to prevent overcharging. But the question remains why this is not a matter left to resolution at the local level.

There is another "level playing field" issue that will disappear over time: the problems associated with the FCC's "must carry" regulations (i.e., the cable system must carry all local TV stations, as defined in the FCC regulations). This poses no issue in the case of the new systems with large capacity. But a large proportion of systems still have 12 or less channels and, until rebuilt, cannot present the new cable services like CNN because of the need to carry many local signals. Broadcasters strongly oppose elimination of the "must carry" rules, and the FCC is unlikely to act in these circumstances (although it is conceivable that some relief could be afforded by not requiring full carriage of all duplicating network affiliates). The cable industry previously lost on this issue in the courts (*Black Hills v. FCC* 1968), but is trying again on the grounds of new circumstances (*Quincy Cable TV v. FCC* 1983; *Turner Broadcasting Co. v. FCC* 1984). The broadcasters meanwhile, are pushing for codification of the rule in Congress.

There is a sound solution: the FCC should eliminate all authorization of distant signals for new cable systems or those in the top 100 markets, and at the same time end the "must carry" and other requirements. Cable today is a parasite on the broadcast system: it carries distant ·broadcast signals under government fiat and at rates fixed by the government; the government therefore also requires cable to observe the bedrock concept of the broadcast system—local service. If a cable system came fully within the competitive TV programming market place, there would be no reason why it should be called upon to give a "special break" to broadcasters. And the government would also then not be skewing the market towards cable: all cable's carriage would be determined in the marketplace (except for smaller systems "grandfathered" to prevent great disruption).

One can expect progress along the above lines, but it will be slow and painful: these are powerful industries, and they will not lightly give up long established advantages. Congress detests clashes of such industries and usually admonishes them to work out a compromise or forget about legislation.

There is still another "level playing field" issue between cable and telephone. Cable in large cities is now entering the data market. The telephone company argues that such entry is unfair in that cable's services are unregulated, while its operations receive the full panoply of local regulation. It contends that either both should be deregulated or both regulated. In response to the telephone industry, some local Public Utility Commissions (PUCs) have sought to regulate cable (*Cox Cable Communications v. Simpson* 1983). The cable industry, in turn, has sought to block PUC regulation through preemptive FCC and congressional action (*Cox Cable Communications* 1983). The 1984 Cable Act does preclude all regulation of cable telecommunications services defined as the one-way transmission of video or other programming, including videotext (U.S. Congress 1984; H.R. 4103, §§602(16); 621(c); 624(f)).

Cable is surely right that there is a difference between a cable system and a *monopoly* telephone company, and that one does not build the same cage for the canary and the gorilla. The canary should go free. But the gorilla, while it needs a keeper (FCC/PUC) and "bells and whistles" (rate regulation; fully separated subsidiaries for competitive endeavors), ought not be caged. Under the Modified Final Judgment (MFJ) in the AT&T antitrust case, the divested Bell Operating companies are, however, caged. They cannot engage in any information services unless they show the district court that there is no substantial possibility that they can use their monopoly power to impede competition in the particular field they seek to enter (*U.S. v. Western Electric* 1982). This issue—the total suppression of BOC competition in the enhanced (data) fields—certainly warrants further consideration, and will be the subject of great controversy over the next decade.

IV. CONCLUSION

Based on the foregoing analysis, I would predict the following patterns of future regulation in this important area:

— The "letting in, letting go" process will continue. The overall trend will be to video publishing—to the print model, with a substantial portion of such publishing occurring over common carrier facilities (telephone and multichannel cable), with rate regulation only of the former.

— New services requiring radio licensing will be allowed to pick their regulatory mode (broadcast, common carrier, private radio, hybrid), subject only to the statutory requirements imposed by Congress. The FCC will wait for the service to mature before considering rules (although it may be politically infeasible to adopt rules once an industry is entrenched).

— In the broadcast field, the public trustee concept will be fought about in Congress, with progress in video only after radio deregulation is tested. In the meantime, the FCC will continue to relax its own rules, consistent with the statute, but will be faced with perennial litigation from those who will charge them with inconsistent or arbitrary agency action.

— In cable, behavioral regulation will fade, as the video publishing (print model) takes firm hold, but the festering issues of access, particularly of a leased (common carrier) nature, will remain.

— As to the many facets of the "level playing field" issue, great difficulties will be encountered in eliminating skewed governmental policies. As Senator Magnusson observed, "all each industry seeks is a fair advantage over its rivals."

In short, we are proceeding in the right direction, but the transition will be difficult. Goethe once observed, "the Devil is in the details." I would amend that to: "the Devil is in the transition."

Notes

1. A caveat should be noted here. While the Commission stresses that the regulatory scheme does not call for regulation of the customers, it nonetheless kept a possible "string" here. Thus, the FCC couched its DBS order in terms of declining to assert jurisdiction, "because the Communications Act does not expressly require that customer-programmers of common carriers be regulated, and because unwarranted regulation would stifle desirable experimentation and development" (FCC 1983e: FCC brief on appeal, p. 8). The brief further states that the Commission "emphasized, however, that it would respond appropriately if circumstances arise to suggest a need for regulation. *Id.* at 77 *Reconsideration,* FCC 83-271 at 2 n.2." The Court reversed, holding that whenever radio facilities are used to disseminate programming directly to the public, this use must come under broadcast regulation (e.g., sec. 315 requiring equal opportunities), either by regulating the common carrier licensee or its customer

(*United States Satellite Broadcasting Co. Inc. v. FCC*, 1984). The FCC may seek further review so the matter remains in doubt. In my view, the key consideration is that the common carrier affords *access* to users, and this negates any resort to broadcast regimen.

It is possible to impose a regulatory scheme upon the customer—by attaching reasonable conditions to the license of the common carrier (see *Carter Mountain Transmission Corp. v. FCC* 1963), imposing carriage and nonduplication requirements on cable systems that are customers of common carriers)—but this indirect method has never been used to impose behavioral content regulation (fairness, equal time) and would be of most dubious validity, if attempted.

2. There are other anomalies. Thus, unlike the MDS operator who is treated as a common carrier, the ITFS licensee can sell its excess capacity to pay TV entrepreneurs without incurring common carrier status. Also, a teletext operation on MDS would not raise the equal time or fairness problems that can be encountered in the broadcast mode (see above). For further treatment of the many anomalies, see Botein, chapter 10 herein.

3. See *Berkshire Cablevision of Rhode Island, Inc. v. Burke* (1983), upholding the constitutionality of access regulations promulgated by the Rhode Island Division of Public Utilities and Carriers. But see Shapiro et al. (1983).

4. These elements are that the material is patently offensive by contemporary standards, is prurient in nature, and lacks serious redeeming social value. See *Community Television of Utah, Inc. v. Roy City* (1982).

5. When *Times-Mirror* began its new pay service, Spotlight, it removed HBO from most of its own systems; HBO did not enlist an STV or MDS to compete; it was simply foreclosed. Similarly, Cable News Network was precluded from access to Westinghouse's Manhattan system and filed an antitrust suit based on Westinghouse's preference for its own cable news service (now defunct).

10

The FCC's Regulation of the New Video Technologies: Backing and Filling on the Level Playing Field

MICHAEL BOTEIN

CONTENTS

 I. Introduction
 II. A Comparative Analysis of the FCC's Regulatory Policies
    A. Procedural Inhibitions on Entry
    B. Structural and Ownership Limitations
    C. Jurisdictional Bases
    D. Degree of Federal Preemption
    E. Program Content Control
 III. Conclusion

I. INTRODUCTION

Like many other federal agencies, during the past few years the Federal Communications Commission (FCC) has engaged in a spree of re-regulation, deregulation, and now unregulation. The basic assumption behind this exercise is that effective competition among rational profit-maximizing entrepreneurs inevitably will produce consumer satisfaction and make regulation unnecessary (Fowler 1982). This tenet produces the regulatory imperative of creating—or at least encouraging—as much competition as possible within an industry. The sole role of governmental intervention is to create a "level playing field" on which firms can compete.

Whether regulation can produce these market conditions is far from clear. As Representative Tim Wirth has quipped, "there's no such thing as a level playing field or airline food" (Wirth 1983). Part of the problem, of course, is that government traditionally has two distinct—and basically inconsistent—ways of promoting competition.

The first, a temptingly logical approach, is simply to impose identical restrictions upon all potential players. This rationale is eminently fair, assuming that all these players have reasonably comparable abilities. If they do not, however, this approach runs into both political and equitable problems. After all, the public and its representatives traditionally get a bit queasy at the sight of a 240-pound professional football player landing on the back of a 140-pound high school athlete. As a result, it is tempting to adjust any game's rules so that everyone can play.

Precisely because of this very human—and very inefficient—tendency, the second and time-honored method of creating a level playing field is to rein in the most effective players. Common examples are handicaps for golfers, weights for jockeys, and separation of professional from amateur athletes. Indeed, much of the New Deal's sometimes murky philosophy derived from this principle. This approach, naturally, is heresy to any ideologically pure deregulator, since it injects government into the marketplace. Nevertheless, it routinely creeps into administrative decision-making because of demands for equity. Classic examples in telecommunications policy include the now declassé anti-siphoning rules, which prevented cable or subscription television from competing with broadcast television to buy motion pictures as well as sporting events (*Home Box Office v. FCC* 1977) and the still operational multipoint distribution service (MDS) rules, which prohibit an MDS operator from controlling more than half of its programming (FCC 1983v:47§21.900).

The current ideologically pure Commission purports to have used only the first approach in bulldozing a level playing field for the new video technologies. In most respects, this probably has been the case. Nevertheless, it is useful to test the Commission's premises by analyzing the consistency of its current regulatory scheme. This chapter thus reviews the FCC's policies toward the new video technologies in several different areas, including ease of entry, ownership restrictions, jurisdictional bases, degree of federal preemption, and content regulation.

These areas merit consideration because they have a heavy impact on each medium's ability to compete effectively. This classification scheme is suggestive rather than scientific, however, since there are no data available on the cost of regulatory burdens. Indeed, some of these media do not even exist, and the Commission's abolition of most reporting requirements will make it difficult to create accurate data bases in the future.

With these considerations in mind, it is appropriate to begin a perhaps pedestrian analysis of the Commission's regulatory approaches to the new video media. On many points, the most relevant observations focus not on what the FCC has stated, but rather on what it has failed to say. In these situations, of course, a certain amount of speculation as to the Commission's intent is necessary.

II. A COMPARATIVE ANALYSIS OF THE FCC'S REGULATORY POLICIES

The primary goal of deregulation is to encourage competition in previously regulated markets. Although perhaps desirable from a logical point of view, completely uniform regulation is often either politically or pragmatically infeasible; after all, most potential competitors are not even roughly comparable in terms of market performance. An operational regulatory goal in many cases is to equalize the effects of regulation on competitors. It is, therefore, less than surprising that the FCC's regulation of the new video technologies shows a notable lack of consistency.

A. Procedural Inhibitions on Entry

Since most of the new video technologies are infant industries, there are few absolute barriers to entry. In all the over-the-air services considered here, a substantial amount of spectrum has been available for initial licensing, even if there has not been enough for every potentially interested user. Moreover, only a few absolute legal bans—such as prohibitions on alien ownership or cross-ownership—currently exist, and the FCC is attempting to abolish most of these.

As is inevitably the case in regulation, however, a variety of procedural requirements may inhibit or delay entry. More important for purposes of this analysis, these potential procedural snares vary significantly from one medium to another. To a certain extent, of course, this situation results from differences in the underlying statutory and case law. For example, conventional broadcast television, LPTV, STV, and any other broadcast use are subject to a wide variety of statutory and judicial doctrines which evolved during the 1950s and 1960s, when the Commission focused most of its regulatory attention upon broadcasting (Krasnow et al. 1982). Moreover, the effect of this historical accident may be exaggerated somewhat by the vagaries of the Commission's current regulatory program. Because of both political and judicial opposition, the Commission has found it harder to repeal existing rules than to avoid adopting new ones. Three areas of the FCC's procedural rules seem particularly noteworthy.

First, the Commission's current application processes effectively require applicants for some services to undergo substantially more steps than applicants for other services. For example, the Commission has proposed eliminating the traditional requirement of a construction permit in processing applications for MMDS stations. Applicants for conventional broadcast, STV facilities, and LPTV stations, however, apparently still must secure a construction permit before applying for a covering license. Applicants for DBS facilities must obtain a construction permit, launch authority, and a covering license.

To be sure, legal and historical reasons explain many of these procedural differences. The Communications Act requires broadcasters to secure a construction permit before applying for a covering license (U.S. Code 47§319), and the Commission has done business in this fashion for fifty years. Moreover, implementation of DBS service requires coordination with other government authorities, which control the nation's publicly operated satellite launch facilities. The Commission's action might flow from an assumption that MMDS's impact on a national scale will be minimal, while DBS's might be substantial. Nevertheless, the requirement of construction permits for DBS but not for MMDS arguably might allow an MMDS station to go on the air substantially before a DBS operation.

A similar phenomenon may exist as to petitions to deny or competing applications. Under the doctrine of *Carroll Broadcasting v. FCC* (1958), the courts have required the Commission to allow an existing broadcaster to oppose a license application by showing that grant of another license would make operation of both the existing and the new stations economically infeasible and thus deprive the public of service. The *Carroll* doctrine's wisdom is questionable, because it eliminates potential competition solely on the basis of economic projections; but until the D.C. Circuit disavows the doctrine, it continues to apply to conventional broadcast television applications. At the same time, the Commission has indicated that it will not apply *Carroll* to LPTV (FCC 1982d:507) and DBS (FCC 1982e:1352–53) applications. The Commission's reasoning seems to be that neither LPTV nor DBS is likely to have any significant impact upon conventional television broadcasting. Still, it is not clear that the Commission can use a general policy statement to avoid case-by-case adjudication (*United States v. Storer* 1956; *FCC v. Texaco* 1964).

The Commission may have good reasons for not applying *Carroll* to the new video technologies. Along these lines, however, it should be noted that the Commission has cautioned LPTV operators against causing direct electrical interference to either MDS or cable operators (FCC 1982d:497–99). After all, *Carroll* may never have made much sense because of its clearly anticompetitive consequences, and it presumably makes even less sense in a video industry of abundance. The continued applicability of *Carroll* to broadcasting, but not to the new video technologies, seems a bit anomalous, however, unless the Commission implicitly is stating that it will not enforce the doctrine as to broadcasting either—a position also with questionable legal validity.

A third procedural difference arises from the Commission's procedure for resolving competing applications for the same frequency. Traditional case law required the Commission to hold comparative hearings (*Ashbacker Radio v. FCC* 1945), which are infamous for their Dickensian length and cost. Under a recent amendment to the Communications Act, however, the Commission may resolve comparative proceedings by means of lotteries (FCC 1983b). Although the Commission has proposed to use the lottery procedure for both conventional broadcast television and comparative MMDS licenses (FCC 1983f:145), it has applied the lottery procedure only to applications for LPTV licenses. As a result, an applicant for a conventional broadcast television station must wade through years of litigation and thousands of dollars in legal expenses, while a potential LPTV operator in the same community would receive comparatively speedy and certainly inexpensive processing.

Once again, there may be sound reasons for this situation. Regardless of its deregulatory philosophy, the Commission may find it difficult to depart from almost forty years of precedent—albeit rather unsatisfactory experience—with comparative hearings for broadcast stations. Moreover, there simply may be less need for concern about picking the "right" licensee for LPTV and MMDS, because of the initially limited public use of these services. (This rationale obviously will not apply if these services—particularly MMDS—become "wireless cable" systems.) In addition, the Commission may be the victim of the regulatory lag inherent in disposing of old rules.

The analysis above conspicuously omits any consideration of cable television for the simple reason that cable systems need not obtain a license or other authorization from the FCC. Instead, a cable operator need only file a "registration statement" when it actually begins operations (FCC 1983v:47§76.12). Cable operators, however, must obtain licenses to operate microwave relay stations (FCC 1983v:47§78.11) which are essential for any large system. In theory, a cable operator can begin operations considerably more expeditiously than any of the over-the-air new video media. In reality, of course, most multiple systems operators have had to wage costly "franchise wars" in order to obtain choice franchises. For example, New York City granted franchises for Manhattan in 1970, but not for the other four boroughs until 1983. Depending upon the disposition of a city's governing authorities, a cable operator may face procedural delays as great as or even greater than those applicable to the other new video technologies.

Precisely because of these difficulties in the local cable franchising process, the Commission showed steadily increasing tendency to preempt local cable regulation. It first took local authorities out of rate regulation (FCC 1983h), and then prevented local authorities from regulating satellite master antenna systems (SMATV's)—i.e., private cable systems which serve only one apartment dwelling or complex (FCC 1983r). Moreover, the Commission informally threatened to preempt all state and local regulation of cable, if the Congress did not pass legislation limiting the regulatory powers of state and local governments—a strategy which apparently created pressure for passage of the Cable Communications Policies Act of 1984, as discussed in Subsection D.

To the extent that abuses in local cable regulation exist, preemption by the Commission may have been sound policy. But while the Commission has invoked preemption to relieve the cable industry from local regulation, it has failed to substitute any federal licensing or certificating requirements. The ultimate result of federal preemption could be that all of the new video media—except cable—would face sometimes convoluted and expensive authorization processes. Although this would be just a side effect of the Commission's and the Congress' attempt to prevent perceived local abuses, it could give cable a substantial procedural advantage over the other new video technologies.

Thus the new video media are subject to different procedural schemes for obtaining operating authorizations. These differences translate into time and money. For example, if a potential STV operator must go through a lengthy comparative hearing while a potential LPTV operator need not, the latter presumably will incur fewer expenses than, and be operational before, the former. Therefore, if a particular geographic market can support only one over-the-air pay television operation, a group of LPTV operators might foreclose future entry by a potential STV operator. There may be good reasons for these seemingly anomalous results, but so far the Commission has failed to articulate them very thoroughly.

B. Structural and Ownership Limitations

Not only may an ownership restriction bar a firm from a market, but it may also make it difficult for other firms to generate capital by means of joint ventures and the like. Thus when Congress abolished the prohibition on alien ownership of cable television systems in 1974 (FCC 1975d:160n.7) it brought a significant—and sorely needed—amount of Canadian capital into the U.S. cable industry. Ownership limitations have comparatively little impact on acquisition of programming, which is essentially a separate business. So even though an English firm cannot own more than twenty-five percent of a U.S. broadcast station, British programmers obviously have done a brisk trade in the United States.

In general, the Commission has imposed comparatively few ownership restrictions on the new video technologies and has attempted to eliminate most existing ones. Perhaps because of the inherent problems of history and regulatory lag, however, the Commission's present ownership policies are less than consistent.

The FCC has retained its traditional prospective ban on cross-ownership of a radio station, newspaper, or cable system by a broadcast television station in the same market (FCC 1983v:47§73.636), but it has not imposed similar cross-ownership requirements upon MMDS, DBS, or LPTV operators. When considering cross-ownership issues in the context of the new video technologies, the Commission merely has repeated its rhetoric that cross-ownership prohibitions are unnecessary in light of multiple video sources (FCC 1982d:486). The contrast between this approach and traditional cross-ownership prohibitions is anomalous. On the one hand, a broadcast television station may not acquire a radio station in its market without a waiver from the Commission (FCC 1982h). On the other hand, it is perfectly free to acquire one or more MMDS, DBS, and LPTV operations serving that same area—even though the latter three operations are likely to garner a larger share of the audience than is one radio station.

There may be an argument in favor of allowing local cross-ownership of MMDS, DBS, LPTV, and cable operations, on the theory that—at least in the very short run—aggregation of these media outlets creates countervailing power to local broadcast television stations and newspapers. However, the Commission obviously has not taken this approach; rather, it allows broadcast television stations to own MMDS and DBS, but not cable (FCC 1983v:47§76.51) operations in their markets. Similar arguments exist for allowing cable/telephone cross-ownership (FCC 1981a).

Conversely, the Commission's policies do not consider possible future growth by the new video technologies. For example, cable and MMDS eventually may supply the vast majority of premium programming (Microband 1984). By permitting cross-ownership of MMDS, DBS, LPTV, and cable operations, the Commission may be creating the risk that it will need to unscramble this omelet at some point in the future—a job which it has found singularly distasteful in the past with cross-ownership of local newspapers and broadcast or cable operations (FCC 1975c, 1980a).

Along similar lines, the FCC traditionally has limited the number of broadcast stations which a multiple owner may acquire (FCC 1983v:47 §73.636). Yet the Commission has disavowed multiple ownership restrictions for MMDS, LPTV, DBS, or cable (FCC 1982g). In the absence of common and cross-ownership restrictions, one firm in theory could own all MMDS, DBS, and cable systems in the country. Still this scenario seems rather unlikely, if only because AT&T has not expressed any interest in it. Instead, ownership of the new video media presumably will follow the historical pattern of oligopoly. Nevertheless, the Commission's liberal postures on both common and cross-ownership have significant implications for the future, depending upon how the new video technologies develop.

Once again, the sharp contrast between the Commission's restrictions on conventional radio or television stations and its relaxed attitude toward the new video media seems to be largely a result of history. After all, the Commission currently is in the process of attempting to repeal its multiple ownership restrictions for radio and television, partially in response to arguments that the emergence of the new video media makes strict multiple ownership rules unnecessary (FCC 1983y).

In terms of alien ownership, the Commission faces a somewhat more complicated problem. Section 310(a) of the Communications Act prohibits a foreign firm from owning more than twenty-five percent of the stock in a U.S. broadcast station or common carrier (U.S. Code:47 §310(a)). Because of low-visibility technical amendments in 1974, however, Section 310(a) applies only to broadcasting and common carriage. Thus, by its terms, the statute does not govern MMDS, DBS, or cable. (To the extent that any of these media elected to operate as a broadcaster or carrier, Section 310(a) presumably would apply.)

If the purpose of Section 310(a) is to restrict foreign control of the U.S. mass media, the current exemption of cable, MMDS, and DBS seems anomalous. Moreover, the rather haphazard coverage of the present statute creates some strange situations. For example, alien ownership of an MMDS operation using leased educational microwave channels presumably would be acceptable, because these facilities are neither broadcasters nor carriers. On the other hand, the same foreign corporation could not acquire more than twenty-five percent of a traditional single-channel MDS operation—which might be folded into an MMDS operation—because the single-channel MDS operation is, technically, a common carrier. Since most MMDS systems probably will combine leased educational channels and existing single-channel MDS stations, the present situation has the potential for endless mischief. The Commission could resolve these anomalies merely by adopting alien ownership restrictions as a matter of discretion as it proposed to do for cable television (FCC 1975d) but has shown no inclination to act.

Finally, the Commission traditionally has reserved both radio and television frequencies for educational and noncommercial uses (FCC 1983v:47§73.606). It has declined to do so, however, for DBS (FCC 1982e:1347–48) or cable (FCC 1981e). MMDS operations presumably will lease educational microwave channels, thus building in an educational component; and since a number of television broadcast channels already are assigned to noncommercial uses, the present reservation of noncommercial frequencies effectively is built into the LPTV service (FCC 1982d:490). The Commission's reasoning seems to be that existing public television stations provide sufficient educational programming, even though many public stations have poor transmission facilities and small coverage areas. Although this rationale has a certain amount of abstract validity, it ignores the current decline in public television funding. The Commission's only response to this problem seems to be that MMDS will provide funding for local educational microwave stations, by leasing channels from them (FCC 1983g:383). The amount of such funds is likely to be quite insubstantial, however, unless and until the MMDS industry grows significantly.

Moreover, the Commission's refusal to reserve noncommercial allocations distributes the burden of providing noncommercial television channels somewhat unequally. The Commission's policy reduces the number of commercial channels available to conventional, LPTV, or STV broadcasters, and increases the number available to DBS and cable operators. Since this position does not change the status quo for broadcasters, there may be no advantages or disadvantages in relieving DBS and cable operators from offering noncommercial channels. But some potential broadcasters might suffer by not being able to use conventional, STV, or LPTV channels for advertiser-supported and pay programming.

Thus the FCC has not been terribly consistent in its ownership policies for the new video technologies. As would be expected, the reasons lie partially with statutory problems and partially with history. If the Commission were to make at least some major changes—e.g., as to alien ownership—it would need to seek amendments to the Act.

C. Jurisdictional Bases

Under the Act, the FCC has at least five different types of regulatory jurisdiction. First, under Title II of the Act, the Commission has jurisdiction over any "common carrier"—a term which is defined rather circularly as "a common carrier for hire in interstate or foreign communication" (U.S. Code: 47§153(h)). The basic notion of common carriage is comparatively simple, focusing on whether a firm either holds itself out by its business practices or is required by law to provide transmission services to any properly qualified customer. The most common types of communications common carriers, of course, are local and long-distance telephone companies.

Second, the Commission also has jurisdiction under Title III of the Act over use of "any apparatus for the transmission of energy or communications or signals by radio" (U.S. Code: 47§301). This jurisdiction in turn breaks down into three distinct subcategories. The most visible is regulation of broadcast stations, of course, and Title III contains special provisions applicable only to broadcasters—such as the fairness doctrine and sponsorship identification requirements. In addition, a license is necessary under Title III for any Title II common carrier spectrum use. Moreover, Title III gives the Commission jurisdiction over spectrum uses which are neither broadcasting nor common carriage. These usually fall under the general rubric of "private radio."

Finally, the FCC has a very vague type of implied or residual power over activities which are not squarely within either Title II or Title III. The most significant example of this type of jurisdiction is the Commission's "reasonably ancillary" jurisdiction over cable television. Although the extent of this jurisdiction is open to continuing question, it appears to be totally separate from—albeit implied by—the Commission's other jurisdiction (*United States v. Southwestern Cable* 1968). Its relationship to the FCC's limited jurisdiction under the new Cable Act is less than clear.

The D.C. Circuit recently seemed to limit the FCC's discretion in choosing jurisdictional bases for the new media, by holding that the Commission could not refuse to regulate either DBS operators or their customers as broadcasters—and thus subject them to the full panoply of fairness, equal opportunities and other traditional broadcast regulations (*National Ass'n of Broadcasters v. FCC* 1984.) The court reasoned that since "DBS systems transmit signals to homes with the intent that these signals be received by the public, such transmissions rather clearly fit the definition of broadcasting." At the same time, the court rejected analogies to regulation of MDS as a common carrier, suggesting that the

Commission's initial classification of MDS may have been incorrect. The case thus casts considerable doubt on the FCC's treatment not only of DBS, but also MMDS and the other new video media.

The FCC's choice of a jurisdictional basis has a significant impact upon the legal status of a medium. If a medium is classified as broadcasting, it becomes subject to a wide variety of statutory requirements, ranging from the fairness doctrine to "equal time" to sponsorship identification (U.S. Code: 47§§315, 317). On the other hand, classification as a common carrier requires an operator to file tariffs, and at least potentially to operate subject to rate-of-return regulation (U.S. Code: 47§214). As a result, regulation as a private radio service is attractive, since it effectively insulates a medium from both common carriage and broadcasting requirements.

The distinctions between common carriers, broadcasters, and private radio services traditionally were bright-line in nature. After all, both broadcasting (in the form of AM radio) and common carriage (in the form of telephone and telegraph) had existed for between one and five decades when the Act was drafted. When the Commission embarked upon regulation of cable television in the mid-1960s, it faced a somewhat more complicated problem. Cable obviously did not fit into either Title II or Title III, since it neither held itself out to the public nor used the electromagnetic spectrum. The Commission fudged the question by treating cable as a "hybrid."

Subject to the fall-out from recent litigation, the Commission has taken a hands-off position with the other new video media, by treating most of them simply as private radio services. To a very real extent, the Commission may have reacted to the problems which it had created for itself by hastily selecting regulatory classifications for MDS and STV, before their development was very clear. Although the courts basically have used a "form follows function" approach in classifying the electronic media (*NARUC v. FCC* 1976a) the Commission presumably can take a wait-and-see position. At the very least, the FCC probably has the discretion to defer the imposition of a regulatory mold until a medium develops (*NARUC v. FCC* 1976b).

Precisely because of its past decisions, however, the Commission faces somewhat of a hodge-podge of regulatory modes for the new video media. Cable television retains its hybrid status, although the Supreme Court has held that FCC common carrier regulations were improper. On the other hand, single-channel MDS is a loosely regulated common carrier; although it must file tariffs, it is not subject to rate-of-return regulation (FCC 1983v:47§21.900). The rationale behind the classification of MDS as a common carrier is a bit murky, but seems to have been based solely upon the fact that MDS frequencies previously had been designated for common carrier purposes (FCC 1974). In contradistinction to MDS, both STV and LPTV are broadcasters; but LPTV is subject to few conventional broadcasting rules, need not provide community service, and realistically may be exempt from the fairness and equal opportunities doctrines (FCC 1982d:518–20). Since all STV stations and many LPTV stations provide pay programming virtually identical to—and often from the same sources as—that offered by MDS, the basis for the distinction seems to be that STV and LPTV use frequencies previously allocated to conventional television broadcast stations.

In the context of totally new services such as DBS and MMDS, however, the Commission was not constrained to follow its own prior decisions, and has refrained from imposing any regulatory classifications. Depending upon the nature of their activities, DBS operators may therefore end up being regulated as broadcasters, common carriers, or private radio services (FCC 1982e:1366–67). Similarly, MMDS operators would be classified as private radio services, although they might be regulated as either broadcasters or carriers if they operated as such—for example, by providing data transmission capability (FCC 1983f:140). Although private radio status may be quite appropriate for MMDS in its formative years, it might subject MMDS operators to both private radio and common carrier regulation. Single-channel MDS retains its traditional common carrier status, and most MMDS operators are likely to combine existing single-channel MDS, newly authorized MMDS channels, and leased educational channels.

Finally, recent amendments to the Communications Act may require common carrier status for at least some of the new video technologies' activities. Section 331(c)(1) of the Act classifies any "service provided by specialized mobile radio, multiple licensed radio dispatch systems, and all other radio dispatch systems" as land mobile radio (U.S. Code: 47§331(c)(1)). A new definition of "mobile service" includes any "radio communications services carried on between mobile stations or receivers and land stations . . . and . . . both one-way and two-way radio services" (U.S. Code:47§153(n)). As the Commission recognizes (FCC

1983f:141–42), the statutory language would include a paging or other service offered on a subcarrier by a television, DBS, MMDS, LPTV, or STV station. (The new provision presumably is irrelevant to cable television, which cannot offer these services over a closed circuit system.)

The Commission's wait-and-see approach to classification of the new video media seems to make sense, but is hardly consistent. Some of the disparities may not be terribly significant in terms of their real world impacts. For example, the Commission is quite unlikely ever to apply the fairness doctrine rigorously to LPTV stations (FCC 1982d:519). Other factors may have far greater impacts, however, in terms of investment decisions. For example, even the potential threat of rate-of-return regulation might deter entry into a common carrier service.

The basic problems are historical and statutory in nature. If the Commission is to leave STV and LPTV as broadcasters and yet give them regulatory parity with DBS and MMDS, it presumably should seek repeal of several provisions in the Act—including the fairness and equal opportunities doctrines. Indeed, the Commission already has proposed eliminating the fairness doctrine, but has met with a rather chilly reception in the Congress (Stern and Krasnow 1984). Neither the fairness doctrine nor the equal opportunities doctrine seems vulnerable at present, because of their substantial backing from both public interest groups and elected officials—the latter of whom naturally have a strong incentive to preserve their right to free or inexpensive air time. Moreover, repeal of Section 331(c) of the Act presumably would be necessary in order to keep the new video media free from common carrier regulation, but would meet stiff opposition from existing land mobile radio operators. As a result, the Commission probably will be unable to reclassify existing media or secure major statutory changes in the near future. As its limited application of the fairness doctrine to LPTV indicates, however, the Commission probably will not apply these statutory provisions very stringently. Whether this type of administrative lawmaking is within the Commission's discretion, of course, remains to be seen.

D. Degree of Federal Preemption

Related to the issue of regulatory status is the question as to which level of government—i.e. federal, state, or local—should administer any regulatory scheme. The level of governmental regulation has a very substantial impact upon a firm in terms of inconsistent regulatory schemes and intensity of regulation. After all, six thousand cities and fifty states are considerably more likely to experiment with regulatory policies—and are much more difficult to control—than a single federal agency (Noam 1980). In a deregulatory federal environment, the absence of state or local regulation effectively translates into no regulation at all—a fact which hardly has escaped the attention of the cable industry.

With the exception of cable television, the new video media are subject to virtually exclusive federal regulation. Since STV, MMDS, LPTV, and DBS use over-the-air transmissions and are interstate in nature, the Commission has ample statutory authority to preempt any state or local regulation. To be sure, the Commission presumably could allow local or state authorities to exercise specified forms of jurisdiction (Wilkie 1980). But it has failed to consider this approach so far—hardly surprising in light of these industries' inherent preferences for federal regulation.

The major exception to this trend was cable television. Local governments traditionally have used both their police power and their ownership of the streets to require cable operators to secure a franchise or other local authorization before constructing systems (New York 1977:§362). Roughly a dozen states have invoked their general police powers to regulate cable, sometimes by cooperating with cities and sometimes by preempting them (Cable Television Bureau 1982). The cable industry did not actively oppose state or local regulation until recently, apparently because it feared intensive federal regulation more than comparatively untutored efforts by local governments. But massive federal deregulation has provided an incentive for the industry to seek federal preemption—and thus effectively no regulation at all.

The Commission has traditionally restricted state and local governments' powers in two significant ways. First, an FCC rule prohibited local governments from charging franchise fees in excess of five percent of a cable operator's gross revenues (FCC 1983v:47§76.31). Although recent litigation has questioned the validity of the rule on both statutory and Tenth Amendment grounds (*GE Cablevision v. Peoria* 1982), it has not produced a definitive decision.

Perhaps more important, in 1983 the Commission preempted local regulation of customer rates except for "basic" service. The FCC's rationale was somewhat unclear, however, since its opinion merely reviewed its past preemption policies and then stated—in one paragraph—that it was preempting local rate regulation (FCC 1983h:1360). The Commission effectively has abolished virtually all rate regulation, since the ability to regulate rates for only basic service is largely meaningless. Under the Commission's decision, a cable operator can define basic service as just local signals, and offer all of its other—and more valuable—programming on a tiered, pay channel, or pay-per-view basis. Moreover, the Commission was threatening to preempt all local regulation of cable television, if the Congress had not passed the legislation discussed below. Whether the FCC had the statutory authority to undertake such broad-brush preemption is less than clear, but the mere threat may have been an effective way of promoting the legislation.

The 1984 Cable Act, which adds a new Title VI to the Communications Act, represents the culmination of a two-year battle by the cable industry for relief from local regulation. In the spring of 1983, the Senate passed S.66, which reflected a highly touted compromise between the National Cable Television Association and the National League of Cities. S.66 ran into serious opposition in the House Subcommittee on Telecommunications, which narrowed the bill's prohibitions and added a leased access channel requirement. The Act limits franchise fees to 5 percent of a system's gross revenues, phases in a prohibition against rate regulation except in areas with virtually no over-the-air television reception, over two years, and largely guarantees renewal of franchises.

The inevitable trend in cable regulation is toward exclusive federal regulation, however, either by statute or by FCC action. Regardless of whether federal, state, or local regulation intrinsically is most effective, cable operators have become national in scale and need uniformity as much as any other national medium. Although preemption of state and local regulation would give cable parity with the other new video media, it would leave one important difference: namely, all media except cable would be federally licensed. Even in a deregulatory environment, licensing serves an important function by allowing an agency to monitor an industry's performance and to police any abuses. It thus might be in order for the Commission to impose some type of licensing or certificating process for cable, in order to insure its parity with the other new video media. Questions may exist as to the Commission's power to license cable systems, however, since Title III's licensing requirements extend only to over-the-air transmissions—not those via cable (*U.S. vs. Midwest Video* 1972). The Commission thus would need to seek legislation in this area, in order to impose a licensing requirement on all of the new video media.

E. Program Content Control

Even aside from First Amendment considerations, regulation of any medium's programming has a number of practical consequences. On a purely noneconomic level, the existence of content control affects managers' self-perceptions and behavior. Thus it is not surprising that newspaper editors place more emphasis upon the message than the medium, while telephone operating company executives reverse these priorities. On an economic level, restraints on speech affect decisions as to whether or not to take a particular risk. The Playboy Channel presumably never would have come into existence if the FCC had prohibited frontal nudity on cable.

The Commission traditionally has regulated programming only on broadcast services, on the theory that by definition a common carrier cannot control—and thus be responsible for—the content of the messages which it transmits. In turn, regulation of broadcast program content has taken two primary forms: first, prohibitions on certain types of offensive material (such as obscenity, indecency, payola, plugola, and lotteries), and, second, affirmative requirements to provide time under the fairness and equal opportunities doctrines.

Commission has indicated that it does not plan rigorous enforcement of even statutory provisions such as the fairness doctrine (FCC 1980b:65; FCC 1982d:519). Finally, in addition to Title III's provisions, federal law provides criminal penalties for the transmission of specified types of material—most notably, obscenity, indecency, plugola, payola, and lotteries (U.S. Code: 18§1464). These provisions would apply to all of the new video media except for cable, since it does not use over-the-air transmissions. (The statute applies to any "means of radio communication," rather than just to broadcasting.) However, the only means for direct enforcement of the Criminal Code is by prosecutions, at the discretion of regional United States attorneys. Although the Commission has the authority to enforce the Criminal Code's policies through appropriate rules, it is not required to do so (*Illinois v. FCC* 1975).

The extent of program content control for each of the new media therefore depends largely upon whether it is a user of over-the-air transmissions or is a broadcaster. Although cable television is neither, the Commission long ago imposed the traditional array of negative and positive broadcast regulations to "origination" material (FCC 1983v:47§§76.205–76.221). While the meaning of this term is less than clear, it apparently refers only to programming produced directly by a cable operator, as opposed to programming received from satellite networks and the like. In any event, the question is probably moot; the Commission never has enforced the rules against a cable operator since their adoption more than a decade ago.

On the other hand, STV and LPTV presumably are subject to all of the Commission's broadcast regulations, since both are broadcast uses. As noted before, however, the Commission already has indicated that it will not enforce the fairness doctrine—and presumably other regulations also—against LPTV stations as rigorously as it enforces them against conventional broadcast stations (FCC 1980b:65; FCC 1982d: 519). DBS and MMDS apparently would be subject to no regulation beyond the Criminal Code's provisions, however, because of their status as private radio services. If a DBS operator were treated as a broadcaster, it would become subject to the full panoply of Title III regulations—including the fairness and equal opportunity doctrines.

Finally, the FCC apparently would subject none of the new video media to access requirements. A DBS operator would be subject to Title II's common carriage requirements if it chose to operate as a common carrier, of course, but Title II contemplates commercial as opposed to free public access. Along similar lines, single-channel MDS operators are theoretically common carriers and must sell time on a nondiscriminatory basis; realistically, however, most MDS operators take the bulk of their programming from established pay television networks. Finally, the FCC clearly lacks jurisdiction to impose access channel requirements on cable television systems (*FCC v. Midwest Video* 1979), but state and local governments are allowed to do so under the new Cable Act.

Except on the access front, the Commission's content regulation are less than a model of consistency. The problems appear to arise from much the same factors already considered in the context of regulatory status: that is, historical and statutory inhibitions. Rationalizing questions of regulatory status thus would solve a number of problems simultaneously.

III. CONCLUSION

Although the Commission is committed to creating a level playing field for the new video technologies, it has left a number of potholes. Indeed, on virtually all of the fronts examined above, significant disparities and inconsistencies exist among the new video media. Equally important, the FCC simply has failed or refused to consider a host of questions— e.g., MMDS's fairness and community programming obligations— without giving any reasoned basis for its positions.

At the present, it is difficult if not impossible to estimate these problems' impact on the new video media. Measuring the cost of a particular type of regulation is speculative at best and downright foolhardy at worst, when two of the industries in question—DBS and MMDS—do not even exist. Nevertheless, these inconsistencies may change the ways in which the new video media evolve.

The problem is not that the FCC deliberately has created this lack of consistency. In almost every instance the Commission has been hampered by historical accidents, legislative lacunae, and inherent regulatory lag. Nevertheless, it seems fair to criticize the Commission for not considering these problems in advance. The FCC's apparent lack of concern naturally complicates any resolution of these issues—particularly resolutions which inevitably must rely upon new legislation. As Judge Bazelon pointedly has noted, "a thorough rethinking of the legal treatment accorded telecommunications is in order. . . . It will not be easy to challenge the investment in the present system, but reform must be far-reaching and far-sighted if the law is ever to catch up with the reality of our times" (Bazelon 1981).

To date, the FCC has embraced the concept but not the details of the level playing field. Perhaps the Commission needs to spend less time on ideology and more time on methodology. But without internal rethinking and external debate, the Commission may find that it has created a host of inequities which ultimately will only stifle potential competition.

Comment: The Regulatory Setting

Stephen A. Sharp

Michale Botein's study conveys the impression that he disapproves of the FCC's deregulatory efforts. His rhetoric makes that clear. What is unclear, however, is the direction in which he believes the Commission should go. The polemic nature of his approach highlights several misunderstandings of the Commission and its current response to technological innovation.

Early in his paper Botein refers to "the current, ideologically pure Commission." It is essential to understand that the FCC, with seven or five members, is a collegial body with members of diverse backgrounds and varied viewpoints. While the Commission acts as an entity, it is a serious error to ascribe to it a unity and consistency of ideology that does not exist.

Each commissioner comes to the question of regulation or deregulation differently and votes on a particular matter in a unique context. In my case, for example, I did not take up the cause of deregulation because Adam Smith appeared to me in a dream or because I was plotting the sacrifice of public interest objectives at the altar of private greed. Having spent nearly a decade inside the FCC and several more years affected by it, it became clear to me that regulation was not always the most efficient means to achieve social goals.

There are ways to achieve social goals by using the marketplace to do what government intervention had been intended to do. The essence of deregulation is to identify the optimal structure which maximizes the private contribution and minimizes governmental participation, while yielding the same result. As Botein points out, "The basic assumption . . . is that effective competition makes regulation unnecessary." Competition is "effective" if it achieves the goals which regulation would have sought to achieve.

If we ask whether competition may be "effective" in achieving a goal, it is important to ask whether government regulation has been "effective" in reaching the same goal. Both means should be held to the same standard of effectiveness in evaluating which should be used or what combination of both is called for. After observing the implementation of many regulatory schemes and their effects on economic and social behavior, I came to doubt that regulation was necessarily the best approach.

These doubts were heightened by measuring what I refer to as "regulatory dysfunction," or impairment of the achievement of other worthy goals created by the existence of government regulation. For example, the costs of compliance with government regulations, both in dollars and in management attention are considerable. Reduction in government forms and detailed rules provides management in the affected industry with the opportunity to devote those resources to serving better the public it has as its customers. Minimizing government intervention also serves to avoid the unintended and usually unanticipated negative side effects of government involvement.

The policy of the current Commission has been to allow the development of new technologies. We resolved not to be branded as electronic-age Luddites, but rather to allow technology to benefit society while trying to minimize sudden economic or social dislocation. The "level playing field" is a figure of speech which essentially tries to describe equity or fairness.

The Commission understands handicaps. Professor Botein's example of government regulation, the antisiphoning rule, was not a handicap which reined in the most effective player. It was a shackle on the new entrant which preserved the status of the most effective player (the broadcaster) at the expense of the new entrants (cable and STV). This Commission has avoided shackling new entrants, having learned the lessons of excessive government regulation in such instances as antisiphoning.

Professor Botein notes that "the FCC has embraced the concept but not the details of fostering the level playing field." Unfortunately, he does not offer any solutions nor provide any of his own details which I had hoped to see.

Comment: Competing Technologies and Inconsistent Regulation

John D. Abel

Communication technologies, consumer choice, and program diversity are advancing more rapidly than policies are changing to assure regulatory parity in the delivery of programming to American households. It is time for a review of the nature of the regulatory environment for communication technologies that deliver information and entertainment to American households.

Most of the major changes in the communications environment are traceable to the astonishing growth in satellite communication. Cable television, for example, would never be the competitive force that it is today without satellite communication that distributes both pay and advertiser-supported services to cable systems. Many, if not all, of the newer delivery technologies rely heavily on satellite communication, none more so than direct broadcast satellites (DBS).

Ten years ago DBS did not exist. In November 1983 United Satellite Communications, Inc. (USCI) launched the first interim DBS operation serving television households in the northeast quadrant of the U.S. through one Canadian satellite. USCI offers five channels of programming directly to homes equipped with a small receiving dish about 4 feet in diameter. It is estimated that there are about 10,000 subscribers to the USCI service. These subscribers tend to be concentrated in un-cabled, although not necessarily rural, areas. The USCI subscribers are believed to be concentrated in large urban areas not yet wired for cable. In September 1984 Satellite Television Corporation (STC), a subsidiary of COMSAT, and USCI tentatively agreed to merge and pursue the DBS business in tandem. In early 1986 the USCI-STC DBS venture will likely expand the service area to the entire continental U.S. Other DBS companies expected to enter the business in 1987–88 are Hubbard Broadcasting's United States Satellite Broadcasting and Dominion Video.

Estimates for the potential growth of DBS in the United States vary from 2.5 to 6 million households by the early 1990s. DBS operators will not only serve homes, but also seek alliances with full-power and low-power television stations, satellite master antenna television systems, and cable systems.

Until very recently, DBS was an excellent example of regulatory inconsistency and confusion. DBS operators had a choice of being regulated as a broadcaster or as a common carrier. In the broadcaster mode, the service provider retains control over the transmission whether or not the service is offered on a subscription basis. If, on the other hand, someone leased the transmission capacity from a DBS operator acting as a common carrier, then the service would be completely unregulated. In a third mode, the FCC approved a transaction between a satellite owner (Satellite Business Systems) and an entity controlled by a news publisher (Rupert Murdoch) without applying the common carrier or the broadcast provisions. This third mode of DBS operation is best called private DBS. Judge Mikva of the Court of Appeals in Washington recently forced the FCC to regulate DBS as a broadcaster.

There are many other inconsistencies in the regulation of DBS. DBS operators obviously have no local service requirements even though terrestrial broadcasters must serve local needs. There are no limits on DBS ownership. There are no multiple ownership restrictions and there are no limits on the ownership of more than one channel on a single satellite serving an area. By contrast, a terrestrial broadcaster cannot own more than a set number of radio and TV stations and cannot own two or more AM, two or more FM, or two or more television stations in the same local market. Some DBS operators, by comparison, are proposing to offer as many as 16 channels, all receivable in a local area.

The FCC decided to let the marketplace set de facto technical standards for DBS. That means that if a home owner purchases one DBS receiving dish, that dish probably will not be able to receive the signals of other DBS services. Terrestrial broadcasters, however, must conform to stringent transmission and reception standards. The current rules will permit DBS to offer both conventional and high definition television.

MDS

Single channel multipoint distribution service was first authorized in the early 1970s and by the summer of 1984 there were between 300,000 and 500,000 single channel MDS subscribers in over 100 different cities. Single channel MDS is a good example of the inability of a single channel provider to survive in the new multichannel environment. In 1982, single channel MDS had over 700,000 subscribers and the subscribing base has been eroding as cable and other multichannel providers are established.

In 1983, the FCC authorized multichannel MDS (MMDS) which will result in at least 8 channels of service in many communities. An indication of the strong entrepreneurial interest in MMDS is that the FCC received 16,500 applications for MMDS systems in 1983. Even though single channel MDS is suffering some loss of subscribers, it appears that MMDS will have about 5% of the pay video market in the early 1990s.

MDS is an even better example of regulatory confusion than is DBS. MDS is regulated as a common carrier even though MDS (and MMDS) operates essentially as any terrestrial broadcaster sending a signal through the air to a receiving antenna. The channels are leased on a first-come-first-served basis. There are no ownership restrictions, no programming requirements or restrictions, and no local service requirements even though MDS systems serve very local areas, usually about a 25-mile radius.

One MMDS operation can offer at least 4 or 8 channels and possibly as many as 31 channels by leasing channels from Instructional Television Fixed Service (ITFS) and private Operational Fixed Service (OFS). This latter option raises even more inconsistencies since ITFS is regulated as a private service and OFS is regulated as a hybrid.

MMDS is sometimes referred to as "wireless cable" because it has the multichannel capacity of cable. The odd thing about MMDS is that it is not regulated as broadcasting even though it looks like broadcasting. In addition, it has none of the local, state, or federal regulations of cable, which is also regulated as an ancillary broadcast service.

STV

Over-the-air Subscription Television (STV) is another example of the problems of a single channel provider in a multichannel environment.

Although STV was authorized in 1968, it took STV until 1982 to reach a high of 28 stations and about 1.3 million subscribers. By 1984 a subscription service was offered by about 20 STV stations and there were less than 800,000 subscribers. By 1990 there will be about 3 STV stations in operation with perhaps 300,000 subscribers in 2 or 3 markets. STV stations are regulated as broadcasters even though they look much like MDS systems since both of these technologies send scrambled signals through the airwaves to receivers.

Perhaps the inconsistency among over-the-air services can be highlighted by an example. If an entrepreneur is interested in providing an over-the-air pay television service, he/she can: (1) obtain an STV license and be regulated as a broadcaster; (2) lease time from an MDS licensee and be unregulated; (3) get an OFS license, in which case the entrepreneur will control the transmission facility and the program content but be exempt from broadcast *and* common carrier regulation; or (4) lease time from an ITFS licensee at privately set rates and conditions and avoid broadcast regulation.

SMATV

Satellite Master Antenna Television (SMATV) is yet another system of video programming delivery that did not exist even ten years ago. Some of these systems offer as many as 36 channels of service and there are an estimated 500,000 subscribers nationwide. By the early 1990s we believe SMATV could have 3 percent of the pay video market.

SMATV systems are essentially unregulated. There are no ownership restrictions, no local franchise is required, there are no program content requirements, no requirements to serve or ascertain or program for local needs, yet one operator can control many channels of service.

CABLE

In 1974, cable was in 12.6 percent of TV households; by 1984 it was in 43 percent of TV households. The number of subscribing households has increased by over 300 percent since 1974. Subscribing households will grow another 50 percent between now and the early 1990s, eventually penetrating about 60 percent of U.S. television households.

Cable is regulated as ancillary to broadcasting, so many of the broadcast regulations apply; however, there are some dramatic distinctions.

Cable has no multiple ownership restrictions even though there are many cable subscribers being served by a relatively small number of companies. For example, about 70 percent of the nation's 36 million cable households are served by the top 50 cable multiple system operators. One cable operator controls many channels in the local area while the local broadcaster can control only a single channel.

BROADCASTING

In the past ten years there has been a 22 percent increase in the number of radio stations, and the number of radio stations is expected to increase another 10 percent between 1984 and the early 1990s. By the early 1990s there will be about 10,500 radio stations on the air.

Since 1974, the number of TV stations has increased by 24 percent. In 1974 low-power television did not exist as a broadcast service. In 1984 there were over 280 LPTV stations on the air. By the early 1990s there should be a 375 percent increase in broadcast television stations including full-power and low-power television stations. There are no real ownership limits for LPTV stations and no local service requirements.

There are multiple and cross-ownership restrictions for broadcasters. There are limitations on the number of channels a broadcaster can control in a single market. There are local program service requirements. Broadcasters must adhere to specific transmission and reception technical standards. Broadcasters must adhere to the Fairness Doctrine and provide access for political candidates. Broadcasters must adhere to and be judged by a public interest standard.

HOME INFOTAINMENT APPLIANCES

In addition to all of these systems and services there are the home information and entertainment appliances. Home videocassette recorders (VCRs) did not exist in 1974. Ten years later they are in 14 percent of all households and will be in about 40 percent of all households in the early 1990s. Video game units are in 22 percent of households. Home computers did not exist in 1974; in 1984 they are in 12 percent of households. Neither videotex nor teletext existed in 1974; but by the early 1990s 20 percent of households will use these services.

According to the Society for Private and Commercial Earth Stations (SPACE), backyard satellite dishes are selling at the rate of 30,000 to 35,000 a month. At the beginning of 1984 there were about 500,000 to 700,000 backyard dishes installed. These receiving dishes are not regulated by the FCC and provide for the reception of about 60 channels of programming.

Nearly every American household is touched in some way by new communication technologies. American consumers, however, do not watch or listen to technologies—they watch or listen to programs. These consumers do not care if the programs come from cable, a direct broadcast satellite, a tape in a VCR unit, a videodisc, an MDS system, a SMATV system, their home computer connected to a telephone line, or a terrestrial broadcast station.

There is regulatory confusion for single channel and multichannel providers delivering programming to American households. From the FCC's experience with the regulation of DBS, it is clear that the courts probably will not permit such confusion and inconsistency. The FCC and Congress need to consider the total communications environment of American consumers and decide on the best regulatory approach for services such that regulatory parity is achieved.

11

Antitrust and Video Markets: The Merger of Showtime and the Movie Channel as a Case Study

LAWRENCE J. WHITE

CONTENTS

   I. Introduction
  II. The Proposed Merger and the Antitrust Division's Procedures
      A. The Venture
      B. The Procedures
 III. The General Legal and Economic Analyses
  IV. A Specific Analysis
      A. A Conceptual Framework
      B. Defining the Product Markets
      C. Defining the Geographic Market
      D. Determining Appropriate Market Shares
      E. Entry
      F. Simple Collusion Upstream?
      G. The Vertical Link
   V. The Outcome
  VI. Conclusions

I. INTRODUCTION

Rapid advances in electronics and telecommunications technology in the past two decades have produced substantial changes in entertainment, and especially video, markets. New opportunities have arisen;

new markets have been created; some firms have entered, others have exited; new business relationships have been established.

Some of these markets, especially television, have been heavily regulated by the Federal Communications Commission (FCC). Cable television services have been subject to controls by the FCC and by local communities. Despite such direct regulation, direct antitrust enforcement has also played a substantial role in affecting the structure of these markets,[1] and recent events have indicated that antitrust is likely to continue to be important.

This paper will report on one recent antitrust action that could have important consequences for these markets: the merger of Showtime and the Movie Channel, the second and third largest providers of pay programming services for cable viewers. This merger, originally quite complex in its proposed structure, was reviewed by the Antitrust Division in 1983 and emerged in a more limited form. This case study should serve as a useful vehicle for understanding the structure of and competition in video markets. It should also be useful for showing the value of the revised Merger Guidelines (U.S. Department of Justice 1982), issued by the Antitrust Division in June 1982 (and modified in 1984), for structuring and illuminating the antitrust analysis of mergers.

Section II of this paper will provide a description of the merger partners, the proposed structure of the merger, and a brief review of procedures within the Division with respect to mergers. Section III will provide the general legal and economic background for the analysis of the case, including a brief description of the 1982 Merger Guidelines. Section IV will provide a more specific analysis of the details of the merger and the antitrust problems that they appeared to raise. Section V reports the Antitrust Division's decision and its aftermath. Section VI provides some conclusions.

II. THE PROPOSED VENTURE AND THE ANTITRUST DIVISION'S PROCEDURES

A. The Venture

As of 1982, Home Box Office (HBO, including its "sister service," Cinemax), Showtime, and The Movie Channel (TMC) were the three leading providers of pay programming service to cable television viewers. HBO accounted for about 60 percent of the subscriptions to pay TV services, Showtime for about 20 percent, and TMC for about 10 percent.[2] HBO was (and still is) a wholly owned subsidiary of Time, Inc. Showtime was a subsidiary of Viacom International, Inc., a leading syndicator of television programs and also one of the ten largest multiple system owners (MSOs) in the cable industry, as well as the owner of the Cable Health Network basic cable service. TMC was a joint venture by Warner Communications, Inc. (parent of Warner Brothers) and the American Express Company. Both are also equal partners in Warner Amex Cable Corp., another of the top ten MSOs, and also the principal owner of the Music Television (MTV) and Nickelodean satellite cable networks.

In November 1982, Paramount Pictures (owned by Gulf & Western), Universal Studios (owned by MCA), Warner, and American Express announced a proposed joint venture for the purpose of owning and operating TMC. The three movie studios involved in the deal accounted for 40–50 percent of theatrical motion picture exhibitions in the late 1970s and early 1980s (based on gross rental fees) and are considered to be three of the six "major" studios;[3] the six accounted for 80–85 percent of theatrical exhibitions in recent years. In January 1983, Viacom entered the picture, and the proposed venture then involved a merger of Showtime and TMC, with Paramount, Universal, Warner, American Express, and Viacom jointly owning the merged entity. The three movie studios and Viacom would each own 22.58 percent of the joint venture; American Express would own 9.68 percent.

B. The Procedures

Under the terms of the Hart-Scott-Rodino (H-S-R) amendments (passed in 1976) to the Clayton Act, the parties to a proposed merger or acquisition that exceeds certain size criteria[4] are required to submit information pertinent to the merger or acquisition to the U.S. Federal Trade Commission (FTC) and to the Antitrust Division of the U.S. Department of Justice; the parties are then required to wait thirty days before consummating the deal. During this time the FTC and the Division make quick scans of the information. If either agency believes that antitrust problems may be involved, that agency asks for "clearance" from the other and begins an investigation. On or before the thirtieth day after submission of the initial information, the investigating agency can make a "second request" for more information and the parties must then wait another twenty days from the time they deliver this information before consummating.[5]

The intent behind the Hart-Scott-Rodino amendments was to give the FTC and the Division more time to investigate proposed mergers before their consummation and to seek preliminary injunctions from the courts for those proposed mergers that appeared to pose antitrust problems. Prior to the amendments, the agencies sometimes did not discover mergers until the last minute or even after the fact and had to rush into court with incomplete information and hastily assembled arguments. Meanwhile, even if the agency eventually were successful in challenging the merger, the untangling of those mergers that had already been completed and the reestablishment of the original entities was often difficult.[6]

The two agencies usually divide responsibility for investigations along lines of historically developed expertise.[7] In this case, the Division had had experience with antitrust cases in movie and video markets stretching back to the 1920s, and the Division had recently (1980) brought and won a case challenging a joint venture ("Premiere") that involved movie studios and other entities and that would have created a new pay programming service;[8] thus, it was natural that the Division would take responsibility for investigating the Showtime-TMC proposal.

The proposed venture described above was submitted to the Antitrust Division for review in January 1983. The procedures of H-S-R were not formally brought into play,[9] but the parties to the venture cooperated with the Division as if the H-S-R requirements had been in effect. The Division's investigation and decision-making processes extended over the following five months. Such extensions beyond the fifty days specified by H-S-R are frequent in complex cases. Sometimes, as was initially true in this case, the parties do not press for a quick decision. Sometimes a significant amount of time is required for the parties to provide the information demanded in the "second request." And sometimes, as the end of the second period approaches, the parties are told by the Division, "We have not yet made up our minds as to whether we will or will not challenge this merger. With more time we may convince ourselves that the merger does not create antitrust problems or that they can be remedied. But our current doubts are sufficiently great so that if you insist on consummating at the end of the second period, we will seek a preliminary injunction to try to stop you." The parties usually prefer to wait. In this case they waited until June.

III. THE GENERAL LEGAL AND ECONOMIC ANALYSIS

The Showtime-TMC proposal involved a somewhat complicated structure for antitrust analytical purposes. It entailed the outright merger of two providers of pay programming services (horizontal competitors), Showtime and TMC; it involved the addition of two movie studios (horizontal competitors), Universal and Paramount, to the joint venture that already involved a third studio (Warner) and controlled one programming service (TMC) and that would now control both; and the programming services were major purchasers of major theatrical films from the studios, so customer-supplier (vertical) relationships were also involved. The specific merger of Showtime and TMC clearly called for merger analysis, under the standards of Section 7 of the Clayton Act. The joint venture aspects of the proposal could either be treated as a type of merger, and hence also fall under the Clayton Act, or be considered as a "contract, combination . . . or conspiracy, in restraint of trade" and hence fall under Section 1 of the Sherman Act.

From the author's economics perspective, merger analysis seems clearest and provides the best framework for understanding the possible competitive consequences of the proposed venture. Accordingly, the remainder of the discussion in this paper will also be in terms of merger analysis.

Section 7 of the Clayton Act instructs the FTC and the Division to challenge mergers and acquisitions, "where in any line of commerce in any section of the country, the effect of such acquisition may be substantially to lessen competition, or to tend to create a monopoly." After a series of Supreme Court victories in merger cases in the 1960s, the Division issued a set of Merger Guidelines (U.S. Dept. of Justice 1968), in 1968, attempting to provide guidance to the private antitrust bar (so that the latter could better advise their clients) as to the ways in which the Division would analyze mergers and the types of mergers the Division would be likely to challenge. In June 1982, the Division issued a revised set of Merger Guidelines (U.S. Dept. of Justice 1982), modified in 1984, which has served as the basis for the Division's analysis of the merger proposals that have come before it, including the Showtime-TMC proposal. Accordingly, a brief review of the 1982 Guidelines is worthwhile.[10]

Which mergers are likely "substantially to lessen competition, or to tend to create a monopoly"? In trying to answer this question, the Guidelines rely heavily on a body of thinking about seller behavior (oligopoly theory) that has been developed over the past half-century. Chamberlain (1956, chapter 3) first expressed these propositions in the early 1930s, and they were later modified and extended by Fellner (1949), Bain (1956), and Stigler (1964), among others.[11] In essence, they argue that sellers in a market are more likely to behave in a non-competitive fashion (i.e., succeed in coordinating their actions so as to raise their prices above, or modify the quality or variety of offerings from, the levels that would prevail in a more competitive industry and hence succeed in earning profits above competitive levels) if a number of structural conditions prevail in the relevant market. Specifically, the following structural features make noncompetitive behavior more likely: fewer sellers in the market; greater inequality in their relative sizes (as measured by sales shares of the relevant market—these first two conditions are usually summarized by a measure of sales concentration in the market); greater difficulty of sales expansion by existing (especially small) sellers; greater difficulty of entry into the market by entities that are not currently selling in it; a larger number of buyers (for any given volume of sales) and less concentration among them; and greater standardization and simplicity of the product being sold.[12] The Guidelines use these propositions—especially the role of seller concentration—to establish the conditions under which the Division is likely to challenge a merger as potentially or actually anticompetitive.

The application of these propositions—again, especially the role of seller concentration—presupposes the delineation of the proper market for antitrust merger analysis. If the market is not properly specified, then the market shares used for concentration measures are unlikely to be correct, entry conditions are unlikely to be correctly stated, etc., and the specific analytical conclusions may well be incorrect. Unfortunately, the economics profession has not applied much specific thought to the problem of market definition, and the general ruminations of economists on market definition, relying on the concepts of cross-elasticities of demand and supply among related goods and services, have not been useful in providing specific guidance for antitrust purposes (Stigler 1982:19; Scherer 1980:60–61). It is, perhaps, in this area that the 1982 Guidelines have been most useful in furthering analytical thought on antitrust merger issues.

Noting that market boundaries must encompass both a product dimension (summarized by the Clayton Act as "in any line of commerce") and a geographic dimension ("in any section of the country"), the Guidelines indicate that a market (for merger analysis purposes) will generally be the smallest group of present or potential sellers (i.e., encompassing the smallest group of products and smallest geographic area) that, if they chose to act in a collective fashion (i.e., tried to act as a monopolist), could succeed in exercising significant market power. "Significant" is defined as the ability of this collective entity to be able to raise selling prices by at least five percent (from where they currently are or could reasonably be expected otherwise to be in the future) and maintain them, profitably, at that level for at least a year. In essence, a market is defined primarily on the basis of demand-side substitutability. The practical question to be asked is, "Would the demanders (of a group of products sold by a specific group of sellers located in a specified geographic area), in response to a significant price rise, switch away (to sellers of other products and/or sellers located in other geographic areas) in sufficient numbers so as to thwart the price rise in the first place?" If the answer to this question is "no," then the products sold by those sellers from those locations constitute a market; if the answer is "yes, the price rise would be thwarted," then the tentative group is too narrow, and a wider group of sellers (in "product space" and/or geographic space) must be included and the question posed again.

The logic behind this general approach can be explained as follows: the purpose of antitrust merger analysis (and of market definition as part of it) is to detect those mergers that pose a threat to competition. If the most anticompetitive merger imaginable among a group of sellers— the combination of all of them into a single entity—could not affect prices significantly (because too many demanders would switch away in response to any attempt to exercise market power), then that group of sellers cannot constitute a market for antitrust merger analysis purposes; the relevant market must be wider.

This procedure implies that the market definition "circle" should be drawn primarily around sellers (since it is sellers who might coordinate their actions and exercise market power). A partial exception would apply to the case in which a group of sellers might not be able to raise their prices generally (because too many customers would switch away) but might be able to raise their prices successfully to a smaller group of their customers (identified by geographic area or by some other characteristic)—i.e., to practice systematic price discrimination against some smaller group of customers. In this case, the appropriate market definition would include both the group of sellers who could exercise this market power and the group of customers who would be subject to the price discrimination.

Supply-side substitutability does not enter directly into the Guidelines' definition of a market, but it enters the Guidelines (as it must in some fashion) at two later points in the analysis. First, any firm that is not now producing the product or products in question but that could do so within six months in response to a 5 percent price rise without a major investment in new plant or equipment (i.e., could begin production primarily by modifying existing facilities) shall be counted as "in the market" (along with existing producers) and assigned an appropriate market share. Second, conditions of entry generally (and specifically within two years in response to a 5 percent price rise) are considered among the extenuating and exacerbating circumstances that could cause the Division to alter judgments drawn from market share criteria alone.

After indicating that the basis (e.g., sales revenues, physical unit sales, or production capacity) for determining market shares should be that which the sellers in the market would most likely choose as the basis for any anticompetitive coordination, the 1982 Guidelines establish "cut point" market share criteria for the likelihood of Division action on a merger. The criteria are expressed in terms of the Herfindahl-Hirschman Index (HHI), which is computed by squaring the market share of each firm in the market (e.g., if a firm's market share is 15 percent, the squared value would be 225) and summing all of these squared values. The HHI for a market can range from a value close to zero (if there are many firms, each with a small market share) to 10,000 (if there is a single firm in the market).

The criteria are as follows: if the postmerger HHI is less than 1,000 (which translates empirically to roughly a four-firm concentration ratio of 50), the Division is unlikely to challenge the merger. If the postmerger HHI is between 1,000 and 1,800 (which translates roughly to a four-firm concentration ratio of 70) and the increase in the HHI caused by the merger (which, algebraically, must be equal to twice the product of the market shares of the merging firms) is above 100, then the Division is more likely than not to challenge the merger, depending on other conditions in the market. Finally, if the post-merger HHI is above 1,800 and the increase in the HHI caused by the merger is above 50, the Division is more likely than not to challenge the merger, and if the increase in the HHI is above 100, the Division is likely to challenge the merger.

The Guidelines then discuss extenuating and exacerbating circumstances—primarily the conditions of entry, the buyers' side of the market, the nature of the product, behavioral practices in the industry, and the antitrust history of the industry.

Next, the Guidelines discuss mergers between a seller in a market and a potential entrant into that market and between customers and suppliers (i.e., vertical mergers). The former area did not appear to be an important issue in the Showtime-TMC proposal (though, as is discussed below, the movie studios could be considered as potential entrants into the programming area), but the latter clearly was. The Guidelines emphasize that a vertical merger should have antitrust significance only if it has *horizontal* consequences in one or more markets—i.e., if it somehow raises barriers to entry or otherwise facilitates coordinated behavior in one or both markets.

Finally, the Guidelines address the question of the possible efficiencies that might be yielded by a proposed merger (the Guidelines state that they will be considered only in exceptional circumstances) and discuss the exceptions that might be made for mergers involving a firm that was near bankruptcy (the "failing firm doctrine," which was not an issue in the Showtime-TMC proposal).

IV. A SPECIFIC ANALYSIS

This section provides the author's analysis of the Showtime-TMC proposal. Since over a dozen attorneys and economists in the Antitrust Division were involved in the investigation and evaluation at some point, it would be improper to present this analysis as "the Division's position." In the end, it was William F. Baxter, the Assistant Attorney General for Antitrust, who made the decisions in this case, and it is only he who truly knows what specific analyses and arguments led to the specific decisions.

A. A Conceptual Framework

It is convenient to have a framework for understanding the roles, positions, and relationships of the major participants in the video industry. Table 11.1 provides a particularly useful framework. At the top are the producer-owners of programming that eventually appears in video markets: the movie studios-distributors, the "independent" producers, producers for television, and syndicators. Next are the wholesale "packagers," who usually buy (or receive licenses for) material from the first group, "package" it into a schedule of entertainment offerings, and sell (or license) the package to the third group. This last group—the cable systems, over-the-air pay stations, and local VHF and UHF television stations—distribute and retail the programming to viewers. The distributors receive payments from viewers, from advertisers directly in return for time devoted to advertising messages, and/or from packagers (who in turn have received payments from advertisers whose messages have been included as part of the package provided to the distributors).

Table 11.1. Schematic Representation of the Video Industry

General Category of Activity	*General Types of Participants*
Programming producers-owners	Movie studios-distributors Independent film producers Producers for television Syndicators
Programming packagers	Pay television programmers "Basic" services programmers Television networks "Super stations"
Distributors of programming to viewers	Cable systems Over-the-air pay channels Local VHF and UHF television stations

These compartments are not air-tight. Many participants in the video industry extend beyond one category. The networks, for example, produce some of their own material[13] and own a few local television stations.[14] A syndicator may also be considered a packager if he tries to sell his programs directly to local stations. And a company like Warner participates in all three levels of the industry, through its movie production, its part ownership of TMC (and now Showtime), and its ownership of cable systems. Nevertheless, the schematic framework is a useful organizing device.

In the context of this framework, it is clear that the main activities of the participants in the Showtime-TMC proposal were concentrated in the first two levels of Table 11.1. (The ownership of cable systems by Warner and by Viacom did not seem important for the analysis.) And it was on these two levels that the author's analysis was focused.

B. Defining the Product Markets

A crucial task for analysis was to determine the relevant product markets. Sales (or licensing) of programming by packagers to distributors was one important focus; the inputs into the packaging level (i.e., the sales or licensing of programming by producers to packagers) was a related, but separate, area that required market analysis. With respect to sales *by* programmers, one could ask whether the relevant market was comparatively narrow (pay programming services that relied primarily on theatrically released movies), somewhat broader (all cable programming services, including free "basic" services), yet broader (all television services, including network and independent stations), or most broad (all forms of entertainment, including watching video cassettes at home, going to theatrical movies or other leisure entertainment, including going bowling or attending sporting events. A very broad definition would have meant that the Showtime-TMC merger would have little expected competitive impact, since the merging of two packagers would involve the loss of only one entity among a large number of providers of entertainment. At the other extreme, a narrow definition would have implied that the merger would yield a significant increase in concentration among current sellers. (Whether this increase would have competitive consequences would still depend on the other structural characteristics discussed below.)

Which market definition was appropriate? In principle, there were varying degrees of substitutability among these services and activities, even extending to substitution possibilities between watching a movie on pay cable at home and going bowling. There was no strictly logical basis for choice in market definition on an *a priori* basis. Fortunately, the Merger Guidelines provided, in principle, the conceptual basis (albeit, a somewhat arbitrary one) for determining the relevant market: find the smallest group sellers who, if they could coordinate their behavior, could raise their prices by five percent and find it profitable to do so for a least a year.

On the basis of this criterion, it appeared to me that pay programming services that relied heavily on theatrically released motion pictures (or, as a paraphrase, "movie-driven pay services") constituted the relevant product market. All of the leading programming services featured and promoted heavily their showing of recently released theatrical films. Though many of them also provided other types of programming (and hence there were some possibilities for substitution between theatrical films and other programming—a crucial point for the argument developed below), recent theatrical films appeared to be crucial to their customer appeal. Marketing studies and general industry perceptions indicated that movies were the major appeal of these services. Unfortunately, there were no econometric or other statistical studies providing estimates of or inferences as to the elasticity of demand for movie-driven pay services, which would have indicated the extent to which demanders would have diverted their purchases to other things in the event of a general price rise for movie-driven pay services. Consequently, one was left relying on impressionistic evidence, but that evidence seemed to point to the narrow definition. Even if the market had been broadened to all pay programming services, the analysis would have been little different, since the movie-driven services accounted for a very large fraction of the viewer subscriptions in this broader category. Impressionistically, it did not appear necessary to extend the market any wider to satisfy the 1982 Merger Guidelines' test for the definition of a market.

The attorneys and experts representing the prospective Showtime-TMC owners naturally argued for a broader definition of the product market. They argued that viewers were interested generally in first-run, network-quality programming and did not particularly care if that programming was in the form of theatrical movies or other types of programs. They cited the fact the HBO and Showtime had recently expanded the amount of nonmovie programming on their services. They also claimed that cable system owners, especially those operating older systems that offered only a comparatively small number of channels, were in a position to limit the market power of the movie-driven pay services by substituting other cable services if the prices of movie-driven services rose. But the arguments in favor of a broad market definition were also based on impressionistic evidence and lacked a statistical or econometrics base.

In the end, at least to me, the impressionistic evidence pointed toward a narrow product market definition.

The identification of the relevant input market for packagers followed easily from this narrow definition of the packaging product market. If movie-driven pay services was the relevant market for the packagers' product, then theatrically released films was the relevant input market. (The two following sections will concentrate largely on the movie-driven pay services market; further discussion of the input market will be left for sections E–G.)

C. Defining the Geographic Market

The definition of the geographic market was less difficult. All of the leading movie-driven pay services distributed their programs nationwide via satellite. Regional location did not seem to matter. Hence, any effort to exercise market power would have to include the nation-wide group of firms. Further, though a group of packagers in principle might have been able to raise prices selectively to one region or even to one cable operator, this type of systematic price discrimination did not appear to be likely in practice. All packagers quoted prices to cable operators from standard "rate cards." Special deals (i.e., unsystematic price discrimination) with some cable operators might be possible, but systematic price discrimination seemed unlikely. And even if it could take place, the market share, entry, and vertical arguments made below would still apply in roughly the same way.

Accordingly, a national market seemed appropriate for movie-driven pay services. (Similar arguments pointed toward a national market for the crucial input, theatrically released films.)

D. Determining Appropriate Market Shares

The subscriber market shares, as of the end of 1982, indicated that HBO accounted for approximately 60 percent of the market, Showtime had about 20 percent, and TMC had about 10 percent, with the remainder divided among a few other services. These data indicated that the relevant market was quite concentrated (with an HHI of about 4,000) and that the merger would increase concentration substantially (the change in the HHI would be about 400).

The attorneys and experts for the joint venturers argued that these market shares vastly overstated the true abilities of these firms to exercise market power. Since virtually all programming services (packagers) did (or would soon) distribute their programs via nation-wide satellite systems, they could expand their sales easily; there were no physical production problems. They only had to convince more cable viewers to subscribe to their service in cases where the cable system offered it, convince more cable systems to offer the service, and/or convince more homeowners to subscribe to cable (and to their particular service) in communities where it was offered. And (according to this argument), since viewer preferences for any given programming service (or even to movie-driven pay services generally) were not strong, these expansions could take place easily in response to any effort by the movie-driven pay services to raise their prices. Hence, one ought to consider each packager (regardless of current market shares) as having a more or less equal capability to attract viewers. Further, there were at least forty or fifty programming services (some pay, some free) in existence and new ones being announced frequently. Accordingly, concentration in this market was quite low, and the merger of Showtime and TMC would not impair competition.

Again, there was no hard evidence to support these assertions. These arguments downplayed the significance of any brand name reputation or recognition among packagers. And they denied the existence of a relevant market consisting of movie-driven pay services. To me, in any event, they did not appear convincing.

E. Entry

Even if one was not convinced by the claims of easy substitution discussed in the previous paragraphs, there was a more limited question that could be asked: with the relevant market limited to movie-driven pay services, how difficult was entry into that market? And here the answer appeared to be "not overwhelmingly." In principle, it appeared possible for current packagers (either of other pay services or of free services) or for de novo entrants to become a movie-driven pay service. They would simply have to obtain the licenses for a package of films from one or more movie distributors and then convince cable operators to offer their service. The entrant might encounter brand-name recognition problems; HBO, especially, appeared to have strong brand-name recognition. But adequate advertising, a good selection of films, and (perhaps) a good brand name in other aspects of the entertainment business (as, for example, the movie studios might bring to this area if they chose to enter it) could probably overcome these difficulties.

Indeed, at the time of the investigation, one firm (Disney) had recently expanded into movie-driven pay services, another (headed by Rupert Murdoch) had announced plans for a direct broadcasting (over the air) service that would feature movies, and a small movie-driven pay service ("Spotlight," owned by five cable operators and offered, at the time, only to their subscribers) had earlier announced plans to "roll out" their service to a national audience. (The Spotlight owners, however, suspended their expansion plans after the Showtime-TMC proposal was announced.)

The experts for the joint venturers argued that entry was quite easy. It is worth noting, though, that this argument conflicted with the arguments made by the executives of the three movie studios involved in the Showtime-TMC proposal. This latter group felt that HBO had been exercising market power—monopsony power—in its purchases of films and hence had been paying prices for films that were too low. Thus, in addition to any direct efficiencies that might be gained through the joint venture, they saw the venture as providing an opportunity to offset (to some extent) HBO's market power. (The same three studios, plus Twentieth Century Fox, had been joint venturers in Premiere, the earlier effort, that the Antitrust Division had successfully challenged in court in 1980; their arguments in support of Premiere had also involved claims of offsetting of HBO's monopsony power.) Monopsony power by HBO and easy entry into movie-driven pay services were logically incompatible.

In any event, to me the question of whether entry into movie-driven pay services was easy enough to provide an adequate check on the exercise of market power was a close one. Entry was surely not as easy as the joint venturers' experts claimed, but recent experience and the simple technology of entry indicated that it could not be impossibly difficult either. In the end, if the supply of theatrically released films were adequate (as will be explained below), it appeared that entry would probably be a sufficient check on the exercise of market power (on either the buying or selling side). Thus, opposition to the simple merger of Showtime and TMC did not seem warranted.

But the proposal before the Antitrust Division was not limited to this simple merger. The proposal also involved the inclusion of Universal and Paramount, joining Warner, as co-owners of the joint venture controlling Showtime-TMC. And it was this strengthened vertical link between the movie studios and the merged packagers that posed more serious competitive problems.

F. Simple Collusion Upstream?

At first glance, it might seem that just the joining of the three movie studios in a joint venture might by itself give rise to added opportunities for coordinated, anticompetitive behavior in the pricing of movies to pay programming services. But the structure of the joint venture was too loose to provide much support for this notion. The studios were not required to provide any or all of their films to the joint venture, nor was exclusivity (the practice of promising that only one programming service would have the right to show a given film, at least for a limited period of time) required for any films provided to the joint venture or forbidden to the studios in their dealings with other packagers. The joint venture might provide studio executives with an extra forum for coordination of their activities, but the industry (like virtually all other industries) already had many other opportunities for coordination (such as industry association meetings and conventions, the conventions of supplier and customer groups, joint ventures for activities outside the U.S., etc.) if they were so inclined. One extra forum did not appear to be important.

Further, even if they did coordinate their behavior among themselves, the three studios together might not be able to exercise market power. That ability would rest on the nature of the demand for the ouput of the three together and the nature of the supply response by the rest of the industry (see Landes and Posner 1981; Reynolds and Snapp 1982). As elsewhere, there were no data that could shed light on this question. The answer was far from clear. The author was prepared to accept the proposition, at least for the purposes of argument, that the three studios together could not exercise market power.

G. The Vertical Link

The Showtime-TMC proposal envisaged a joint venture in which three movie studios, accounting for 40–50 percent of theatrical rentals (and about the same percentage of license revenues to pay programming services), would own (along with Viacom and American Express) a major packager (Showtime-TMC) accounting for about 30 percent of the relevant downstream market and using movies as a crucial input to its service. Thus, the joint venture created a major vertical (customer-supplier) link between these two groups of producers. Was there potential competitive harm that could develop from this vertical link, and how could it arise?

Unfortunately, much of the traditional legal thinking (and some economic thinking) on vertical relationships has not been productive. In the merger area, specifically, theories of "foreclosure" and of "leverage" have been developed that (too simplistically) argue that vertical mergers will allow a firm (or firms) with market power in one market to enhance its market power (and profits), more or less automatically, through expansion into the second, vertically related market (see Posner 1976: 197–201; Bork 1978:229–38; Kaserman 1978). Unfortunately, the means by which this enhancement occurs is frequently not specified. And, for the simplest case—that in which the customer (downstream) industry uses the input from the supplier (upstream) industry in fixed proportions with the other inputs it buys from other sources—the leverage argument is simply wrong. With fixed proportions, a monopolist in the upstream industry, facing a competitive downstream industry, can fully capture all of the potential monopoly profits inherent in the final product by charging the appropriate wholesale price to the downstream competitors. The upstream monopolist cannot gain more by integrating into (and monopolizing) the downstream industry (see Westfield 1981; McGee and Bassett 1976).

Thus, even if one believed that the three movie studio joint venturers could exercise market power individually or jointly, if one also believed that the downstream packagers used movies in roughly fixed proportions with other inputs, then the joint venture could not enhance their market power and could not be anticompetitive on those grounds.

If the assumption of fixed proportions in the use of inputs downstream does not hold—if some substitutability among inputs is possible—the case becomes more complicated. The downstream firms, in response to the high (monopoly) price charged by the upstream monopolist, will try to substitute away from the overpriced input toward other inputs. This substitution causes a reduction in sales and profits for the monopolist and causes him to maintain a price lower than it would be in the absence of substitution. The substitution also represents a social inefficiency, since the substitution takes place only because of the high monopoly price; if competitive prices were charged for this input, the substitution would not take place.

In these circumstances, the upstream monopolist can enhance his control over the downstream market by integrating into and monopolizing it. In so doing, he prevents the inefficient substitution, and this capture of the improvement in efficiency becomes one source of increased profits for him. Further, his elimination of the substitution possibilities also enhances his monopoly power over the sales of his upstream product, providing another source of increased profits. After integration, social efficiency (including both the improved production efficiency downstream and any change in allocative efficiency from the enhanced monopoly power, but ignoring any direct transfer of profits from demanders of the downstream product to the monopolist as a pure transfer) may increase or decrease. If the downstream product price decreases as a consequence of integration, social welfare surely improves; if the downstream price increases, the social welfare change can go in either direction. In any event, the outcome is theoretically indeterminate, depending on a crucial set of empirical parameters (such as the elasticity of substitution among the inputs and the elasticity of demand for the downstream product) (Westfield 1981).

Did this more complicated scenario provide a good fit with the proposed joint venture? The downstream packagers were able to do some substituting of other programming inputs for movies, as the recent experience of HBO and Showtime had indicated. But the three movie studio joint venturers, by themselves or jointly, arguably could not exercise market power. Further, it was not clear how they could achieve the monopolization of the downstream market solely through the ownership of a firm accounting for only 30 percent of the downstream market. And, finally, even if the two previous conditions were met, the social efficiency consequences and even the direction of the price change that might face cable operators and viewers of a possibly monopolizing vertical merger of this kind could not be predicted. This complicated scenario did not appear to me to provide a solid basis for deciding that the joint venture was anticompetitive.

Instead, a more novel theory, partially encompassing the complicated substitution scenario from above and partially encompassing the "raising costs-to-rivals" theory of Salop and Scheffman (1983), provided a better basis for fears that the joint venture could be anticompetitive.[15] This new theory was consistent with the 1982 Merger Guidelines' admonition that the anticompetitive effect of a vertical merger should occur through enhanced opportunities for horizontal coordinated behavior.

The theory requires a number of circumstances to be present. First, there need to be some possibilities for substitution of inputs by the downstream industry.[16] Second, the downstream merger partner should be a sizable (but not necessarily dominant) entity in its market (or a small firm that could readily expand its market share); but neither high concentration nor difficulty of entry downstream need be present. Third, the upstream industry should be at least moderately concentrated, with moderate-to-high barriers to entry, so that increased market power (i.e., increased coordinated behavior) among the upstream firms is a realistic possibility. And, fourth, the upstream merger partner should be a sizable (but not necessarily dominant) entity in its market.

Under these circumstances, a vertical merger could well be anticompetitive. The merged (integrated) entity would have an increased incentive to seek coordinated behavior among its upstream rivals that would raise prices to the downstream industry. The increased incentive arises because the downstream integrated entity does not have to buy its input at the high (noncompetitive) price that results from the upstream coordinated behavior but instead buys from its upstream partner at the true opportunity cost of the input. It thus avoids the higher costs that its downstream rivals experience as a consequence of the higher price of the input (and it avoids any inefficiency of substitution that the higher upstream price might induce). In essence, the integrated entity remains efficient and makes extra profits at the expense of its downstream rivals, whose costs have been raised.[17] The profits of the integrated entity are greater than those that the upstream entity alone would earn from the coordinated behavior in the upstream market. (Whether the integrated entity records the higher profits as accruing at the upstream or downstream level is purely an accounting technicality; the incentives of the integrated entity are unaffected.)

Note that, unlike either the simple or the complicated foreclosure theories, this scenario does not require that the upstream entity have market power at the time of the merger nor that coordinated behavior is occurring generally in the upstream industry at the time of the merger. Instead, it points to the heightened incentive of the integrated entity to engage in coordinated behavior with its upstream rivals and hence the increased likelihood of coordinated behavior upsteam, as a consequence of the vertical merger. It is true that profit-seeking firms always have an incentive to seek coordinated behavior with their rivals, so as to enhance their joint profits. This is the essence of modern oligopoly theory that, as was mentioned in section III of this paper, stands at the heart of the 1982 Merger Guidelines. But there are always risks to a firm's efforts to induce coordinated behavior by its rivals. The rivals may miss the signals provided by the initiating firm, or they may deliberately "cheat" on or "double-cross" the initiator. Further, these efforts may encourage entry that had not been expected. Or they may attract antitrust attention. Consequently, in this risks-and-benefits situation, a firm will engage in efforts to induce coordination only to a level at which marginal costs equal marginal benefits. The vertical merger should increase marginal benefits and thus induce more efforts at achieving coordinated behavior upstream.

How well did the Showtime-TMC proposal fit this yet-more-complicated scenario? First, downstream substitutability was a possibility. Second, the downstream partner (the merged Showtime-TMC) accounted for 30 percent of the downstream market; it was definitely a sizable entity. Third, the upstream market was moderately concentrated, with sizable barriers to entry. Though film production appeared to be competitive (with easy entry), film distribution was the bottleneck. As was noted above, the six major studios accounted for 80–85 percent of theatrical rentals in the late 1970s and early 1980s. No new major distributors have arisen since the end of World War II to challenge the position of the existing majors.[18] Finally, the upstream entities (Paramount, Universal, and Warner) were, collectively, a sizable entity, accounting for 40–50 percent of theatrical rentals.

Accordingly, the circumstances of the joint venture appeared to fit the model quite well. Further, at the time that the Division was evaluating the Showtime-TMC proposal, HBO had an exclusive distribution agreement with Columbia Pictures; and HBO, Columbia, and CBS had proposed a joint venture ("Tristar," which the Division was also evaluating) to create a new production and distribution entity.[19] Though there are pro-efficiency arguments to support exclusive distribution arrangements (they encourage greater downstream advertising and other enhancement of the product), they may also achieve, through long-term contracts, many of the same results achieved through vertical merger. Thus, it appeared that if the Division approved both the Showtime-TMC joint venture and the HBO-Columbia-CBS joint venture, four of the six major studios would be tied to the two major packagers in some fashion, and the incentives for upstream coordinated behavior would be yet greater.

The attorneys and experts for the Showtime-TMC joint venture argued that the provisions of the joint venture greatly reduced the likelihood that coordinated behavior upstream would occur. First, the management of the joint venture was insulated, to some extent from the managements of the movie studios. Second, the upstream studios were not required to bring their films to the joint venture. Thus (it was claimed), they would still have strong incentives to compete actively and would be unlikely to induce or engage in coordinated behavior. Third, in some cases the studios did not own the pay-cable rights to the films that they had theatrically distributed, or key figures in the production of those films had negotiated special pay-cable profit shares for themselves; thus, the studios' ability to exert market power in the sale of films to the pay-cable (packager) market was not as great as their theatrical market shares indicated.

Fourth, suppose the movie studios tried to coordinate their behavior by withholding films from other packagers and providing them only to the joint venture, thereby earning extra profits through the higher prices that Showtime-TMC could charge. But the studios each had fixed ownership and profit shares in the joint venture, which thereby provided each with an incentive to "free ride" and let the others withhold from the packagers and provide to the joint venture, while it tried to sell to the other packagers. This free riding would cause any coordinated price-raising efforts to unravel. Fifth, if the coordinated behavior took the form of simply raising the price of films, the additional profits would be earned upstream, by the movie studio joint venturers, at the expense of the downstream joint venture itself. Hence, Viacom and American Express, the other joint venturers, would be hurt by any such behavior and would surely complain and try to thwart these efforts.

These arguments were not convincing. So long as the three movie studios ultimately controlled the joint venture (through their majority ownership) and profited from its actions, their incentives to induce coordinated behavior among all upstream industry participants were clear (Reynolds and Snapp 1982). No management structuring could prevent this incentive from arising, and any free-riding possibilities could only offset this basic incentive for coordinated behavior to a limited extent. Further, other pay-cable profit participants would be the beneficiaries of coordinated behavior by the studios and would be unlikely to thwart that behavior; and the bottleneck position of the studios in theatrical distribution, where the primary value for pay-cable distribution was created, ensured that the studios would ultimately be able to extract (from the other participants) the gains from coordinated behavior. Finally, Viacom and American Express could quite possibly be mollified through side payments, special purchases, or "creative accounting" within the joint venture; if there were extra profits to be made, the studios could find some way of sharing some of them with the other joint venturers so as to keep them contented.[20]

In sum, this complicated model of the vertical link created by the joint venture appeared, to me, to provide a reasonable basis for fearing that the venture could have an anticompetitive impact and hence would constitute a violation of the Clayton Act.

V. THE OUTCOME

In June 1983, after a series of meetings with the representatives of the joint venturers, the Antitrust Division decided that the joint venture, in the form it had been proposed, raised potential anticompetitive problems. The Division informed the parties that they would be challenged in court if they tried to consummate the arrangement.[21]

A few weeks later the joint venturers returned to the Division with a set of proposals (a possible consent decree) that would have limited the joint venturers' behavior and possibly reduced the possibilities for coordinated behavior. After a few days' consideration, the Division rejected the modifed proposal. So long as Paramount and Universal were part of the proposal,[22] the inherent structure of the joint venture provided unavoidable incentives for upstream coordination that behavioral restrictions could never erase. Further, the Division was generally reluctant to enter into consent decrees that involved an extensive amount of "regulatory" supervision of an industry's behavior, which the proposal would now require.

In August, the parties proposed a simple merger of Showtime and TMC, keeping Warner, Viacom, and American Express as the joint venturers but excluding Paramount and Universal. The Division indicated that it would not challenge the merger.

In December the cable system owners of Spotlight decided to abandon their plans to expand the service and instead sold it to Showtime-TMC. And also in December, Paramount entered into a five-year exclusive distribution arrangement with Showtime-TMC.

VI. CONCLUSION

The Antitrust Division's treatment of the Showtime-TMC proposal provides a good example of the fruitful use of the Division's 1982 Merger Guidelines. It also demonstrates a solid reason for being suspicious of vertical mergers in situations in which the upstream industry is at least moderately concentrated and entry is not easy. The possible efficiency gains from such mergers should not be neglected (at least in economics, if not in law), but neither should the possibilities of heightened incentives for anticompetitive conduct upstream.

In this author's view, the Division's decisions in this case, though not easy, were correct. It would have been useful to have had more information on which to base the decisions. But, in the time periods usually available for investigation and evaluation, complete information (however defined) is rarely available. In light of the limited information that was available, the decision appeared sensible.

The aftermath, though, raises one disquieting possibility. Paramount has entered a five-year exclusive distribution arrangement with Showtime-TMC. Will other studios follow? Will the movie studios achieve through long-term contracts what they failed to achieve through more direct means? Again, there are pro-efficiency reasons for exclusive distribution arrangements in this industry, but they can also create the same incentives for coordinated behavior upstream as do vertical mergers. In the absence of any knowledge of the details of the Paramount arrangement, I should (and will) remain agnostic. But continued antitrust vigilance in these markets does appear to be warranted.

Notes

Much of the information and analyses contained in this paper were generated while the author was the Director of the Economic Policy Office in the Antitrust Division of the U.S. Department of Justice. Many economists and attorneys in the Division contributed to the information and analytical insights that were developed as part of the investigation and evaluation of this case, including economists Bruce K. Snapp, I. Curtis Jernigan, Margo B. Faier, Timothy J. Brennan, and Sheldon Kimmel; and attorneys William F. Baxter, Wayne D. Collins, Stanley M. Gorinson, Robert E. Hauberg Jr., Seymour H. Dussman, Gordon G. Stoner, Monica R.H. Roye, David Schertler, Mark P. Leddy, and Neil E. Roberts. Thanks also are due to Steven C. Salop for helpful suggestions. The contents of this paper, however, are solely the responsibility of the author and do not necessarily reflect the views of the above named individuals or of the U.S. Department of Justice.

1. The "Paramount decrees" substantially altered the structure of the motion picture business. See *U.S. vs. Paramount Pictures* (1948). In television, consent decrees limiting the three networks' abilities to produce and own programming were entered in 1977 and 1980. And in 1980 the U.S. Department of Justice successfully challenged a joint venture ("Premiere") that involved four movie studios and other entities and that would have established a new programming service for cable viewers. See *U.S. vs. Columbia Pictures* (1980).

2. These figures can be derived from data found in various issues of *CableVision*.

3. Twentieth Century Fox, Columbia Pictures, and MGM-United Artists are considered the other major studios; Orion and Disney are considered to be second tier, or "mini-majors" (Waterman 1978). The share figures can be derived from data found in various issues of *Variety*; see also Waterman (1984).

4. Disclosure is required if the acquiring firm has total assets or annual sales of at least $100 million; if the acquired firm has assets or sales of at least $10 million; and if the acquiring company acquires at least $15 million in assets or 15 percent of the voting securities of the acquired company.

5. If the transaction involves a tender offer, the time periods are reduced from 30 and 20 days to 15 and 10 days, respectively. Also, consummation can occur earlier if the investigating agency indicates that it will not challenge the merger.

6. A common antitrust expression in the merger area is that "it is difficult to unscramble the eggs."

7. For example, cases involving companies in the petroleum and food manufacturing industries are usually taken by the FTC; cases involving companies in the steel industry and in regulated industries are usually taken by the Division.

8. See *U.S. vs. Columbia Pictures* (1980).

9. The reasons for the absence of formal H-S-R procedures in this case are not entirely clear to me; apparently, under some circumstances, H-S-R does not apply to joint ventures.

10. For a further discussion of the 1982 Guidelines, see Fox (1982), Symposium (1983), and Werden (1983).

11. The 1982 Guidelines also acknowledge the "dominant firm" model developed by Landes and Posner (1981), but the main theory underlying the Guidelines is that of a group of oligopolists coordinating their actions.

12. Other factors encouraging oligopolistic coordination can be found in Scherer (1980), chs. 5–8.

13. They are restricted in this respect by the Division's consent decrees of 1977 and 1980.

14. They are restricted in this respect by FCC regulations.

15. This theory was suggested to me by Steven Salop.

16. The possibilities of substitution of inputs needs to be present, at least, for the downstream merger partner; it need not be present for the rivals of the downstream partner.

17. The extra profits could occur purely from the higher input costs that the downstream merger partner avoids but that its downstream rivals face. To the extent that its lower costs allow the downstream partner to expand at its rivals' expense, yet higher profits will be gained. In this latter (and probably more general case), the disadvantaged position of the other downstream firms would decrease the profitability of, and hence incentives for, upstream coordination by the other *upstream* firms. But the total profits from coordinated behavior by the upstream firms (including the integrated entity) should be higher than in the absence of any vertical integration, because of the added efficiency (and hence profitability) created by the integration in the presence of upstream coordination. Hence, the overall incentives for upstream coordination should still increase.

18. See Waterman (1978). The source of the barriers is unclear; it may be in economies of scale in risk absorption (since each movie is a costly and highly uncertain venture) or in maintaining a nation-wide network of sales offices and representatives.

19. The Division subsequently approved the HBO-Columbia-CBS joint venture.

20. Also, if Viacom and American Express were unhappy with their position, they might sell their ownership interests to the studios; it would then be an interesting question as to whether the Division could or would sue the parties concerning this sale.

21. The Division issued a press release to this effect shortly after it informed the parties; the Division also issued press releases after it informed the parties of its subsequent decisions.

22. The logic of the argument developed in section IV of this paper indicates that even Warner's presence alone in the venture could have an anticompetitive effect. But Warner had the advantage of already being a co-owner of TMC. And the possible anticompetitive effect from Warner alone seemed, to me, to be much less serious than the effect from the joint presence of the three studios.

12

Regulation of Broadcast Station Ownership: Evidence and Theory

STANLEY M. BESEN and

LELAND L. JOHNSON

CONTENTS

I. Introduction.
II. Group Ownership
  A. Anti-Competitive Behavior
    1. What Does the Evidence Show?
    2. Is There Reason to Expect Anti-Competitive Behavior?
  B. Economic Efficiency
  C. Diversity
  D. Conclusions
III. The Regional Concentration Rule
IV. The Duopoly and One-to-a-Market Rules
  A. Advertising Rates
  B. Syndicated Program Prices
  C. Conclusions
V. The Broadcast Television-Cable Cross-Ownership Rule
  A. The Benefits of Joint Ownership
  B. The Losses from Joint Ownership

I. INTRODUCTION

Seeking to increase program diversity and to prevent undue economic concentration, the Federal Communications Commission has imposed a number of restrictions on the ownership of broadcasting stations. Among these are (a) the group ownership rule, which prohibits a single entity from owning more than seven stations nationwide in the same service (AM, FM, or TV) with no more than five of the seven television stations being VHF, (b) the regional concentration rule, which prohibits common ownership of three commercial AM, FM, or television stations where any two are located within 100 miles of the third, and where the primary service contours of any of the stations overlap, (c) the duopoly rule, which prohibits ownership of more than one station in the same service in a market, (d) the one-to-a-market rule, which prohibits the acquisition of more than one station in any service in a market (although AM-FM combinations are allowed and UHF television-radio combinations are permitted on a case-by-case basis), and (e) the television station-cable cross ownership rule, which prohibits common ownership of a television station and a cable system in the same market.[1]

Whatever justifications may have existed when these rules were adopted, striking changes occurring in the electronic mass media highlight the need for their reassessment. Indeed, at this writing the FCC has a proceeding under way to determine whether the group ownership rule should be amended or abolished (FCC 1983u, 1984a) and recently has eliminated the regional concentration rule. Our purpose in this paper is to examine the empirical evidence on the effect of joint ownership—drawn from a body of literature that, unfortunately, is severely limited—and to supplement this evidence with additional economic analysis. We are concerned with how changes in ownership might affect (a) the prospects for anti-competitive behavior, (b) economic efficiency, including economies in program production and marketing of advertising, and (c) diversity in the range of viewpoints available to the American public.

We conclude that, over a wide range, changes in these ownership rules are likely to have little effect. For example, either continuation of the group ownership rule or its abolition is unlikely to affect economic efficiency, anti-competitive behavior, or diversity, at least in the larger markets. A better case can be made for retaining the duopoly and one-to-a-market rules, but even these rules might be relaxed in markets that are unconcentrated. Moreover, our conclusions are drawn largely from empirical evidence that does not take into account the growing availability of competing media such as cable, multipoint distribution services, and direct broadcast satellites. Continuing development of services using these technologies will only reinforce these conclusions.

II. GROUP OWNERSHIP

Broadcast groups may be able to provide services to their stations, including production and acquisition of programs and selling of advertising, at a lower cost than the combined costs of each of the stations operated independently. To the extent that current limitations on group size prevent these economies from being fully realized, costs are higher than necessary. Of course, whether singly-owned stations have higher costs depends on their ability to purchase services from networks, program syndicators, and spot advertising representatives at prices similar to the costs at which these services are provided by groups to their members.

Group ownership also raises issues of anti-competitive behavior. One possibility involves "leveraging"—the threat by a group owner to deny access by advertisers or program suppliers to some of its stations in order to obtain more favorable terms than those obtained by its singly owned rivals.

The leverage argument is asserted most clearly by Coffey:

Independent stations compete with each other to purchase 'off-network' syndicated programs. . . . Those independents which are part of a group have a distinct competitive advantage over single-owned independent stations in the same market by virtue of their buying power. The leverage may be illustrated by the hypothetical top fifty group owner with independent stations in markets one, two and eight. Such an owner is in a position to tie his purchase of a syndicator's programs in markets one and two to the supplier's promise to sell the same program to him in the less lucrative market eight. A single station owned independent station in market eight is thereby at a competitive disadvantage. (1979:322–323)

Another possible form of anti-competitive behavior involves collusion among groups. If groups expand in size, the number of separate station owners could fall sufficiently below the number of stations within relevant markets for advertising and programming, to facilitate collusive agreements.

Finally, there is the issue of diversity. In enacting the group ownership rules, the goals of the Commission were "to maximize diversification of program and service viewpoints as well as to prevent any undue economic concentration contrary to the public interest." (FCC 1983u:32) Thus, the Commission is concerned not only with the economic effects of concentrated ownership but also with its effects on the range of views available to the public.

In this section, we assess the available empirical evidence on the effects of group ownership on anti-competitive behavior, economic efficiency, and diversity. As we show, this evidence is severely limited. But the pattern of evidence, and our own analysis, suggest that either keeping or eliminating the group ownership rule would have little effect except, perhaps, in small markets.

A. Anti-Competitive Behavior

If groups collude, we would expect advertising rates to rise, and program prices to fall as a function of the market shares of groups in the markets under investigation. If an individual group applies leverage or exercises market power against advertisers and program suppliers, we would expect the group's advertising rates to rise and the prices it pays for programs to fall relative to those of other stations in the same markets.

1. What Does the Evidence Show?[2]

With respect to the issue of collusion, two studies are notable. One, by Peterman (1971), takes as the dependent variable the discounted 20-second national spot advertising prime time rate. After controlling for homes reached and market income in a 97-market sample, Peterman finds no evidence of collusion, since neither the percentage nor the number of group-owned stations in a market is significant in explaining advertising rates.

Although Peterman's analysis is the most useful we have seen with respect to the issue of collusion and advertising rates, it is subject to an important caveat. Like other investigators, Peterman implicitly defines the relevant geographic market as a single city or metropolitan area. Thus, his tests may fail to detect collusion if relevant markets for advertising are larger than the city or metropolitan area.

To demonstrate, consider four cities, each containing group owners drawn from the set A, B, C, D, E, F, G, H, I. These groups are distributed as follows:

City: 1   2   3   4
Groups: A,B,C   A,B,C   D,E,F   G,H,I

Suppose that cities 1 and 2 form one market for selling advertising while cities 3 and 4 form another. Looking at each city separately, one would conclude that groups are equally represented, with three stations in each city. However, the market consisting of 1 and 2 contains only three separate owners while the market containing 3 and 4 contains six. Thus, the former market is more concentrated. Even if these differences in ownership produce higher rates in the advertising market containing 1 and 2, there will be no correlation between group ownership and advertising rates, since all of the stations are group owned. Thus, Peterman's tests would not be able to explain why rates are higher in cities 1 and 2.

A second study, by Fournier and Martin (1983), tests whether the presence of a network-owned station in a market affects spot advertising rates. They find no significant difference in advertising rates, suggesting that the networks do not collude in setting local advertising rates. This finding is notable because the major networks with their owned stations face each other in several major metropolitan markets such as New York, Chicago, and Los Angeles. If these cities together constitute a sufficiently distinct advertising market to permit broadcasters there to collectively exercise market power against advertisers, the networks would be in a particularly good position to exploit this opportunity. If they do so, rates in markets with network-owned stations would be higher (again with everything else held constant) than the rates elsewhere.

A study by Wildman (1978) also bears on the question of the effect of network station ownership on advertising rates. After controlling for a number of other factors, Wildman tests whether a station that is network-owned or competes with a network-owned station has higher spot advertising rates. He finds that network-owned stations have significantly higher rates, other things equal, but that stations with which they compete have rates that are not significantly different from those of other affiliates.

However, Wildman does not attribute the higher rates of network-owned stations to collusion among the networks. Instead, he hypothesizes that, since network-owned stations will "clear" (carry) a larger proportion of the network lineup than other affiliates, other things equal, there will be fewer spot advertisements to be sold where such stations are in the market. The result will be higher spot rates. In Wildman's view, therefore, higher rates result not from coordinated behavior among the networks but from differences between the behavior of network-owned stations and affiliates. He does not attempt to explain why other stations in the market fail to benefit from the restricted supply of spots on network-owned stations.

A larger number of studies address the issue of leveraging. The earliest, by Cherington et al. (1971), involves comparisons of advertising rates between group-owned and singly-owned stations. The authors conclude that "there was no difference in the overall averages [of prime 20-second spot rates] for the group-owned stations vs. the single-owner stations ($3.27 and $3.28, respectively, in 1965). . . . For market group 101–150, group-owned station averages were slightly, but not significantly, higher, while for the market group with the smallest audiences the single-owner stations showed higher cost-per-thousand figures" (p. 54).

Although this evidence suggests that groups do not exert leverage against advertisers, the study has a number of weaknesses. It reports averages of rates for group-owned and singly-owned stations within particular ranges of market size (like markets 51–100) rather than differences within specific markets. Large differences could exist in some markets without much affecting the average for the category. Moreover, the study fails to assess the statistical significance of the observed differences in rates. Nor does it control for other variables, such as the age of stations, family incomes, and differences in market competition.

In another study, Levin (1980) estimates a number of regressions that explain a station's 20-second spot rate. The large number of equations and the wide variety of specifications makes it difficult to briefly summarize Levin's findings. In one set of results, group ownership has no significant effect on advertising rates, in another the effects are mixed, and in others, group ownership significantly raises advertising rates. In all cases, ownership by a network significantly raises a station's rates. It is impossible to identify why the effect of group ownership varies from equation to equation, since Levin's equations are complex and he does not conduct explicit sensitivity tests.

The FCC's Network Inquiry Special Staff (FCC 1980f 2:641–50) tested the hypothesis that group-owned stations are able to obtain more favorable terms than singly owned stations from program suppliers, by analyzing the determinants of the prices paid by stations per viewer-minute for syndicated off-network programs. Controlling for the amount of competition for programs, the staff found that the price per viewer minute is significantly *higher* when the purchaser was owned by a large group or by a network. These results fail to support the hypothesis that group owners are able to take advantage to their position to acquire programs at lower prices than those of their singly owned rivals.

The finding that groups pay more for programs is, however, a puzzle. One possible explanation stems from the linear relationship assumed between program prices and the number of viewers. If this relationship is nonlinear, and if group owned stations tend to be in larger markets and thus command larger audiences than the average station, a variable representing group ownership will show a positive effect on price per viewer.

Leverage by groups could also be manifested in compensation paid to network affiliates. The Barrow Report (U.S. Congress 1958:565), in particular, asserted that network-affiliated stations owned by large groups are able to obtain greater compensation from the networks than their singly-owned rivals.

The Network Inquiry Special Staff examined this assertion. After controlling for (a) the audience delivered by the affiliate, (b) the strength of the network with which it is affiliated, and (c) the presence and strength of independent stations that might compete for the affiliation, the staff found no significant difference between compensation received by stations that are members of the 10 largest stations groups and all other stations (FCC 1980f:259–260, 269–283). This result, like that for syndicated program prices, further weakens the case for the proposition that group-owned stations exercise leverage to the disadvantage of their singly-owned rivals.

The exercise of bargaining power by station groups might also be manifested in their ability to obtain better network affiliations than their singly-owned rivals. Again, the Barrow Report asserts that group owners have this advantage. However, the Cherington study challenges this claim. Presumably, if groups were able to exert such influence, they would tend to be affiliated with the stronger networks—NBC and CBS at that time (1971) rather than ABC. Yet, in the top 50 markets ABC "had the same proportion (33 percent) of stations affiliated with it for both group and single owners" (Cherington et al. 1971:46). Moreover, for both the top 50 markets used and for all markets, the percentage of network affiliated group stations was not much greater than the percentage for nongroup stations—79 percent vs. 73 percent in the top 50, and 93 percent vs. 86 percent in all markets.

Differences in profit margins is another way that the exercise of market power by groups (as well as group economic efficiencies) would be manifested. The Cherington study concludes, however, that, except for the smallest markets, no substantial differences arise in profit margins between group-owned and singly owned stations (pp. 60–65). Using the FCC's data for 1964, the study shows consistently higher profit margins for group-owned stations for all size markets. But the differences are small except for markets below 150 where group-owned stations showed a profit ratio of 15.1 percent as against a loss of 1.7 percent for singly owned stations. Among network affiliated stations classified by net weekly circulation, singly owned stations outperform group-owned stations in markets with more than 500,000 net weekly circulation while group-owned stations show an advantage in the smaller markets.

As in its inquiry into advertising rates, the Cherington study failed to assess the statistical significance of the differences in profit margins reported, or to control for other factors. Moreover, the quality of the underlying data is subject to substantial question (Park et al. 1976). Nevertheless, this pattern of results is intuitively plausible. If groups bargain unfairly or collude, they would likely do so in smaller, less competitive markets.

Levin also examines whether the presence of group owned stations in a market significantly increases station profitability. His results are generally negative. He reports, for example, that "group ownership [has] only weakly significant effects . . . on the market averages of income" (1980:150). Moreover, when the effect of public television is taken into account, he finds no effect of group ownership (p. 255). However, Levin's results are consistent either with the hypothesis that group owned stations do not have higher profits than singly owned ones or with the hypothesis that group ownership redistributes profits among the stations in a market without affecting the amount to be divided among them.

2. Is There Reason to Expect Anti-Competitive Behavior?

On theoretical grounds the leverage hypothesis is an implausible one. Suppose that a hypothetical group owner is willing to pay more for a program than his rivals in markets 1 and 2, but that the rivals are willing to pay more for the program in market 3. We show in our earlier study (Besen and Johnson 1984) that the group owner, rival stations, and the program supplier can each be made better off if a rival obtains the program in market 3 than if the group owner, using leverage, threatens to withhold purchasing in markets 1 and 2 in order to obtain the program in market 3.

However, might not the group owner find it in his long-term interest to accept a short-term loss in order to deny programming to the non-group owner in market 3 and, possibly, drive him out of business? Such behavior by the group owner seems implausible because of the stringent conditions that must be met for the group's short-term losses to be more than offset by the increase in long-term profits. First, either the market must contain few or no other stations, or these stations must be able to collude in order to share the costs of exclusionary behavior. Second, the elasticity of program supply must be low—a condition particularly hard to meet in small markets where all commercial stations are network affiliates and where the amount of syndicated programming available per station is greater than in large markets. Third, the barriers to reentering the market must be large enough to permit the predator to more than cover his earlier losses before his victim can return. Finally, since the program supplier would, in the long run, also be disadvantaged if the group owner were to exclude his rival, program suppliers must fail to anticipate the effects of predatory behavior and not enter into long-term contracts with threatened stations.[3]

With respect to collusion, a number of conditions must be met for it to be facilitated by group ownership. First, the geographic areas in question must be a single (relevant) market in which prices for advertising or programs are related. Second, the number of station owners in the relevant market must be significantly smaller than the number of stations in the market. Finally, overlapping group ownership must reduce the number of owners *sufficiently* below the number of stations to render collusion a feasible option. If the relevant geographic market is large, ownership by some entities of more than a single station may not pose a threat of collusion because of the presence of many other competing stations.

Where, then, would we expect group station ownership to facilitate collusion? A likely candidate would be a collection of cities in relatively close geographic proximity to one another, where several owners operate in more than one city and where the total number of stations (and other media outlets) is small. Of particular relevance, therefore, is the Commission's regional ownership concentration rule discussed in section III.

B. Economic Efficiency

If group ownership confers efficiencies, we would expect profit margins to be higher for groups than for others, regardless of whether groups engage in anti-competitive behavior. However, both the Levin (1980) and Cherington studies find that these margins do not differ significantly between group owned and other stations, suggesting that the cost advantages of group ownership are low.

We would also expect advertising rates to be reduced if there are efficiencies in group marketing. However, this proposition can be tested only by comparing rates in group-only markets either with rates in markets containing both groups and singly owned stations (mixed markets), or with rates in markets containing only singly owned stations. Comparisons *within* mixed markets would be inappropriate because since advertisers are concerned with cost per viewer reached, rates for all stations would tend to be identical.[4] These rates would be just high enough to cover the cost of the singly-owned stations (which are the "marginal" stations) while group owners would enjoy higher profit margins because of their lower costs. Unfortunately, the studies of advertising rates discussed earlier include mostly or only mixed markets and, therefore, do not shed light on group efficiencies.

We would also expect group efficiencies (as well as anti-competitive behavior) to show up in larger audiences. A study by Parkman (1982) suggests that local news programs produced by group-owned stations do tend to attract larger audiences. He uses a multiple regression analysis in which the dependent variable is audience rating and the independent variables include joint ownership with other television stations. The ratings data, for the years 1965 and 1975, are drawn from local television news programs in the top 100 markets. Parkman finds that, for 1965, group ownership has a positive but statistically insignificant effect on local television news ratings. However, for 1975 there is a positive and statistically significant effect. Indeed, the coefficient of the group ownership variable is the largest of the three ownership variables and is the only statistically significant one. In 1975 the group ownership coefficients are of substantial size, showing that group ownership increases ratings by 2.65 and 1.99 for the early and late news programs respectively, compared with average market ratings of 12.02 and 9.97.

Parkman's study covers only local news which is produced by the station, rather than including also syndicated programming where any effects of leveraging or collusion would more likely show up. But the study is useful in suggesting that groups do enjoy cost advantages, at least for local news production.[5]

The findings by Levin and Wildman, discussed earlier, that network-owned stations have higher advertising rates than do their rivals may also constitute evidence of group efficiencies. Differences in rates would arise if economies permit the group-owned station to provide programs that attract larger audiences, and if advertising rates rise faster than audience, i.e., the relationship is nonlinear.

Trends in group ownership also provide useful evidence about the advantages of group ownership. If there were large efficiencies, or opportunities for anti-competitive behavior, we would expect strong incentives for groups to purchase singly-owned stations. If so, we probably would have seen rapid growth of groups after the FCC's 1954 decision increasing the ownership limit to 7 stations, with many or most groups up to the limit. Yet, according to Howard (1983:6), by the end of 1982, only 9 of the 174 television station groups owned 7 stations. Only two had the full complement of 7 television, 7 AM radio and 7 FM radio stations. A total of 23 groups held the limit of 5 VHF stations, at the same time that 20 percent of the nation's 518 VHF remained singly owned (FCC 1983u:25).

The growth of group-owned stations has proceeded at a steady, but not strikingly rapid pace. During the 26-year period from 1956 to 1982, the percentage of group-owned television stations grew from 45 percent to 72 percent, with a substantial number of stations—219 out of 790— remaining in the hands of individual owners.

Overall, the evidence suggests that while group efficiencies may exist, they do not seem to be large except possibly in the production of local news programs.[6]

C. Diversity

The final category of evidence about the effects of group ownership concerns program diversity. Again, the Cherington study is one of the few that shed light on this issue. The analysis involved (a) sending questionnaires to all of the 532 commercial stations in the country, of which 15.2 percent were returned, and (b) conducting 35 interviews "with a representative cross-section of station managements, a majority of which had not answered the questionnaire" (Cherington et al. 1971:82).

The authors conclude that group ownership has little effect on opinion molding or on editorializing. Responses from both group-owned and singly-owned stations disclosed that the station manager and news director have "moderate" to "great" influence on editorial positions. For group-owned stations "headquarters" and the "owner" played "very little" role while, for single-owner stations, in contrast, the "owner" played a "moderate role" (p. 93). For both types of stations, the national wire services, network news organizations, and station reporting staff were of "moderate or great importance"; while group news organizations for the group-owned stations was of "very little" importance (p. 87). The interviews also disclosed a high degree of autonomy by station managers in the selection of programming.

If there were significant group efficiencies, one would expect them to arise in part from the economies of centralized management, news collection and presentation. However, if station managers operate as autonomously as is described in the Cherington study, and if they rely so little on headquarters for news content, the economies of group ownership are likely to be small.[7]

The Cherington study is subject to the obvious criticism that the low response rate of 15.2 percent to the questionnaire could have introduced a self-selection bias. And the evidence is based on self-reporting by station respondents rather than on data about how stations actually behave. A content analysis of programs carried by group and singly-owned stations, while tedious and costly to perform, would provide a far better measure of differences in programming.

More recently, Levin reports that

a reduction in group ownership would have no impact on diversity, however measured, so long as network affiliations remained unchanged. . . . Loss of a group tie would have deprived viewers of no more than 3.5 minutes of news daily, and of 5.5 minutes of non-network shows, whereas public affairs, fine arts, and local programming would each have remained unaffected (1980:170–171)[8]

He also concludes that "the loss of group ties . . . has no significant programming effect, nor any even approaching significance" (p. 205).

D. Conclusions

Our review of the empirical evidence does not leave us with much confidence that the effects of group ownership are well understood, since many of the studies have important shortcomings. The best that can be said is that the studies are consistent with the view that the economies of joint station operation are small and that, as suggested by theory, group ownership does not create market power. Only Parkman's study demonstrates that costs are significantly lower for group-owned stations, although the Levin and Wildman findings are consistent with the presence of group efficiencies. Nor is there evidence that groups, other than those controlled by the networks, significantly raise advertising rates. In the case of network-owned stations, the evidence is mixed, with the Wildman and Levin studies suggesting that they charge higher rates than do other stations in their markets, the Fournier and Martin study indicating that rates are no higher in *markets* with network-owned stations, and the Wildman study concluding that rates are no higher for *other stations* in markets containing network-owned stations.

In view of the limited utility of the evidence, one must place more weight on *a priori* analysis than is perhaps desirable. Our analysis, which is broadly consistent with the empirical evidence, indicates that group ownership is unlikely either to enhance efficiency or create market power. The issue of collusion, which may be a problem if group ownership becomes regionally concentrated, with overlapping group ownership occurring within relevant markets—especially small ones—for advertising and programming, is still an open one, however. Thus, it is important to examine the Commission's regional concentration rule, a subject to which we now turn.

III. THE REGIONAL CONCENTRATION RULE

Group ownership increases the likelihood of collusion if (a) the stations are in the same relevant market, e.g., advertisers regard purchases on the two stations as substitutes, (b) the relevant market is concentrated, and (c) the existence of a station group substantially increases concentration in the market. Therefore, a combination of stations in adjacent cities, each of which contains a relatively small number of stations, is more likely to create market power than a combination in widely separated cities or in cities that contain many other stations. The Commission's regional concentration rule was important to the extent that it assured that stations under common ownership were not in the same market.

Even if the rule had been retained, a group would probably not have been seriously handicapped since it could have purchased stations in other "regions." Perhaps the most serious loss would have been those economic efficiencies that result when groups are regionally concentrated. Unfortunately, no empirical studies shed light on this issue.

On the other hand, little is likely to be lost as a result of the abolition of the rule, as long as relevant advertising and program markets are no larger than the markets defined in the Commission's one-to-a-market rule, discussed below. If this is the case, elimination of the regional concentration rule will have no effect on the ease with which groups can collude. And even if relevant markets *are* larger, no market power will be created if those markets have many stations and other competing media.

A major difficulty with the regional concentration rule is that it accorded no recognition to the extent of media concentration in the markets in question. Whether these markets had only one, or many, stations was of no consequence to the rule's enforcement. Thus, the rule probably prevented some combinations where the relevant market would have remained unconcentrated even if the combination were permitted.

With the elimination of the rule, a reasonable substitute would be reliance on a case-by-case approach based on guidelines similar to those adopted by the Department of Justice for evaluating proposed mergers.[9] Use of these guidelines would avoid the arbitrary nature of the previous regional concentration rule, by emphasizing the need to define the relevant market and to examine the level of concentration in that market.

While recognizing its arbitrariness, the Commission initially adopted the regional concentration rule to avoid the extensive showings and determinations typically involved in a case-by-case approach. Yet, we believe that the Commission could substitute the more flexible case-by-case approach for the regional concentration rule without the difficulties that it faced prior to adoption of the rule in 1975.

Our proposed approach would have several key features. First, when station acquisitions are contemplated, the applicant would, of course, notify the Commission. Second, the Commission staff would be required, within a limited period of time, to determine whether or not to challenge the acquisition. If it did not, this would be prima facie evidence that the transaction was acceptable so that outside challengers would face a heavy burden in opposing it. Third, rejection by the staff would either produce a hearing, if the applicant chose to proceed, or to the withdrawal of the application. Over time, as the outlines of the Commission's policy became clear, applicants would be able to determine the likelihood that a particular application would be approved. Fourth, no one would be foreclosed from defending a combination before the staff or the Commission if it felt that the particular circumstances warranted. Fifth, the Commission would be free to issue guidelines for combinations in order to inform parties in advance about the kinds of combinations likely to be permitted. These guidelines would be based on analyses taking into account what is known about concentration and its effects in broadcasting, and they would be periodically revised as new knowledge became available.

IV. THE DUOPOLY AND ONE-TO-A-MARKET RULES

In the case of multiple ownership—where Commission rules have limited, but not prevented, the formation of broadcast groups—one can compare the behavior of group-owned and singly-owned stations. But one cannot examine the behavior of jointly owned stations in the same service in a market because they do not exist. The FCC has always prohibited joint ownership of television stations in the same market. A similar prohibition applies to FM radio and, since 1941, to AM radio when the FCC adopted its chain broadcasting rules.[10]

However, a limited basis exists for examining the effects of common ownership of stations in *different* services within a market. Some combinations of television and AM radio stations, which are now prohibited, were grandfathered when the Commission adopted its one-to-a-market rule. Moreover, the one-to-a-market rule permits AM-FM combinations and allows combinations of UHF television stations and FM radio stations on a case-by-case basis. Thus, routinely permitted and grandfathered combinations are potential sources of information about the effect of concentrated ownership within a local market.

In addition, even in markets without such combinations, relationships between ownership concentration and economic behavior may shed light on the likely effect of common ownership of stations in the same service. For example, if markets with 20 AM radio stations behave as competitively as those with 10 AM stations, one may infer that some combinations in the former markets would not substantially lessen competition.

A. Advertising Rates

Peterman (1971) addresses the question of whether joint ownership of radio and television raises advertising rates. For each market he assumes that "the proportion of the total number of radio stations jointly owned by TV firms . . . represents the degree of control over radio by TV stations." (p. 78) He relates the average discounted advertising rates summed over all TV stations for each of 204 markets to the number of homes, family income, and the percent of radio stations owned by TV stations in these markets. The analysis shows that homes and incomes are both positively and statistically significantly related to advertising rates, but that there is no effect of cross-ownership between radio and television stations. Peterman obtains essentially the same result when he limits the analysis to markets with exactly three television stations, and to the 51 markets containing only a single station (where cross-ownership is measured by a dummy variable equal to one when the lone TV station also operates a radio station).

Unfortunately, Peterman's price data are from station rate cards and thus do not necessarily reflect transaction prices. Moreover, his model considers only a limited number of factors besides radio-television cross-ownership. For example, the analysis of all 204 markets does not control for the number of television stations in each.

Fournier and Martin (1983), using actual transactions price data, examine the effect of market concentration on the (logarithm of the) price of 30-second television spot advertisements. Controlling for a number of other variables, they use various measures of concentration including entropy—the sum over all stations of market share times the logarithm of (1/market share); the Herfindahl index—the sum of the squared market shares of all stations; and the two-firm concentration ratio.

The results are either not significant or suggest that rates *fall* with an increase in concentration. The only significant measure is entropy, indicating that advertising rates are *higher* the *less* concentrated is the market. The two-firm concentration ratio, which approaches statistical significance, similarly indicates that the more concentrated is the market the lower are advertising rates. However, when the equations were reestimated treating the two-firm concentration ratio, the Herfindahl index, and the entropy measure as endogenous, none was significantly related to advertising rates. These findings suggest that, at least for the observed levels of market concentration, little or no adverse effect on advertising rates would occur if combinations of television stations were permitted in the *same* market.

In paper 4 of this book Wirth and Bloch present statistical evidence relating the highest 30-second spot rate for a sample of CBS affiliates to, among other variables, the number of households in the station's market, the station's audience share when it carries *MASH,* and a Herfindahl index for the market based on average daily viewing. They find that market concentration, as measured by the Herfindahl index, is significantly and positively related to advertising rates and conclude, as a result, that television markets are oligopolistic.

Wirth and Bloch also find that audience share is *not* significantly related to advertising rates, a result that is very surprising. A possible explanation for this result, and of the correlation between rates and market concentration, is that a station will have a larger share the more concentrated is its market, i.e., share and the Herfindahl index are correlated. We conjecture that this multicollinearity is affecting their results and are, therefore, somewhat skeptical about the finding linking market concentration and advertising rates.

Wildman (1978) relates the spot television advertising rates of network affiliates and network-owned stations to a number of variables including those that measure whether there are more than three VHF stations or more than three stations of any type in the markets of the stations he analyzes. The purpose of including these variables was "to provide a measure of the effect of competition from independent stations on the price of spot time sold by affiliated stations" (p. 339).

Rather than finding the expected negative coefficients for these variables, they are generally positive, although rarely significant, in the different equations Wildman estimates. He interprets these results as evidence that in markets with more than three stations the networks are able to get their affiliates to behave like network-owned stations because the stations fear the loss of their affiliations. Thus, for the same reason that he argues that the spot advertising rates will be higher for network-owned stations than for similarly situated affiliates, he contends that rates will be higher for affiliates faced with the possibility that they will be displaced on the network. This reasoning suggests that advertising rates would decline if the number of stations in a market is reduced.

Levin (1980) also finds that rates are higher if there are four or more stations in a market, even after controlling for station audience. One possible explanation is that this variable, as well as network-ownership, are picking up the effect of a mis-specified audience variable. If advertising revenues are related to audiences nonlinearly, with rates rising faster than audience, a linear equation will impart a spurious positive coefficient to variables that are present only in the larger markets. This possibility applies to the Wildman study as well.

Although they are concerned primarily with the effects of newspaper-television station cross-ownership, Wirth and Allen (1980) report findings relevant to our purposes. Using 1973 data for 534 commercial stations, they separately regress television list-price advertising rates and total television station advertising revenues (both per thousand viewers) against a number of explanatory variables including whether the station is owned by a newspaper in the same market, the number of households in the station's market, and whether the television station owns a radio station in the same market.

Wirth and Allen obtain a generally positive and occasionally significant relationship between a television station's advertising rate and its joint ownership with a radio station in the market. Wirth and Allen interpret this finding as evidence that radio-television combinations create market power. However, their finding is also consistent with the hypothesis that ownership generates economies that produce larger audiences, and that the relationship between rates and audiences is non-linear. A test of the market power hypothesis would require examining whether rates are higher for stations that compete with radio-television combinations. Unfortunately, Wirth and Allen do not carry out this test.[11]

They also include in their analysis a variable measuring the number of AM radio stations in a market, expecting that "an increase in the number of [radio] competitors in a market leads to lower prices." (p. 32) They find, however, that advertising rates are always *positively* and usually significantly related to the number of radio stations in the market.[12]

In an earlier study (1979) Wirth and Allen analyze market data in order to determine the effect of local market concentration on advertising rates. They employ 1973 FCC advertising revenue data for 124 markets divided by the market's prime time audience to obtain a measure of the "price" of advertising. Among their explanatory variables are the number of television stations and the number of AM radio stations in the market. They conduct separate analyses for different sources of revenues—network, national-regional, and local—and for the top 50 and all other markets as well as for all 124 markets combined.

Although the number of television stations usually has the expected (negative) sign, the coefficient is only occasionally significant. The variable for the number of radio stations is negative in only slightly more than half the regressions and significant only when it is *positive*. The results, therefore, do not indicate any strong relationship between market concentration and advertising rates.[13]

B. Syndicated Program Prices

The Network Inquiry Special Staff (FCC 1980f: 2:643–650) analyzed the effect of the structure of local broadcast markets on the prices paid by stations for off-network syndicated programming. In one set of equations, which measured competition for syndicated program by the presence or absence of an independent station and whether the independent was "comparable" to the weakest affiliate, the study found that "the price paid per viewer is significantly lower [where there is not a 'technically comparable' independent] than where at least one independent is technically comparable" (p. 647). In another set of equations, which also took into account the numbers of various types of independents, "the results clearly indicate that the larger is the number of independent VHF stations in a market, the higher is the price paid per viewer [for syndicated programs.] The effect of the number of independent UHF stations is mixed, however. In three of the equations, the number of UHF stations in a market is positively and significantly related to the price per viewer. In the other equation, while the measured effect is positive, it is not significant"(p. 650). These results show clearly that a reduction in the number of stations competing for syndicated programming would reduce the price per viewer obtained for these programs. The effect on the price of the *program* of an increase in the number of competing stations is, however, ambiguous. While additional competition may raise the price per viewer, it may also reduce the number of viewers a program attracts.

C. Conclusions

As in the case of multiple station ownership, the empirical studies do not provide convincing evidence of adverse effects of local market concentration. The only evidence that joint ownership creates market power is Wirth and Allen's finding that television stations jointly owned with radio stations in the same market have higher advertising rates. However, this result is also consistent with the existence of economies of joint operation and, because the effect of these combinations or rivals' rates was not examined, the market power hypothesis has not been fully tested. Moreover, the various studies of the effect of concentration of television station ownership on advertising rates indicate that there is no effect—or that rates are higher the *less* concentrated is the market. Finally, none of the studies demonstrates the existence of significant economies of joint operation.

Nonetheless, we would be reluctant to urge abandonment of the duopoly and one-to-a-market rules with nothing to take their place, because the analytic case for these rules is far stronger than that for the group ownership rule. This does not mean, however, that present restrictions are ideal. Rather, we believe that, as a substitute, the case-by-case approach we discussed with respect to group ownership would be appropriate here as well. The major difference is that more group acquisitions in separate markets would likely be approved than would new combinations in the same market. Here, establishing that proposed jointly owned stations are in the same market should be straightforward (although it might be argued in some cases that particular radio and television stations are in different markets). Consequently, no combinations of local stations would be approved on the grounds that they are in different markets. The effect of the combination on concentration would, therefore, have to be confronted in every case. Many local markets are sufficiently concentrated so that proposed combinations in them would be denied. But some markets are presently quite unconcentrated, so that even combinations of stations in the same service in these markets would probably not create market power. Therefore, the FCC might well approve a combination of two AM radio stations in the Los Angeles market, for example, under the case-by-case approach we suggest.

V. THE BROADCAST TELEVISION-CABLE CROSS-OWNERSHIP RULE[14]

When the FCC banned combinations of television stations and cable systems in the same market in 1970, it feared that common ownership would be used by station owners to inhibit the growth of cable. Reduced cable signal quality, relatively high monthly rates to subscribers, and carriage of fewer or less popular distant signals, were among the possible strategies available to a station owner. Conversely, if the owner believed the opportunities for additional profits in cable to be higher than in broadcasting, he would have incentives to let his over-the-air service deteriorate in order to favor cable growth. As Barnett expresses it: "Either way, existence of the television-cable duopoly would tend to impair the television service available to the public. The public would be better served with two outlets striving competively to maximize their respective audiences" (1970:299). With the ban having been in effect for more than a decade, and few combinations grandfathered, no empirical studies have compared the behavior of cross-owned and independently owned outlets. Consequently, one can draw only on a priori analysis to assess the rule.

A. The Benefits of Joint Ownership

We see only very limited benefits to relaxing or abolishing the rule. Local broadcasters have no particular expertise in coping with the many facets of cable operation—negotiating with telephone companies for pole attachments, designing, building, and maintaining trunk and drop lines, marketing cable services, handling customer complaints, and dealing with local franchise authorities. Similarly, cable operators are not experienced in building and maintaining over-the-air transmitters or complying with FCC broadcasting regulations.

However in two areas—program origination and advertising—the same functions are carried out. A jointly owned system might enjoy economies by sharing studio space and equipment for broadcasting and cable program origination. To our knowledge, no studies have addressed the magnitude of the possible savings. Useful here would be analysis of the costs that cable systems incur in program origination; the extent to which these costs would be reduced by using broadcast station facilities; the additional costs that the station would incur in taking on these cable functions; and the additional costs of linking the broadcast station to the cable headend.

For three reasons, we conjecture that the net savings of shared use would be low. First, cable program origination facilities, consisting largely of character generators, automated services, and relatively cheap cameras and other studio equipment, generally do not involve large costs. Second, a broadcast station would have to incur at least some of these costs if it took over these functions. Third, if potential cost savings were substantial, one would expect to see instances where separately owned cable systems and broadcasting stations have worked out shared-use or rental agreements to their mutual benefit. However, such arrangements apparently are rare.[15]

With the growing sales of advertising by cable operators, one might expect that economies would also flow from joint ownership.[16] However, the strategy of selling advertising for the small audiences that view advertiser-supported cable channels varies from that of selling for the

entire audience within the service area of a broadcasting station. Moreover, media conglomerates with holdings in both cable and broadcasting
may be able to exploit at least some economies, even though they
cannot hold more than one such property in a single market.

B. The Losses from Joint Ownership

At the same time, we see little to be lost by relaxing or eliminating the
rule, at least in large markets. The notion of a broadcaster inhibiting the
growth of his cable system (or for a cable owner to similarly behave
toward his broadcast station) strikes us as unlikely.[17] The benefits to the
broadcaster from this strategy would be reduced to the extent that cable
extends the broadcaster's signal to additional audiences, and they would
be further reduced because they would be shared with competing broadcasters.[18]

But what about diversity? Would not common ownership reduce the
number of "voices" in the market, contrary to the Commission's often
stated goal? We think that this danger is exaggerated. With its multiple
channels, cable surely brings many voices into the market. But, to what
extent does cable ownership *itself* make a difference? Unless ownership
by a broadcaster would lead to a more restricted menu—and our preceding argument suggests that such ownership would not—there is little to
fear.

One would have more reason for concern if cable owners were editorializing and in other ways expressing their own views to any notable
degree. In this case, common ownership with a station might mute this
voice (or mute the voice of the station). But one is hard pressed to
identify cases where cable operators are doing this, as against carrying
the voices of others.

Of course, one might argue that as cable further develops, their
owners will increasingly perform this function. But competing media
will also develop so that in any event, diversity will likely continue to
expand.

The problem posed by cross-ownership, if it exists, is most likely to
occur in small markets. Here, the owner might reduce the quality of his
broadcast signal, especially if he has the only station in the market. By
transmitting a weaker signal than allowed by the FCC, and by carrying
less attractive programming than would a separately owned station, he

may gain more from increased cable penetration than would be lost from the smaller over-the-air audience. Moreover, the jointly owned system might be able to exercise greater market power against advertisers and program suppliers.

Thus, while the FCC would be unwise to abandon the cross-ownership rule in one-station markets, situations exist in which joint ownership may produce operating economies without creating market power. For example, a modified rule might stipulate that joint ownership would be permitted (a) if the market contains no fewer than a specified number of stations, or (b) if the jointly owned station has a market share no greater than a specified maximum, or (c) if the station is a UHF in a mixed market.

Even better, we believe, would be the case-by-case approach discussed earlier. This more flexible approach would facilitate accounting for the growing competition from other media and the additional diversity of viewpoints that they provide.

Notes

This paper is based on work supported by a grant from the John and Mary R. Markle Foundation. Views expressed here do not necessarily reflect the opinions or policies of The Rand Corporation or its research sponsors.

1. Additional rules prohibit new television broadcasting–newspaper combinations in the same market, ownership of cable systems by national television networks, ownership by a single entity of more than one television broadcast network, and cross-ownership between telephone companies and cable systems in the same market. The television-newspaper cross-ownership rule is extensively analyzed in Baer et al. (1974).

2. For a more detailed critique of the studies of the effects of group ownership see Besen and Johnson (1984).

3. See Easterbrook (1984:270–271). The predation argument does not require that the predator be a group owner. Conceivably, even the owner of a single station could bid more for a program than it is worth to him in order to deny it to his rivals in the hope that they will be driven out of business.

4. However, if advertisers are willing to pay higher rates per viewer to stations with larger audiences, group-owned stations will have higher rates if their greater efficiency produces larger audiences.

5. One might suppose that group efficiencies (as well as anti-competitive behavior) would show up in station selling prices, which would be higher when a station is purchased by a group than by a nongroup. Indeed, both the Levin (1979, 1980) and the Cherington studies extensively analyze station selling prices by type of buyer and seller in order to test this proposition. However, this evidence is irrelevant to the question. Even if groups have advantages over non-groups, they would not pay higher prices when purchasing stations. If groups have advantages, they would tend to outbid others and, thus, buy more stations than would non-groups.

6. For this reason, we do not believe that group owners are more likely to be *de novo* entrants than are others.

7. It is possible, of course, that station managers claim more autonomy than they actually have.

8. Obviously, program minutes is not the only possible measure of diversity.

9. The guidelines appear in U.S. Department of Justice (1982). For a useful commentary, see Werden (1983).

10. Prior to the adoption of the Chain Broadcasting rules by the Commission in 1941, NBC owned two AM radio stations in each of four markets (FCC 1980 2:35).

11. In examining the effect of combinations of newspapers and television stations, Wirth and Allen do include a variable indicating whether a television station competes with such combinations.

12. They do not include the number of television stations, presumably because that variable has already been employed to estimate the share of total market advertising revenues captured by a particular station. Therefore, they do not test the hypothesis that an increase in the number of competing television stations lowers advertising rates.

13. Wirth and Allen do not really examine advertising rates but rather revenues per thousand viewers. In doing so they fail to note that these revenues are sensitive to the numbers and types of stations in the markets, quite apart from any effect of market structure on competition. Thus, markets with independent television stations will generate different spot advertising revenues than ones with only network affiliates because much of the time of affiliates is occupied by network programming. This will, to be sure, be reflected in differences in network revenues but the offset will be incomplete because the networks bear the costs of network programming. Precisely how this affects the authors' results is unclear, but it suggests that their findings should be regarded with skepticism.

14. Much of the analysis in this section can be applied to combinations of broadcast stations and multipoint distribution systems (MDS). The principal difference between MDS and cable is that, because of the latter's much larger channel capacity, subscribers are likely to obtain all of their television service

over the cable, while households taking MDS will continue to view over-the-air signals.

15. The research department of the National Cable Television Association reports that, to its knowledge, only two or three instances have arisen of cooperative arrangements. No formal survey of such practices has ever been undertaken.

16. The fact that most advertising sales on cable are made at the network level, i.e., by the providers of program services, limits these economies. The economies of joint marketing activities would be increased if there were a strong national spot market for advertising on cable.

17. However, in paper 5 of this book Thorpe finds a small but statistically significant effect of the presence of an STV station on the market power of a cable system.

18. This assumes that cable carriage of all local signals will continue to be mandated by the Commission. Hence a broadcast-owned cable system could not be used to discriminate against other local broadcasters. Robert Pepper points out, however, that justifying the elimination of the must-carry rule would be easier if the ban on cross-ownership were retained.

Comment: Antitrust, Concentration, and Competition

Harvey J. Levin

This review of the articles by Lawrence White, Kenneth Thorpe, and Stanley Besen and Leland Johnson, will focus on three issues: the definition of the relevant market, program diversity, and the data.

I. DEFINITION OF THE RELEVANT MARKET

Market boundaries, Lawrence White explains, must encompass both a product dimension and a geographic dimension. A market is defined by the 1982 Justice Department Guidelines as "the smallest group of present or potential sellers (sellers which encompass the smallest group of products in the smallest geographic area) that, if they chose to act in a collective fashion. . . . could succeed in exercising significant market power." "'Significant' is defined as the ability of this collective entity to be able profitably to raise selling prices by at least five percent (from where they . . . are or could. . . be expected to be in the future), and maintain them at that level for at least a year." "The practical question," he tells us, is: "Would the demanders (of a group of products sold by a specific group of sellers located in a specified geographic area), in response to a significant price rise, switch away (to sellers of other products and/or sellers located in other geographic areas)? . . . If the answer . . . is 'no,' then the products sold by those sellers, at those locations, constitute a market; if the answer is 'yes,' the price rise would be thwarted, and the tentative group is too narrow." A wider group of sellers (in product space and/or geographic space) must then be included, and the question posed again.

How would Kenneth Thorpe's analysis and tests have looked if he had undertaken as refined an analysis of cable TV's relevant market as White did on the Movie Channel–Show Time merger proposal? The closest Thorpe comes to defining the relevant geographic market in his study is the simple statement that such markets are "the market area where cable TV is available."

Thorpe distinguishes between metro area markets (like Baltimore and Washington) and smaller autonomous cities within those metro areas; he uses the Area of Dominant Influence (ADI) in his table 5.2. But which is the best measure of the cable operator's relevant market: the ADI, the SMSA, Dominant Market Area (DMA), or the city, county, or franchise area? He also criticizes seller concentration ratios which are admittedly no adequate measure of market power without information on exit and entry barriers. Nevertheless, seller concentration is a good starting point—a presumption of market power—yet one on which market power cannot really be grounded without reference to the factors mentioned by White, or better still, the thirteen factors identified by William G. Shepherd.[1] Concerning the product market, Thorpe notes that "the ability to raise prices above costs is constrained if substitute products are available. [And that] no one would deny that STV and other video technologies are to some degree substitutes for cable TV." But are they good substitutes? Also, at what point do close substitutes become part of the relevant market and included when markets are calculated?

In their article, Besen and Johnson write: "If groups expand in size, the number of separate station owners could fall substantially below the number of stations within relevant markets for advertising and programming, thereby facilitating collusive agreements." But actually, *three* relevant markets are pertinent to their study—one for advertising or time sales, another for programming, and a third for a composite of these, viz., audience circulation. The authors in fact make these markets explicit in an earlier report (Besen and Johnson 1984a).

Besen and Johnson's best discussion of the relevant market is when they note that group ownership is most likely to result in collusion where a) the geographic areas in question are in a single market in which prices for advertising or programming are related; where b) the number of station owners is significantly smaller than the number of stations in that market; and where c) overlapping group ownership reduces the number of station owners sufficiently below the number of stations to make the above-mentioned collusion feasible. "A likely candidate (for a relevant market)," Besen and Johnson helpfully conclude, "would be a collection of cities in relatively close geographic proximity to one another, where several owners operate in more than one city and where the total number of stations (and other media outlets) is small. Of particular relevance, therefore (they note), is the Commission's regional concentration rule."

The authors' treatment of group acquisitions is deficient in one other possibly serious regard. There is virtually *no* discussion *anywhere* of group acquisitions of TV stations as market-extension conglomerate mergers, where the stations are located in two geographically separate cities. There should at least be references to the need to analyze mergers in terms of their effects on *potential* entry. Even if stations are located in separate geographic regions, preventing a merger might induce a group owner in one market to build a *new* station in the second market, or, at least, to hover at the market's threshhold, posing a potential threat of entry (that may or may not materialize). When I examined this issue in 1970 (Levin 1970), I found few if any VHF outlets available in the top fifty markets, or elsewhere. Hence the likelihood then that preclusion of a group acquisition would generate net *new* entry depended largely on the potential viability of unused UHF channels in the second market. I did find numerous unoccupied UHFs at that time, but deficient viability to support the potential entry hypothesis. Today, thirteen years later, the situation could well be decisively different. The authors do in any case owe us at least some scrutiny of that issue, and a direct review of group acquisitions as a form of market-extension conglomerate mergers in geographically separate areas.

II. DIVERSITY

Besen and Johnson refer to diversity at several points, but do not make any effort to explore it at the length it deserves in either theoretical or empirical measurement terms (Besen and Mitchell 1975; Levin 1980). Nor do they take even a passing look at most of the empirical evidence in the literature that they do in fact peruse. Two even more limited references to diversity are made by White and Thorpe. White's point is that the industrial organization literature (Chamberlin, Fellner, Bain, Stigler) argues that, under certain structural conditions, "sellers in the market are more likely to behave in a noncompetitive fashion (viz., . . . coordinating their actions so as to raise their prices above, or modify the *quality or variety* of offerings from, the levels that would prevail in a more competitive industry)."

The question is how to relate such structural conditions to program diversity in TV broadcasting and cable TV. This is discussed by Wildman and Owen. But, is there any place in antitrust review to analyze the likely impact on program diversity as well as on market power and economic efficiency, of changes in relative market shares and the number and size of sellers in the market due to mergers like that between The Movie Channel and Showtime? If so, how can we measure the program diversity in question? Or is it enough that the FCC has authority to weigh program diversity as well as the anti-competitive effects of TV group acquisitions of other TV or radio stations?

Thorpe notes that "cable firms could deter entry through program decisions which offer more programming than other cable firms, thereby precluding any product differentiation advantages of potential competitors." Thus, Thorpe sees increased diversity as a strategy to maximize profits, or preclude entry.

Thorpe explains that cable TV firms will add additional program sources "if marginal program revenues exceed the marginal programming costs," marginal revenues being derived from a) new, first-time cable subscribers, b) existing cable subscribers who produce more (or fewer) services, and from c) new subscribers switching from STV—or other competing technologies—to cable TV. He concludes that "the difference in perceived marginal revenues across different markets (implies that) both the number and diversity of programs would be greater in monopolistically competitive markets than in the isolated monopoly market." But again, we need a far more refined comment on the theories of diversity and viewer behavior, and still more important, explicit consideration of the empirical constructs by which competitive and noncompetitive effects on program diversity can be assessed.

III. THE DATA

Besen and Johnson alert us to the "poor quality of the evidence which they review," but literally never mention the poor quality of the data all investigators under their scrutiny had to work with. We should have had some speculation on the latter's implications for research strategy and policy results. The individual company data cited by Besen and Johnson in this literature are generally worthless as, also, the profit margins (i.e., income to revenue or to time sales ratios) analyzed in Cherington et al. (1971:8). So much so that FCC has sometimes contracted to have such data assessed by outside contractors. Even estimating the rate of return on total assets is a demanding task, though by no means impossible. (Levin 1980:4).

For those reasons alone, my colleagues and I felt compelled to diversify our dependent economic variables in *Fact and Fancy,* using discounted 20- or 30-second time rates, estimated station audiences and revenues, as well as market averages of income, revenues, and time sales, and sales prices of TV stations. That indeed is a major reason for the plethora of equations in *Fact and Fancy* which Besen and Johnson mention, though many of the results they see as "mixed" (p. 6) in fact reveal a more distinctive pattern than they recognize.

Thus, evidence in my table 6.8 (Levin 1980) clearly shows that group impact (when interacted with TV homes) significantly raises rates in the large markets (when interacted with TV homes), even though not in small markets (250,000 homes). The same is true for estimated station revenue and, for audience, group impact is significant in both small and large markets. Therefore, when considered with its positive impact on advertising rates, group ownership does act to raise station income significantly. In fact, I found a significant positive impact when group ownership was interacted with TV homes (Levin 1980: tables 6.4, 6.5), even though my simpler additive model revealed no impact at all (table 5.3). Actually, then, the more refined my statistical model (Levin 1980: table 6.5) or my data (table 5.4), the clearer the evidence that group ownership significantly raises advertising rates.

In sum, total income to all stations appears to remain *constant* even though group owners enjoy *higher income* than nongroup stations. And all of this seemingly points to a significant redistribution of income from nongroup to group owned stations.

In Besen and Johnson's discussion of advertising rates, finally, they should at least have taken note of the relation between transactions prices and published card rates, with and without discounts. Transactions prices are mentioned here only once, and nowhere in their earlier report; nor are discounts mentioned virtually anywhere in the present paper, and only once (without comments) in the longer report. Nor in either paper do the authors consider whether the discounted published card rates (which Peterman and I both use) may better reflect transactions prices than undiscounted card rates do.

In contrast with Besen and Johnson's data, Thorpe's data are in some ways more refined. At least, P-MC/P as an index of market power and economic efficiency, is far more explicit than any comparable data on group economic efficiency assessed in Besen and Johnson. Furthermore, Thorpe looks directly at subscriber rates and hence avoids any transactions price problem or the discounted rate issue. Indeed, P-MPC/P is a more direct measure of market power and economic efficiency than inferences drawn from advertising rates alone.

True, Thorpe limits his estimates of marginal cost to marginal programming cost and deliberately omits any consideration of marginal labor costs, converter prices, installation charges, etc., or of other factors he cites. However, he notes that, for cable TV, the most important marginal cost incurred is the marginal license fees TV stations pay to programmers. Nonetheless, it would have helped clarify the proper weight to place on marginal *programming* cost as a proxy for marginal cost, if Thorpe had provided some illustrative breakdown of his *other* components of marginal cost.

IV. POLICY IMPLICATIONS

Thorpe draws no explicit policy conclusions from his interesting analysis. But suppose his cable TV "natural monopoly" does indeed lack the market power to exact supernormal profits due to competition from near substitutes. There would then seem to be far less possibility of dedicating or earmarking special channels for exclusive use by governmental, educational, or cultural organizations, or by public access groups without external subsidies from governments, foundations, or industry public service grants. At present, such channels and services are supported by internal cross-subsidy from a cable company's more lucrative operations.

Besen and Johnson mainly find that the group ownership literature reveals no statistically significant impact on the economic efficiency, competitive behavior, and program diversity of TV broadcast operations. Therefore, they conclude that, with few exceptions, the rules which limit multiple station ownership in different markets, could as well be removed as retained. But the reverse is equally true. By Besen and Johnson's own assessment, retention of the rules would have no anti-competitive, anti-efficiency, or anti-diversity effects. One unstated premise, however, does in that instance argue strongly for retention in some form. Until we have far more systematic and definitive content analysis of group and nongroup impact on diversity, there lurks at least the *possibility* of adverse group impact on diversity, fairness, and balance. Therefore, the able Besen and Johnson review clearly reveals that *retention* of at least some of the rules would best enable us to be "safe rather than sorry." This is especially true until group owner acquisitions of TV stations in other markets are systematically analyzed as market-extending conglomerate mergers the disallowance of which could conceivably strengthen the chances for net entry in the market the acquiring group owner was trying to enter.

Note

1. In his appendix table 8, Shepherd (1970) adjusts four-firm concentration ratios for markets that are mainly regional and local in scope; for census definitions that are too broad or too narrow; and for imports that are a significant fraction of total sales. In his appendix table 13, in addition to adjusted concentration ratios, Shepherd (1970) includes five other internal structural elements—assymmetry of firm size, divergence between 8-firm and 8-plant concentration, stability of market shares of leading firms, entry barriers and tariff rate. His external structural elements further include: size of industry, diversification by leading firms, and buyer type or structure.

Comment: Antitrust, Concentration, and Competition

Nolan A. Bowie

Lawrence White's paper, "Antitrust and Video Markets: The Merger of Showtime and The Movie Channel As a Case Study," is an excellent tutorial on antitrust law as applied to the video industry and it reveals how the process really works: affirmative inaction. Dribbling, but no baskets.

Notwithstanding the logic and thoroughness of the Antitrust Division's highly touted guidelines and procedures, or that over a dozen attorneys and economists in the division were involved in the investigation and evaluation of the proposed Showtime–TMC merger, or the division's conclusion that the joint venture constituted a violation of the Clayton Act, in the end, Showtime and The Movie Channel obtained, almost intact, the result which they originally sought. Rather than reap common control of the market through merger, the parties achieved common control through a more informal affiliation. Following a year's worth of investigation, evaluation, negotiation, and counter proposals, the cable system owners of Spotlight, Showtime's former competitor, decided to abandon their plans to expand their service and instead sold it to Showtime–TMC. Simultaneously, Paramount entered into a five-year exclusive distribution agreement with Showtime–TMC. The result was greater concentration of control in the video programming market. Therefore, the Antitrust Division's apparent premises that "antitrust has played a substantial role in affecting the structure of these markets, and recent events have indicated that antitrust is likely to continue to be important," are wrong. The Showtime–TMC case study clearly shows how the antitrust laws, as presently administered, do not really protect trade and commerce against what appears to be an unlawful restraint. If the Showtime–TMC model represents the norm, then the public is provided with an invaluable look at the process of antitrust litigation at the Department of Justice.

The division's antitrust activities in the Showtime–TMC case seem to have been effective only to the extent that they served to educate at public expense possible violators of the antitrust laws. While the division may have gone through all the right moves and motions in their investigation and evaluation, the game concluded with "no baskets" and, moreover, without the benefit of full public disclosure regarding the real reasons why certain decisions were reached.

This observation is not mere cynicism but is based on White's revelation that: "In the end, it was William F. Baxter, the Assistant Attorney General for Antitrust, who made the decision in this case, and it is only he who truly knows what specific analysis and arguments led to the specific decisions."

Kenneth Thorpe, in "The Impact of Competing Technologies on Cable Television," puts the reader on notice right from the beginning that little is in fact known about the subject, and that the recent debate over the regulation of cable television is characterized by a lack of an empirical foundation. Surely, however, some additional empirical information concerning this area must exist within the industries involved, though it is made available or accessible only on terms set by the organization possessing it. Such proprietary information, i.e., marketing research data, long-term projection studies, etc., is normally exchanged only for compensation. The implications of this "privatization" of information on the research community are made clear in Thorpe's paper. His attempt to show the nature of the multichannel video distribution industry is hampered by the lack of empirical information.

Thorpe finds that STV appears to have a moderate impact on the price-cost margin of cable operation *provided* "it is suitably differentiated from cable," *provided* it had entered an area before cable television, and further *provided* that it is not owned and operated by the very same cable operators attempting to protect the market for themselves. The nature of the conditions and provisos leads to the conclusion that "most cable operators do not face competition from another distributor of pay programming. Further, even when competition is technically feasible, it often does not occur." This conclusion is the inescapable result of comparing single tier pay services with multichannel options. Why would an educated consumer pay for a single video channel when multichannel pay cable services are also available offering similar programming, more choices, and better reception for a similar price?

Cable, unlike other pay video services, is a monopoly, since cable franchises are usually granted on some de facto exclusive basis. The real issue therefore is whether any business can fairly compete with a monopoly? If not, then regulation is justified, at least when a cable monopolist begins to abuse its market power. Thus, if cable operators begin to overprice their services to reflect their monopoly power, rate regulation, common carriage regulation, content regulation, or even municipal ownership may be necessary to protect the public.

"Regulation of Broadcast Station Ownership: Evidence and Theory," by Stanley Besen and Leland Johnson, presents a pro-deregulation brief in support of undermining or eliminating government restrictions on ownership of broadcast stations. In their zeal to promote the relaxation or elimination of the rules concerning group ownership, regional concentration, and broadcast television-cable cross-ownership as well as the duopoly and one-to-a-market rules, they base their conclusions on a number of questionable and still untested assumptions. They acknowledge that the available empirical evidence on the effects of group ownership on anti-competitive behavior, economic efficiency, and diversity is severely limited, yet they nevertheless speculate, based on "the pattern of evidence, and our own analysis," that either keeping or eliminating the rule would have little effect, except, perhaps, in small markets. This conclusion, if it is to be believed, would demand less speculation and more hard data especially since it so directly challenges the public interest tradition of United States information policy.

U.S. policy has traditionally encouraged diversity in both the source and the content of information because of the belief that a sufficient diversity of source and content will lead to a diversity of ideas. The broadcast ownership rules were, and still are, intended to encourage a number of sources in the dissemination of information to a particular audience. This rationale was reflected in 1940 when the Federal Communications Commission first adopted a rule that ownership or control of more than six FM stations would be considered "contrary to the public interest" (FCC 1940). Again in 1953, the Commission reaffirmed this principle in its *Rules and Regulations Relating to Multiple Ownership* wherein it stated:

It is our view that the operation of broadcast stations by a large group of diversified licensees will better serve the public interest than the operation of broadcast stations by a small and limited group of licensees. . . .

The fundamental purpose of this facet of the multiple ownership rules is to promote diversification of ownership in order to maximize diversification of program and service viewpoints *as well as to prevent any undue concentration of economic power contrary to the public interest. In this connection, we wish to emphasize that by such rules, diversification of program services is furthered without any governmental encroachment on what we recognize to be the prime responsibility of the broadcast licensee.* (FCC 1953)

In 1956, the U.S. Supreme Court upheld the 7-7-7 multiple ownership rule as "reconcilable with the Communications Act as a whole" (*U.S. v. Storer,* 1956).

Nothing is offered in the Besen and Johnson economic analysis either to show why elimination of the group ownership rule would have but "little effect" on the market or to successfully undermine the above-stated rationale affirmed by the Supreme Court. Moreover, nothing is mentioned about the possible consequences that elimination of the group ownership rule would have on minority ownership opportunities, or on the concept of "localism," or concerning the preservation of important democratic values.

It is worth noting here that in its *Statement of Policy on Minority Ownership of Broadcasting Facilities,* the Commission only six years ago said:

It is apparent that there is a dearth of minority ownership in the broadcast industry. Full minority participation in the ownership and management of broadcast facilities results in a more diverse selection of programming. In addition, an increase in ownership by minorities will inevitably enhance the diversity of control of a limited resource, the spectrum. And, of course, we have long been committed to the concept of diversity of control because "diversification . . . is a public good in a free society, and is additionally desirable where a government licensing system limits access by the public to the use of radio and television facilities." (FCC 1978b)

Elimination of the ownership limitation rule would most surely result in fewer ownership opportunities for minorities (who currently own less than 2 percent of existing broadcast facilities) since they (as well as any new entrants) would be in direct competition with rich and powerful corporations attempting to garner the lion's share of broadcast properties. In addition, the selling prices for broadcast stations are apt to increase beyond even the record setting prices at which some stations are selling today (e.g., VHF television station KHOU-TV Houston, sold for $342 million in 1983) as ever larger group owners compete for choice stations to add to their networks. Such a free-market in broadcast stations is bound to drive the price threshold beyond the economic reach of minorities, whose greatest existing barrier to broadcast ownership is the lack of sufficient economic clout.

If the ownership rules were eliminated, the concept of "localism," would soon follow in its wake.

The tradition of favoring localism is accurately stated by Christopher Sterling (1979):

> The FCC and its predecessors have clearly held that the "best" broadcast station is locally owned and operated. Such ownership was deemed in the public interest as it would presumably be closer to local needs and concerns, and thus the station would more adequately reflect and project that community than some absentee-owned operation or central network.

Localism not only enhances diversity in programming but also in ownership. Yet, Besen and Johnson would have one believe that abolition of the ownership rules is unlikely to influence diversity and that changes in these ownership rules are likely to have little effect on social welfare.

In its decision in *Associated Press v. United States* (1945), the Supreme Court declared that the First Amendment "rests on the assumption that the widest possible dissemination of information from diverse and antagonistic sources is essential to the welfare of the public." This policy was reiterated in *FCC v. National Citizens Committee for Broadcasting:* "If our democratic society is to function, nothing can be more important than insuring that there is a free flow of information from as many divergent sources as possible" (1978).

Has competition in the video market become so intense during the past ten years to justify removal of the ownership restrictions and their public interest benefits? Is there no linkage between broadcast ownership and the power to influence public opinion? Less than a decade ago, the FCC, in its *Second Report* on TV-Newspaper Cross-Ownership said: "The significance of ownership from the standpoint of "the widest possible dissemination of information" lies in the fact that ownership carries with it the power to select, to edit, and to choose the methods, manner and emphasis of presentation, all of which are a critical aspect of the Commission's concern with the public interest" (1975a).

Besen and Johnson's conclusions generally support policies which would result in the limited spectrum being concentrated and controlled by fewer players rather than more. Such a course would ultimately lead to oligopolistic or monopolistic patterns in the broadcast field, especially in light of what Lawrence White has shown us about the effect of the Antitrust Division's policies and enforcement approach.

Besen and Johnson admit that relaxing or abolishing the various ownership rules would not "confer any notable benefit on society." Thus, there is no valid reason or legal basis to change the rules. Simply put, Besen and Johnson fail to consider the potential detrimental costs to the public interest nor do they show that such costs are outweighed by any anticipated benefits as would be required under the holding in *Citizens Communications Center v. FCC* (1971).

PART THREE

The International Outlook

A European View of Competition and Control in a Multimedia Society

HELMUT SCHÄFER

Europe is presently undergoing a revolution in the field of television. Its major component is the remarkable and rapid success with which the video cassette recorder (VCR) is penetrating the European consumer market. The revolution is also characterized by the rapid growth of cablecasting—although not as rapid as optimists predicted—and will soon also include satellite TV. These developments confront politicians with a number of serious problems; problems which were not even foreseen a few years ago.

Experts in the Federal Republic of Germany and other European countries argued for years about cablecasting, pay-TV, and direct satellite broadcasting, and about the pros and cons of the theoretically increased choice of programs that these technologies offer to the consumer. And politicians did likewise, if only because the experts failed to supply alternative scenarios. West Germany, for example, is only starting to test the viability of TV cablecasting, eight years after an original recommendation to do so was made. Of the four cities for which pilot projects are planned, only two have started to operate them by mid 1984.

This is the result of an ideological debate, itself based on historical experience. Whereas the Anglo-American tradition of freedom of the press, and by extension freedom of information, is a long one, it is relatively new to Germany. The misuse to which the information media were put during the fascist era resulted in a search for a system in which political extremism could no longer get a foothold. Because of the technical and financial restrictions on the number of channels available for broadcasting purposes, particularly in television, a concept of "balance" was introduced in postwar West Germany which would not allow any single school of opinion or interest group to dominate. This situation has been radically changed by the availability of more channels in the form of cablecasting networks and, in the near future, of satellite broadcasting systems.

The German Left wished to preserve the status quo which had proved its worth—hence the delay in the introduction of new broadcasting technology. It also feared extensive control by newspaper owners, the only group initially interested in the new media. Furthermore, there was a feeling that new developments would be to the detriment of quality, for instance in the form of more light entertainment and less cultural programs. Traditionally in Germany, information has not been considered a consumer good; it has been regarded as a public service with an educational bias.

The force of necessity, however, has recently led to a fundamental change. The increased number of channels have reduced the opportunity for manipulation. The interests of German industry are also at stake. If Germany does not take a lead, foreign enterprise will certainly take over, even to the extent of supplying German households with programs, via direct broadcasting satellites. The only dispute that now remains is whether to establish a coaxial broadband cable network or to wait for optical fiber technology when it becomes an economically viable proposition a few years from now.

The relevance of cablecasting projects has, at least in part, been overtaken by events. The VCR-boom was not foreseen, even as late as 1980. A number of German experts even attribute its success to the failure to innovate in the TV field until it was too late. One commentator has described the present state of affairs with the following observation, applicable to other countries as well: "It is not unusual for a group of people to spend all day discussing satellite and cable, which they do not watch, and then to go home and watch video, which they do not discuss."

The impact of VCRs exceeds that of the greater choice offered by cablecasting and direct satellite broadcasting, at least until well into the 1990s. The impact of VCR is not a passing phenomenon, mainly due to the fact that the present TV networks throughout most European countries do not provide for a greater choice in entertainment. VCRs have already fundamentally affected the economics of both cable and satellite TV in ways many advocating both do not yet realize.

A few facts and figures: an estimated 20 percent—perhaps even more—of West German TV households already have VCRs; this percentage is one of the highest in Europe—with the notable exception of the United Kingdom with more than 30 percent—and far greater than in the United States. VCR penetration in Western Europe as a whole will probably be 50 percent by 1986. An interesting aside: the country with the greatest TV choice in Europe—Italy—also has the lowest VCR penetration within the European community—barely 2 percent of all TV households.

Is this VCR revolution the result of shortcomings in media policy? In the past German surveys have frequently pointed out that there is yet relatively little public interest in the new media or in greater choice in TV programming (this is, however, probably the result of a lack of information about what such media will actually be like and how high their costs will be). And yet the public is obviously buying VCRs to satisfy demand for something that broadcasting services are not providing or cannot provide. Every day nearly 40 percent of VCR households watch videocassettes either through rentals or by broadcast programs recorded for later viewing.

Where do we go from here?—in a situation in which the public is increasingly enthusiastic about VCRs while policy makers are still primarily concerned with regulating TV cablecasting and satellite broadcasting? What does or should a media policy in Europe aim at?

European broadcasting systems see themselves primarily as public services under public law. This is true whether they are financed by advertising revenue (for instance, the Independent Broadcasting Authority in the United Kingdom), by license fee revenue, or by both. This self-perception, which the various broadcasting laws and regulations have enforced or at least promoted, has entailed restrictions on the time available to advertisers including many cases of an outright ban on advertising and control of content. Perhaps most important of all, it has led to a balance of programming both in political terms and in terms of content (in Germany this is the ruling of the supreme court). This balance frequently means that 40 percent or more of total programming time is devoted to nonentertainment fare, much to the discontent of TV viewers. These might find that at certain points in the evening they do not have a choice between informational and entertainment programs but between informational and cultural, social or political discussion programs.

With VCRs in the home, any attempts by broadcasters, private or public, to balance their programming, as legally required, or to dictate viewer choices at any particular time, become a farce. When 50 or more percent of European TV households have VCRs (as will soon be the case), what can the broadcasting authorities do? Those dependent on income from commercials cannot continue to assume enough people will be watching at peak viewing hours to make TV advertising an attractive proposition to the consumer goods industry more or less irrespective of what is shown. If people can switch on their VCRs when they are not interested in what is being broadcast the TV advertising market might decline significantly. To state the problem differently: programmers will face a hitherto unaccustomed pressure to fill their peak viewing hour schedules with mass entertainment. This will come at the expense, perhaps, of quality, but certainly of diversity as far as the major broadcast channels are concerned.

I believe that people should be able to choose what they want. I also believe in the citizen's ability to decide for himself, better than political rivals on the left and right could. But I also believe in promoting minority rights and interests, and here new developments are worrying. There are many minority interests. Every TV viewer is part of both a mass audience and of a program minority audience in accordance with his interests. Here politicians have a major responsibility: to ensure that, in the spectrum of video/TV services available, such interests are provided for. And free market mechanisms can achieve this.

Europeans should consider structural changes at the regulatory level now, before it is too late. VCRs are here to stay, and traditional TV may well decline in its relative importance. Economically this is already being manifest in the difficulties broadcasters are experiencing in purchasing movie material in the face of competition from videocassette distributors. Videocassette distributors in Germany are already paying at least $200,000 for the right to distribute a good movie. It is here, and not in the field of video material for minority audiences, that distributors are finding a lucrative market, to the detriment of broadcasters.

We should begin to reorganize the traditional broadcasting authorities so that they are given the prime responsibility for catering to program minorities in addition to their role in news and sports—which they will not lose. The British system with its minority channels BBC2 and Channel 4, provides a good example of the kind of direction in which the rest of Europe could go.

Progress in the field of cable TV in Europe will continue to be relatively slow, even now that in a number of West European countries the PTT authorities are making great efforts to provide a comprehensive cable distribution network as quickly as possible. Recent market research suggests that at best ony 19.5 percent of West European households will have cable TV in 1992; a pessimistic forecast suggests only 13 percent. Income from cable TV fees in Western Europe will amount to $2.6 billion in that year, compared to only $475 million from advertizing. The lesson to be drawn, as far as cable enthusiasts are concerned, is to prepare for low-cost budgeting in cablecasting production. The lavish standards set by the traditional TV broadcasters would, if adopted by cablecasters, jeopardize their own existence and allow for only a bare minimum of original production.

The idea of opening the field of television to increase program choice is a good one. Television in Europe does not yet fully serve all interests. Most of the time it only caters to the "average man." Of course, there are exceptions in the form of minority channels, but no one would claim that more could not be done. The only question is whether sufficient revenue can be raised for it. This is the question behind perhaps the most interesting cablecasting project in Europe: in Ludwigshafen, a project which, besides the three usual TV services (ARD, ZDF, and the local Third Program) supplies the viewer with additional out-of-area Third Programs, foreign TV programs and, when and if all those who expressed their interest become active, eight further *original* services, including an open channel.

The same applies to satellite television: within the European Community, direct satellite broadcasting technology opens up the prospect of European television, with its inherent advantages for furthering the European idea, European understanding, and language teaching. Indeed, an initiative has been launched to establish a "European" service over and above the various national TV services that would be transmitted via satellite. In 1982, the report of the Committee on Youth, Culture, Education, and Information to the European Parliament, proposing an all-European community television service in order to improve citizens' knowledge of European affairs and promote a greater sense of European commitment, was endorsed by all political groups within the European Parliament. The European Commission and European Parliament proposed that the respective fifth channels of domestic direct broadcasting satellites be devoted to transmitting such a service. Rather than establish a separate new European TV authority, however, both community institutions want to use the long-established European Broadcasting Union, which successfully tested the viability of a Euro-program in late 1982.

Of course direct satellite broadcasting has great potential, particularly for West Germany, for increasing the free flow of information between Eastern and Western Europe in accordance with the aims set out in the third basket of the Final Act of the Conference for Security and Cooperation in Europe in 1975. The technical conditions today already permit the television programs of the two German states to be received in the territory of both. DBS could make such coverage complete.

Further interesting possibilities abound. For instance, both the ZDF and a private German consortium have received channels on the European Communication Satellite. The latter will be recruited from those interests already participating in the cablecasting project in Ludwigshafen, and the objective of the project will be to test the viability of a combined satellite-cable service.

We have to accept the possibility that within the next decade a radically new concept of financing traditional TV broadcasting will have to be devised. If there are competing media in the field of TV, the slice of the advertising revenue cake made available will be smaller in real terms for each entity involved in that competition. It is entirely conceivable that video distributors, faced with rising costs and the kind of cutthroat competition that is already beginning to arise (in Germany it is often possible to rent a movie tape for as little as a dollar a day), might resort to inserting commercials into the prerecorded tapes they offer to the public.

The present concepts for cablecasting and DBS are little more than to retransmit what is available elsewhere; there is yet relatively little experimentation with new types of programs, even in cablecasting pilot projects in Germany, where pay TV has yet to be introduced. Furthermore, community programming—one of the opportunities cable TV offers—has failed in many instances. And the U.K.'s community cable TV ventures have not proved very successful. Another point with respect to satellite TV and cablecasting: technically and *solely* for the purpose of television, another technology for distributing the same programs already being distributed over the air is not really necessary. Finally, in terms of advertizing revenue, the trend—if existing services could be established on a European-wide basis—will be to the detriment of certain national broadcasters, especially those with few resources at their disposal. This is a problem that the European community, the European Commission in particular, is looking at at the moment, especially with respect to the European community policy of internal free trade in goods and services. In summary, the economics of new services are shaky, and if one particular service is feasible, it will be to the detriment of others!

Establishing a nationwide broadband cable network—as Germany is doing—is unnecessarily expensive if it is used only for television. However, this is *not* the only reason why Germany is installing cable. As far as television is concerned, the decision was taken rather late, but now that the decision has been taken, it is difficult to see that cheaper alternatives such as MDS (multiple distribution services) will play an important role in the future.

To conclude, as far as Germany is concerned, regulation of the new media will most probably follow three lines:

— The German PTT authorities will remain in control of the cable network which is presently being installed: cable and satellite networks will continue to be planned and organized under monopoly conditions in order to maintain so called "network neutrality" with its inherent advantages in terms of standardization and maintenance of a comprehensive and unbiased technical service for its customers.

— Private, commercial, and public cablecasting services and programmes will be controlled by nongovernmental boards under public law. Their purpose will be, as in the case of the present public broadcasting authorities, to guarantee the neutrality and political balance in programming.

— There will be a certain control over video producers and distributors so as to tackle the present problem of the enormous number of cassettes devoted to horror and brutality which concerns the nation as a whole, at present. In doing this we have to avoid censorship on the one hand but at the same time it is also necessary to limit total free access to such productions, particularly in the case of young people.

Perhaps this is to propose new regulation, but a liberal broadcasting policy cannot promote diversity, true diversity—minority programming and the like—necessary elements of what we regard to be a pluralist society, without any sort of regulation. Perhaps it sounds paradoxical to say this but regulation and the right to freedom of information or the right to communicate go hand in hand, if regulation is designed to promote these rights. Market forces left to themselves have yet to demonstrate that they can meet such requirements.

Some of the phenomena discussed above are not restricted only to Western industrialized countries. VCRs have made a highly successful start in all of the Arab countries, parts of Latin America, and even some of the least economically developed countries such as India and Pakistan.

The UNESCO-inspired discussion on how to promote development in the field of communication without irreparable cultural damage to smaller and less advantaged countries in particular has not yet taken this phenomenon into account. I am referring to the many efforts to establish a so-called New World Communication and Information Order. The report of the MacBride Commission published in 1980 failed to mention VCRs as a consumer media; perhaps it could not foresee the phenomenon.

With VCR sales making such great inroads, TV broadcasting policies are being questioned. Why have television programs aimed at development support (if the idea was ever feasible) when there is little or no captive audience left? Pakistani and Sudanese migrant workers in the Gulf states buy, among other things, precisely such consumer goods for their families at home. But home video is not on the developmental policy agenda yet, and I fear it will not be until new structures have been firmly established. Of course there are advantages in this. Most developing countries have highly authoritarian political structures, and television was accordingly conceived to serve such structures. Traditional television allows itself to be used for nondemocratic purposes.

The situation is different for home video. It is next to impossible for governments to control the VCR revolution, both with respect to importing such consumer goods and, more importantly, with respect to controlling the cassettes that are circulated. Competition occurs in the media field whether governments like it or not. This is actually an opportunity for introducing democracy in such countries.

The TV authorities in Third World countries are faced with two problems: either TV has to compete and thus become highly irrelevant to the development needs of the country; or it can carry on as before, but without an incentive to improve its attractiveness because nobody watches anyway. Are there alternative policies?

In view of the situation in many Third World countries we need new ideas on how to bring the development message across effectively. This is a classical UNESCO task. I wonder whether the organization will do so, particularly without the membership of the USA. Europeans won't have as much of a voice as Europeans and Americans could have together!

Such future-oriented research is sadly lacking. A new enterprising spirit is needed. Perhaps those involved in communication and development should encourage research for this very purpose.

There are, of course, many other serious problems that the Third World faces in the field of broadcasting. The situation is such that television in many such countries is there to stay, even if often restricted only to the élites. The overall gap in broadcasting technology between the First and Third Worlds is widening, however. Media diversity in the field of television does not exist in the hardware sphere to the extent that it does in the West and is not likely to in the near future, simply because of the costs involved (with the exception of basic traditional television and the VCR inroads that have been referred to).

The important problem, over and above the software problem, is that of access. In many countries television can still only be watched in urban areas and the provinces, as it is still too expensive for the overwhelming majority. Methods to ease the situation, for instance by community viewing facilities, remain to be explored fully. In some countries, such as India and Indonesia, the use of satellites to create a nationwide infrastructure for television broadcasting rather than a terrestrial transmission system is a cost-effective policy. Of course, it could be said that the VCR dispenses with the need for transmission facilities completely, but it should also be remembered in this connection that the broadcasting media in many Third World countries also have a nation-building function.

Communications policy in many countries is simply the result of almost arbitrary decisions taken by the former colonial powers; a sense of inner cohesion still has to develop. The broadcasting media are one of the very few tools available for this purpose. Research in the media field should include developing new strategies for increasing access with such requirements in view.

Unfortunately, development assistance in the field of broadcasting, as in the telecommunications field as a whole, still ranks low in the list of priorities of both donor and recipient nations. UNESCO's International Programme for the Development of Communication is both fragmentary and short term in character. Unfortunately, there are too few organizations worldwide (such as the Friedrich Naumann Foundation) which provide long-term media assistance including specialized training in the audiovisual field appropriate for a particular country on a six- to eight-year basis. Efforts in the field, if one starts from scratch, can only be successful if they are conceived on a long-term basis. A complicated technology cannot be mastered with pitiful sums and through three-month courses.

Most developing countries advocate protective measures in the media field mainly as a result of a sense of inadequacy in broadcasting. This may certainly be true of the efforts in trying to obtain acknowledgement of the principle of prior consent in the field of direct satellite broadcasting, which affects Western countries that traditionally advocate free flow of information. Although not legally binding, the new United Nations' resolution on the matter makes things more difficult for those who, like myself, advocate free flow.

In conclusion, it is important to focus on something that affects everyone whether in the so-called "First" or "Third" World. It is a question frequently lost sight of. All the different forms of transmitting or distributing film or video material, whether VCR, DBS, MDS, SMATV, cable, or whatever, all depend on the same basic software (which movie film distributors and broadcasters have discovered to their great horror). Our most serious difficulties—and this applies to smaller countries in particular—are not in the hardware but in the software field. It is only necessary to look at the incredible worldwide dependence on the USA and, to a certain extent, on the U.K. for TV program material to realize this fact. Who else has the resources to produce *Dallas, Dynasty,* and *Falcon Crest*? What is the effect of such material on an Asian or a Latin American? What kind of values are being transmitted? Sales of such program material should not be restricted, but more should be done to encourage the production of attractive alternatives at home.

The most effective way of doing this is by investing in manpower and not in technology. Journalists and creative personnel are the basic ingredients of success in the media field. A bad actor, a bad singer, a dull newscaster do not become more attractive with stereo-sound TV. For the particular benefit of Third World partners, efforts must be made to think of ways and means of cutting production costs while maintaining quality. Public funds in broadcasting should be targeted to fund those interests that commercial sources cannot or will not provide for, e.g., minority programming. U.S. television enterprises might even look into the possibility of producing TV products specifically designed to cater to the needs of developing countries rather than supplying them with programs having great mass appeal but irrelevent to such needs.

New Media in the Third World

ERNEST JOUHY

Being a European "egghead," I try to systematize all occurring problems before examining the facts. As such, I attempt to understand the
various systems of new media and their impact on society and the
individuals, particularly in the Third World, as parts of a wider and
more comprehensive system of reference, that is, a national culture,
which is itself part of the all-inclusive and comprehensive system of
world culture.

I understand "culture," in the American sense of the term, to be a
system of technology, language, attitudes, beliefs, and sociopolitical
means of power and interaction within a historically bound community.
I put "technology" first, because man, being a "tool-making animal,"
structures his culture according to technology before modeling it along
social, political, and ideological patterns (Ribeiro 1971). Consequently,
when speaking about the role of the new media in the Third World, we
have to ask ourselves:

1. How does it interfere with the traditional systems of economic, social, political, and personal interaction?
2. How does it influence the prevailing overt and hidden trends of development?

These questions have to be considered from various angles, the most
important being the communicative aspect of the new technology in the
public as well as in the private sphere.

Television allows us to witness physically a reality which is actually
far from our eyes. Being trained, as we are, from early childhood to
believe that reality is what we see and what we hear, we are induced to
believe that what we see and hear on the television and via videotape is
real even if we know that we are, in fact, watching a piece of fiction.

This fundamental notion is of course much older than the modern tool
of audiovisual technology. The traditional media, for instance, theater,

makes use of the very same mechanisms of perception, emotions, and consciousness for interaction. However, there is a basic difference between traditional media and the moving images created by modern media. The spectator of traditional media understands what is involved in the performance, who produced it, how, and for what purpose. The production of reality produced by modern media is based on an economic, social, and especially technological system of which the viewer remains oblivious. When people watch a puppet theater in Java, when they see and listen to the epic poem of Ramajana, they are confronted with a reality which is as far removed from theirs as that of a cowboy movie which comes to them via videocassette. Through their cultural system, they learned in their early childhood to distinquish the reality of the play from the experience of their daily lives. In contrast to this, American fiction is foreign to them. They are ignorant of its roots and therefore absolutely incapable of incorporating what they see into their internalized conceptions of reality and fiction. I will return to this problem in more detail later.

Films made for television and video cassettes are sophisticated technological and cultural systems of production which cannot be made transparent, especially when the audience is made up of people in the Third World. To do so one is forced to analyze the interconnection between producers and users of the new media. That is, one is impelled to examine the system that creates and represents a new cultural identity which contrasts to the reality of the Third World.

By definition "to analyze" means to separate the facts and to search for the causal or correlational link between them. Herein lies the first major difficulty concerning the use of modern media in the Third World. Compared to the past and to former technology, it is much more difficult to isolate the different aspects and phenomena surrounding the mass media. In the words of one of the foremost experts in this field, Armand Mattelart:

The convergence of a number of networks, through which travels a flux of information onto a television screen, no longer allows for the isolation of domains that were once dissociable: newsreel information—entertainment information—education information—social control information. (Mattelart et al. 1983:13)

The new technology makes it very difficult to determine the cause-effect relationship between the mode of production and the ways of consumption. On the production end you have technical innovations, commercial trends, power, and profit. On the consumer end, the needs, expectations, social, and cultural background of the viewer. How the two worlds interrelate is not at all clear. Where once we could blame imperialism or transnational companies for the creation of a particular mode of production, now we have to look elsewhere to understand why television and video films are consumed in the Third World so eagerly by people whose needs, materially speaking, clearly do not lie amongst the fruits of Western industrial culture.

In order to face the difficulties of analysis, let us choose a method which was elaborated by Donald McGranahan (director of the United Nations Research Institute for Social Development in Geneva) especially for arriving at an understanding of Third World development. It involves the use of an "indicator." An indicator is a variable that points to something quite different than that which it measures. A thermometer, for example, measures the body's temperature. The measurement of an abnormally high temperature becomes the indicator for something not quantifiable, namely illness. In a similar manner, the statistics measuring the use and diffusion of television and video cassettes in the Third World can serve as a valuable indicator for the health or the illness of the Third World's social body.

The profound changes which are occurring throughout the Southern Hemisphere did not, of course, originate with the emersion of the new media, nor can they be considered as the cause of the revolutionary transformations which are shaking the whole system of interaction in the developing countries, and yet through the indicator "TV-video" we can better comprehend the general trend of economic, social, and psychological changes in world culture.

Taking the diffusion and use of the new media throughout the Third World as an indicator of development, it would be naive to equate its increasing presence in the urban areas of the Third World with the general progress of developing societies. It is evident that in any society the linear growth of one particular factor within the global system, in this case that of the number of television receivers or video recorders, does not necessarily indicate progress. Furthermore, it may even accentuate preexisting economic, social, political, and cultural disparities and contradictions, so that a continuation of growth in this area could even provoke the collapse of an already precarious balance in the social system. For this reason, the widespread application of a new means of communication or any other technological innovation has to be put into perspective and weighed against the improvement or worsening of the general economic and social conditions. More specifically, such factors as food, work, health, and distribution of the gross national product must be compared to the mobility, autonomy, and freedom of the individual, to his potential and his expectations. In other words, the rapid increase of television sets and video recorders, the multiplicity of offered programs and cassettes in Caracas, Lagos, or Jakarta is by no means an unequivocal indicator of general progress among these societies. As we shall see, this kind of "progress" creates immense problems and so far has done more to contribute to the economic, social, and cultural crisis than to alleviate it.

In order to demonstrate how new media may indicate actual and predictable development, it is useful to consider a 1960 UNRISD study of eight countries that shows that completely different indices such as life expectancy, average number of person per room, percentage of households that were electrified, as well as number of newspapers, number of radios and telephones all correlate with per capita income. And without any reference to the internal social stratification, the difference between radio and newspaper diffusion is much higher in the $300 annual income bracket than in the $1,500 one. The higher the income, the narrower is the discrepancy between the amount of newspapers which are read and the degree to which radios are listened to. This may be due to a number of economic and technical reasons, two of which are the extent of press distribution and the level of literacy. What appears certain is that information which needs a mental translation from reception to understanding, let us call this "digital," has a much wider market in the higher income bracket and correlates with a higher degree of education.

The analog type of information, the audiovisual one, if it still correlates with the income rate because it needs a receiver, correlates inversely to the rate of education. One needs to be literate to read a newspaper. Less education is necessary to understand the message of a comics magazine. One need not be literate at all to watch a television film. Moreover, the audiovisual message transmitted via television or video will reach the illiterate viewer by the visual alone and not by the accompanying language for the simple reason that either he does not understand the language in which it was produced (e.g., English) and even if he does understand it (e.g., when the subject is a national product), he doesn't comprehend the meaning of the text because the cultural background of the spoken universe does not correspond to the one in which he grew up. McLuhan's "the medium is the massage" may be placed in doubt, but one cannot refute the gap between the perception of messages which require digital training of thought and those of an audiovisual nature, which need none. Thus far his theory has proven to be correct and applies fully to the study just discussed.

Nonetheless, in this study of international comparison, the most important indicator for our topic, that of the discrepancy in income within individual nations, is missing. It seems that in the Third World, the greater these differences are, the more the usage of new media becomes concentrated in the very narrow strata of high incomes. At the same time, but for other reasons, the longing for them becomes especially urgent among the poor. If it is true that the have-nots of modern media, who are the very large majority in the Third World, are not about to tolerate being deprived of such innovations, then we can conclude that the introduction of the former in the Third World is a potentially explosive catalyst of social unrest with unpredictable political consequences.

To illustrate the meaning of social disparity in Third World countries by the indicator "use of new media," let me take an example which illustrates the situation in all developing countries with the exception of Singapore, Hongkong, and Taiwan. The average income of the owner of a video recorder in Latin America is $52,500 compared to only $32,950 in the United States and $27,450 in Europe. This means that the buyer of a video recorder in Latin America needs an income ten times superior to the average of his countrymen, while in the United States and in Europe the ratio is only 2 to 1. It can be said that the gap between the social classes in the Third World is indicated more by the access of the latter to the new media than by the accumulation of such status symbols as housing and cars.

As to the use of such apparatus, Mittelart and Schmucler estimate that 75 percent of Latin American videocassette owners purchase prerecorded fiction. In the United States this number is 48 percent and in Europe, 41 percent. This ratio points to the disturbing fact that until now the new communication technology has been adopted by the Third World in a purely consumptive way without any attempt to use it to increase personal culture or to encourage individual development. The two authors cite a marketing study of Time Review which came to two interesting conclusions. First, the introduction of modern media accentuates the social division within the already small minority in the Third World between those who own electronic media and those who do not. Second, all the publicity around the liberating function of television usage and video recorders has proven to be an illusion because almost nobody in Latin America records television programs through personal choice or makes any other creative use of the possibilities offered by the new technology (Mattelart 1983).

Now let us come to the important problem of the promotion of the new media as an indicator of the growing economic and cultural dependency of developing countries on the industrial ones. The extent to which the promotion of modern communication's technology is monopolized by the First World is an indicator of the degree to which the Third World is deprived of its own cultural power and technology. Take as an example the following descriptions of two Latin American enterprises, which upon first view give the impression of being autonomous and very successful:

The first is Rede Globo the major television chain in Brazil, with headquarters in Rio de Janeiro. The second is Televisa in Mexico. Both are corporately connected, multimedia enterprises with chains of newspapers, a radio station, book publications, audiovisual and audiocassettes. Globo owns the largest television chain in Brazil with five broadcasting stations and thirty-six affiliated stations, plus hundreds of retransmission stations. It has an AM and FM system, an audiovisual recording studio, the electronics firm, Telecom, a theater, an art gallery, and still more. The latest statistics indicate that their programs reach 58 percent of the total population of Brazil.

Mexico's Televisa, in existence since 1973, owns four television chains with sixty-one stations of retransmission. According to 1979 statistics Televisa reaches 41 million of Mexico's 55 million television viewers. The company owns forty-seven enterprises within the cultural industry; with a total of 70,000 television hours of fiction and documentation at its disposal, Televisa annually exports 24,000 hours of television viewing for the 18 million members of the Spanish-speaking population of the United States. Furthermore, it owns five of the biggest radio stations in Mexico, five publishing houses for books and magazines, nine show business enterprises, three film studios, four record studios, a tourist agency, and more.

These two impressive examples would not suffice as an indicator if Rede Globo and Televisa were considered simply as successful national enterprises. The penetration and diffusion of modern media technology in the Third World serves as an indicator of the profound economic and social changes only when considered internationally. It is impossible, within the limitations of this article, to present an exhaustive account of the dependency imposed on the Third World in this realm. Instead I have chosen an example.

In the very country where Televisa is a powerful, independent, national enterprise, the United States, Japan, West Germany, France, and the Netherlands established around 500 electronic plants in the Free Trade Zones of Mexico precisely for the purpose of producing new media technology. In 1982 these employed 120,000 workers, 85 percent of whom were women between the ages of 17 and 23. Their output represents 10 percent of the world's production under foreign contract and 30 percent of the whole Third World market. The United States alone established 370 plants for electronic products in Latin America, 193 of them in Mexico and 140 in Puerto Rico. In South East Asia, 226 other U.S. plants are established, 90 of them in Hongkong and Taiwan, 62 in India and Singapore. In 1975 already 7 out of 11 enterprises controlling the color television market in Brazil belonged to international companies and 80 percent of their components were imported from industrial countries. In Venezuela 89 percent of the capital invested in the cultural industries was of foreign origin and the 11 percent of national origin served only for the production of unsophisticated goods such as wood, cardboard, paint, etc.

The problem of dependency is aggravated still further by the one-way transfer of advanced technology. Out of a sample of 29 contracts for media production and diffusion made for Venezuela, 62.5 percent were of U.S. origin, 16.7 percent Dutch, 12.5 percent Japanese, and 4.2 percent West German and French. The stipulations for these contracts are still more revealing: 37 percent prohibit the production of derived products, 43 percent prohibit the export of goods produced with the help of the transferred technology, 65 percent comprise legal clauses which severely limit the access to technical information, and 62 percent limit the use of these technological innovations once the contracts are broken off.

Mattelart points out that Sony has produced its semiprofessional U-matic in cooperation with the Brazilian company Motoradio since 1981 and intends to produce the series of Betamax-type cameras, monitors, and video reporters outside Japan (Tirado 1983).

These are some examples of the way in which Third World countries are driven to become dependent on the hardware of new communication media produced by the industrial nations. They are significant indicators of the degree of dominance claimed by one part of the world over the other. They demonstrate how this dominance clearly lies in the monopolization of advanced technology by a few centers of the Northern Hemisphere.

The concentration of technical know-how is invariably followed by the concentration of corresponding software production in the studios of the industrial powers. Monopolization of the new media industry also follows because those countries which export their studio creations to the Third World are the former colonial or imperialist powers, who once imposed their language and culture on the small corrupt native minority, today ruling most of the officially independent former colonies. Hence, most developing countries import the broadcasting systems of their former colonial rulers or, in Latin America, those of the United States. For example, India's broadcasting system is a close imitation of Britain's; that of the francophone countries of Africa is modeled after France's; and TV in the Philippines it is based on the style of U.S. broadcasting. Intangible elements, such as broadcasting norms, styles of production, professional codes, and expectations are all strongly influenced by those of the former colonial rulers. This is even more relevant to cassette production, especially where subject matter and style are concerned. Training courses, technical assistance contracts, advisers sent from the centers of technology and economic power virtually guarantee the continuity of cultural dependency.

In addition, there is a simple economic reason why Third World countries continue to rely on others for technical leadership and materials. The following passage taken from a study on "media imperialism in the Philippines" makes five points:

At an average cost of only $500.00 per hour, a country would require a production budget of close to one million dollars a year. Third World countries, with the exception of OPEC countries, do not have this kind of money—nor do many of them have the necessary trained manpower or production facilities. Consequently, in order to maintain a daily schedule, programmes must be imported and, for poor countries, American programmes are available at an unbelievably low cost. For instance, the price range of half-hour episodes of American series in 1980 was $150–200 in Thailand, $130–150 in Korea and $225–260 in Hong Kong. (Mercada and Buch 1981)

A further quotation from H. J. Schiller (1977:33–43) also taken from the above-mentioned study demonstrates the subtle way in which Third World audiences are caught up in the craze of new media consumerism:

The production of movies, television programmes, games, records, magazines, and books is consolidated in a few corporate superstructures and made part of multiproduct lines of profit-maximizing combines. . . . The transformation of national media structures into conduits of the corporate business system and the heavy international traffic of commercial media products flowing from the center to periphery are the most prominent means by which weaker societies are absorbed culturally into the modern world system. (Schiller 1977:33–43)

Economic and especially cultural domination is indeed a much more complex phenomena than would appear at first—let us say—materialist glance. While statistical indicators prove the technical dominance of the United States, Japan, and Europe, they fail to explain why mass audiences in the Third World do not choose to ignore the instruments of their further oppression. Instead, no matter what the message is, whether it proclaim the revitalizing efficacy of Coca-Cola, the lightning speed of the latest model of a brand-name car, whether it be a Western, a horror film, a sequence in the long-running *Dallas* series, if it comes from the Northern Hemisphere it seems to fascinate a public living in the most dire conditions of malnutrition, shabby housing, and unemployment. This phenomenon is still more baffling when one considers that the very same audience that feeds on the shallow products of industrial media, possesses its own rich indigenous culture.

In order to arrive at an explanation to this seemingly incomprehensible dilemna, we must have a closer look at the revolutionary change in the cultural needs of two billion members of the world's population.

"Basic needs" is the term that socioeconomic scientists use when refering to food, housing, health, work and education. Never, however, do they include the viewing of television or video recorders in this category. When speaking about that part of the world's population which lives below the poverty line and whose only goal can be to survive, there is no doubt that those needs listed above are the major concerns. However, I am less certain that when refering to those living above the poverty line, one can so easily divide basic human requirements into those that are "primary" and those that are "secondary" to survival. The following passage from Mattelart should illustrate more clearly the difficulty I see in trying to rank human needs hierarchically:

> More and more often one can spot in the Iquique Zone a Brazilian Indian pulling out from underneath her sixth skirt a roll of dollars with which to buy electronic devices which she then sells as contraband in her own country.
>
> In the South of Bolivia whole villages are beginning to see their daily lives being transformed by the introduction of sophisticated technical apparatus, whose acquisition was considered impossible just a short time ago. Overnight little islands of transnational culture are being implanted in the midst of thousand year old traditions and are beginning to gnaw these away. (1953:58)

The question here is why this simple Bolivian Indian wants to buy electronic gadgets and why her village or poverty-stricken neighborhood agrees to spend the little money that they have or that they can borrow on the purchase of U.S.-produced video recordings and the like. If there is indeed a hierarchy of needs, one would think that these people would first think of bettering their water supply and establishing some kind of sanitation facilities, investing in agricultural equipment, or seeking training for a skilled job. Instead, the Indonesian taxi driver, the Nigerian oil field worker, the Indian shopkeeper choose to remain for a lifetime in debt for the satisfaction of being able to watch television programs. How can these needs be more urgent to them than the alleviation of their miserable conditions? To answer this question by blaming advertising for creating such absurd needs or by accusing the consumers for their lack of education and common sense is too easy. This kind of reasoning ignores the sociopsychological link between fiction and reality, which I mentioned at the outset.

When we think of our needs and the way they are satisfied, what comes to mind are the goods and services which we have learned to regard as valuable within our specific social group. Inside our cultural environment we have learned to eat a certain kind of food and to respond to a particular manifestation of love and tenderness. More precisely, any behavior is goal-oriented. The goals, in turn, represent collective and individual means of satisfying needs. These may be basically organic, but they are shaped and historically produced by the expectations of the group or the culture to which we belong.

To use an example, research has been published expounding upon the needs and sources of gratification of young American and European TV viewers and on the reasons why they desire video equipment. The interpretations that social researchers have come up with to explain these needs are not only quite different from one another, they are often contradictory. On one point, however, they all agree: The satisfaction derived from watching television and other media productions serves as a compensation for the need of active communication and interaction, like play, work, and tenderness, which remain unsatisfied. What appeals in this case to children applies in general to the Third World customers of modern media. The need to watch the screen and the satisfaction that goes along with this activity is inversely proportional to the opportunity which the watcher believes he has before him to cope with his expectations or to fulfill culturally determined goals by planned activity. Put in a different way, television viewing is compensation for frustration in social communication and interaction and such frustration is the consequence of economic, political, and cultural conditions.

In this light, we can define needs as feelings whose conscious expression arises in response to the distance between social goals and self-expectations and the capacity which each individual imagines himself as having in order to fulfill these expectations. When a need is felt by an individual or by a group it is necessarily linked to the goal which is strived for. It is historically and socially irrelevant to judge such goals as being "right" or "wrong." The ambition of a 12-year-old U.S. boy to one day become President of the United States and that of his Iranian contemporary to go directly to the seventh sky of Allah by running into the Iraqian mine fields are both based on the same ground of human psychology. They vary only in their degree of realistic or fictive thinking when considered in their cultural context. Keeping in mind this hierarchy of needs in the Third World, it would therefore be a typical example of Western ethnocentric prejudice to judge as "wrong" the Indian Sikh who purchases a television on heavy credit.

The distance separating the individual's or the group's real situation from the pursued goals, be these economic, social, political, or ideological is considered by those who seek them to be needs. The size of the gap depends itself on the actual situation of the individual and of his group. The greater this distance is conceived to be, the more urgently it requires a fictive solution. By a "fictive" solution I mean any answer which seems to satisfy the felt need without actually attaining the goal which is sought after. A fictive solution shifts the goal from something which is longed for, but which is somehow unattainable—be the hindrance real or imagined—to a dream of a goal. From this, we can conclude that:

1. The greater the distance separating a need and the possibility to fulfill it, the more fictitious must be the individual's attitude and behavior.
2. The fictive solution must effectively compensate for the disability, whether it be real or imagined, to reach the goal created by the need.

Historically and as can be judged from individual biographies the fictitious answer to a need is as effective as the real solution. One can say that the whole production of thought, of fantasy and art, of literature, and of religious ideas and rituals are the fictive solutions or the compensation for real needs, that is, of internalized goals. One can also say that the industry of culture understands perfectly well this need to compensate. It sells its products with increasing success precisely because it excels in promoting its market of dreams on a worldwide scale.

Perhaps this may all seem like very abstract thinking. Such reasoning, however, explains the fads which allow for the penetration of new media in the Third World in the first place.

Let us consider first the social group toward which the marketing of electronic hardware is geared to primarily. It is composed of the higher income brackets, a very small minority of indigenous urban commercial administrative and military agents of national or foreign power. These are people who educated themselves in the West, which means that their internalized goals are to be active consumers in the manner of the former political heads and actual economic rulers of the world. They see no possibility of attaining the position of their dominators. That is to say, they will never be the managers, politicians, generals, scientists, or artists of New York, London, Paris, or Tokyo. Nonetheless, they can compensate for this frustration by driving the same kind of cars, by playing golf, by sending their children to the same exclusive schools that the elite send their offspring and above all, by storing all the information and the fiction produced by the cultural industry. Through television and video viewing they feel that they can partake in the active life of those in power from which they otherwise find themselves excluded. They resemble those European and North American children who are mesmerized by horror films and space vessel commandos because they are deprived of actively shaping their own daily lives.

This is not the whole story. I already mentioned the fact that a television receiver and even more so a video recorder are very important status symbols. They separate the few "haves" from the innumerable "have nots." Now, for the "haves" in the Third World, the simple fact that they possess such a sophisticated tool, whatever it may be—the car, the color TV set—it is proof to themselves and to the world around them of their success. Usage of a television or video machinery is analogous to the sense of satisfaction that their children derive upon receiving a grade of "A" at school or college. It is something like a certificate guaranteeing to all who can see them that they indeed belong to the mighty, successful world of the elite from which they are actually excluded because they live in Lagos instead of New York, in Lima instead of Paris, in Jakarta and not Tokyo.

But, let us now turn to the much larger group of those who are forced to strive for physical and social survival. This is the overwhelming majority of the very poor, especially the deprived youth in the Third World countries. These young people emerge from the patterns of traditional societies and are accosted by the reality and the fictitious aspirations of industrial society, which mark the economic and social trends of today's world.

In pre-industrial cultures the needs of the group and the individual were internalized within a traditional framework of communication and interaction. So too, were the compensatory mechanisms. Thus, the real solutions as well as the fictitious ones fit into the context of the social group and individuals pursuing them. The expectation of a girl in an African tribal culture, for instance, conformed with her real and compensatory means to achieve the internalized goals and thus to satisfy her basic needs. Not so, when the needs she learned to recognize while growing up in the African tradition clash with those nurtured by industrial and post-industrial culture. The traditional forms and modes of communication and interaction inside her family and her village are violently intruded upon by the products of industrial culture—be it a transistor radio, Western music and language, school, or what her brothers relate of their attempts to earn a living in town. The girl's self-estimation of her ability to cope with these newly felt needs, stemming from industrial culture, is extremely low and yet her craving to belong to this irruptive style of life is inversely proportionately strong. Since she sees no chance of obtaining the real goals of industrial society, she must seek compensatory satisfaction.

The most effective source of compensation comes across audiovisual devices. The visions and sounds they produce allow the spectator to participate emotionally and therefore "really" in this fictive world of abundance, ambitions, and conflict. The longer our African girl is separated from her authentic social and individual situation by the reality presented to her on video, the greater is her need for this kind of compensatory fiction.

Television viewers in the Third World are as excited by anything that appears to them on their screens as children are in the Northern Hemisphere when watching television commercials. The major difference is that, being adult, the needs of this audience are all the more urgent. However, instead of working for the satisfaction of their needs—a task which their low self-esteem assumes to be impossible—they compensate for them by living them on television. As long as these adults are convinced that they can never belong to the industrial culture, which they admire so much, at least they can hope to be able to one day purchase the hardware for audiovisual dreaming.

One of the most serious studies undertaken on the connection between poor youth and communications systems, was conducted by two Indonesian social scientists and published in the English edition of the influential Indonesian magazine, *Prisma*. The subjects under consideration were the youth of the poor kampong of Jakarta. In order to be classified in the low income bracket, the subjects of the study had to meet at least one of the following criteria: 1) those living in areas of illegally erected houses; 2) those living . . . near railroad tracks, riverbanks, under bridges, etc.; 3) those living in the parts of the city with minimum facilities, where housing is crowded and where sanitation facilities are wanting; 4) the unemployed, regardless of whether they have a home and are supported by others or not.

If the assumption was true that compared to that of other media the impact of television is relatively greater among the youth and that much of the behavior of the youth is influenced by information sources such as movies and television, there would be good reason to say that there is a widening cultural gap between the youth and the well-to-do on the one hand and the elders on the other hand. This asymmetrical cultural growth may be able to explain the increasing alienation of the youth, the formation of limited groups, the widening generation gap and the conflict between generations. The alienation of the youth is also noticeable from their participation in religious activities and their views on these activities. Generally speaking, the youths relatively seldom attend the mosque or *langgar* together with their elders except on special occasions during religious festivities.

The most obvious impact of communication with the metropolitan centers around the poor kampongs is the formation of a certain pattern of consumption among the poor youths. The discrepancy between the ever-increasing hope and the ugly daily reality surrounding the youth is being bridged by various forms of emulation of sumptuous conditions they notice of their neighbor, the modern metropolitan center. This consumption pattern manifests itself in the imitation of the newest thing in fashion, in talks about luxurious topics or things and in the emulation of attitudes they see around them. The emulation is frequently over-done and is more for demonstration effect than to reflect the reality of their daily lives. For example, the imitation of dressing with such conspicuous colors, thick powder and cosmetics, long hair, the use of symbols of youth like necklaces, bracelets, chains or excessive scribblings, pictures and attitudes. (Karamoy and Sablie 1975)

In order to underpin this sociopsychological approach, a number of our correspondents at the Institute for Education in the Third World in Frankfurt were contacted. I sent them a short questionnaire and requested of them statistical material or their own estimations (see Appendix A). In the very short time that I had at my disposal, I received responses from Singapore with most valuable statistics of the "Survey Research Group" under contract with the "Asian Mass Communication Research and Information Center," Singapore. It is recorded in a "General Report, 1982, on Cinema and Television." It covers Singapore, Malaysia, and Indonesia. Another response came by telex from Jakarta with short but most significant data, answering the questions in our inquiry. Finally, we received data from our Senegalese correspondent. The latter gave a short comment concerning the general aspects of television and video in Dakar. For Latin America I relied on two publications of Mattelart's and the personal accounts of contacts in Peru and Columbia.

The preliminary results gathered from the bulk of this material indicate that television as well as video recorders are distributed throughout the urban areas and that their presence is increasing at a high rate. The progress of telematics largely exceeds that of any other productive activity in the Third World at least in as far as urban areas are concerned. A brief scan of the statistics, however, shows that this rapid expansion of the television and video market is out of proportion with the increase in national and per capita income. The following is a sample of this data:

The cost of a color television set compared to monthly income:
  in Indonesia: 20 months' wages of a peasant
                  10 months' wages of a teacher
  in Senegal: 24–30 months' wages of a peasant
                  12–14 months' wages of a teacher

The cost of a video recorder compared to monthly income:
  in Indonesia: 30 months' wages of a peasant
                  15 months' wages of a teacher

The distribution of television sets and video equipment:
  in Indonesia: 1 TV for every 25 inhabitants in urban districts
                  1 TV for every 80 inhabitants on the whole population
  in Senegal: 1 TV for every 12 inhabitants in Dakar
                  none in the villages
  in Indonesia: 100,000 video recorders
  in Senegal: 80,000 video recorders

Regarding the rate of increase in the distribution of television sets and video equipment:
  in Indonesia: yearly official increase in registered TV sets: 100,000
  in Senegal: No statistical data, but "the interest in owning such apparatus is very strong and increasing rapidly"

To adequately judge this data we have to remember that in Indonesia the yearly per capita income is $450. In Senegal for the year 1981 the per capita income was $436. The cost of a television set is about $1,250. Calculating very roughly, this would mean that the yearly increase of color televisions in Indonesia is equivalent to the combined yearly income of 6 million peasants, representing about 5 percent of the national income from the agrarian sector. In Senegal, with a much lower rate of industrial production, the ratio is still more frightening. These statistics support the thesis presented above regarding the revolutionary transformation in the so-called hierarchy of basic needs.

The second striking revelation produced by this information was the fact that household income and the extent of education are not determinants of television and video consumption.

The Singapore statistics point out that in regard to Malaysia, Indonesia, and Singapore, on the average 60 percent of television and video viewers watch their screens from five to seven days a week for one to four hours, which means that when they are not working this is their major pastime.

Finally, our Senegal correspondent reports that 40 percent of the programs available are of an informational, documentary, or educational nature, most of them coming from foreign trained producers: 45 percent of the programs are films, serials, plays, Westerns, and gangster movies. Of these 60 percent are imported from Western producers; 35 percent are produced in Senegal and 5 percent in other African countries.

Further evidence supporting this thesis came from another series of data from Singapore. A report on the "Frequency and Recency of Viewing Network Programs" in Malaysia shows that among women in low income households, there is a greater rate of television viewing than among women coming from high income households. Only among the 15-to-24-year-olds in the $1,000 annual income bracket is the rate of television viewing lower than in the $1,000 to $2,000 annual income bracket. Between the $1,500 to $2,500 annual income range, the rate of television viewing among the 15-to-24-year-age group drops to less than half. From 25 to 29 years of age the rate of television viewing is more than twice as frequent as among the same age group belonging to the next higher income bracket and nearly three times that of the highest income level.

The corresponding table for men between the ages of 15 and 24 years of age shows no deviance from the general rule applied to women. For all ages the frequency of watching television decreases with the increase in income. The difference that does exist in the amount of time spent in front of the television set between the two sexes in this age group is due to the patriarchal base of Third World society. Within the poor income bracket young women are too busy with household duties to reach the same viewing rate as their male counterparts.

The statistics for Singapore, comparing women and men, are slightly different. This is because the population is almost exclusively urban and the average household income is much higher than that of Malaysia. For all ages and all income brackets, the frequency of viewing is more or less equally high and in comparison to the viewing habits of Europeans and North Americans, it reaches Western standards. One reason for this could be that once the need for television as an escape from poverty becomes less urgent, people of different income rates and education become choosier as to what they will watch. Television becomes less of a drug and more a source of pleasure corresponding to the tastes of the viewer and his social group.

The statistics that I received on the type of programs watched in Jakarta read as follows: 35 percent of the programs are documentaries, informational, and educational shows; 35 percent are better action films, theater, and folklore; 20 percent are films of crime, Westerns, spy films and science fiction. The remaining 10 percent of television time is filled by sports. The same ratios apply to bought or borrowed video showings. Recalling to mind the information about the attitude of the poor kampong youth toward the programs, my thesis is entirely confirmed: the poorer the real situation, the more it produces the need of fictive gratification.

Our Jakarta correspondent's response to question 11 of the questionnaire reads "TV runs permanently," and to number 12, "Everybody watches when the opportunity is available." In other words, it doesn't matter what the message is, the essential thing is that the spectator be saved from having to face the miserable reality of his condition and its exigency.

Two Philippine experts on the subject state: "In terms of programming, television schedules tend to be heavily weighted toward entertainment programs (70 to 75%) at the expense of more serious programs such as news, documentaries and talk shows (25–30%)" (Mercado and Buck 1981:77).

"General Report's" detailed statistical analysis of Indonesia discloses slightly different results than those for Singapore and Senegal. For both sexes of all ages and income brackets the type of programs which are preferred are fiction (40%) and home and world news (47%).[1] If one contemplates the distance separating the censored and ideologically intended home and world news broadcastings and the average viewer's daily uncensored existence, one is led to conclude that what he seeks when watching the news is the kind of thrill that he could just as well derive from a Western or a crime film. The "reality" which he sees on the news is nothing less than the glamour, the horror, the "action" of a universe to which he does not belong, but yearns to join.

There remains still another aspect of the contradictory impact of television and video on the Third World. As fictive as the heroes of the United States, European, and Japanese films and newsreels may be in comparison to the daily reality of the masses in the Third World, they represent earthly men and earthbound situations rather than mythological men and women in fantastic places. Their dwelling places, their fast-moving cars, the glamour and despair of their love affairs or conflicts over money, the influence and power that these heroes of the industrial world command is real to them because they witness it with their own eyes in the streets of their towns or villages every time a political or military figure of some importance makes his appearance in their neighborhoods.

In traditional cultures the heroes and the masters were supernatural, heavenly gods and goddesses, clearly beyond the human experience. The characters of Gilgamesh, of the Trojan War, of the Mahabarata or the Ramajana were looked upon as possessing superhuman faculties. They fought with magic and invincible weapons, they moved swifter than any living creature, flew higher than any bird, and could watch sights far beyond their eyes. The tales created around the deeds of these extraordinary beings procured a sense of deep satisfaction among the spectators, who were able to share in the magical mood of the accounts not just by listening and watching, but by actually partaking in the religious beliefs and rituals of their heroes.

The heroes of the modern world, as they appear on television, are endowed with very human characteristics and at the same time with the powers of the deities of traditional societies. They love, they fight and kill, and they succeed in gaining power over nature and other men. The tales of their bold exploits, however, allow for no route to success other than by individual or collective effort. The fiction which comes over the TV screen blocks out any possibility of spectator participation. There is no hope. There is no ritual to join in, other than that of imitating the manner, thc dress, and the habits of the white hero.

The active communication between producer and spectator that was aroused by traditional media in the form of figurative art, story-telling, theater, dance, and music was a very efficient means of maintaining sociopsychological balance. As such, traditional media was a stabilizing factor in a world pervaded by misery, cruelty, ignorance, and oppression.

To the contrary, modern media, especially the audiovisual kind, induces an ever-increasing sociopsychological imbalance. Not only does the compensatory escape fail to provide an occasion for participating in and acting out one's needs, it adds to the feeling of frustration and craving. For this reason modern media is an enormously powerful instrument in disrupting the traditional course of social interaction and of intruding upon the class structure and the relationship between the generations as well as of the sexes. Audiovisual media destroys traditional values and norms. It dismisses the social hierarchy. Finally, it nullifies all ethical and moral beliefs and robs its victims of any religious consolation.

With each television set or video recorder that we export via the one-way path to the Third World, with each show or cassette that we sell in these parts, we transport the germ of unrest, of instability, revolt, delinquency, and violence, because the practical means of attaining the fictive goals that the media delivers are missing.

Nevertheless, there is perhaps one redeeming aspect to the impact of telematic imperialism which is of great importance and which is certain to become even more significant in the near future. In order to counteract the catastrophic predicament of two-thirds of the human race, I am convinced that the only effective weapon is creative thought, not only and not even primarily from the centers of science and technology, but from the workers and oppressed masses all over the world. The new media, the latest devices in communication and information technology are, in fact, capable of opening up this opportunity for creative thought among the poor. Which isn't to say that we musn't remain very critical admirers of the wonders that these modern means of communication are opening up to us every day.

First of all, we must ask ourselves, what are the positive effects which could come from the diffusion of television programs bought in the United States or Europe. One outcome is the emergence of a mythology which is neither local nor tribal nor national, but of cosmopolitan origin and orientation. The United States and European cultural industry produces the same feelings, goals, hopes, attitudes, and behavior all over the world. The same rhythms of music, a cerain standard in clothing fashions, identical status symbols are gradually being spread on an international scale. From Lima to Rio, from Lagos to Nairobi, from Bombay to Jakarta and to Manila an international language is being spoken. It is a tongue communicating identical notions from the centers of imperialism to the farthest corners of the earth. The propaganda that is a good part of this idiom is responsible for transforming the traditional norms and values.

All those responsible for cultural policies regret and resist this development. They try to preserve the traditional principles of their respective cultures. Their struggle is, however, to a large degree hypocritical and futile. I call it hypocritical because when all is said and done, the government, its military and civil servants, are in fact the economic agents of the large transnational companies. Even if they make an attempt to include elements of tradition and folklore into their programming, in truth those in power seek to eradicate the traditional mentality in order to insure for themselves political and economic supremacy. This is so because their own education shaped them into people who must calculate everything in terms of input and output. No longer do they trust in the magic cosmic powers of their traditions. In order to secure their position the national elite depends on schools, universities, industrial technology, and know-how. Further, they rely on the power, arms, and concepts of their former colonizers. Hence, while these agents of the industrial centers claim to be fighting for an autonomous culture, in reality they support the dissemination of the standardized profit-making culture of technological rationality. This is the hypocritical aspect of their "fight." The reason their pretended combat is futile is because the population has already adopted the new mythology of the industrial culture and has placed their trust in its gods. The gods of Coca-Cola, of Suzuki motorbikes, and of the Denver Saga have replaced, to a large degree, their own indigenous deities.

How can anyone possibly refer to these terrifying worldwide changes which are rapidly destroying thousands of years of old cultures and upsetting the delicate balance between frustration and compensation as being positive, the reader must be wondering. Are not the Third World's hungry peasants and jobless urban youth simply being handed over to the manipulative power of the transnational companies and their cultural industry? The answer is yes, but there is something else that the changes can bring with them.

A fundamental idea, however perverted, transported by modern media is making its way into the hearts and heads of the Third World masses. The essence of it is that the general conditions of individual and collective life are not shaped in the heavens, off limits to human endeavor, but here on earth in human hands. There is no doubt that the needs and expectations of the Third World population are being manipulated. Invariably, though, the poor of this world will be forced to ask themselves the reason for the harsh contradictions between the happy faces that appear on the television screen and the desolation which is the reality of their surroundings. It is only a matter of time before they become convinced that the misery of their lives is not a matter of fate, but of the human potentials of good and evil. The result of this realization could be creative thought. It is precisely the most advanced devices in communication technology which could open up such progressive perspectives. For instance, closed-circuit television and cable television allow the spectator to act out the feelings and thoughts experienced during the viewing of a preselected piece of reality. The filmed reactions give way in turn to group-learning, group-dynamics, and to finding new solutions. The latest technological innovations in communication enable viewers geographically or socially separated from one another to see a common sight, to hear the same information, and even to feel similar emotions. In this way people have the possibility of together experiencing new and tentatively better ways of thinking, feeling, and behaving. In a word, the new media hauls the spectator out of the isolation and hopelessness which is inherent in the contradiction in which he lives between reality and manipulated dreams.

If this opportunity for creative thinking, brought on by the new media is to be taken advantage of, then the power structure of production and the diffusion of cultural industry must undergo far-reaching changes. A change would require that the seat of know-how in the technological production of hardware and software be shared with the Third World. Scientific as well as economic cooperation must evolve on an equal footing between the metropoles and the peripheral nations. Not the short-sighted, profit-seeking interests of competing companies or government agencies should determine the goals of research and its technological outcome, but rather the long-range perspectives for development.

If, with the help of low-energy running media on a local and national scale we are able to join the Pakistani peasant with the young inhabitant of a Brazilian favela in coming up with new solutions to satisfy their needs, then the market for new technology could turn out to be the most promising branch of industrial production.

This perspective is more than just the dream of a European "egghead" in search of utopian solutions to world problems. It is an actual occurrence going on at present in the Third World. Allow me to cite some final examples from Mattelart and Schmucler:

A group of researchers in Social Sciences, with assistance from engineers of informatics and with the help of a minicomputer, have tried to "systematize and

disseminate the basic information on the Brazilian and international reality."
This information is spread and addressed in particular to base movements and
organizations, such as trade unions, professional associations and local voluntary groups. But at the same time, it is meant for institutions like the universities, the political parties and the churches which are all linked to social
development and to the transformations of society. IBASE in its pledge to aim
for the "democratization of information" tries to "collect the socioeconomic
information produced by already existing agencies and by popular currents or
movements. "We aim," they declare, "to integrate, generalize and transform
such information into practical know-how. We will translate it into accessible
language in order that it be made available to base movements who can use it in
seeking political alternatives and in guiding action . . ."

Some Venezuelan engineers in the professional movement, Antonio José de
Sucre, reflected in 1976 on the attitudes of professionals towards society and the
state. "We believe that the scientist and the technician can adopt a style of life, in
which money is not the parameter of success and where administrative corrup-
tion and the distortion of values—so rampant today—are absent. We believe that
governmentally run enterprises inside an economic and social system which
tends to accord them quite a new importance are able to and should demonstrate
their technical as well as administrative efficiency. Finally, we believe that a
scientific and technical development that responds to the real needs of humanity
and to all humans is possible." (1983:145–146)

Appendix A

QUESTIONNAIRE

1. Number of television receivers per number of inhabitants, when
   possible according to city or town.
2. Increase in the number of television receivers per year within the
   last 5 years.
3. The number of video recorders per number of inhabitants, if possible with the same information as in 1 or 2.
4. The price of a television set in comparison with the average wage
   earnings of a farmer and of a teacher.

5. The same for video apparatus.
6. What is the percentage of Western produced programs in comparison to those produced in the native land, either per week or per year.
7. The same for video cassettes.
8. The amount and kind of national production in governmental and nongovernmental studios for television and cassettes.
9. The percentage of broadcasting time for the following kinds of programs:
   —Information/ Documentaries/ Education
   —Action films/ theater/ folklore/ crime films/ westerns/spy films
   —Sport
10. The same for videocassettes.
11. How many hours of television are watched on the average every day? Which programs are the most popular?
12. How do viewing habits differ according to salary, sex, and age?
13. What kind of videocassettes sell best?

Note

1. Obviously video recording will never cover the news the way television does. Developing along the same lines as television minus the news coverage, video is bound to accentuate the trend of contemporary fiction.

References

A. C. Nielsen Co. 1981. Nielsen Cable Status Report. May.

A. C. Nielsen Co. 1982a. Cable Television Audience Distribution Report by Designated Market Areas. Northbrook, Ill.

A. C. Nielsen Co. 1982b. Videocassette Recorder Special Report, May 20–June 16.

Adams, W. J. and J. L. Yellen. 1976. "Commodity Bundling and the Burden of Monopoly." *Quarterly Journal of Economics* 90:475–98.

Altman, E. and S. Katz. 1976. "Statistical Bond Rating Classification Using Financial and Accounting Data." In Michael Schiff and George Sorter, eds., *Proceedings of the Conference on Topical Research in Accounting*. New York: New York University School of Business.

Anthony, R. A. 1971. "Towards Simplicity and Rationality in Comparative Broadcast Licensing Procedures." *Stanford Law Review* 24:1–115.

Applebaum, E. 1982. "The Estimation of the Degree of Oligopoly Power." *Journal of Econometrics* 19:287–99.

Arbitron Television. 1983. *1982–1983 Television Markets and Rankings Guide*.

Arnold & Porter. 1982. *New York City Cable Action Plan*. Washington, D.C.: Arnold and Porter.

Asatani, K., R. Watanabe, K. Nosu, T. Matsumoto, and F. Nihei. 1982. "A Field Trial of Fiber Optic Subscriber Loop Systems Using Wavelength-Division Multiplexers." *IEEE Transactions on Communications*, pp. 2172–84.

Ashbacker Radio Corp. v. FCC. 1945. 326 *U.S.* 327.

Babe, Robert E. 1975. "Cable Television and Telecommunications in Canada." Michigan State University Graduate School of Business Administration, East Lansing, Mich.

Baer, W. S., H. Geller, J. A. Grundfest, and K. Possner. 1974a. "Concentration of Mass Media Ownership: Assessing the State of Current Knowledge." R-1584-MF. Santa Monica, Calif.: Rand Corporation.

Baer, W. S., H. Geller, and J. A. Grundfest. 1974b. "Newspaper-Television Station Cross Ownership: Options for Federal Action." R-1585-MF. Santa Monica, Calif.: Rand Corporation.

Bailey, E. E. and A. Friedlaender. 1982. "Market Structure and Multiproduct Industries." *Journal of Economic Literature* 20:1024–48.

Bain, J. S. 1956. *Barriers to New Competition*. Cambridge: Harvard University Press.

Baker, J. 1983. "Cable and the Telcos: From Confrontation to Détente." *Cablevision Plus*, August 1, pp. 8–22.

Barnett, S. R. 1970. "Cable Television and Media Concentration: Part I. Control of Cable Systems by Local Broadcasters." *Stanford Law Review* 22:221–329.

Barten, A. P. 1969. "Maximum Likelihood Estimation of a Complete System of Demand Equations." *European Economic Review* 1:7–73.

Baseman, K. C. and B. M. Owen. 1982. *A Framework for Economic Analysis of Electronic Media Concentration Issues*. Washington, D.C.: Economists Incorporated.

Baumol, W. J. 1977. "On the Proper Cost Tests for Natural Monopoly in a Multiproduct Industry." *American Economic Review* 67:809–22.

Baumol, W. J., E. E. Bailey, and R. D. Willig. 1977. "Weak Invisible Hard Theorems on the Sustainability of Multiproduct Natural Monopoly." *American Economic Review* 67:350–68.

Baumol, W. J., J. C. Panzar, and R. D. Willig. 1982. *Contestable Markets and the Theory of Industry Structure*. New York: Harcourt Brace Jovanovich.

Bazelon, D. 1981. Foreword, Student Symposium: "Communications Regulation." *California Law Review* 69:443.

Bednarski, P. J. 1984. "Living with Telelst." *Channels*, May–June, pp. 55–56.

Beebe, J. H. 1977. "Institutional Structure and Program Choices in Television Markets." *Quarterly Journal of Economics* 91:15–37.

Belinfante, A. 1978. "The Identification of Technical Change in the Electricity Generating Industry." In M. Fuss and D. McFadden, eds., *Production Economics: A Dual Approach to Theory and Applications*. Vol. 2. Amsterdam: North-Holland.

Belsley, D. A., E. Kuh, and R. E. Welsch. 1980. *Regression Diagnostics*. New York: Wiley.

Berkshire Cablevision of Rhode Island, Inc. v. Burke. 1983. 571 *F. Supp.* 976 (D.R.I.).

Berndt, E. R. and M. S. Khaled. 1979. "Parametric Productivity Measurements and Choice among Flexible Functional Forms." *Journal of Political Economy* 87:1220–45.

Besen, S. M. 1976. "The Value of Television Time." *Southern Economic Journal* 42:435–41.

Besen, S. M. and L. L. Johnson. 1982. *An Economic Analysis of Mandatory Leased Channel Access for Cable Television*. Santa Monica, Calif.: Rand Corporation.

Besen, S. M. and L. L. Johnson, 1984. *An Analysis of the Federal Communication Commission's Group Ownership Rules*. N–2097–MF. Santa Monica, Calif.: Rand Corporation.

Besen, S. M. and B. Mitchell. 1975. "Watergate Television: An Economic Analysis." R–1712–MF. Santa Monica, Calif.: Rand Corporation.

Besen, S. M., B. M. Mitchell, R. M. Noll, B. M. Owen, R. E. Park, and J. N. Rose. 1977. "Economic Policy Research on Cable Television: Assessing the Costs and Benefits of Cable Deregulation." In P. W. MacAvoy, ed., *Deregulation of Cable Television*. Washington, D.C.: American Enterprise Institute.

Bhusri, G. S. 1984. "Considerations for ISON Planning and Implementation." *IEEE Communications* 22(1):18–32.

Black Hills Video Corp. v. FCC (1968). 399 *F.2d* 65. 8th Cir.

Bloch, H. and M. Wirth. 1982. "Demand for Pay Television and Its Impact on Expansion of Cable Availability." Denver, Colo.: University of Denver Center for Mass Communications Research and Policy.

Bohn, P. P., M. J. Bucker, and T. N. Rao, 1983. "Bringing Lightwave Technology to the Loop." *Bell Laboratories Record*, April, pp. 6–10.

Bork, R. H. 1978. *The Antitrust Paradox: A Policy at War with Itself*. New York: Basic Books.

Bortz, P., J. Pottle, and M. Wyche. 1983. "An Analysis of the Television Programming Market." Denver, Colo.: Browne, Bortz, and Coddington. Prepared for the American Broadcasting Companies, Inc.

"Broadcasters Show Profit Margin Drop in Last Five Years." 1984. *Broadcasting,* February 13, p. 210.

Brookhaven Cable TV, Inc. v. Kelley. 1978. 573 *F.2d* 765 (2d Cir.), cert. denied, 441 *U.S.* 904.

Browne, Bortz, and Coddington. 1981. "Demand for Multiple Television Channels." Denver, Colo. Prepared as an appendix B–1 of Microband MDS proposal.

Burrill, J. R. 1981. "Optimum Service to Rural Subscribers Goal of Telco-Owned Cable Systems." In "CATV Operators vs. Telcos: Debating the Public Interest." *Telephony,* May 4, pp. 23, 35–41.

"Cable Ad Network Sues Times Mirror." 1984. *Multichannel News,* May 7, p. 39.

"Cablecasting." 1983. *Broadcasting,* October 24, p. 8.

"Cable Stats." 1984. *CableVision,* February 6, p. 5.

Cable Television Bureau, FCC. 1982. Cable Television Legislation 1982. FCC, Washington, D.C.

Cable Television Information Center (CTIC). 1972. *Cable Television Options for Jacksonville.* Washington, D.C.: Urban Institute.

Capuzzi, C. 1984. "Cable Homes Lead in VRC Use, Nielsen Says." *CableVision,* May 14, p. 20.

Carey, J. and M. Moss. 1984. *Telecommunications Technologies and Public Broadcasting.* Washington, D.C.: Corporation for Public Broadcasting.

Carroll Broadcasting Co. v. FCC. 1958. 258 *F.2d* 440 (D. C. Cir.).

Carter Mountain Transmission Corp. v. FCC. 1963. 32 *F.2d* 359 (D.C.Cir.), cert denied 375 *U.S.* 951.

Caves, D. W., L. R. Christensen, and M. W. Tretheway. 1980. "Flexible Cost Function for Multiproduct Firms." *Review of Economics and Statistics* 62:477–81.

Century Federal, Inc. v. Palo Alto, 1983. *Multichannel News* September 19, p. 3.

Chamberlain, E. H. 1956. "The Theory of Monopolistic Competition." 7th ed., Cambridge: Harvard University Press.

Chang, K. Y. and E. H. Hara, 1983. "Fiber-Optic Broad-Band Integrated Distribution—Elie and Beyond." *IEEE Journal on Selected Areas in Communications,* pp. 439–44.

Channels. 1983. "1984 Field Guide to the New Media. *Channels* November–December Supplement.

Charles River Associates. 1978. "Analysis of Demand for Cable TV." CRA Report No. 178–2. Boston.

Cherington, P. W., L. V. Hirsch, and R. Brandwein 1971. *Television Station Ownership: A Case Study of Federal Agency Regulation.* New York: Hastings House.

Chow, G. C. 1967. "Technological Change and the Demand for Computers." *American Economic Review* 57:1117–30.

Christensen, L. R. and W. H. Green. 1976. "Economies of Scale in U.S. Electric Power Generation." *Journal of Political Economy* 84:655–76.

Circulation. 1984. Washington, D.C.: American Newspaper Markets.

Coffey, A. 1979. "The 'Top 50 Market Policy': Fifteen Years of Non-Policy." *Federal Communications Law Journal* 31:303–39.

Cohn, L. 1984. "Investment by U.S. Studios in 1984 Releases To Be Up 36% from Past Two Years." *Daily Variety,* February 15, p. 1.

Comanor, W. S. 1970. "Should Natural Monopolies Be Regulated?" *Stanford Law Review* 22:510–18.

Comanor, W. S. and B. M. Mitchell. 1972. "The Costs of Planning: The ICC and Cable Television." *Journal of Law and Economics* 15:177–206.

Community Communications Co. v. City of Boulder. 1981. 660 *F.2d* 1370 (10th Cir.). cert dismissed, 102 *S.Ct.* 2287 (1982).

Community Television of Utah Inc. v. Roy City. 1982. 555 *F.Supp.* 1164. (D. Utah).

Conant, M. 1960. *Antitrust in the Motion Picture Industry: Economic and Legal Analysis.* Los Angeles: University of California Press.

Cook, R. D. 1977. "Detection of Influential Observation in Linear Regression." *Technometrics* 19.

Cowling, K. and M. Waterson. 1976. "Price-Cost Margins and Market Structure." *Economics* 43:267–74.

Cox Cable Communications. 1983. Petition FCC No. CCB DFD 83-1.

Cox Cable Communications, Inc. v. Simpson. 1983. No. CV 83–L240. (D. Neb).

Crandall, R. W. and L. L. Fray. 1974. "A Reexamination of the Prophecy of Doom for Cable Television." *Bell Journal of Economics and Management Science* 5:264–89.

Crandall, R. W., R. G. Noll, and B. M. Owen. 1983. "Economic Effects of the Financial Interest and Syndication Rule: Comments on the ICF Report." Washington, D.C.: Economists Inc.

Cronin, F. J. et al. 1983. "An Analysis of the Economic Benefits and Harm from Videocassette Recorders and Related Products." Richland, Wash.: Battelle Northwest. Prepared for the Motion Picture Association of America, Inc.

Demsetz, H. 1968. "Why Regulate Utilities?" *Journal of Law and Economics* 13:293-306.

Demsetz, H. 1969. "Information and Efficiency: Another Viewpoint." *Journal of Law and Economics* 12:1–22.

Denny, M. and M. Fuss. 1977. "The Use of Approximation Analysis to Test for Separability and the Existence of Consistent Aggregates." *American Economic Review* 67:492–97.

Denny, M., M. Fuss, C. Everson, and L. Waverman. 1981a. "Estimating the Effects of Diffusion of Technological Innovation in Telecommunications: The Production Structure of Bell Canada." *Canadian Journal of Economics* 14:34–43.

Denny, M., M. Fuss, and L. Waverman. 1981b. "The Measurement and Interpretation of Total Factor Productivity in Regulated Industries, with an Application to Canadian Telecommunications." In T. Cowing and R. Stevenson, eds., *Productivity Measurement in Regulated Industries.* New York: Academic Press.

Dertouzos, J. and K. Thorpe. 1982. "Newspaper Groups: Economies of Scale, Tax Laws and Merger Incentives." R–2878–SBA. Santa Monica, Calif.: Rand Corporation.

Dhrymes, P. J. and M. Kurz. 1964. "Technology and Scale in Electricity Generation." *Econometrica* 32:287–315.

Dickson, V. A. 1981. "Conjectural Variation Elasticities and Concentrations." *Economics Letters* 7:281–85.

Diewert, W. E. 1976. "Exact and Superlative Index Numbers." *Journal of Econometrics* 4:115–45.

Dixit, A. 1979. "A Model of Duopoly Suggesting a Theory of Entry Barriers." *Bell Journal of Economics* 10:20–32.

Dobell, A. R., L. D. Taylor, L. Waverman, T. H. Lium, and M. D. G. Copeland. 1972. "Communications in Canada." *Bell Journal of Economics and Management Science* 3:175–219.

Dougherty, P. H. 1984. "Advertising: Using QUBE to Market Cosmetics." *New York Times,* April 13, p. D17.

Dunmore, K. R. and M. M. Bykowsky. 1982. "Cable Television Demand and Its Implications for Cable Copyright." Boulder, Colo.: Office of Policy Analysis and Development, National Telecommunications and Information Administration, Dept. of Commerce.

Easterbrook, F. H. 1981. "Predatory Strategies and Counterstrategies." *University of Chicago Law Review* 48:263–337.

Eaton, C. and R. Lipsey. 1979. "The Theory of Market Preemption: The Persistence of Excess Capacity and Monopoly in Growing Spatial Markets." *Economica* 46:149–58.

Eldor, D., C. H. Shami, and E. F. Sudit. 1979. "Production-Cost Elasticities in Product and Factor Markets: The Case of Telecommunications." *Journal of Economics and Business* 37:84–89.

Electronic Industries Association. 1983. "Consumer Electronics Annual Review." Washington, D.C.

Ely, R. T. 1937. *Outlines of Economics.* New York: Macmillan.

"Encyclopedia of Exhibition." National Association of Theater Owners, New York.

FCC. 1940. 5 *Fed. Reg.* 2382.

FCC. 1953. Rules and Regulations Relating to Multiple Ownership. 18 *F.C.C.* 288.

FCC. 1969. First Report and Order in Docket 18397. 20 *F.C.C.2d* 201.

FCC. 1970. Section 214 Certificates, Docket 18509, 21 *F.C.C.2d* 307.

FCC. 1971. Moline Television Corp. 31 *F.C.C.2d* 263.

FCC. 1972. Use of Broadcast and Cablecast Facilities by Candidates for Public Office. 34 *F.C.C.2d* 510.

FCC. 1974. Report and Order. 29 *Rad.Reg.2d* 382.

FCC. 1975a. Second Report in Docket 18110 on TV-Newspaper Ownership. 50 *FCC 2d* 979.

FCC. 1975b. First Report and Order in Dockets 19554 and 18893. 52 *F.C.C.2d* 1.

FCC. 1975c. Second Report and Order. 55 *F.C.C.2d* 540.

FCC. 1975d. Notice of Proposed Rule Making. 56 *F.C.C.2d* 159.

FCC. 1976. Ascertainment of Community Problems. 57 *F.C.C.2d* 418.

FCC. 1978a. Enforcing Sec. 312(a) (7). 68 *F.C.C.2d* 1079.

FCC. 1978b. Statement of Policy on Minority Ownership of Broadcasting Facilities. 78 *F.C.C. 2d* 979.

FCC. 1980a. Further Notice of Proposed Rulemaking. 81 *F.C.C.2d* 150.

FCC. 1980b. Notice of Proposed Rule Making. 82 *F.C.C.2d* 47.

FCC. 1980c. Table of TV Channel Allotments. 83 *F.C.C.2d* 52.

FCC. 1980d. Notice of Inquiry and Proposed Rule Making in CC Docket No. 80–116. 45 *Fed.Reg.* 29335 (May 2); FCC 80–141.

FCC. 1980e. *Report and Order* in Dockets 20988 and 21284, 45 *Fed. Reg.* 60186.

FCC. 1980f. Network Inquiry Special Staff. *New Television Networks: Entry, Jurisdiction, Ownership, and Regulation.* Vol. 2. Washington, D.C.: U. S. Federal Communications Commission.

FCC. 1980g. Network Inquiry Special Staff. "The Determinants of Television Station Profitability." Preliminary Report. Washington, D.C.

FCC. 1980h. "The Market for Television Advertising." Network Inquiry Special Staff Preliminary Report. Washington, D.C.

FCC. 1981a. Notice of Proposed Rulemaking. 84 *F.C.C.2d* 335.

FCC. 1981b. Deregulation of Radio. 84 *F.C.C.2d* 968, aff'd in part, remanded in part, *Office of Communications of the United Church of Christ v. FCC.* 707 *F. 2d* 1413 (D.C.Cir. 1983).

FCC. 1981c. Private Microwave Facilities. 86 *F.C.C.2d* 299.

FCC. 1981d. Radio Broadcast Services: Revision of Application for Renewal of Licenses. 49 *Rad.Reg.2d* 740 aff'd, *Black Citizens for a Fair Media v. FCC.* 54 *Rad.Reg.2d* 1151 (D.C.Cir. 1983) pet. for cert. pending, Case No. 83–1498 (Oct. Term 1983).

FCC. 1981e. Memorandum Opinion and Order. 49 *Rad.Reg.2d* 1696.

FCC. 1981f. 9 KHz Channel Spacing. 46 *Fed.Reg.* 56214.

FCC. 1981g. "Cable Television and the Political Broadcasting Laws." Report to Senator Barry Goldwater.

FCC. 1982a. Direct Broadcast Satellite. 90 *F.C.C.2d* 676, appeal pending sub nom. *NAB v. FCC,* 82–1926 (D.C.Cir).

FCC. 1982b. GTE Satellite Corp., 90 *F.C.C.2d* 1009. recon. denied, FCC 83–271.

FCC. 1982c. AM Stereophonic Broadcasting. 51 *Rad.Reg.2d* 1.

FCC. 1982d. Low Power Television Service. 51 *Rad.Reg.2d* 476.

FCC. 1982e. Report and Order. 51 *Rad.Reg.2d* 1341.

FCC. 1982f. Competitive Common Carrier Services. 52 *Rad.Reg.2d* 187.

FCC. 1982g. Report and Order. 52 *Rad.Reg.2d* 257.

FCC. 1982h. Report and Order. 52 *Rad.Reg.2d* 401.

FCC. 1982i. Code of Federal Regulations.

FCC. 1982j. Third Report and Order, in Docket 21502. 90 *F.C.C.2d* 341.

FCC. 1983a. Broadcast Auxiliary Facility Service. 53 *Rad.Reg.2d* 1101.

FCC. 1983b. Memorandum Opinion and Order. 53 *Rad.Reg.2d* 1270.

FCC. 1983c. Teletext Transmission. 53 *Rad.Reg.2d* 1309.

FCC. 1983d. FM Subsidiary Communications Authorizations. 53 *Rad.Reg.2d* 1519.

FCC. 1983e. WARC Implementation. 54 *Rad.Reg.2d* 101, appeal pending, *United States Satellite Broadcasting Co., Inc. v. FCC, Case* No. 83–1692. (D.C. Cir.).

FCC. 1983f. Instructional Television Fixed Service (MDS Reallocation). 54 *Rad.Reg.2d* 107.

FCC. 1983g. Notice of Proposed Rulemaking. 54 *Rad.Reg.2d* 381.

FCC. 1983h. Memorandum Opinion and Order. 54 *Rad.Reg.2d* 1351.

FCC. 1983i. Memorandum Opinion and Order, Declaratory Ruling and Order, Earth Satellite Communication, Inc. 54 *Rad.Reg.2d* 1427, appeal pending *New York State Commission on Cable TV v. FCC,* Case Nos. 83–2190, 83–2196 (D.C.Cir.).

FCC. 1983j. Notice of Proposed Rule Making in MM Docket 83–670. 48 *Fed.Reg.* 37239.

FCC. 1983k. Notice of Proposed Rule Making in Gen. Docket 83–1009. 48 *Fed.Reg.* 49438.

FCC. 1983l. Private Microwave Facilities. FCC 83–245.

FCC. 1983m. Notice of Proposed Rule Making. FCC MM Docket 83–331.

FCC. 1983n. FCC 83–364.

FCC. 1983o. Notice of Proposed Rule Making in Gen. Docket 83–484.

FCC. 1983p. Fourth Report and Order in Docket No. 21502. 54 R.R.2d 1401.

FCC. 1983q. Memorandum Opinion and Order. FCC 83–525.

FCC. 1983r. Memorandum Opinion and Order. FCC 83–526.

FCC. 1983s. Notice of Proposed Rulemaking in CC Docket No. 83–1096. FCC 83–460 (October 28).

FCC. 1983t. Notice in CC Docket 83–1096.

FCC. 1983u. Multiple Ownership Rules. 56 *R.R.2d* 859, 887.

FCC. 1983v. Code of Federal Regulations. Washington, D.C.: General Services Administration.

FCC. 1984a. Notice of Proposed Rule Making. MM Docket 84–19 bj.

FCC. 1984b. FCC 84–293.

FCC. 1984c. FCC 84–350.

FCC v. Midwest Video Corp. 1979. 440 *U.S.* 689.

FCC. v. National Citizens Committee for Broadcasting. 1978. 436 *U.S.* 775.

FCC. v. Pacifica. 1978. 438 *U.S.* 726.

FCC. v. Texaco. 1964. 377 *U.S.* 33.

Fellner, W. 1949. *Competition Among the Few.* New York: Knopf.

Ferguson, M. 1983. "Daily Newspaper Advertising Rates, Local Media Cross-Ownership, Newspaper Chains, and Media Competition." *Journal of Law and Economics* 26:635–54.

Fischelson, G. 1977. "Telecommunications: CES Production Function." *Applied Economics* 9:9–18.

Fischer, S. 1971. "Puzzles and Problems." *Journal of Political Economy* 79:1178–79.

Fisher, F. 1979. "Diagnosing Monopoly." *Quarterly Review of Economics and Business* 19(2):7–33.

Fisher, F. and J. McGowan. 1983. "On the Misuse of Accounting Rates to Infer Monopoly Profits." *American Economic Review* 73:82–97.

Fisher, F. M., J. J. McGowan, and D. S. Evans. 1980. "The Audience-Revenue Relationship for Local Television Stations." *Bell Journal of Economics* 11:694–708.

Fogarty, J. R. 1980. "Exploring the Question of CATV Cross-Ownership." *Telephony,* August 4, pp. 28–31.

Fournier, G. M. and D. L. Martin. 1983. "Does Government-Restricted Entry Produce Market Power? New Evidence from the Market for Television Advertising." *Bell Journal of Economics* 14:44–56.

Fowler, Mark. 1982. "The Public's Interest." *Communications and the Law* 4(1):51–58.

Fox, E. M. 1982. "The New Merger Guidelines—A Blueprint for Microeconomic Analysis." *Antitrust Bulletin* 27:519–91.

Fox, J. R., D. I. Fordham, R. Wood, and D. J. Ahern. 1982. "Initial Experience with the Milton Keynes Optical Fiber Cable TV Trial. " *IEEE Transactions on Communications,* pp. 2155–63.

Friendly, H. J. 1962. *The Administrative Agencies.* Cambridge: Harvard University Press.

Frisch, R. 1965. *Theory of Production.* Dordrecht, Holland: D. Reidel.

Fuss, M. 1981. "The Regulation of Telecommunications in Canada." Technical Report No. 7, Economic Council of Canada.

Fuss, M. and L. Waverman, 1982. "Multi-Product Multi-Input Cost Function for a Regulated Utility: The Case of Telecommunications in Canada." In G. Fromm, ed. *Studies in Public Regulation*. Cambridge: MIT Press.

Geller, H. 1978. Testimony on H. R. 13015, Before the House Communications Subcommittee (September 11).

Geller, H. and D. Lampert. 1983. "Cable, Content Regulation and the First Amendment." *Catholic University Law Review* 32:603–31.

Geller, H. and J. Yurow. 1982. "The Reasonable Access Provision (312) (a) (7) of the Communications Act: Once More Down the Slippery Slope." *Federal Communications Law Journal* 34:389–430.

General Electric Cablevision Corp. v. Peoria. 1982. 51 *Rad.Reg.2d* 603.

Goldberg, V. 1976. "Regulation and Administered Contracts." *Bell Journal of Economics* 7:426–48.

Gollop, F. M. and M. J. Roberts. 1981. "The Sources of Economic Growth in the U.S. Electric Power Industry." In T. G. Cowing and R. E. Stevenson, eds., *Productivity Measurement in Regulated Industries*. New York: Academic Press.

Good, L. 1974. "An Econometric Model of the Canadian Cable Television Industry and the Effects of CRTC Regulation." Ph.D. dissertation, University of Western Ontario, London.

Gordon, K., J. D. Levy, and R. S. Preece. 1981. "FCC Policy on Cable Ownership." Washington, D.C.: FCC Office of Plans and Policy.

Greater Freemont, Inc. v. City of Freemont. 1968. 302 F.Supp. 652 (N.D. Ohio).

Griliches, Z. and V. Ringstad. 1971. *Economies of Scale and the Form of the Production Function: An Econometric Study of Norwegian Manufacturing Establishment Data*. Amsterdam: North-Holland.

Hanneman, G. and R. LaRose. 1983. "Cable Television: A New Business Communications Medium." *Business Communications Review*, May–June, pp. 23–29.

Hanoch, G. 1975. "The Elasticity of Scale and the Scope of Average Costs." *American Economic Review* 65:492–97.

Harberger, A. 1954. "Monopoly and Resource Allocation." *American Economic Review* (Papers and Proceedings), 44:77–87.

Harmetz, A. 1984. "Hollywood Thriving on Video-Cassette Boom." *New York Times*, May 7, pp. A1, C17.

Hausman, R. M. 1984a. "Credibility of Basic Cable Needs a Lift, Agencies Say." *CableAge*, March 19, pp. 10–14.

Hausman, R. M. 1984b. "Hefty System Ad Rates Often Surpassing Broadcast." *CableAge*, April 30, pp. 30–32.

Home Box Office, Inc. v. FCC. 1977. 567 F.2d 9, 46 (D.C. Cir.) (per curium), cert. denied, 434 U.S. 829.

Homet, R. S., Jr. 1984. "Getting the Message: Statutory Approaches to Electronic Delivery and the Duty of Carriage." Washington, D.C.: Roosevelt Center for American Policy Studies.

Home Video Yearbook 1981–82. 1982. White Plains, N.Y.: Knowledge Industries Publications.

Horrigan, J. O. 1966. "The Determination of Long-Term Credit Standing with Financial Ratios." *Journal of Accounting Research (Suppl.)*, 4:44–62.

Howard, H. H. 1983. *Group and Cross-Media Ownership of Television Stations in 1983*. Washington, D.C.: National Association of Broadcasters.

Hymes v. Mayor of Oradell. 1976. 425 U.S. 610.

Ibbotson, R. G. and R. A. Sinquefield. 1979. *Stocks, Bonds, Bills, and Inflation: The Past (1926–1976) and the Future (1977–2000)*. Charlottesville, Va.: Financial Analysis Research Foundation.

Illinois Citizens Committee for Broadcasting v. FCC. 1975. 515 *F.2d* 397.

"Indies Looking Profitable Today and Tomorrow." 1984. *Broadcasting*, January 23, p. 64.

IRD (International Resource Development). 1983. "Fiber Optic Markets." Norwalk, Conn.: International Resource Development.

Johnston, J. 1972. *Econometric Methods*. New York: McGraw-Hill.

Jones, W. V. 1962. "Licensing of Major Broadcast Facilities by the FCC." Washington, D.C.: Administrator of the United States Committee on License and Authorizations.

Jorgenson, D. W., L. R. Christensen, and L. J. Lau. 1971. "Conjugate Duality and the Transcendental Logarithmic Production Function." *Econometrica* 39:225–56.

Kaatz, B. 1982. *Cable: An Advertiser's Guide to the New Electronic Media*. Chicago: Crain Books.

Kahn, A. E. 1966. "The Tyranny of Small Decisions: Market Failures, Imperfections, and the Limits of Economics." *Kyklos* 19:23–47.

Kahn, A. E. 1971. *The Economics of Regulation: Principles and Institutions*. New York: Wiley.

Kahn, H. 1983. "The Cable Subscriber Speaks: Channels, Choice or Chaos?" Paper presented at the Advertising Research Foundation, December 15.

Kahn, I. 1983. Address to the Cable TV Summit Conference, October 27, Washington, D.C.

Kalba, K. 1977. *Separating Content from Conduit*. Cambridge, Mass.: Kalba Bowen Associates.

Kalba, K. 1980. "Executive Summary of Findings of State Regulation, Program on Information Resources Policy." Cambridge: Harvard University.

Kaplan, R. S. and G. Urwitz. 1979. "Statistical Models of Bond Ratings: A Methodological Inquiry." *Journal of Business* 52:231–61.

Karamoy, A. and A. Sablie. 1975. "The Communication Aspect and Its Impact on the Youth of Poor Kampongs in the City of Jakarta." In *Drioma Indonesian Journal of Social and Economic Affairs*, vol. 1, no. 1.

Karp, A. 1984. "Selling Video in the Theatre." *Boxoffice*, June, p. 9.

Kaserman, D. L. 1978. "Theories of Vertical Integration: Implications for Antitrust Policy. " *Antitrust Bulletin* 23:483–510.

Kaysen, C. and D. F. Turner. *Antitrust Policy*. Cambridge: Harvard University Press.

Kmenta, J. 1971. *Elements of Econometrics*. New York: Macmillan.

Kniepts, G. and I. Vogelsang. 1982. "The Sustainability Concept Under Alternative Behavioral Assumption." *Bell Journal of Economics* 13:234–41.

Koga, T., Y. Iijima, K. Iinema, and T. Ishiguro. 1981. "Statistical Performance Analysis of an Interframe Encoder for Broadcast Television Signals." *IEEE Transactions on Communications*, pp. 1868–76.

Kostas, D. J. 1984. "Transition to ISDN—An Overview." *IEEE Communications* 22:11–17.

Krasnow, E. G., L. D. Longley, and H. A. Terry. 1982. *The Politics of Broadcast Regulation*. New York: St. Martin's Press.

450 *References*

Landes, W. M. and R. A. Posner. 1981. "Market Power in Antitrust Cases." *Harvard Law Review* 94:937–96.

Lence, R. 1978. "Theories of Television Program Selection: A Discussion of the Spence-Owen Model." Discussion Paper, Stanford University, Studies in Economics, No. 94.

Leventhal, J. 1969. *Star Television, Inc. v. FCC.* 416 *F.2d* 1086, 1089–95 (D.C.Cir.) (dissenting opinion).

Levin, H. J. 1970. "Competition, Diversity and the Television Group Ownership Rule." *Columbia Law Review* 70:791–834.

Levin, H. J. 1980. *Fact and Fancy in Television Regulation.* New York: Russell Sage Foundation.

Levy, J. and F. Setzer. 1982. *Measurement of Concentration in Home Video Markets.* Washington, D.C.: FCC Office of Plans and Policy.

Liebowitz, S. J. 1982. "The Impacts of Cable Retransmission on Television Broadcasters." *Canadian Journal of Economics* 15:503–24.

Lintner, J. 1965. "Security Prices, Risk, and Maximal Gains from Diversification." *Journal of Finance* 20:587–616.

Lloyd, F. W. 1983. "Cable Television's Emerging Two-Way Services: A Dilemma for Federal and State Regulators." *Vanderbilt Law Review* 36:1045–91.

Londoner, D. J. 1980. *The Motion Picture Industry.* New York: Wertheim.

Lowry, E. D. 1973. "Justification for Regulation: The Case for Natural Monopoly." *Public Utilities Fortnightly,* November 8, 28:1–7.

MacAvoy, P. W., ed. 1977. *Deregulation of Cable Television.* Washington, D.C.: American Enterprise Institute for Public Policy Research.

McCloskey, D. 1982. *The Applied Theory of Price.* New York: Macmillan.

McGee, J. S. and L. R. Bassett. 1976. "Vertical Integration Revisited." *Journal of Law and Economics* 19:17–38.

Maddala, G. A. 1977. *Econometrics.* New York: McGraw Hill.

Marks, J. 1983. "Power Bases: Clustering for Numbers." *Cable Television Business,* April 15, pp. 18–26.

Mattelart, Armand and Hector Schmucler. 1983. *L'Ordinateur et le Tiers Monde.* Paris: Maspero Editions.

Mercado, O. and E. Buck. 1981. "Media Imperialism in Philippine Television." *Media Asia,* vol. 8, no. 7.

Miami Herald Publishing Co. v. Tornillo. 1974. 418 *U.S.* 241.

Microband Corporation of America. 1984. "Fact Sheet." New York: Microband.

Midwest Video Corp. v. FCC. 1978. 571 *F.2d* 1025, 1056 (8th Cir.), aff'd on other grounds, 440 *U.S.* 689.

Milgrom, P. and J. Roberts. 1982. "Predation, Reputation and Entry Deterrence." *Journal of Economic Theory* 27:280–312.

Mill, J. S. 1848; 1909 ed. *Principles of Political Economy.* London: Longmans, Green.

Miller v. California. 1973. 413 *U.S.* 15.

Millimeter. 1984. Anniversary Issue: 1974–1984.

Mitchell, B. M. and R. H. Smiley. 1974. "Cable, Cities, and Copyrights," *Bell Journal of Economics and Management Science* 5:235–63.

Mitre Corporation. 1974. Office of Telecommunications Policy. "Cable Television Financial Performance Model Description and Detailed Flow Diagram." Bedford, Mass.: Mitre Corporation.

Moody's Investor Services. 1981. *Moody's Bond Survey.* New York: Moody's.

Moozakis, C. 1983. "Return on Your Ad Sales Investment." *Cable Television Business,* April 15, p. 28–43.

Motion Picture Association of America. 1982. *Videocassette Recorders and the Law of Copyright.* Washington, D.C.: MPAA, Inc.

Motion Picture Association of America. 1984a. Mimeo., January 24.

Motion Picture Association of America. 1984b. Unpublished data.

Motion Picture Association of America. 1984c. "1983 Estimates of Population, Television Sets, and VCRs." Washington D.C.: MPAA, Inc.

NAACP v. Button. 1963. 371 *U.S.* 415.

Nadel, M. S. 1983. "COMCAR: A Marketplace Cable Television Franchise Structure." *Harvard Journal on Legislation* 20:541–73.

Nadel, M. S. 1984. "Editorial Freedom: Editors, Retailers, and the First Amendment." Manuscript.

Nadiri, M. I. and M. A. Schankerman. 1981. "The Structure of Production, Technological Change, and the Rate of Growth of Total Factor Productivity in the U.S. Bell System." In T. Cowing and R. Stevenson, eds., *Productivity Measurement in Regulated Industries.* New York: Academic Press.

NARUC v. FCC. 1976a. 525 *F.2d* 630 (D.C.Cir.).

NARUC v. FCC. 1976b. 533 *F.2d* 601 (D.C.Cir.).

National Association of Broadcasters v. FCC. 1984. 56 Rad. Reg. 2d 1105. (D.C. Cir.).

National League of Cities. 1981. *Regulating Cable Television.* Washington, D.C.

NBC v. U.S. 1943. 319 *U.S.* 190.

NCTA. 1983. *White Paper: Cable and Telephone Companies: A History of Confrontation.* Washington, D.C.: National Cable Television Association.

Needham, D. 1978. *The Economics of Industrial Structure, Conduct and Performance.* New York: Holt, Rinehart and Winston.

Nerlove, M. 1968. "Returns to Scale in Electricity Supply." In Arnold Zellner, ed., *Readings in Economic Statistics and Econometrics.* Boston: Little, Brown.

New Union Pact on Ads To Benefit Smaller Ops. 1984. *Multichannel News,* March 19, p. 21.

New York Times v. Sullivan. 1964. 376 *U.S.* 254.

Noam, E. M. 1980. "The Interaction of Federal Deregulation and State Regulation." *Hofstra Law Review* 9:199–206.

Noam, E. M. 1982a. "Economies of Scale and Scope in Cable Television." Working Paper, Columbia University, New York.

Noam. E. M. 1982b. "Towards An Integrated Communications Market: Overcoming the Local Monopoly of Cable Television." *Federal Communications Law Journal* 34:209–57.

Noam, E. M. 1983a. "Local Distribution Monopolies in Cable Television and Telephone Service: The Scope for Competition." In Noam, ed. *Telecommunications Regulation Today and Tomorrow.* New York: Harcourt, Brace, Jovanovich.

Noam, E. M. 1983b. "Federal and State Roles in Telecommunications: The Effects of Deregulation." *Vanderbilt Law Review* 36:949–83.

Noll, R. G. and B. M. Owen. 1983. *The Political Economy of Deregulation: Interest Groups in the Regulatory Process.* Washington, D.C.: American Enterprise Institute.

Noll, R., M. Peck, and J. McGowan. 1973. *Economic Aspect of Television Regulation.* Washington, D.C.: Brookings Institute.

NPD Electronic Media Tracking Service. 1983a. "Wave II Study." Port Washington, N.Y.

NPD Special Industry Services. 1983b. "The VCR Market: Owners/Attitudes/ Usage." Port Washington, N.Y. (Prepared for the Motion Picture Association of America.

Oettinger, A. G. and C. L. Weinhaus. 1983. "The Once and Future Telephone Plant and Costs: At the Heart of Debate." Cambridge: Harvard University Program on Information Resources Policy.

Omega Satellite Products Co. v. City of Indianapolis. 1982. 694 *F.2d* 119, 128 (7th Cir.).

Owen, B. M. 1975. *Economics and Freedom of Expression: Media Structure and the First Amendment.* Cambridge, Mass.: Ballinger.

Owen, B. M. and P. R. Greenhalgh. 1983. Options for Cable Television. Hearings. U.S. House of Representatives, Committee on Energy and Commerce, Subcommittee on Telecommunications, Consumer Protection and Finance. 98th Cong., 1st Sess. (May 25, June 22 and November 3), Serial 98-73, pp. 69–117.

Owen, B. M., J. H. Beebe, and W. G. Manning. 1974. *Television Economics.* Lexington, Mass.: Lexington Books.

Pacific Telephone. 1983. Mid-Peninsula Wideband Proposal. Palo Alto, Calif.

Pacific West Cable Co. v. Sacramento. 1983. *Multichannel News,* September 19, p. 3.

Panko, R. R., G. C. Edwards, K. Penchos, and S. P. Russel. 1975. *Analysis of Consumer Demand for Pay Television.* PB-250–51. U.S. Dept. of Commerce, National Technical Information Service, Washington, D.C.

Panzar, J. and R. Willig. 1977. "Free Entry and the Sustainability of Natural Monopoly." *Bell Journal of Economics* 8:1–22.

Panzar, J. 1979. "Economies of Scope, Product-Specific Economies of Scale, and the Multiproduct Competitive Firm." Bell Laboratories Economic Discussion Paper No. 152, Murray Hill, N.J.

Park, R. E. 1971. "Audience Diversion Due to Cable Television: Statistical Analysis of New Data." R-2403-FCC. Santa Monica, Calif.: Rand Corporation.

Park, R. E., L. L. Johnson, and B. Fishman. 1976. "Projecting the Growth of Television Broadcasting: Implications for Spectrum Use." R-841-FCC. Santa Monica, Calif.: Rand Corporation.

Parkman, A. M. 1982. "The Effect of Television Station on Local News Ratings." *Review of Economics and Statistics* 64:289–95.

Paul Kagan Associates. 1983a. "Cable TV Franchising." December 23, pp. 1–2.

Paul Kagan Associates. 1983b. "Cable TV Investor." June 2, p. 2.

Paul Kagan Associates. 1983c. *Census of Pay Television.* Carmel, Calif.: Paul Kagan Associates.

Paul Kagan Associates. 1983d. *The Pay TV Newsletter.* Census Issue.

Paul Kagan Associates. 1983e. *Cable TV Program Databook.*

Paul Kagan Associates. 1983f. *Cable TV Databook.*

Pepper, R. 1983. *Competition in Local Distribution: The Cable Television Industry.* Cambridge, Mass.: Harvard University Program on Information Resources Policy.

Peterman, J. L. 1971. "Concentration of Control and the Price of Television Times." *American Economic Review* (Papers and Proceedings) 61:74–80.

Phillips, O. 1980. "Product Bundles, Price Discrimination, and a Two-Product Firm." Working Paper, Department of Economics, University of Texas.

Phlips, L. 1983. *The Economics of Price Discrimination.* London: Cambridge University Press.

Pinchas, G. E. and K. A. Mingo. 1973. "A Multivariate Analysis of Industrial Bond Ratings." *Journal of Finance* 28:1–18.

Pinchas, G. E. and K. A. Mingo. 1975. "A Note on the Role of Subordination in Determining Bond Ratings." *Journal of Finance* 30:201–6.

Pogue, T. F and R. M. Saldofsky. 1969. "What's in a Bond Rating?" *Journal of Financial and Quantitative Analysis* 4:201–28.

Posner, R. 1969. "Natural Monopoly and Its Regulation." *Stanford Law Review* 21:548–643.

Posner, R. 1970. "Cable Television: The Problem of Local Monopoly." RM-6309-FF. Santa Monica, Calif.: Rand Corporation.

Posner, R. 1976. *Antitrust Law: An Economic Perspective.* Chicago: University of Chicago Press.

Pottle, J. and P. Bortz. 1982. *The Impact of Competitive Distribution Technologies on Cable Television.* Denver: Browne, Bortz and Coddington.

Preferred Communications v. Los Angeles. 1983. *Multichannel News,* September 19, p. 3.

Price, M. E. 1984. "The Videotape Revolution." *Wall Street Journal,* March 5, p. 28.

Quincy Cable TV, Inc. v. FCC. 1983. D.C. Cir. No. 83-1283.

Red Lion Broadcasting Co. v. FCC. 1969. 395 *U.S.* 367.

Reynolds, R. J. and B. M. Snapp. 1982. "The Economic Effects of Partial Equity Interests and Joint Ventures." Washington, D.C.: Economic Policy Office, Antitrust Division, U.S. Department of Justice.

Rivera, Henry. 1984. "Communications Law: The New Regulatory and Technological Framework." Remarks before the American Law Institute, March 29.

Robinson, John O. 1979. "Assignment of Radio Channels in the Multipoint Distribution Service by Auction." In *Proceedings of the Sixth Annual Telecommunications Policy Research Conference,* Lexington, Mass.: Lexington Books.

Rosenthal, E. M. 1984. "Ad Sales: Stepchild Status Under Attack by MSOs," *CableAge,* March 19, pp. 6–8.

Rosse, J. 1970. "Estimating Cost Function Parameters Without Using Cost Data: Illustrated Methodology." *Econometrica* 38:256–75.

Rothenberg, J. 1962. "Consumer Sovereignty and the Economics of TV Programming." *Studies in Public Communication* 4:45–54.

Rubin, P. E. 1984. "Wideband Window to the Information Age." *AT&T Bell Laboratories Record,* January, pp. 5–12.

Salinger, M. 1984. "Tobin's Q, Unionization, and the Concentration-Profits Relationship." *Rand Journal of Economics,* 15:159–70.

Salop, S. C. and D. T. Scheffman. 1983. "Raising Rivals' Costs." *American Economic Review* 73:267–71.

Scherer, F. M. 1979. "The Economics of Product Variety: An Application to the Ready-to-Eat Cereals Industry." *Journal of Industrial Economics* 28:113–34.

Scherer, F. M. 1980. *Industrial Market Structure and Economic Performance.* 2d ed. Chicago: Rand McNally.

Schiller, H. J. 1977. "Transnational Media and National Development." In J. Richstad, ed., *New Persepctives in International Communications.* Honolulu: University of Hawaii Press.

Schink, G. R. and S. Thanawale. 1978. *The Impact of Cable TV on Local Station Audience.* Prepared for the National Association of Broadcasters. Philadelphia: Wharton EFA.

Schley, S. 1984. "CCTA Seeks to Prevent Telco Entry into Cable." *Multichannel News,* February 27, p. 8.

Schmalensee, R. 1979. *The Control of Natural Monopolies.* Lexington, Mass.: D. C. Heath.

Schmalensee, R. 1982. "Product Differentiation Advantages of Pioneering Brands." *American Economic Review* 72:349–65.

Setzer, F. O., B. A. Franca, and N. W. Cornell. 1979. "Policies for Regulation of Direct Broadcast Satellites." Washington, D.C.: FCC Office of Plans and Policy.

Shapiro, G. H., P. B. Kurland, and J. P. Mercurio. 1983. *Cablespeech.* New York: Harcourt Brace Jovanovich.

Sharkey, W. 1982. *The Theory of Natural Monopoly.* Cambridge: Cambridge University Press.

Sharpe, W. F. 1964. "Capital Asset Prices: A Theory of Market Equilibrium Under Conditions of Risk." *Journal of Finance* 19:425–42.

Shephard, R. W. 1970. *Theory of Cost and Production Functions.* Princeton, N.J.: Princeton University Press.

Shepherd, W. G. 1970. *Market Power and Economic Welfare.* New York: Random House.

Shew, W. B. 1984. *Costs of Cable Television Franchise Requirements.* White Plains, N.Y.: National Economic Research Bureau, Prepared for the National Cable Television Associates, Inc.

Sloan Commission. 1971. *On the Cable: The Television of Abundance.* New York: McGraw-Hill.

Smith, I. V. 1984. "Local Research for Advertisers." *Cable Television Business,* April 1, pp. 30–32.

Smith, J. C. 1984. *Financial and Economic Analysis of the Cable Television Permit Policy of the City and County of Denver.* Portland, Ore.: Touche, Ross.

Smith, R. L. and R. B. Gallagher. 1980. *The Emergence of Pay Cable Television.* PB 80-209-968, Washington, D.C.: U.S. Dept. of Commerce, National Technical Information Service.

Sony Corp. of America v. Universal Studios, Inc. 1984. 104 S.Ct. 774.

Spence, A. M. 1976. "Product Selection, Fixed Costs and Monopolistic Competition." *Review of Economic Studies* 43:217–36.

Spence, A. M. 1977. "Entry, Capacity, Investment, and Oligopolistic Pricing." *Bell Journal of Economics* 8:534–44.

Spence, M. A. and B. M. Owen. 1977. "Television Programming, Monopolistic Competition and Welfare." *Quarterly Journal of Economics* 91:103–26.

Standard & Poor. 1981. *Standard & Poor's Fixed Income Investor.* New York: Standard & Poor.

Standard Rate and Data Services. 1983. *Spot TV Rates and Data.* March.

Steiner, P. O. 1952. Program Patterns and Preferences, and the Workability of Competition in Radio Broadcasting. *Quarterly Journal of Economics* 66:194–223.

Sterling, C. H. 1979. "Television and Radio Broadcasting." In B. Compaine, ed., *Who Owns the Media? Concentration of Ownership in the Mass Communications Industry.* White Plains, N.Y.: Knowledge Industry.

Stern, J. A. and E. G. Krasnow. 1984. *The New Video Marketplace and the Impending Identity Crisis.* Cambridge, Mass.: Harvard University Program on Information Resources Policy.

Stern, J. A., E. G. Krasnow, and R. M. Senkowski. 1983. "The New Video Marketplace and the Search for a Coherent Regulatory Philosophy." *Catholic University Law Review* 32:529–602.

Stigler, G. J. 1963. "*United States v. Loew's Inc.*: A Note on Block Booking." In P. Kurland, ed., *The Supreme Court Review: 1963.* Chicago: University of Chicago Press.

Stigler, G. J. 1964. "A Theory of Oligopoly." *Journal of Political Economy* 72:44–61.

Stigler, G. J. 1982. "The Economists and the Problem of Monopoly." *American Economic Review* 72:1–11.

Stoller, D. 1982. "The War Between Cable and the Cities." *Channels,* April–May, p. 36.

Sudit, E. F. 1973. "Additive Non-Homogeneous Production Function and Application to Telecommunications." *Bell Journal of Economics and Management Science* 4:495–514.

Sutherland, S. 1984. "Movie Theatres Eye Video Entry." *Billboard,* March 10, p. 3.

Switzer, I. 1983. "What To Do in the U.K." Paper presented to the Society of Cable Television Engineers, London, April 7.

Symposium. 1983. "1982 Merger Guidelines." *California Law Review* 71:280–672.

Taub, S. 1984. "Cable TV: The End of the Shakeout?" *Financial World,* May 2–15, pp. 14–19.

Television Audience Assessment, Inc. 1983. *The Multichannel Environment: A Study of Television Viewing in Two Cable Markets.*

Television Digest, Inc. 1980. *Television Factbook.* Washington, D.C.

Television Digest, Inc. 1983. *Television and Cable Factbook 1982–83.* Washington, D.C.

Terry, K. 1984. "1990 Homevideo Market Put At Near $10 Bill." *Daily Variety,* February 16, p. 1.

Theil, H. 1971. *Principles of Econometrics.* New York: Wiley.

Thorpe, K. 1984. "Cable Television Market Power and Regulation." Ph.D. dissertation, Rand Graduate Institute.

Tirado 1976. "Analisis de la industria electronica y de telecommunicaciones en Venezuela." In A. Mattelart and H. Schmucler, *L'Ordinateur et le Tiers Monde.* Paris: Maspero Editions.

Tusher, W. 1984. "Film Security Office Head Raises Financial Red Flag in Address At ShoWest '84." *Daily Variety,* February 24, p. 1.

U.S. Code. 1976. Various sections cited.

U.S. Congress. 1958. House of Representatives, Committee on Interstate and Foreign Commerce. *Network Broadcasting.* 85th Cong., 2d sess.

U.S. Congress. 1972. Public Law 92-225. *Statutes* 86:3.

U.S. Congress. 1982. House Report 97-975. 97th Cong., 2d sess.

U.S. Congress. 1983a. Public Law 98-214.

U.S. Congress. 1983b. S.66., 98th Cong., 1st sess.

U.S. Congress. 1983c. H.R. 4103, 98th Cong., 1st sess.

U.S. Congress. 1983d. House of Representatives, Committee on the Judiciary, *Hearings on Home Recording of Copyrighted Works.* 97th Cong., 2d sess.

U.S. Congress. 1983e. House of Representatives. *Hearing Before the Committee on Energy and Commerce Regarding H.R. 4103.* 97th Cong., 2d sess.

U.S. Congress. 1983f. Senate. *Hearings Before the Subcommittee on Communications of the Committee on Commerce, Science and Transportation, on Cable Television Regulation.* 97th Cong., 1st sess.

U.S. Dept. of Commerce. 1978. *City and County Databook, 1977.* Washington, D.C.: GPO.

U.S. Dept. of Commerce. 1983a. Bureau of the Census. *Current Population Survey,* Series P-20 (no. 381).

U.S. Dept. of Commerce. 1983b. Bureau of the Census. *1980 Census of Population. General Population Characteristics: United States Summary.*

U.S. Dept. of Commerce. 1983c. Bureau of Economic Analysis. "State Personal Income, 1980–82: Revised Estimates." *Survey of Current Business* 63(8):49–51.

U.S. Dept. of the Interior. 1970. *The National Atlas.* Washington, D.C.: Geologic Survey.

U.S. Department of Justice. 1968. Antitrust Division. *Merger Guidelines.* May 30. Washington, D.C.: GPO.

U.S. Dept. of Justice. 1982. "U.S. Department of Justice Merger Guidelines Issued June 14, 1982." *The Antitrust Bulletin* 27:633–65.

United States Satellite Broadcasting Co. Inc. v. FCC. 1984. July 24 (D.C. Cir.).

United States v. Columbia Pictures. 1980. 334 U.S. 131.

United States v. Midwest Video Corp. 1972. 406 U.S. 649.

United States v. Paramount Pictures. 1948. 507 F. Supp. 412. aff'd 659 F. 2d 1063.

United States v. Southwestern Cable Co. 1968. 392 U.S. 157.

United States v. Storer Broadcasting Co. 1956. 351 U.S. 192.

U.S. v. Western Electric Co., Inc. and AT&T. 1982. 47 Fed. Reg. 7170.

Vernon, J. and D. Graham. 1971. "Profitability of Monopolization by Vertical Integration." *Journal of Political Economy* 79:925–26.

VCR Sales to Dealers. 1983. *Television Digest with Consumer Electronics,* June 27, p. 9.

Video Week. 1983. Vol. 5, no. 1.

Vinod, H. D. 1972. "Non-Homogeneous Production Functions and Applications to Telecommunications." *Bell Journal of Economics and Management Science* 3:531–43.

Waterman, D. 1978. "Economic Essays on the Theatrical Motion Picture Industry." Ph.D. dissertation, Stanford University, Stanford, Calif.

Waterman and Associates. 1984. Unpublished data.

Webb, J. K. 1983. *The Economics of Cable Television.* Lexington, Mass.: Lexington Books.

Webbink, D. W. 1977. "The Elasticity of Demand for Fuel: Some Comments." *Industrial Organization Review* 5:121–27.

Webbink, D. W. 1980. "Frequency Spectrum Deregulation Alternatives." Washington, D.C.: FCC Office of Plans and Policy.

Webster, J. G. 1983. "The Impact of Cable and Pay Cable Television on Local Station Audiences." *Journal of Broadcasting* 27:119–26.

Weinberg, G. 1972. *Cost Analysis of CATV Components*. PB 211-012. Washington, D.C.: U.S. Dept. of Commerce, National Technical Information Service.

Werden, G. J. 1983. "Market Delineation and the Justice Department's Merger Guidelines." *Duke Law Journal*, 1983:514–79.

Westfield, F. M. 1981. "Vertical Integration: Does Product Price Rise or Fall?" *American Economic Review* 71:334–46.

Wheeler, T. E. 1981. "Possible Cross-Subsidization Renders Telcos 'Unfair' Competitors in CATV." In "CATV Operators vs. Telcos: Debating the Public Interest." *Telephony*, May 4, pp. 27–34.

Wienski, R. M. 1984. "Evolution to ISDN Within the Bell Operating Companies." *IEEE Communications* 22(1):33–41.

Wildman, S. 1978. "Vertical Integration in Broadcasting: A Study of Network Owned and Operated Stations." In *Proceedings of the Symposium on Media Concentration*. Washington, D.C.: Federal Trade Commission.

Wildman, S. 1980. "A Spatial Model of Entry Deterrence." Working Paper, Department of Economics, UCLA.

Wildman, S. W. 1984. "A Note on Measuring Surplus Attributable to Differentiated Products." *Journal of Industrial Economics* 33:123–132.

Wiles, P. 1963. "Pilkington and the Theory of Value." *Economic Journal* 73:183–200.

Wilkie, J. 1980. "The Radio Reference and Onward: Exclusive Federal Jurisdiction over Content Control in Broadcasting?" *Osoode Hall Law Journal* 18:76–86.

Williams, M. J. 1984. "Slow Life off for Satellite-to-Home TV." *Fortune*, March 5, p. 100.

Wirth, Timothy E. 1983. Remarks in New York City, January 10.

Wirth, M. O. and B. T. Allen. 1979 "Another Look at Crossmedia Ownership." *Antitrust Bulletin* 24:87–103.

Wirth, M. O. and B. T. Allen. 1980. "Crossmedia Ownership, Regulatory Scrutiny, and Pricing Behavior." *Journal of Economics and Business* 33:28–41.

Wirth, M. O. and J. A. Wollert. Forthcoming. "The Effects of Market Structure on Local Television News Pricing." *Journal of Broadcasting*.

Yankee Group. 1983. "Cable and the Telcos: From Confrontation to Detente." *Home of the Future Planning Service*. Cambridge, Mass.: The Yankee Group.

Zellner, A. 1962. "An Efficient Method of Estimating Seemingly Unrelated Regression and Tests for Aggregation Bias." *Journal of American Statistical Association* 57:348–68.

Ziegler, P. 1984. "Nielson Rating Numbers Point to Sharp Increase in Basic Cable Viewing." *Multichannels News*, April 16, p. 31.

Contributors

JOHN D. ABEL. John D. Abel is senior vice-president for Research and Planning for the National Association of Broadcasters. Prior to his appointment at NAB in June 1983, Dr. Abel was chairman and professor of the Department of Telecommunication at Michigan State University. Dr. Abel served as a consultant with the Federal Communications Commission in Washington during 1977–78. He was also a founding partner of the ELRA Group, a media research and consulting firm. As senior vice-president, Dr. Abel is responsible for the Research and Planning projects at NAB including preparing assessments of the growth and development of communication technology, marketing, audience and policy research, and strategic planning for the industry and the Association. He is the author of more than fifty journal articles, books, and research reports, and has done extensive consulting within the telecommunications industry. Dr. Abel holds M.A. and Ph.D. degrees from Indiana University in Bloomington.

WALTER S. BAER. Walter S. Baer is director of Advanced Technology at the Times Mirror Company. He is responsible for developing new business activities in telecommunications, electronic publishing, and other information technologies. Prior to joining Times Mirror, he was director of the Energy Policy Program at the Rand Corporation. He has published widely in the fields of energy, telecommunications, and science and technology policy. His *Cable Television: A Handbook for Decisionmaking* received a 1975 Preceptor Award from the Broadcast Industry Conference. He co-authored and edited five other books for Rand and Aspen Institute of Humanistic Studies. Dr. Baer has worked as an independent consultant and served on the Office of Science and Technology staff in the Office of the President. He is currently a member of the faculty of the Rand Graduate Institute. Dr. Baer holds a B.S.

degree from the California Institute of Technology and a Ph.D. degree in physics from the University of Wisconsin.

STANLEY M. BESEN. Stanley M. Besen is a senior economist at the Rand Corporation. He was co-director of the Network Inquiry Special Staff at the FCC and the Allyn R. and Gladys M. Cline Professor of Economics and Finance at Rice University. Dr. Besen has written numerous articles on telecommunications, law, and economics. His recent work includes analyses of the economics of mandatory leased access to cable television, the effects of the Federal Communications Commission's group ownership rules, and the impact of new technologies on the supply of intellectual property. He received a B.B.A. from the City College of New York, and an M.A. and Ph.D. from Yale.

HARRY BLOCH. Harry Bloch is associate professor of economics at the University of Denver, and has previously taught at Illinois Institute of Technology, the University of British Columbia, the University of Manitoba, and Queen's University. An expert in econometrics and industrial economics, including the economics of advertising, international competition, and television economics, Dr. Bloch has conducted research under grants from a number of organizations, including the National Science Foundation and the Public Utilities Institute. His articles have appeared in *Journal of Political Economy,* the *Canadian Journal of Economics,* and the *Journal of Industrial Economics,* as well as scholarly books. Dr. Bloch has also done consulting work for such organizations as American Television and Communications Corporation; Browne, Bortz and Coddington; Frontier Airlines; and the National Basketball Association. Dr. Bloch's undergraduate degree is from the University of Michigan (A.B. in economics, 1967), and his graduate degrees are from the University of Chicago (A.M. in economics, 1969; Ph.D. in economics, 1971).

MICHAEL BOTEIN. Michael Botein is a professor of law and director of the Communications Media Center at New York Law School as well as counsel to the Washington D.C. law firm of Verner, Liipfert, Bernhard, McPherson & Hand. He previously taught at Brooklyn Law School and Rutgers Law School. Professor Botein has been a consultant for the Federal Communications Commission and Rand. He has served on a number of bar committees relating to communications law. His articles have appeared in numerous scholarly journals, and he has co-authored a number of books on cable television law and regulation. Professor Botein received his B.A. from Wesleyan, his J.D. with distinction from Cornell, and his J.S.D. and L.L.M. degrees from Columbia University.

NOLAN A. BOWIE. Nolan A. Bowie is a telecommunications policy analyst, consultant, and attorney. He is currently affiliated with the Aspen Institute for Humanistic Studies' Program in Communications and Society as a Fellow. Mr. Bowie was formerly executive director of Citizens Communications Center, the Washington, D.C.-based public interest law firm and educational center that is now part of Georgetown University Law Center. He serves on the American Civil Liberties Union policy committees on Privacy and Communications/Media and is a member of the N.Y. State Legislative Commission on Science & Technology's Computer Technology Advisory Group. He is currently a Section Editor of the *International Encyclopedia of Communications,* and his work is represented in a number of anthologies and journals. He was a member of the U.S. Delegation to the World Administrative Radio Conference in 1979. Mr. Bowie received his J.D. degree from the University of Michigan Law School.

STUART N. BROTMAN. Stuart N. Brotman is a communications lawyer and management consultant based in Brookline, Massachusetts. He formerly served as special assistant to the director of the National Telecommunications and Information Administration in Washington, D.C. Mr. Brotman is a member of the State Bar of California and the Federal Communications Bar Association. He received undergraduate and graduate degrees in Communications from Northwestern University and the University of Wisconsin, respectively, and a law degree from the University of California, Berkeley, where he served as Note and Comment editor of the *California Law Review.*

HENRY GELLER. Henry Geller is the director of the Washington Center for Public Policy Research, part of Duke University. He has held the positions of assistant secretary for Communication and Information and administrator of the National Telecommunications and Information

Administration. Most of his career, however, was spent at the FCC, where he served as general counsel from 1964 to 1970, and as a special assistant to the Chairman of the FCC. In 1970, Mr. Geller received the National Civil Service Award. He has taught at the Georgetown and the University of Pennsylvania law schools, and at George Washington University. He received a B.S. from the University of Michigan in 1934 and a J.D. from Northwestern School of Law in 1949.

JOHN K. HOPLEY. John K. Hopley is assistant vice-president, rate administration, of the New York Telephone Company and is responsible for the pricing and rate administration of all telephone services. He pioneered the rate design in the Bell System for such charging concepts as directory assistance, local usage sensitive pricing, access charges and multi-element connection charges; he testified frequently before the state regulatory and legislative bodies on pricing and policy issues. He has consulted with the governments of Israel, England, Japan and Finland on a broad range of pricing, economic, policy, and operation matters in the field of telecommunications. He received a degree in electrical engineering from Iowa State University.

JANE B. HENRY. Jane B. Henry is an entrepreneur and independent consultant specializing in the management of emerging communications technologies. She worked with McKinsey & Co., in New York for three years, consulted independently to Time Inc.'s Video Group, and most recently was associated with CSP International in New York. Her work concentrates on changes in the television marketplace, particularly the new pay TV media and the emergence of independent television stations. Recent speeches were before the American Press Institute, on new video technologies, and the American Bankers' Association, on video banking. Dr. Henry holds an M.B.A. with honors and a Ph.D. from Harvard University.

LELAND L. JOHNSON. Dr. Leland L. Johnson is a senior economist at the Rand Corporation, where he is involved in telecommunications research. He has completed studies dealing with issues of monopoly and competition in the telephone industry and with the economics of mandated leased access to cable television systems. Dr. Johnson was Associate Administrator for Policy Analysis and Development in the

National Telecommunications and Information Administration in Washington, D.C. Prior to that, he was manager of Rand's Communications Policy Program in Santa Monica. Earlier, he served as Director of Research for the President's Task Force on Communications Policy. Dr. Johnson holds a Ph.D. degree in economics from Yale University.

ERNEST JOUHY. Ernest Jouhy took his abitur in Berlin. In 1933 he left Germany for France where he studied child psychology at the Sorbonne. He participated in the French resistance. After the war, he received his Ph.D. and became a professor and educator in Germany. Professor Jouhy has worked for UNESCO, where he undertook a study on education in boarding schools in postwar Germany. He has taught at the famous private boarding school, Odenwaldschule, where he directed higher studies. He was appointed to the Goethe University in Frankfurt, where he taught sociology and psychology of childhood and youth at the faculty of educational science and where he started the Institution on Education in the Third World. He has been a consultant on education to Third World projects for various organizations including the Friedrich Naumann Foundation and the Germany Ministry for Economic Cooperation. Professor Jouhy has published widely.

HARVEY J. LEVIN. Harvey J. Levin is an Augustus B. Weller Professor of Economics and director of the Public Policy Workshop at Hofstra University. He is an economic specialist, consultant, and author on broadcast organization and regulatory policy, and economic aspects of the radio spectrum resource. He has held special consultantships relating to telecommunications economics and public policy for the Office of Technology Assessment of U.S. Congress, the General Accounting Office, the Bureau of Economics/Federal Trade Commission, the Ford Foundation, and the Brookings Institute. Professor Levin is the author of *Fact and Fancy in Television Regulation* (1980), *The Invisible Resource* (1971), and *Broadcast Regulation and Joint Ownership of Media* (1960). He has written some thirty articles on related issues, and is the recipient of numerous grants and awards.

JONATHAN D. LEVY. Jonathan D. Levy is an economist in the Office of Plans and Policy at the Federal Communications Commission, specializing in mass media issues. Prior to joining the F.C.C. in 1980, Dr.

Levy taught economics at the University of Wisconsin-Milwaukee. He holds a Ph.D. in economics from Yale University.

MARK S. NADEL. Mark S. Nadel is an adjunct assistant professor at Benjamin Cardozo and New York Law Schools and a research associate at the Columbia University Research Program on Telecommunications and Information Policy. He teaches and does research on the issues of economics and the First Amendment in the media. His publications comprise book reviews and articles, including "A Unified Theory of the First Amendment: Divorcing the Medium from the Message," "COMCAR: A Marketplace Cable Television Franchise Structure," and "Antitrust Issues in the New Media." He holds a B.A. from Amherst College and a J.D. from Harvard Law School.

ELI M. NOAM. Eli M. Noam is an associate professor at the Columbia Business School and the director of its Research Program in Telecommunications and Information Policy; he has also taught at the Columbia Law School and has been a visiting professor at Princeton. Among his publications are articles in the *Journal of Political Economy,* and the *Quarterly Journal of Economics;* articles in law reviews and interdisciplinary journals; and the volume *Telecommunications Regulation: Today and Tomorrow.* Dr. Noam serves on the editorial boards of several journals, and is the general editor of the Columbia University Press series "Studies in Business, Government, and Society." He received an A.B. in 1970 from Harvard, and a Ph.D. in economics and a J.D. from the same university in 1975.

BRUCE M. OWEN. Bruce M. Owen is president of the consulting firm of Economists Incorporated and adjunct professor of Business and Public Policy at Duke University. He previously served as chief economist of the Department of Justice and the White House Office of Telecommunications Policy. Dr. Owen has taught economics at Stanford University, and business and law at Duke. He has been a fellow of the Brookings Institute, the Hoover Institution, and the Aspen Institute for Humanistic Studies. His extensive publications on media and regulation include several books, including *The Political Economy of Deregulation* (with Roger Noll). Dr. Owen received his B.A. from Williams and his Ph.D. from Stanford University.

PETER K. PITSCH. Peter K. Pitsch received a B.A. degree in economics from the University of Chicago in 1973 and a law degree from the Georgetown University Law Center in 1976. While at University of Chicago, he received a National Science Foundation grant to do independent research in economics. In 1976, he joined the Office of Policy and Planning in the Federal Trade Commission. In 1977, he was selected by Commissioner Calvin J. Collier to work on his personal staff. In 1978, he joined the FTC's Bureau of Consumer Protection where he worked as a staff attorney. From 1979 to 1981, he worked as a general regulatory attorney in the Washington, D.C., legal office of Montgomery Ward and Co. In the fall of 1980, Mr. Pitsch served on the Reagan Transition Team for the FTC. Since June 1, 1981, he has served as the chief of the Office of Plans and Policy at the FCC.

HELMUT SCHÄFER. Helmut Schäfer has, since 1977, been a member of the Deutscher Bundestag. He is also a member of the Free Democratic Party (F.D.P.) and serves on the Executive Board of the F.D.P. of Rhineland Palatinate. He was national vice-chairman of the German Young Democrats between 1966–68; was appointed Expert in Media in the Ministry of Culture of Rhineland Palatinate between 1967 and 1977; and, between 1972 and 1982, served on the Federal Executive Board of the F.D.P. He presently also serves on the F.D.P. Commission for Media; the Media Commission of the European Liberal Parties; the Executive Commission of the Liberal International; and the Executive Board of the Friedrich-Naumann-Foundation. Mr. Schäfer studied German literature and English at the Universities of Mainz, Innsbruck, and Dayton, Ohio.

STEPHEN A. SHARP. Stephen A. Sharp is a partner in the Washington office of Skadden, Arps, Slate, Meagher and Flom. Immediately prior to joining the law firm in 1983, he served as a member of the Federal Communications Commission. Commissioner Sharp held a number of positions at the FCC since 1972, including the office of General Counsel and that of Commissioner. He has taught communications law at the University of Virginia and George Mason University. Commissioner Sharp has served as chairman of a number of American Bar Association committees, and is currently chairman of the ABA Special Committee on Election Law and Voter Participation. In 1974 he was counsel to the Impeachment Inquiry, Committee on the Judiciary, U.S. House of Representatives. Commissioner Sharp received his B.A. from Washington and Lee University and his J.D. from the University of Virginia.

KENNETH THORPE. Kenneth Thorpe is an assistant professor of Public Health and Public Policy at Columbia University. He is also a consultant to the Rand Corporation and has taught business and management at Pepperdine University. Dr. Thorpe's research has centered on regulation in the cable television, newspaper, and health industries. He has served with the Human Resources and Community Development Division of the Congressional Budget Office and with the Department of Commerce. He received a B.A. from the University of Michigan in Political Science, an M.A. in Public Policy from Duke University and a Ph.D. in Public Policy from the Rand Graduate Institute.

DAVID WATERMAN. David Waterman is president of Waterman and Associates, a Los Angeles consulting firm serving government and private industry clients in the mass communications field. Dr. Waterman is also adjunct professor at the Annenberg School of Communications, University of Southern California, and was formerly a research economist for the National Endowment for the Arts. He holds a B.A. from the University of Southern California and M.A. and Ph.D. degrees in economics from Stanford University.

DOUGLAS W. WEBBINK. Douglas W. Webbink is an economist at the Federal Trade Commission, Bureau of Economics, Division of Regulatory Analysis. He taught at the University of North Carolina at Chapel Hill, and spent a year at the FCC as a Brookings Institution Economic Policy Fellow. Dr. Webbink then spent a number of years at the Federal Trade Commission, Bureau of Economics, Division of Industry Analysis. Following that, he spent four years at the FCC, three of them as Deputy Chief of the Office of Plans and Policy. He was later associated with the consulting firm of Cornell, Pelcovits and Brenner Economists, Inc. He is the author of articles and reports on a variety of subjects such as the use of the frequency spectrum, common carrier regulation, the semiconductor industry, and competition in the energy industries. He received his B.A. in physics from Brown University and his Ph.D. in economics from Duke University.

LAWRENCE J. WHITE. Lawrence J. White is professor of economics at the New York University Graduate School of Business Administration. During 1982–83 he was on leave to serve as director of the Economic Policy Office, Antitrust Division, U.S. Department of Justice. Dr. White is the author of *The Automobile Industry Since 1945*; *Industrial Concentration and Economic Power in Pakistan*; *Reforming Regulation: Processes and Problems*; *The Regulation of Air Pollutant Emissions from Motor Vehicles*; *The Public Library in the 1980s: The Problems of Choice*; and articles in leading economics journals. He is the coeditor of two conference volumes, *Deregulation of the Banking and Securities Industries* and *Mergers and Acquisitions: Current Problems in Perspective*. He also served on the Senior Staff of the President's Council of Economic Advisers during 1978–79. He received a B.A. from Harvard, an M.Sc. from the London School of Economics, and a Ph.D. from Harvard.

STEVEN S. WILDMAN. Steven S. Wildman is an economist with the consulting firm of Economists Incorporated. He was previously an assistant professor in the Department of Economics at UCLA and a consultant to the Rand Corporation. He held a National Science Foundation Fellowship from 1974 to 1977. Dr. Wildman has published a number of articles and working papers on competition in the broadcasting industries and other communications-related issues. He holds a B.A. in economics from Wabash College and a Ph.D. from Stanford University in the same subject.

MICHAEL O. WIRTH. Michael O. Wirth is an associate professor and director of Graduate Studies in the Department of Mass Communications at the University of Denver. Dr. Wirth has received grants from the National Science Foundation and the National Association of Broadcasters and has published articles and essays in the *Journal of Economics and Business, Telecommunications Policy, Quarterly Review of Economics and Business, The Denver Law Journal*, and the *Journal of Broadcasting*. He has also done consulting work for many leading firms in the communications industry. Dr. Wirth received a B.S. from the University of Nebraska-Lincoln and both an M.A. in television and radio, and a Ph.D. in Mass Media from Michigan State University.

JOHN R. WOODBURY. John R. Woodbury is vice-president of Research and Policy Analysis at the National Cable Television Association. Prior to this, Dr. Woodbury was senior economist of the Regulatory Analysis Division for the Bureau of Economics of the F.T.C. He was the chief of the Economics Division of the Common Carrier Bureau of the F.C.C.; and industry economist, Network Inquiry Special Staff of the F.C.C. He has been an assistant professor of economics at the University of New York at Albany and lecturer at Southern Illinois University. He received a B.A. from the College of Holy Cross and a Ph.D. from Washington University, St. Louis.